P9-CKV-609

34

· MILET ·
BILINGUAL VISUAL
DICTIONARY
ENGLISH · GUJARATI

Library Resource Center
Renton Technical College
3000 N.E. 4th St.
Renton, WA 98056

DISCARDED

491.47317 CORBEIL 2001

Corbeil, Jean Claude.

Milet bilingual visual
  dictionary Gujarati

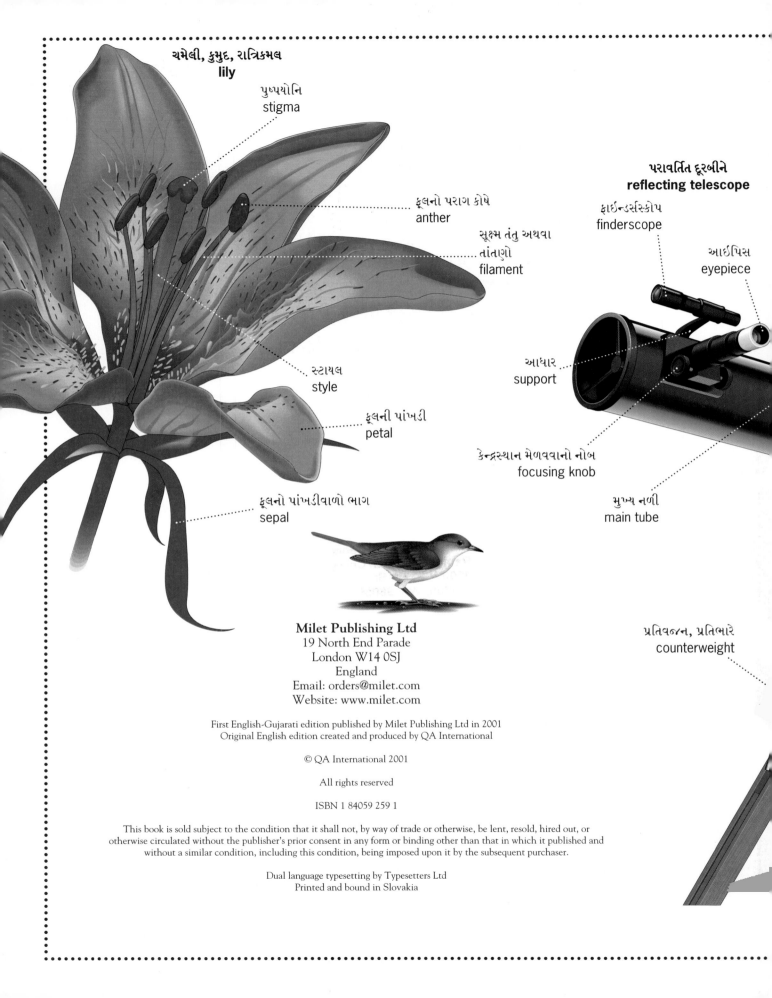

ચમેલી, કુમુદ, રાત્રિકમલ
lily

પુષ્પયોનિ
stigma

ફૂલનો પરાગ કોષ
anther

સૂક્ષ્મ તંતુ અથવા
તાંતાણો
filament

સ્ટાયલ
style

ફૂલની પાંખડી
petal

ફૂલનો પાંખડીવાળો ભાગ
sepal

પરાવર્તિત દૂરબીને
reflecting telescope

ફાઇન્ડર્સ્કોપ
finderscope

આઇપિસ
eyepiece

આધાર
support

કેન્દ્રસ્થાન મેળવવાનો નોબ
focusing knob

મુખ્ય નળી
main tube

પ્રતિવજન, પ્રતિભારે
counterweight

Milet Publishing Ltd
19 North End Parade
London W14 0SJ
England
Email: orders@milet.com
Website: www.milet.com

First English-Gujarati edition published by Milet Publishing Ltd in 2001
Original English edition created and produced by QA International

© QA International 2001

All rights reserved

ISBN 1 84059 259 1

This book is sold subject to the condition that it shall not, by way of trade or otherwise, be lent, resold, hired out, or
otherwise circulated without the publisher's prior consent in any form or binding other than that in which it published and
without a similar condition, including this condition, being imposed upon it by the subsequent purchaser.

Dual language typesetting by Typesetters Ltd
Printed and bound in Slovakia

Jean-Claude Corbeil • Ariane Archambault

• MILET •
BILINGUAL VISUAL
DICTIONARY
ENGLISH • GUJARATI

Authors
Jean-Claude Corbeil, Ariane Archambault
Director of Computer Graphics
François Fortin
Art Directors
Jean-Louis Martin, François Fortin
Graphic Designer
Anne Tremblay
Computer Graphic Designers
Marc Lalumière, Jean-Yves Ahern,
Rielle Lévesque, Anne Tremblay, Jacques Perrault,
Jocelyn Gardner, Christiane Beauregard,
Michel Blais, Stéphane Roy, Alice Comtois,
Benoît Bourdeau
Computer Programming
Yves Ferland, Daniel Beaulieu
Data Capture
Serge D'Amico
Page Make-up
Lucie Mc Brearty, Pascal Goyette
Technical Support
Gilles Archambault
Production
Tony O'Riley

Gujarati translation supplied by Typesetters Ltd

Editorial Note: For objects whose English terms are
different in North America and Britain,
we have used both terms: the North American term
followed by the British term. In the
index, these dual terms are listed alphabetically
by the first term.

Translation Note: In cases where there is no direct
Gujarati term for an object, the translator has
used an approximate term or a descriptive term. In
cases where the English term is commonly
used in Gujarati, or where there is no Gujarati term,
the translator has used a transliteration
of the English term.

ROAD TRANSPORTATION

RAIL TRANSPORTATION

MARITIME TRANSPORTATION

AIR TRANSPORTATION

SPACE TRANSPORTATION

SCHOOL

MUSIC

TEAM GAMES

WATER SPORTS

WINTER SPORTS

GYMNASTICS

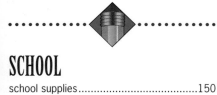

CAMPING

INDOOR GAMES

MEASURING DEVICES

ENERGY

HEAVY MACHINERY

SYMBOLS

5

સૌર પ્રણાલિ
SOLAR SYSTEM

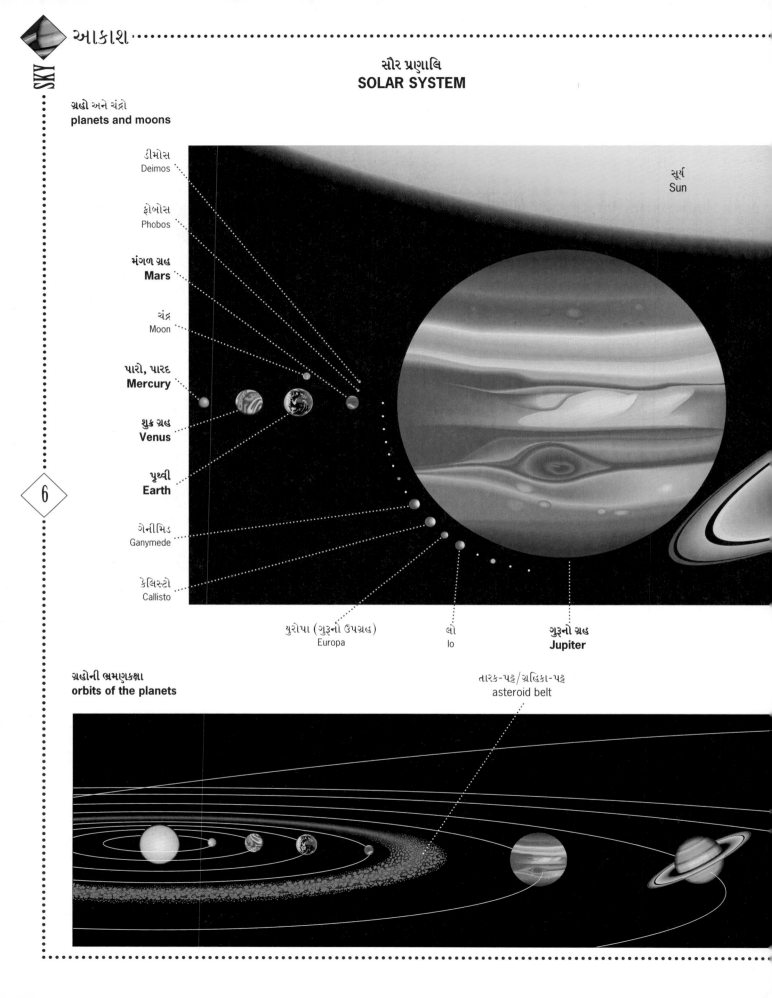

ગ્રહો અને ચંદ્રો
planets and moons

ડીમોસ
Deimos

ફોબોસ
Phobos

મંગળ ગ્રહ
Mars

ચંદ્ર
Moon

પારો, પારદ
Mercury

શુક્ર ગ્રહ
Venus

પૃથ્વી
Earth

ગેનીમિડ
Ganymede

કેલિસ્ટો
Callisto

સૂર્ય
Sun

યુરોપા (ગુરુનો ઉપગ્રહ)
Europa

લો
Io

ગુરુનો ગ્રહ
Jupiter

ગ્રહોની ભ્રમણકક્ષા
orbits of the planets

તારક-પટ્ટ/ગ્રહિકા-પટ્ટ
asteroid belt

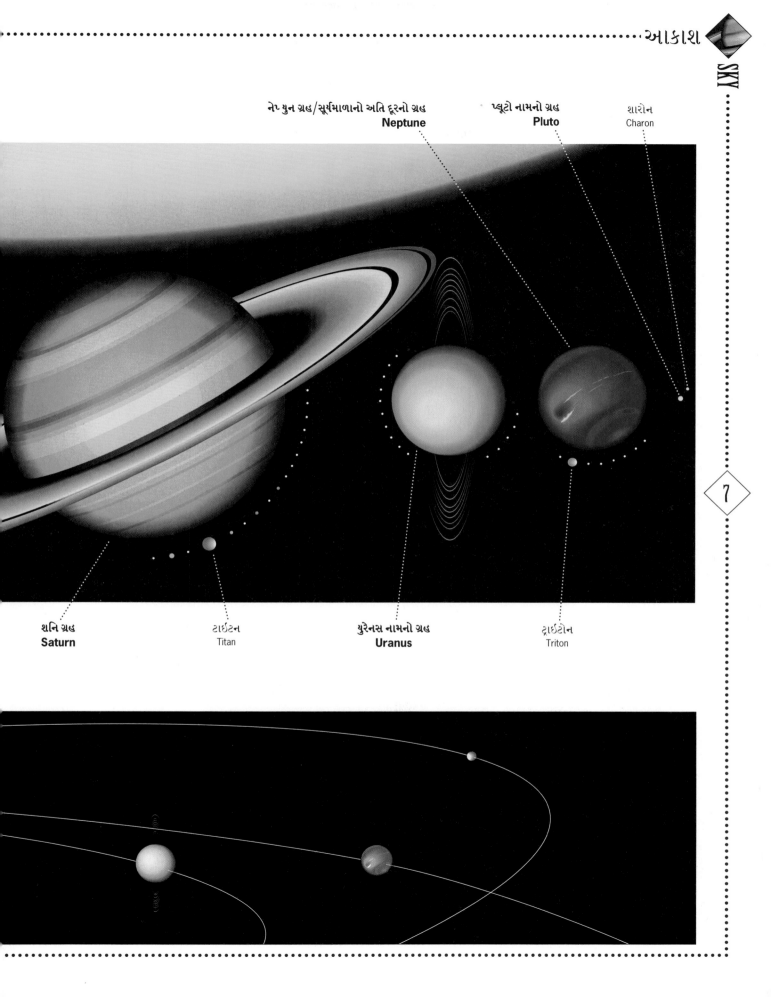

નેપ્ચુન ગ્રહ/સૂર્યમાળાનો અતિ દૂરનો ગ્રહ
Neptune

પ્લૂટો નામનો ગ્રહ
Pluto

શારોન
Charon

શનિ ગ્રહ
Saturn

ટાઇટન
Titan

યુરેનસ નામનો ગ્રહ
Uranus

ટ્રાઇટોન
Triton

સૂર્ય
SUN

સૂર્યની સંરચના
structure of the Sun

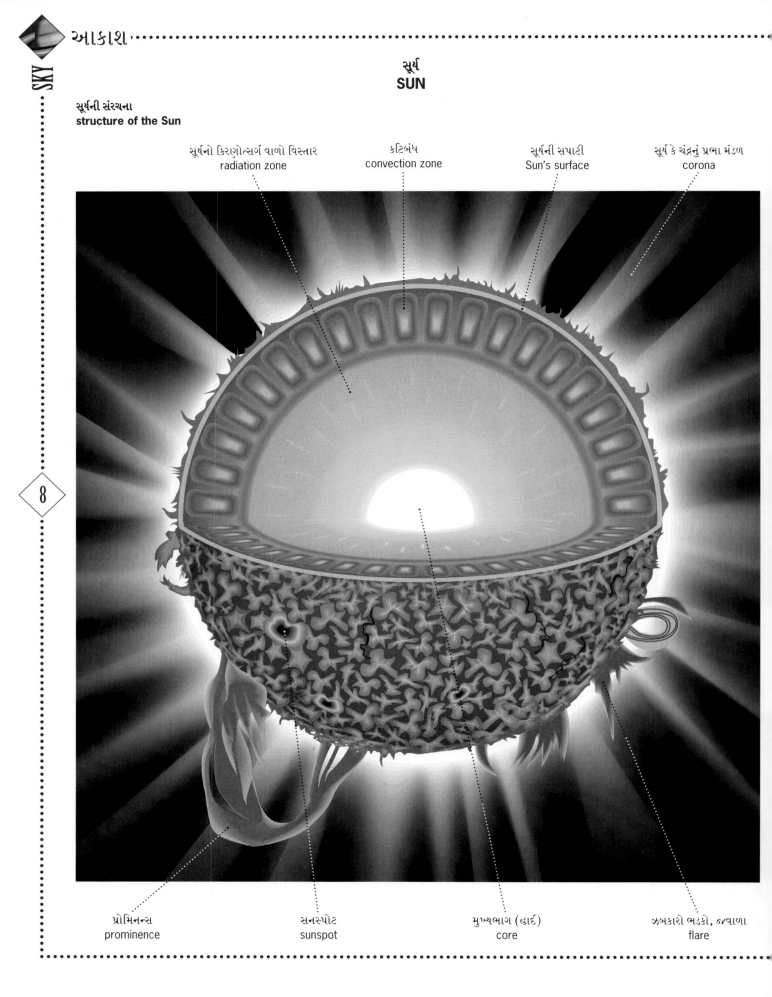

સૂર્યનો કિરણોત્સર્ગ વાળો વિસ્તાર
radiation zone

કટિબંધ
convection zone

સૂર્યની સપાટી
Sun's surface

સૂર્ય કે ચંદ્રનું પ્રભા મંડળ
corona

8

પ્રોમિનન્સ
prominence

સનસ્પોટ
sunspot

મુખ્યભાગ (હાર્દ)
core

ઝબકારો ભડકો, જ્વાળા
flare

ચંદ્ર
MOON

ચંદ્રની લાક્ષણિકતાઓ
lunar features

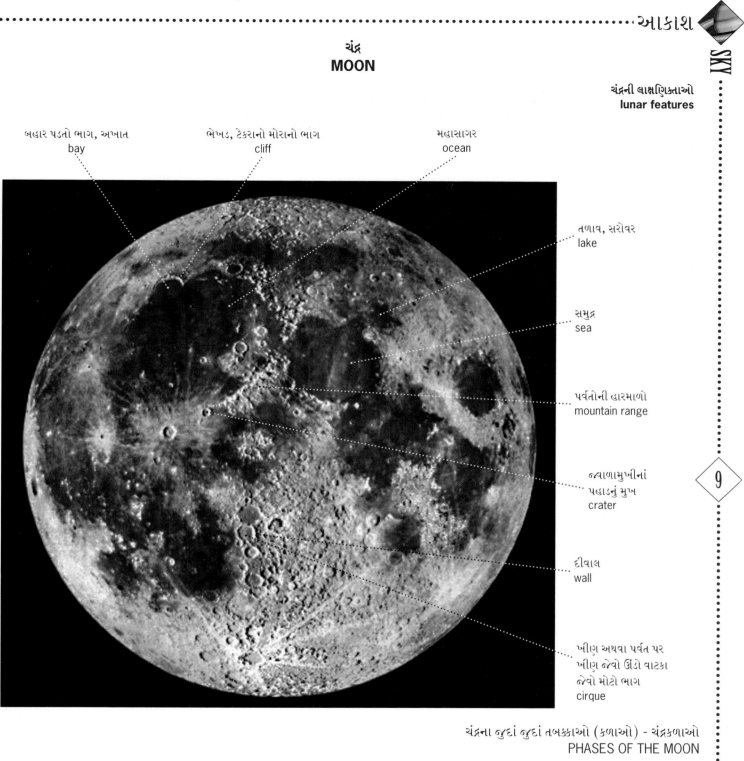

બહાર પડતો ભાગ, અખાત
bay

ભેખડ, ટેકરાનો મોરાનો ભાગ
cliff

મહાસાગર
ocean

તળાવ, સરોવર
lake

સમુદ્ર
sea

પર્વતોની હારમાળો
mountain range

જ્વાળામુખીનાં
પહાડનું મુખ
crater

દીવાલ
wall

ખીણ અથવા પર્વત પર
ખીણ જેવો ઊંડો વાટકા
જેવો મોટો ભાગ
cirque

ચંદ્રના જુદાં જુદાં તબક્કાઓ (કળાઓ) - ચંદ્રકળાઓ
PHASES OF THE MOON

નવો અર્ધચંદ્રાકાર
new crescent

બહિર્ગોળ ચંદ્ર
waxing gibbous Moon

બહિર્ગોળ ચંદ્ર
waxing gibbous Moon

જૂનો અર્ધચંદ્રાકાર
old crescent

નવો ચંદ્ર
new Moon

પ્રથમ ચતુર્થાંશ
first quarter

પૂર્ણ ચંદ્ર
full Moon

ચતુર્થાંશ
last quarter

પૂંછડિયો તારો, ધૂમકેતૂ
COMET

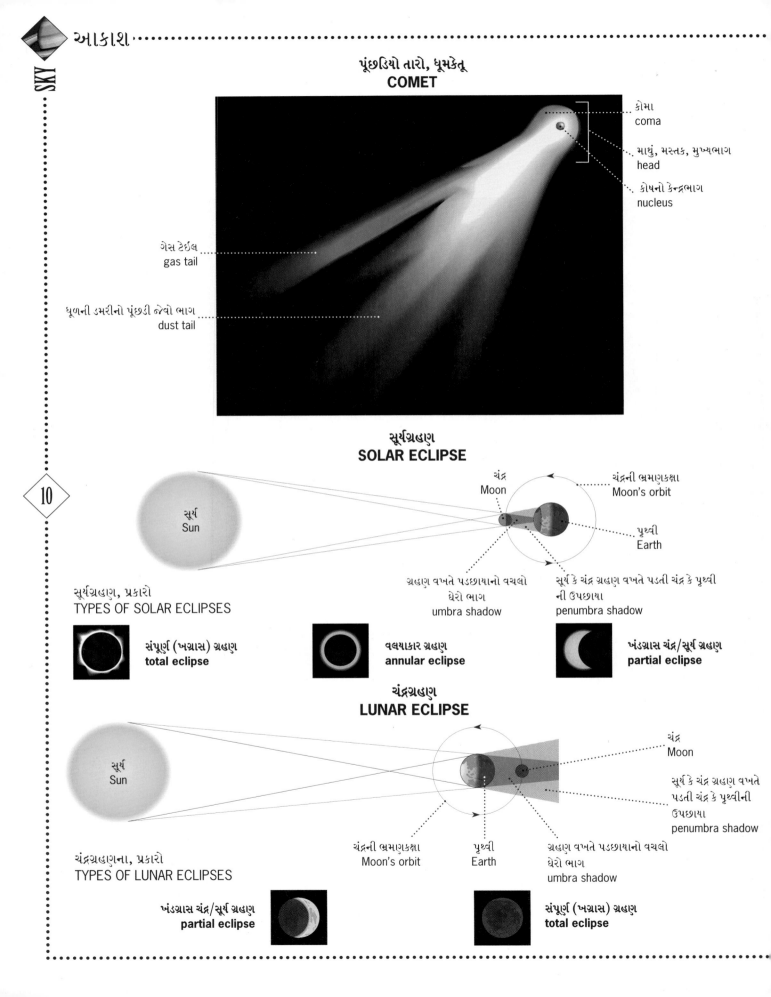

કોમા
coma

માથું, મસ્તક, મુખ્યભાગ
head

કોષનો કેન્દ્રભાગ
nucleus

ગેસ ટેઈલ
gas tail

ધૂળની ડમરીનો પૂંછડી જેવો ભાગ
dust tail

સૂર્યગ્રહણ
SOLAR ECLIPSE

ચંદ્ર
Moon

ચંદ્રની ભ્રમણકક્ષા
Moon's orbit

સૂર્ય
Sun

પૃથ્વી
Earth

ગ્રહણ વખતે પડછાયાનો વચલો ઘેરો ભાગ
umbra shadow

સૂર્ય કે ચંદ્ર ગ્રહણ વખતે પડતી ચંદ્ર કે પૃથ્વી ની ઉપછાયા
penumbra shadow

સૂર્યગ્રહણ, પ્રકારો
TYPES OF SOLAR ECLIPSES

સંપૂર્ણ (ખગ્રાસ) ગ્રહણ
total eclipse

વલયાકાર ગ્રહણ
annular eclipse

ખંડગ્રાસ ચંદ્ર/સૂર્ય ગ્રહણ
partial eclipse

ચંદ્રગ્રહણ
LUNAR ECLIPSE

ચંદ્ર
Moon

સૂર્ય
Sun

સૂર્ય કે ચંદ્ર ગ્રહણ વખતે પડતી ચંદ્ર કે પૃથ્વીની ઉપછાયા
penumbra shadow

ચંદ્રની ભ્રમણકક્ષા
Moon's orbit

પૃથ્વી
Earth

ગ્રહણ વખતે પડછાયાનો વચલો ઘેરો ભાગ
umbra shadow

ચંદ્રગ્રહણના, પ્રકારો
TYPES OF LUNAR ECLIPSES

ખંડગ્રાસ ચંદ્ર/સૂર્ય ગ્રહણ
partial eclipse

સંપૂર્ણ (ખગ્રાસ) ગ્રહણ
total eclipse

Library Resource Center
Renton Technical College
3000 N.E. 4th St.
Renton, WA 98056

પરાવર્તિત દૂરબીન
REFLECTING TELESCOPE

ફાઇન્ડરસ્કોપ
finderscope

આઇપિસ
eyepiece

મુખ્ય નળી
main tube

કેન્દ્રસ્થાન મેળવવાનો નોબ
focusing knob

સોયની હલચલને નિયત કરવાની આંકપટ્ટી
declination setting scale

દિગંશીય ચાપડો
azimuth clamp

ઉપર કરવાની જમણી આંખપટ્ટી
right ascension setting scale

ઊંચાઇ પરની જગ્યાએ ચઢવા માટેનો ક્લેમ્પ
altitude clamp

દિગંશીય સૂક્ષ્મ અનુકૂલન
azimuth fine adjustment

ચઢાઇ માટે નાજુક/સુક્ષ્મ સાનુકૂલન
altitude fine adjustment

પરાવર્તિત દૂરબીનનાં અન્ય વિભાગો
cross section of a reflecting telescope

આઇપિસ
eyepiece

મુખ્ય નળી
main tube

મુખ્ય અરીસો
main mirror

ચપટો અરીસો
flat mirror

પ્રકાશ
light

11

પ્રત્યાવર્તિત દૂરબીન
REFRACTING TELESCOPE

આધાર
support

આઇપિસ હોલ્ડર
eyepiece holder

વિકર્ણ તારક (સ્ટાર ડાયગોલ)
star diagonal

વાસ્તવિક કાચ
objective lens

આવરણ
dew shield

ઘોડિયું, ઝૂલો
cradle

પ્રતિવજન, પ્રતિભાર
counterweight

કાંટો
fork

ત્રણ પાયાવાળી ઘોડી
tripod

ચીજવસ્તુ રાખવાનાં ખાનાં વાળી ત્રણ પાયાવાળી ઘોડી
tripod accessories shelf

પ્રત્યાવર્તિત દૂરબીનનાં, અન્ય વિભાગો
cross section of a refracting telescope

આઇપિસ
eyepiece

વાસ્તવિક કાચ
objective lens

મુખ્ય નળી
main tube

પ્રકાશ
light

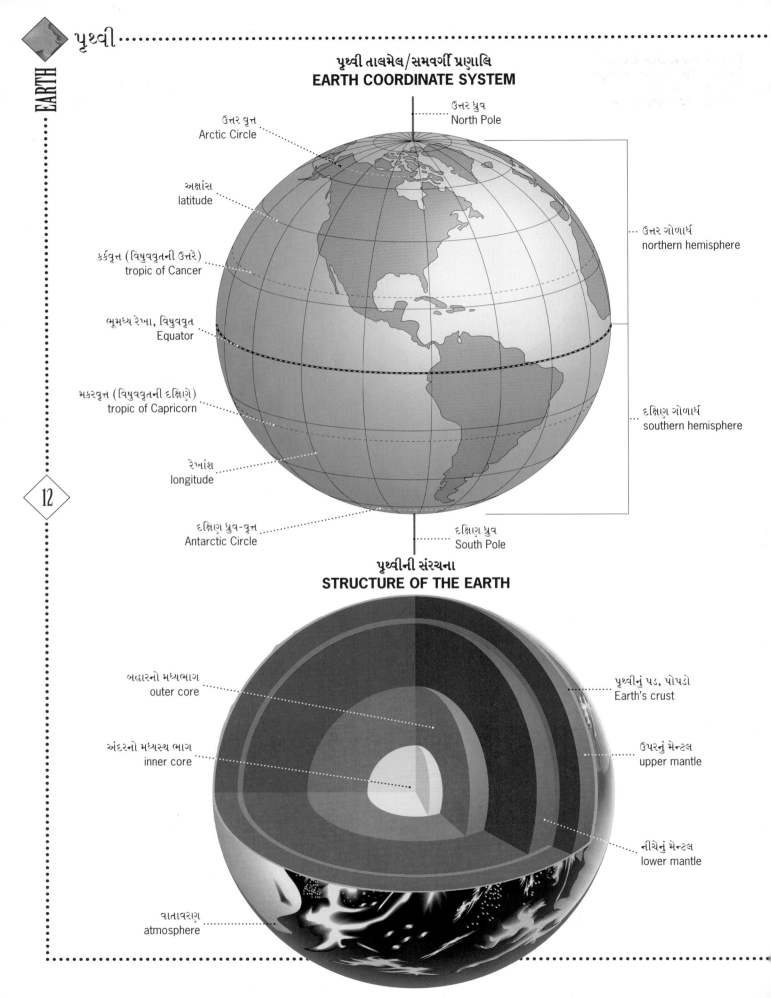

પૃથ્વી તાલમેલ/સમવર્ગી પ્રણાલિ
EARTH COORDINATE SYSTEM

ઉત્તર વૃત્ત
Arctic Circle

ઉત્તર ધ્રુવ
North Pole

અક્ષાંસ
latitude

ઉત્તર ગોળાર્ધ
northern hemisphere

કર્કવૃત્ત (વિષુવવૃતની ઉત્તરે)
tropic of Cancer

ભૂમધ્ય રેખા, વિષુવવૃત
Equator

મકરવૃત્ત (વિષુવવૃતની દક્ષિણે)
tropic of Capricorn

દક્ષિણ ગોળાર્ધ
southern hemisphere

રેખાંશ
longitude

દક્ષિણ ધ્રુવ-વૃત્ત
Antarctic Circle

દક્ષિણ ધ્રુવ
South Pole

પૃથ્વીની સંરચના
STRUCTURE OF THE EARTH

બહારનો મધ્યભાગ
outer core

પૃથ્વીનું પડ, પોપડો
Earth's crust

અંદરનો મધ્યસ્થ ભાગ
inner core

ઉપરનું મેન્ટલ
upper mantle

નીચેનું મેન્ટલ
lower mantle

વાતાવરણ
atmosphere

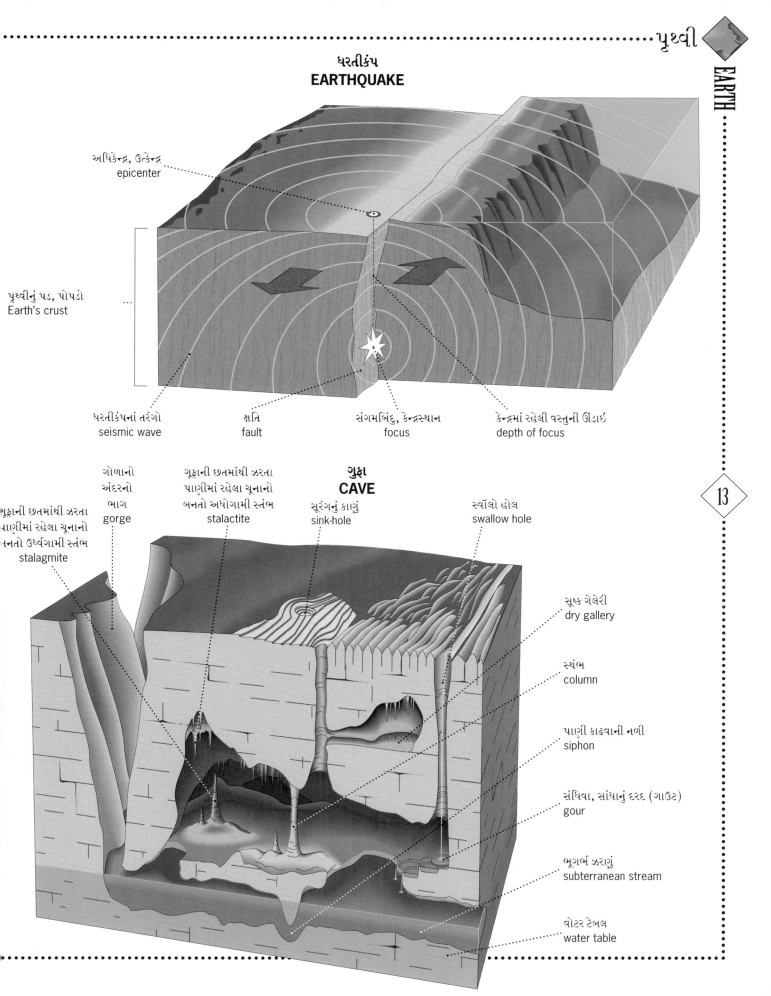

ધરતીકંપ
EARTHQUAKE

અધિકેન્દ્ર, ઉત્કેન્દ્ર
epicenter

પૃથ્વીનું પડ, પોપડો
Earth's crust

ધરતીકંપનાં તરંગો
seismic wave

ક્ષતિ
fault

સંગમબિંદુ, કેન્દ્રસ્થાન
focus

કેન્દ્રમાં રહેલી વસ્તુની ઊંડાઈ
depth of focus

ગોળાનો
અંદરનો
ભાગ
gorge

ગૂફાની છતમાંથી ઝરતા
પાણીમાં રહેલા ચૂનાનો
બનતો અધોગામી સ્તંભ
stalactite

ગૂફા
CAVE

સુરંગનું કાણું
sink-hole

સ્વૉલો હોલ
swallow hole

ગૂફાની છતમાંથી ઝરતા
પાણીમાં રહેલા ચૂનાનો
બનતો ઊર્ધ્વગામી સ્તંભ
stalagmite

સૂષ્ક ગેલેરી
dry gallery

સ્થંભ
column

પાણી કાઢવાની નળી
siphon

સંધિવા, સાંધાનું દરદ (ગાઉટ)
gour

ભૂગર્ભ ઝરણું
subterranean stream

વોટર ટેબલ
water table

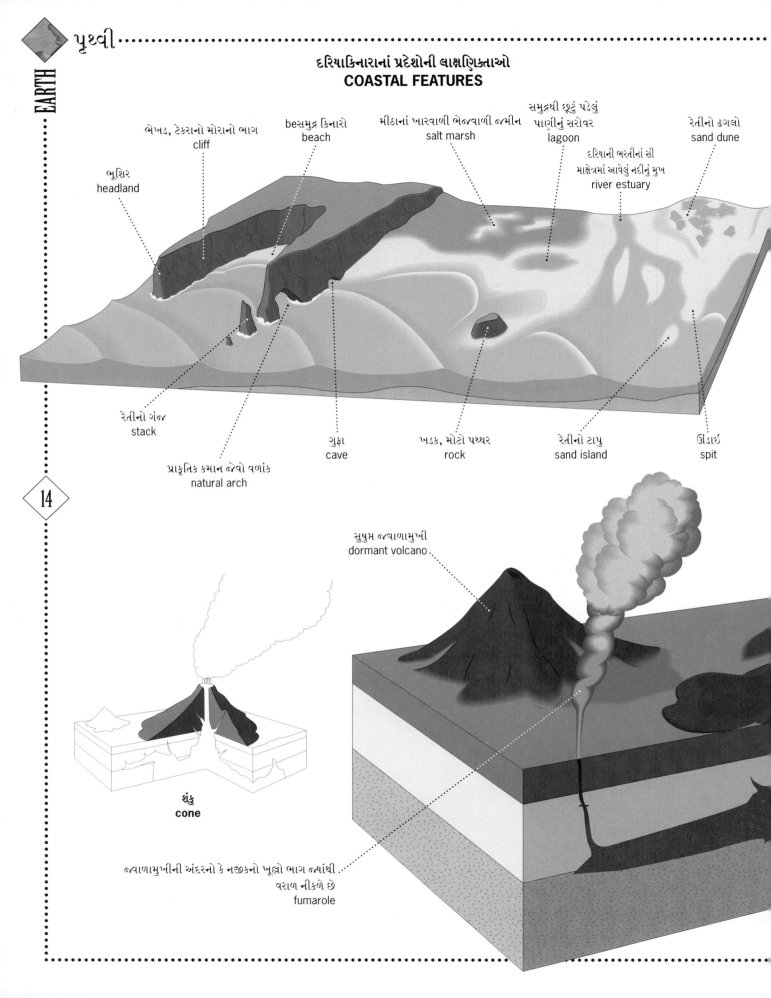

દરિયાકિનારાનાં પ્રદેશોની લાક્ષણિક્તાઓ
COASTAL FEATURES

ભૂશિર
headland

ભેખડ, ટેકરાનો મોરાનો ભાગ
cliff

besમુદ્ર કિનારો
beach

મીઠાનાં ખારવાળી ભેજવાળી જમીન
salt marsh

સમુદ્રથી છૂટું પડેલું
પાણીનું સરોવર
lagoon

દરિયાની ભરતીનાં સી
માક્ષેત્રમાં આવેલું નદીનું મુખ
river estuary

રેતીનો ઢગલો
sand dune

રેતીનો ગંજ
stack

પ્રાકૃતિક કમાન જેવો વળાંક
natural arch

ગુફા
cave

ખડક, મોટો પથ્થર
rock

રેતીનો ટાપુ
sand island

ઊંડાઇ
spit

સુષુપ્ત જ્વાળામુખી
dormant volcano

શંકુ
cone

જ્વાળામુખીની અંદરનો કે નજીકનો ખૂલ્લો ભાગ જ્યાંથી
વરાળ નીકળે છે
fumarole

જ્વાળામુખી
VOLCANO

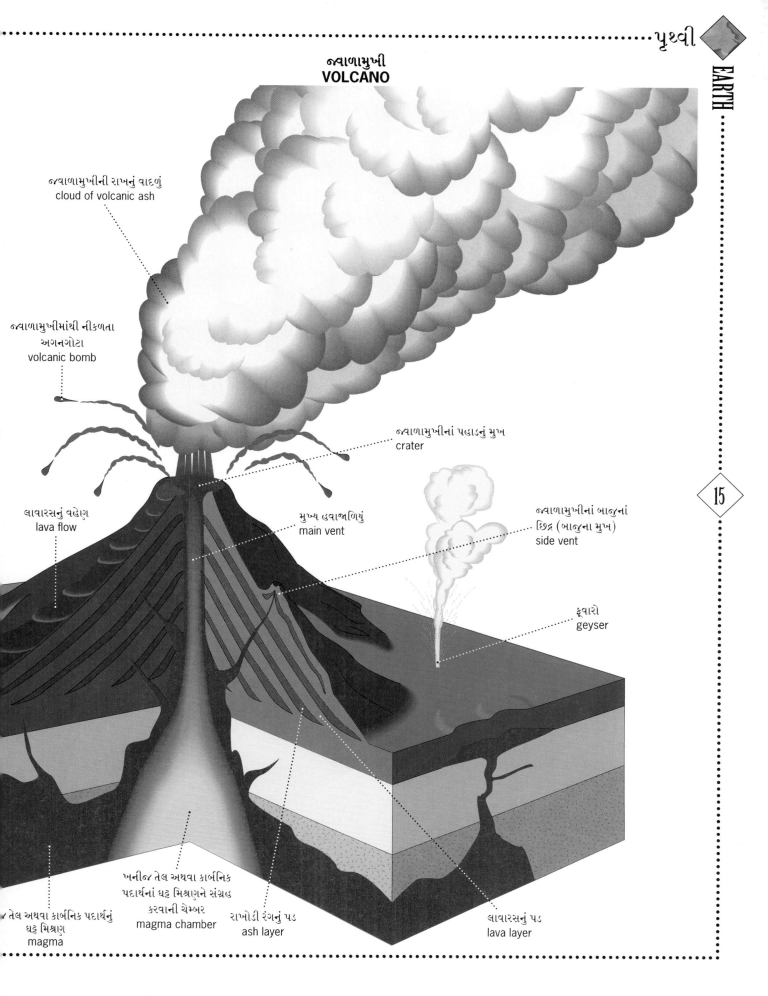

જ્વાળામુખીની રાખનું વાદળું
cloud of volcanic ash

જ્વાળામુખીમાંથી નીકળતા
અગનગોટા
volcanic bomb

જ્વાળામુખીનાં પહાડનું મુખ
crater

લાવારસનું વહેણ
lava flow

મુખ્ય હવાજાળિયું
main vent

જ્વાળામુખીનાં બાજુનાં
છિદ્ર (બાજુના મુખ)
side vent

ફૂવારો
geyser

તેલ અથવા કાર્બનિક પદાર્થનું
ઘટ્ટ મિશ્રણ
magma

ખનીજ તેલ અથવા કાર્બનિક
પદાર્થનાં ઘટ્ટ મિશ્રણને સંગ્રહ
કરવાની ચેમ્બર
magma chamber

રાખોડી રંગનું પડ
ash layer

લાવારસનું પડ
lava layer

હિમનદી
GLACIER

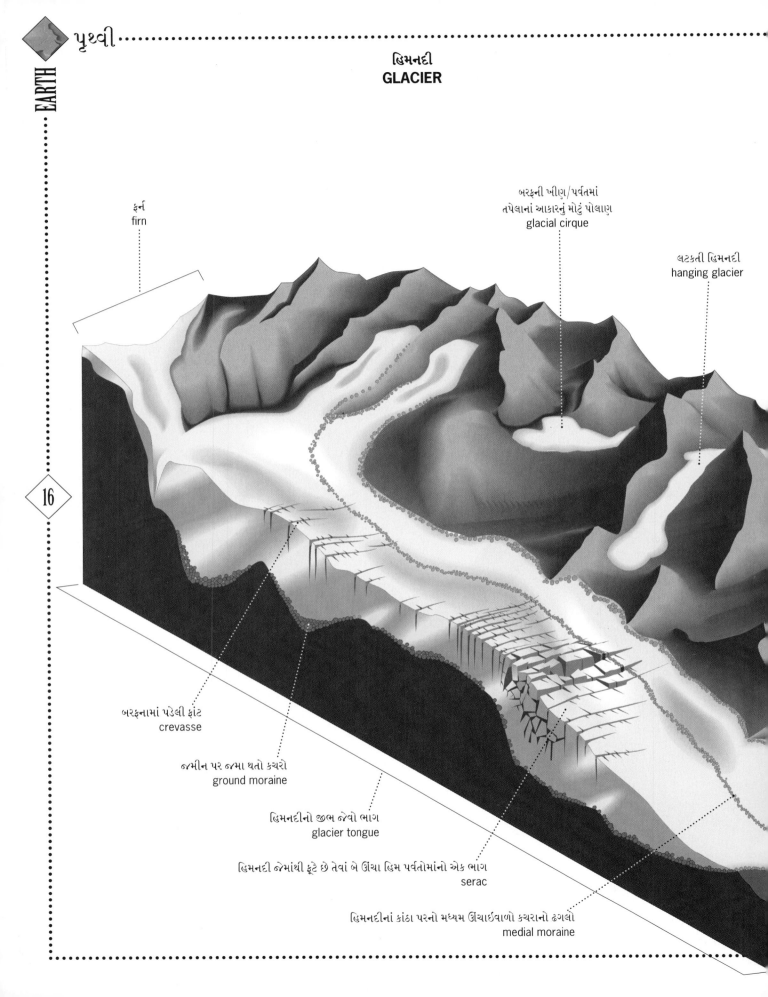

ફર્ન
firn

બરફની ખીણ/પર્વતમાં
તપેલાનાં આકારનું મોટું પોલાણ
glacial cirque

લટકતી હિમનદી
hanging glacier

બરફનામાં પડેલી ફાંટ
crevasse

જમીન પર જમા થતો કચરો
ground moraine

હિમનદીનો જીભ જેવો ભાગ
glacier tongue

હિમનદી જેમાંથી ફૂટે છે તેવાં બે ઊંચા હિમ પર્વતોમાંનો એક ભાગ
serac

હિમનદીનાં કાંઠા પરનો મધ્યમ ઊંચાઇવાળો કચરાનો ઢગલો
medial moraine

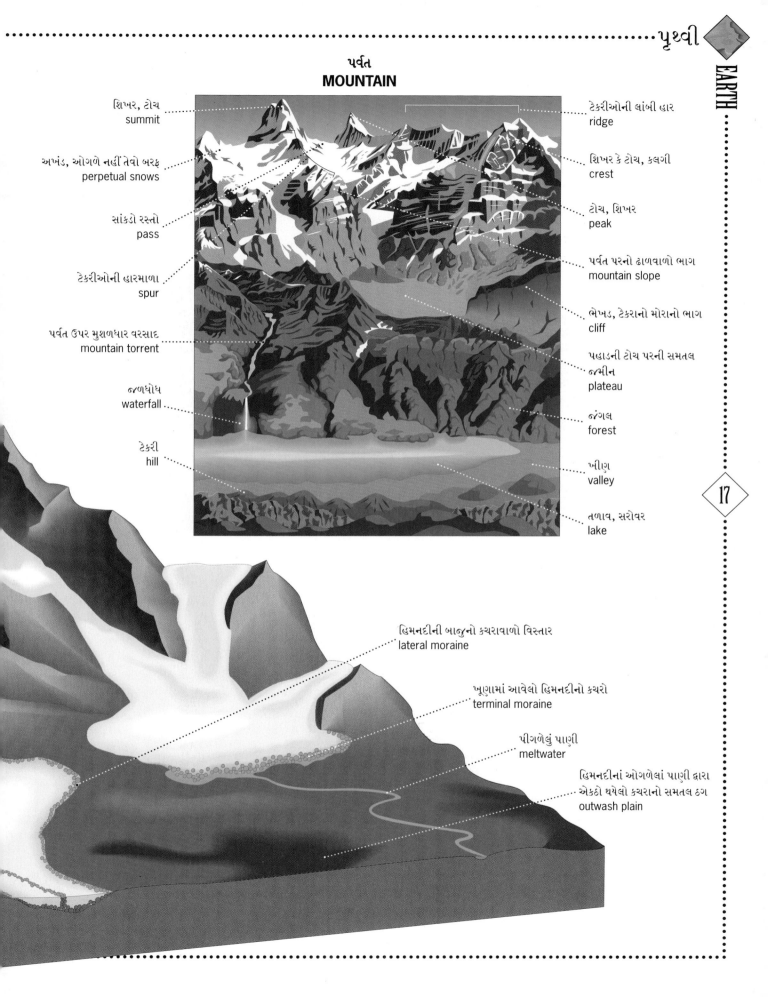

પર્વત
MOUNTAIN

શિખર, ટોચ
summit

અખંડ, ઓગળે નહીં તેવો બરફ
perpetual snows

સાંકડો રસ્તો
pass

ટેકરીઓની હારમાળા
spur

પર્વત ઉપર મુશળધાર વરસાદ
mountain torrent

જળધોધ
waterfall

ટેકરી
hill

ટેકરીઓની લાંબી હાર
ridge

શિખર કે ટોચ, કલગી
crest

ટોચ, શિખર
peak

પર્વત પરનો ઢાળવાળો ભાગ
mountain slope

ભેખડ, ટેકરાનો મોરાનો ભાગ
cliff

પહાડની ટોચ પરની સમતલ જમીન
plateau

જંગલ
forest

ખીણ
valley

તળાવ, સરોવર
lake

હિમનદીની બાજુનો કચરાવાળો વિસ્તાર
lateral moraine

ખૂણામાં આવેલો હિમનદીનો કચરો
terminal moraine

પીગળેલું પાણી
meltwater

હિમનદીનાં ઓગળેલાં પાણી દ્વારા એકઠો થયેલો કચરાનો સમતલ ઠગ
outwash plain

ખંડો
THE CONTINENTS

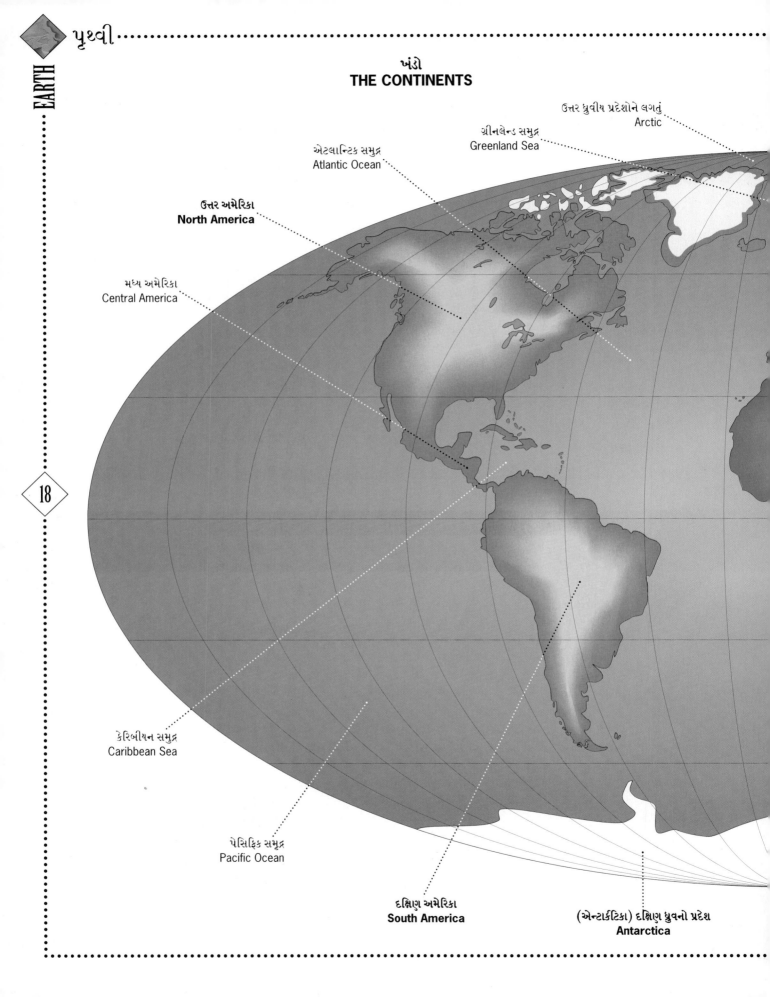

ઉત્તર ધ્રુવીય પ્રદેશને લગતું
Arctic

ગ્રીનલેન્ડ સમુદ્ર
Greenland Sea

એટલાન્ટિક સમુદ્ર
Atlantic Ocean

ઉત્તર અમેરિકા
North America

મધ્ય અમેરિકા
Central America

18

કેરિબીયન સમુદ્ર
Caribbean Sea

પેસિફિક સમુદ્ર
Pacific Ocean

દક્ષિણ અમેરિકા
South America

(એન્ટાર્કટિકા) દક્ષિણ ધ્રુવનો પ્રદેશ
Antarctica

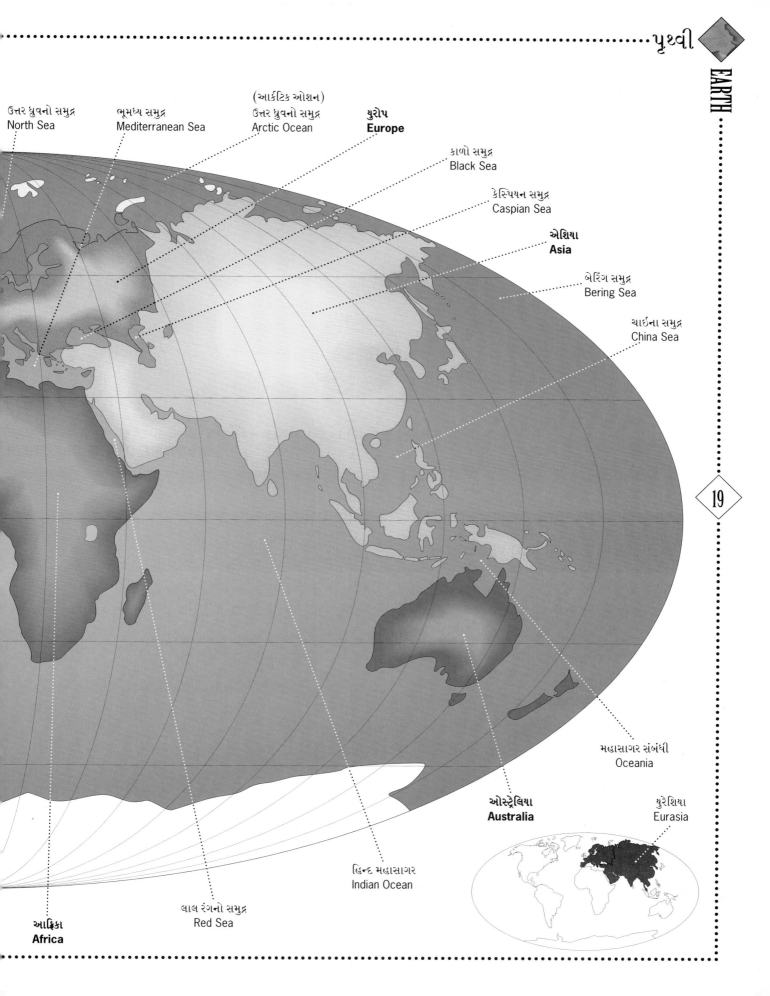

ઉત્તર ધ્રુવનો સમુદ્ર
North Sea

ભૂમધ્ય સમુદ્ર
Mediterranean Sea

(આર્કટિક ઓશન)
ઉત્તર ધ્રુવનો સમુદ્ર
Arctic Ocean

યુરોપ
Europe

કાળો સમુદ્ર
Black Sea

કેસ્પિયન સમુદ્ર
Caspian Sea

એશિયા
Asia

બેરિંગ સમુદ્ર
Bering Sea

ચાઈના સમુદ્ર
China Sea

મહાસાગર સંબંધી
Oceania

ઓસ્ટ્રેલિયા
Australia

યુરેશિયા
Eurasia

હિન્દ મહાસાગર
Indian Ocean

લાલ રંગનો સમુદ્ર
Red Sea

આફ્રિકા
Africa

વર્ષની ઋતુઓ
SEASONS OF THE YEAR

વસંતઋતુનો સંપાત સમય (વાસંતિક સંપાત); વસંત ઋતુનો સંપાત સમય
vernal equinox; spring equinox

વસંત ઋતુ
spring

શિયાળો
winter

શિયાળાનો અયનકાળ
winter solstice

ઉનાળાનો અયનકાળ (આશરે 21 મી જૂન)
summer solstice

ઉનાળો
summer

પાનખર ઋતુનાં સમય દરમ્યાન આવતો સંપાત સમય
autumnal equinox

પાનખર ઋતુ
autumn

બાયોસ્ફીયરની સંરચના (પૃથ્વીનાં પોપડાનાં પ્રદેશો અને જૈવિક પ્રાણીઓ દ્વારા વપરાતો વાતાવરણનો ભાગ)
STRUCTURE OF THE BIOSPHERE

વાતાવરણ
atmosphere

જળમંડળ
hydrosphere

સ્થળ મંડળ
lithosphere

ઊંચાઈનાં વિસ્તારો અને વનસ્પતિઓ
ELEVATION ZONES AND VEGETATION

હિમનદી યા હિમક્ષેત્ર
glacier

હિમાછાદિત ધ્રુવ પ્રદેશ
tundra

શંકુદ્રમ વર્ગનું જંગલ
coniferous forest

સંમિશ્રિત જંગલ
mixed forest

પાંદડા ખેરવનારું જંગલ
deciduous forest

ઉષ્ણકટિબંધનાં જંગલો
tropical forest

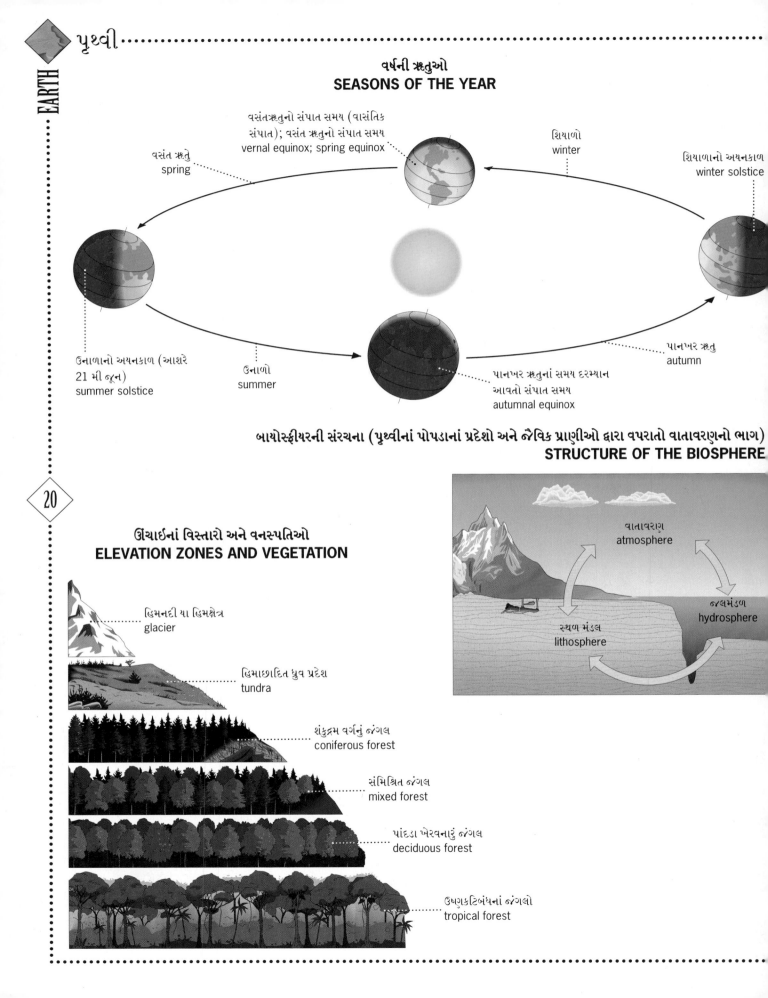

વિશ્વનાં હવામાનો
CLIMATES OF THE WORLD

ઉષ્ણકટિબંધનાં હવામાન
tropical climates

ખૂબ વરસાદ આવતો હોય તેવાં
ઉષ્ણકટિબંધનાં જંગલો
tropical rain forest

ઉષ્ણકટિબંધ પરના વૃક્ષહીન મોટા ઘાસનો પ્રદેશ
tropical savanna

વૃક્ષવિહીન ઘાસવાળું મેદાન
steppe

રણ
desert

સમશીતોષ્ણ હવામાન
temperate climates

ભેજવાળો, લાંબો ઉનાળો
humid - long summer

ભેજવાળો, ટૂંકો ઉનાળો
humid - short summer

દરિયાઈ
marine

ઉત્તર/દક્ષિણ ધ્રુવનું હવામાન
polar climates

ઉત્તર/દક્ષિણ ધ્રુવનો
હિમા છાદિત પ્રદેશ
polar tundra

ઉત્તર/દક્ષિણ ધ્રુવ પર બરફનું શિખર
polar ice cap

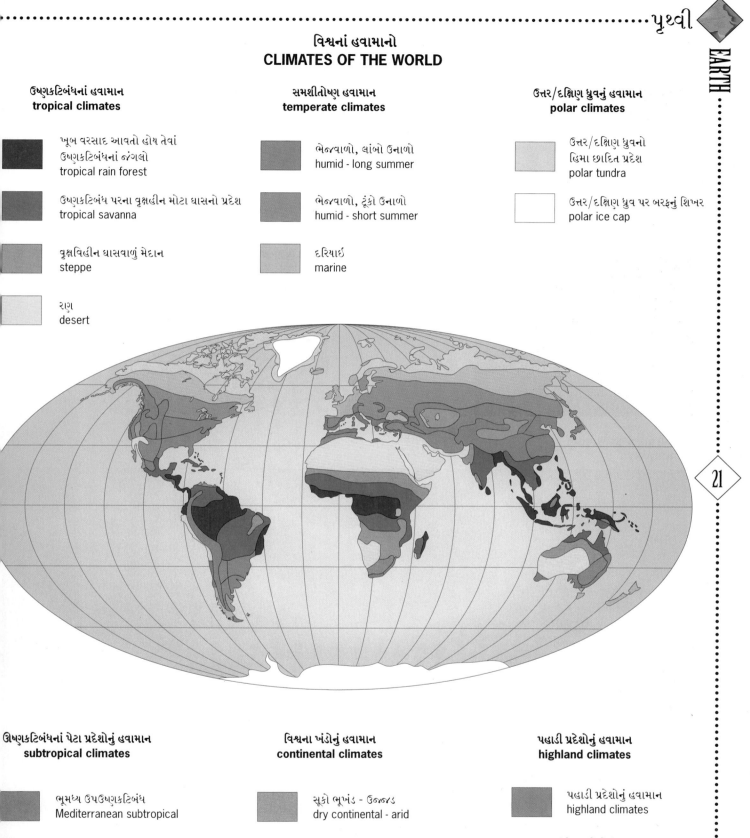

ઉષ્ણકટિબંધનાં પેટા પ્રદેશોનું હવામાન
subtropical climates

ભૂમધ્ય ઉપઉષ્ણકટિબંધ
Mediterranean subtropical

ભેજવાળો, ઉપ-ઉષ્ણ કટિબંધ
humid subtropical

સૂક્ષ ઉપઉષ્ણ કટિબંધ
dry subtropical

વિશ્વના ખંડોનું હવામાન
continental climates

સૂકો ભૂખંડ - ઉજ્જડ
dry continental - arid

સૂકો ભૂખંડ - અર્ધ ઉજ્જડ
dry continental - semiarid

પહાડી પ્રદેશનું હવામાન
highland climates

પહાડી પ્રદેશોનું હવામાન
highland climates

ઉત્તર ધ્રુવનાં પેટા પ્રદેશોનું હવામાન
subarctic climates

ઉત્તર ધ્રુવનાં પેટા પ્રદેશોનું હવામાન
subarctic climates

હવામાન
WEATHER

ઝાકળ
mist

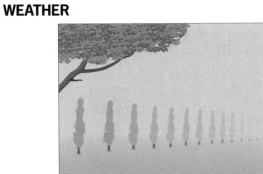

ધુમ્મસ
fog

ઝાકળ
dew

ચમકતો હિમ (ગ્લેઝ્ડ ફ્રોસ્ટ)
glazed frost

તોફાની વાદળાંઓવાળું આકાશ
stormy sky

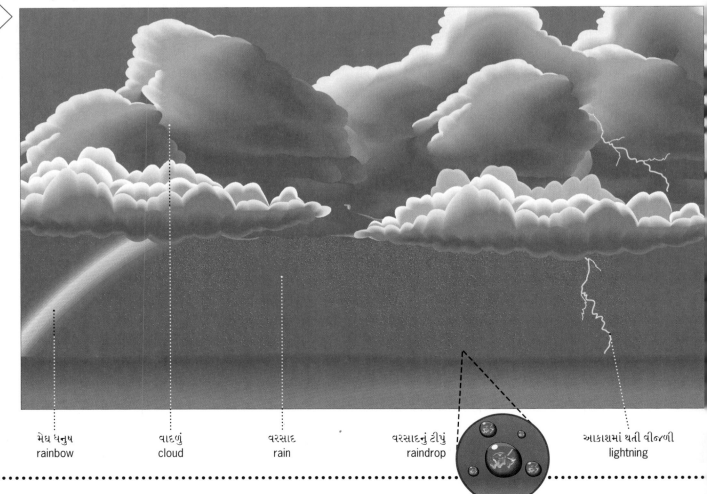

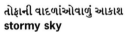

| મેઘ ધનુષ
rainbow | વાદળું
cloud | વરસાદ
rain | વરસાદનું ટીપું
raindrop | આકાશમાં થતી વીજળી
lightning |

હવામાનશાસ્ત્રને લગતા માપવાનાં સાધનો
METEOROLOGICAL MEASURING INSTRUMENTS

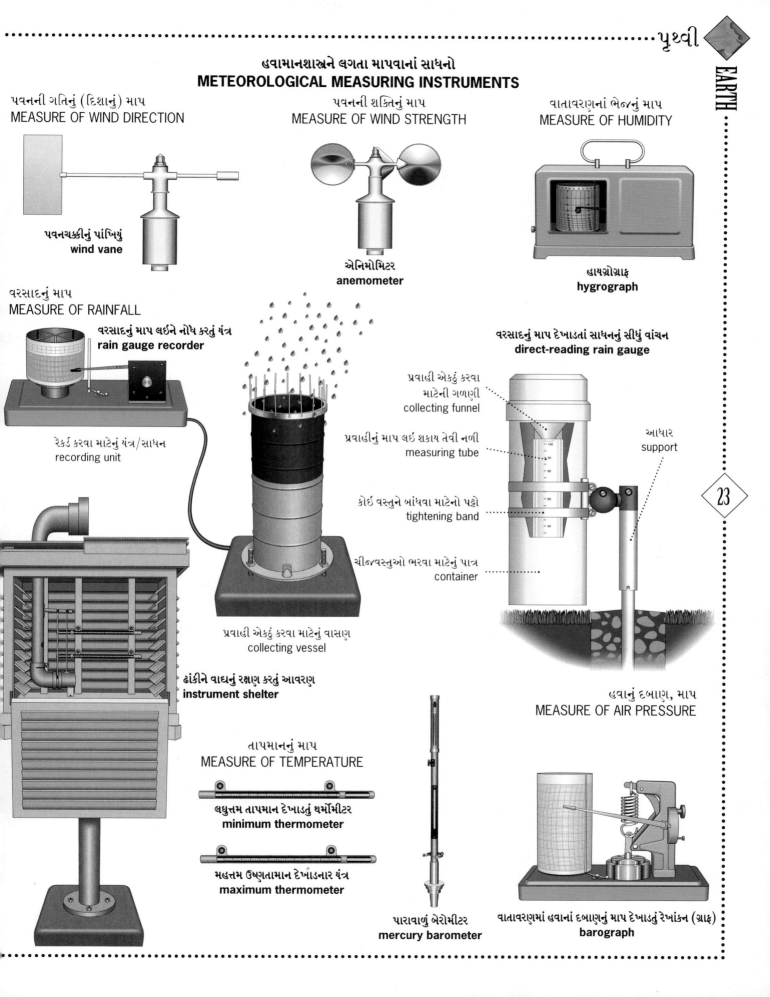

પવનની ગતિનું (દિશાનું) માપ
MEASURE OF WIND DIRECTION

પવનચક્કીનું પાંખિયું
wind vane

પવનની શક્તિનું માપ
MEASURE OF WIND STRENGTH

એનિમોમિટર
anemometer

વાતાવરણનાં ભેજનું માપ
MEASURE OF HUMIDITY

હાયગ્રોગ્રાફ
hygrograph

વરસાદનું માપ
MEASURE OF RAINFALL

વરસાદનું માપ લઈને નોંધ કરતું યંત્ર
rain gauge recorder

રેકર્ડ કરવા માટેનું યંત્ર/સાધન
recording unit

વરસાદનું માપ દેખાડતાં સાધનનું સીધું વાંચન
direct-reading rain gauge

પ્રવાહી એકઠું કરવા
માટેની ગળાણી
collecting funnel

પ્રવાહીનું માપ લઈ શકાય તેવી નળી
measuring tube

કોઈ વસ્તુને બાંધવા માટેનો પટ્ટો
tightening band

ચીજવસ્તુઓ ભરવા માટેનું પાત્ર
container

આધાર
support

પ્રવાહી એકઠું કરવા માટેનું વાસણ
collecting vessel

ઢાંકીને વાયુનું રક્ષણ કરતું આવરણ
instrument shelter

તાપમાનનું માપ
MEASURE OF TEMPERATURE

લઘુત્તમ તાપમાન દેખાડતું થર્મોમીટર
minimum thermometer

મહત્તમ ઉષ્ણતામાન દેખાડનાર યંત્ર
maximum thermometer

પારાવાનું બેરોમીટર
mercury barometer

હવાનું દબાણ, માપ
MEASURE OF AIR PRESSURE

વાતાવરણમાં હવાનાં દબાણનું માપ દેખાડતું રેખાંકન (ગ્રાફ)
barograph

નકશા બનાવવાનું કામ
CARTOGRAPHY

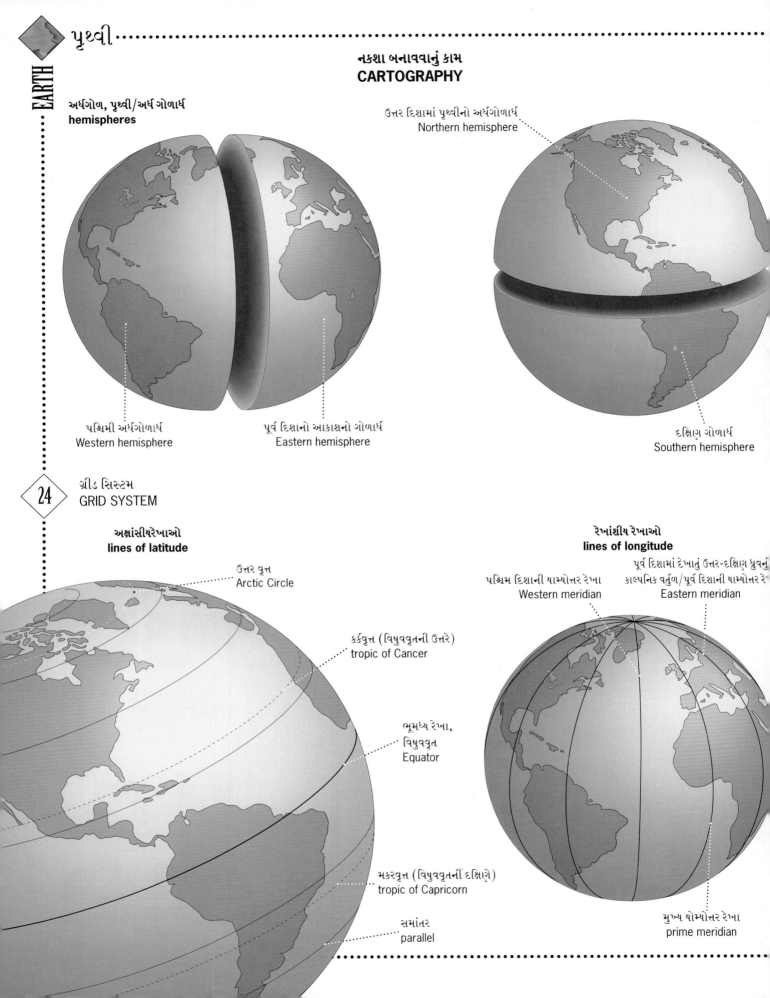

અર્ધગોળ, પૃથ્વી/અર્ધ ગોળાર્ધ
hemispheres

ઉત્તર દિશામાં પૃથ્વીનો અર્ધગોળાર્ધ
Northern hemisphere

પશ્ચિમી અર્ધગોળાર્ધ
Western hemisphere

પૂર્વ દિશાનો આકાશનો ગોળાર્ધ
Eastern hemisphere

દક્ષિણ ગોળાર્ધ
Southern hemisphere

ગ્રીડ સિસ્ટમ
GRID SYSTEM

અક્ષાંસીયરેખાઓ
lines of latitude

ઉત્તર વૃત્ત
Arctic Circle

કર્કવૃત્ત (વિષુવવૃત્તની ઉત્તરે)
tropic of Cancer

ભૂમધ્ય રેખા,
વિષુવવૃત્ત
Equator

મકરવૃત્ત (વિષુવવૃત્તની દક્ષિણે)
tropic of Capricorn

સમાંતર
parallel

રેખાંશીય રેખાઓ
lines of longitude

પૂર્વ દિશામાં દેખાતું ઉત્તર-દક્ષિણ ધ્રુવનું
કાલ્પનિક વર્તુળ/પૂર્વ દિશાની યામ્યોત્તર રે
Eastern meridian

પશ્ચિમ દિશાની યામ્યોત્તર રેખા
Western meridian

મુખ્ય યોમ્યોત્તર રેખા
prime meridian

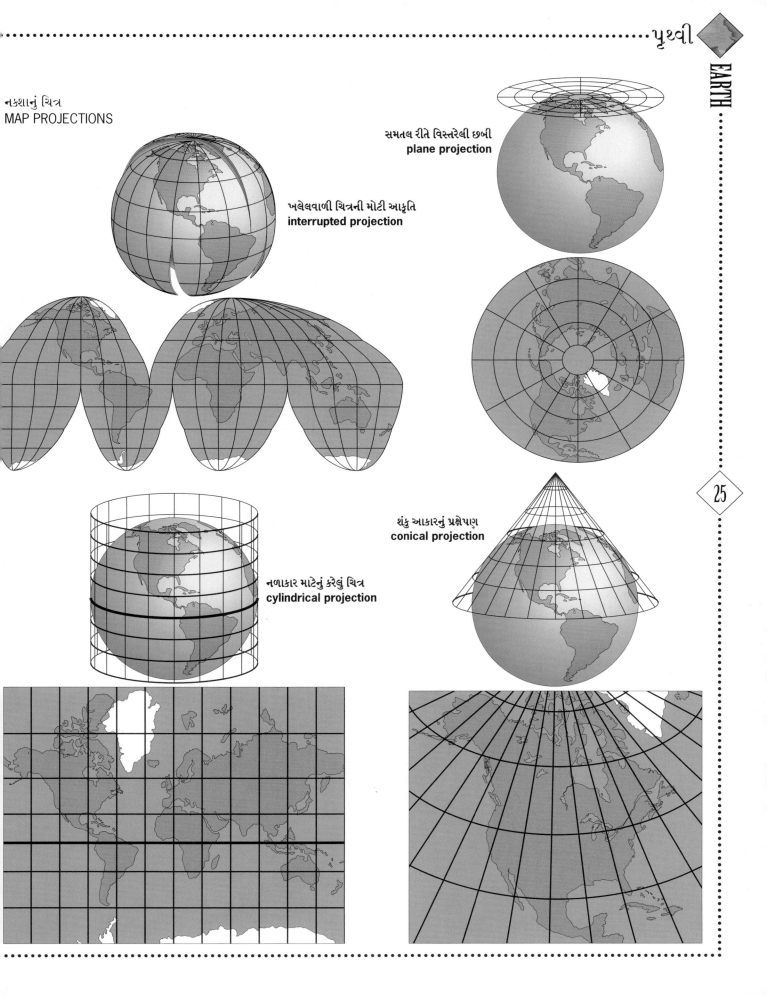

નકશાનું ચિત્ર
MAP PROJECTIONS

ખલેલવાળી ચિત્રની મોટી આકૃતિ
interrupted projection

સમતલ રીતે વિસ્તરેલી છબી
plane projection

નળાકાર માટેનું કરેલું ચિત્ર
cylindrical projection

શંકુ આકારનું પ્રક્ષેપણ
conical projection

EARTH

નકશા બનાવવાનું કામ
CARTOGRAPHY

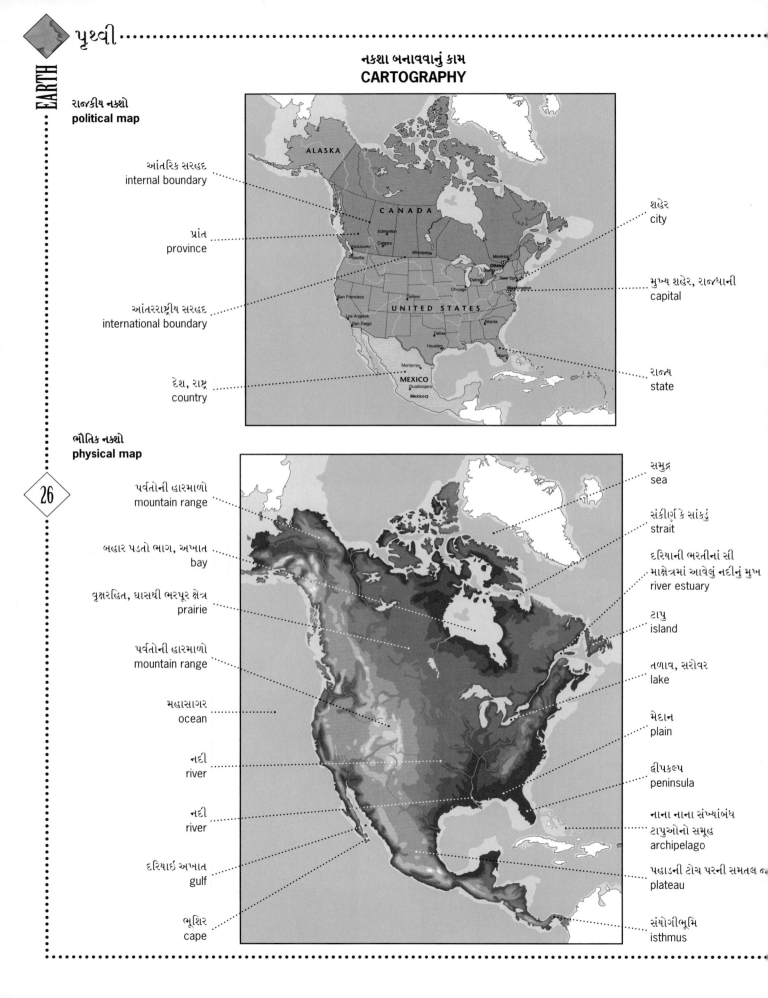

રાજકીય નકશો
political map

આંતરિક સરહદ
internal boundary

પ્રાંત
province

આંતરરાષ્ટ્રીય સરહદ
international boundary

દેશ, રાષ્ટ્ર
country

શહેર
city

મુખ્ય શહેર, રાજધાની
capital

રાજ્ય
state

ભૌતિક નકશો
physical map

પર્વતોની હારમાળો
mountain range

બહાર પડતો ભાગ, અખાત
bay

વૃક્ષરહિત, ઘાસથી ભરપૂર ક્ષેત્ર
prairie

પર્વતોની હારમાળો
mountain range

મહાસાગર
ocean

નદી
river

નદી
river

દરિયાઈ અખાત
gulf

ભૂશિર
cape

સમુદ્ર
sea

સંકીર્ણ કે સાંકડું
strait

દરિયાની ભરતીનાં સી
માક્ષેત્રમાં આવેલું નદીનું મુખ
river estuary

ટાપુ
island

તળાવ, સરોવર
lake

મેદાન
plain

દ્વીપકલ્પ
peninsula

નાના નાના સંખ્યાબંધ
ટાપુઓનો સમૂહ
archipelago

પહાડની ટોચ પરની સમતલ જ
plateau

સંયોગીભૂમિ
isthmus

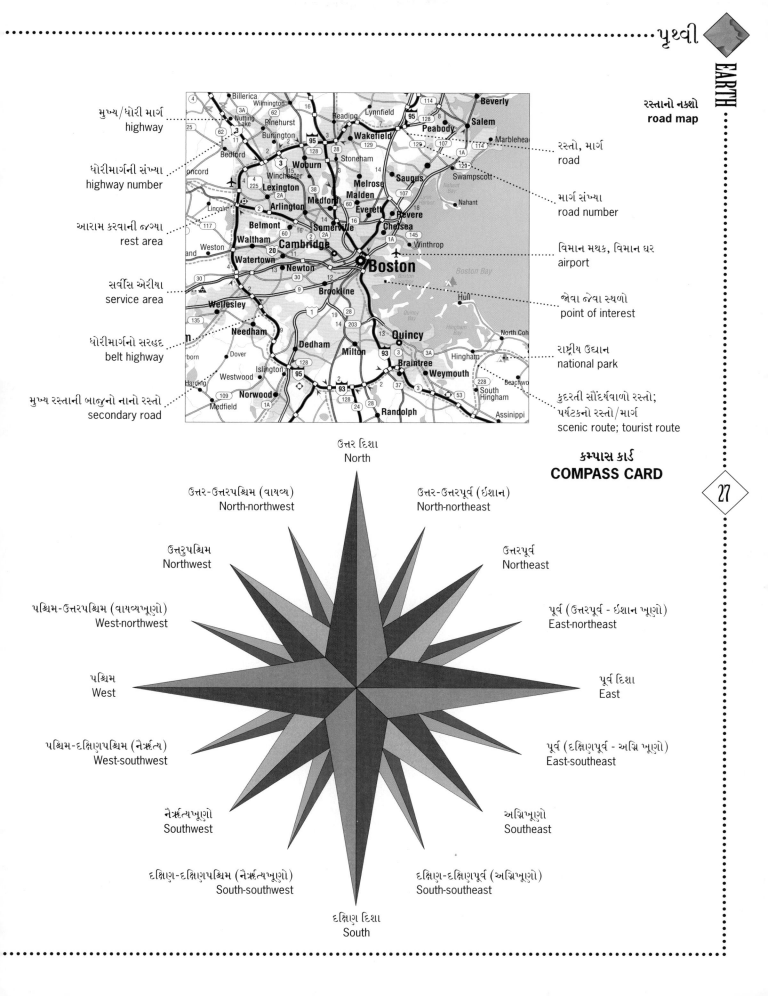

મુખ્ય/ધોરી માર્ગ
highway

ધોરીમાર્ગની સંખ્યા
highway number

આરામ કરવાની જગ્યા
rest area

સર્વિસ એરીયા
service area

ધોરીમાર્ગનો સરહદ
belt highway

મુખ્ય રસ્તાની બાજુનો નાનો રસ્તો
secondary road

રસ્તાનો નકશો
road map

રસ્તો, માર્ગ
road

માર્ગ સંખ્યા
road number

વિમાન મથક, વિમાન ઘર
airport

જોવા જેવા સ્થળો
point of interest

રાષ્ટ્રીય ઉદ્યાન
national park

કુદરતી સૌંદર્યવાળો રસ્તો;
પર્યટકનો રસ્તો/માર્ગ
scenic route; tourist route

કમ્પાસ કાર્ડ
COMPASS CARD

27

ઉત્તર દિશા
North

ઉત્તર-ઉત્તરપશ્ચિમ (વાયવ્ય)
North-northwest

ઉત્તર-ઉત્તરપૂર્વ (ઈશાન)
North-northeast

ઉત્તરપશ્ચિમ
Northwest

ઉત્તરપૂર્વ
Northeast

પશ્ચિમ-ઉત્તરપશ્ચિમ (વાયવ્યખૂણો)
West-northwest

પૂર્વ (ઉત્તરપૂર્વ - ઈશાન ખૂણો)
East-northeast

પશ્ચિમ
West

પૂર્વ દિશા
East

પશ્ચિમ-દક્ષિણપશ્ચિમ (નૈર્ઋત્ય)
West-southwest

પૂર્વ (દક્ષિણપૂર્વ - અગ્નિ ખૂણો)
East-southeast

નૈર્ઋત્યખૂણો
Southwest

અગ્નિખૂણો
Southeast

દક્ષિણ-દક્ષિણપશ્ચિમ (નૈર્ઋત્યખૂણો)
South-southwest

દક્ષિણ-દક્ષિણપૂર્વ (અગ્નિખૂણો)
South-southeast

દક્ષિણ દિશા
South

EARTH

જીવન પધ્ધતિઓ અને તેના વાતાવરણનું વિજ્ઞાન
ECOLOGY

કાર્બન ડાયોક્સાઇડનાં વધારાનાં કારણે પૃથ્વી પર સૂર્યની ગરમીનું શોષણ થવું
greenhouse effect

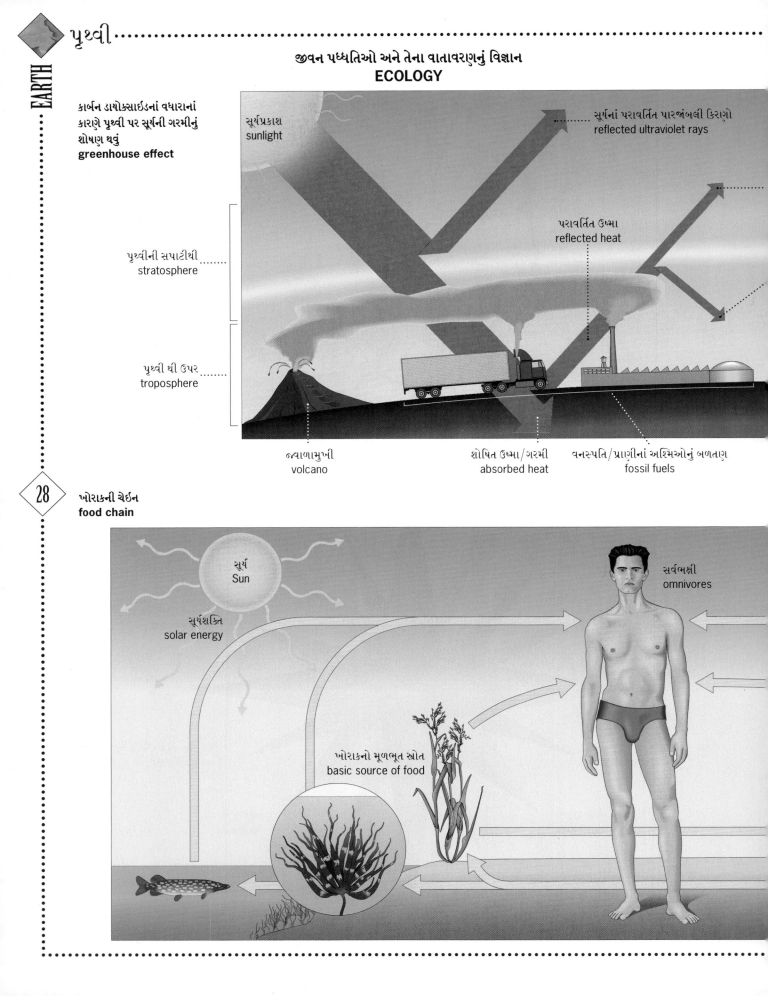

સૂર્યપ્રકાશ
sunlight

સૂર્યનાં પરાવર્તિત પારજંબલી કિરણો
reflected ultraviolet rays

પરાવર્તિત ઉષ્મા
reflected heat

પૃથ્વીની સપાટીથી
stratosphere

પૃથ્વી થી ઉપર
troposphere

જ્વાળામુખી
volcano

શોષિત ઉષ્મા/ગરમી
absorbed heat

વનસ્પતિ/પ્રાણીનાં અશ્મિઓનું બળતાણ
fossil fuels

ખોરાકની ચેઇન
food chain

સૂર્ય
Sun

સૂર્યશક્તિ
solar energy

સર્વભક્ષી
omnivores

ખોરાકનો મૂળભૂત સ્રોત
basic source of food

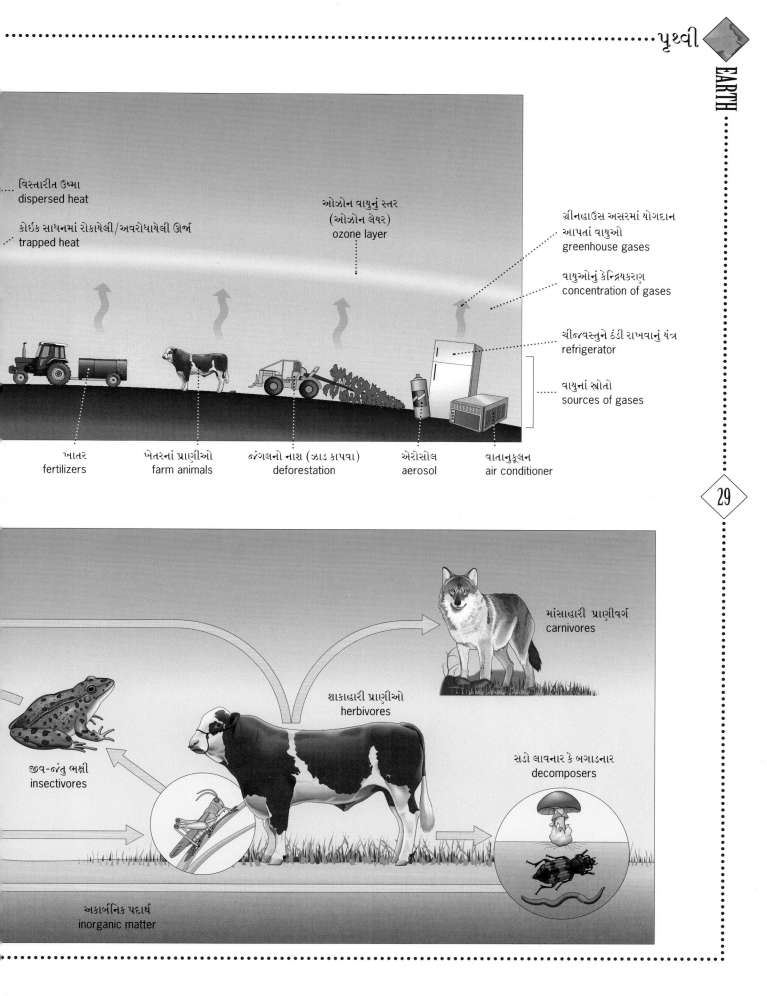

વિસ્તારીત ઉષ્મા
dispersed heat

કોઈક સાધનમાં રોકાયેલી/અવરોધાયેલી ઊર્જા
trapped heat

ઓઝોન વાયુનું સ્તર
(ઓઝોન લેયર)
ozone layer

ગ્રીનહાઉસ અસરમાં યોગદાન
આપતાં વાયુઓ
greenhouse gases

વાયુઓનું કેન્દ્રિયકરણ
concentration of gases

ચીજવસ્તુને ઠંડી રાખવાનું યંત્ર
refrigerator

વાયુનાં સ્રોતો
sources of gases

ખાતર
fertilizers

ખેતરનાં પ્રાણીઓ
farm animals

જંગલનો નાશ (ઝાડ કાપવા)
deforestation

એરોસોલ
aerosol

વાતાનુકૂલન
air conditioner

માંસાહારી પ્રાણીવર્ગ
carnivores

શાકાહારી પ્રાણીઓ
herbivores

સડો લાવનાર કે બગાડનાર
decomposers

જીવ-જંતુ ભક્ષી
insectivores

અકાર્બનિક પદાર્થ
inorganic matter

જીવન પધ્ધતિઓ અને તેના વાતાવરણનું વિજ્ઞાન
ECOLOGY

વાતાવરણનું પ્રદૂષણ
atmospheric pollution

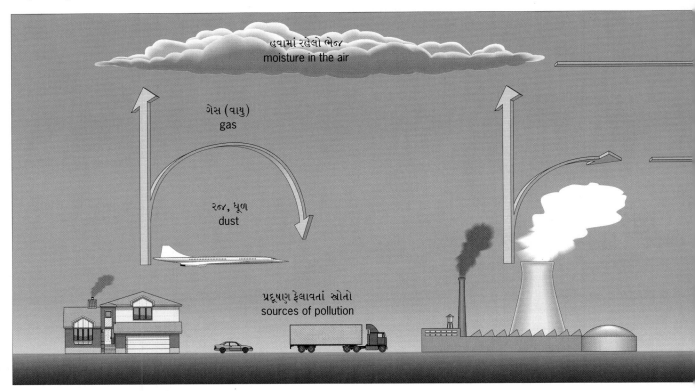

હવામાં રહેલો ભેજ
moisture in the air

ગેસ (વાયુ)
gas

રજ, ધૂળ
dust

પ્રદૂષણ ફેલાવતાં સ્ત્રોતો
sources of pollution

પાણી દ્વારા ચાલતી રાસાયણિક પ્રક્રિયા (વોટર સાયકલ)
water cycle

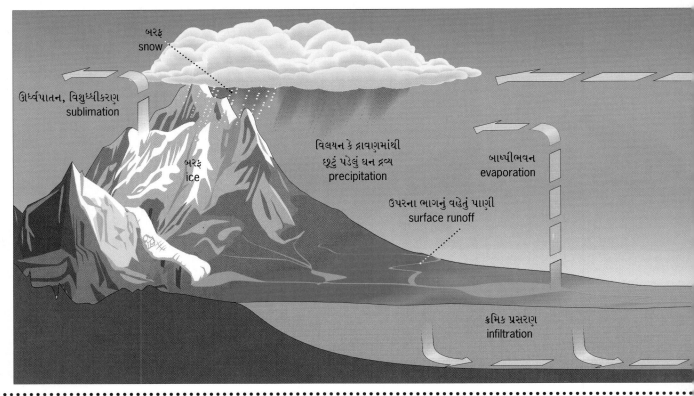

બરફ
snow

ઉર્ધ્વપાતન, વિશુધ્ધીકરણ
sublimation

બરફ
ice

વિલયન કે દ્રાવણમાંથી
છૂટું પડેલું ઘન દ્રવ્ય
precipitation

બાષ્પીભવન
evaporation

ઉપરના ભાગનું વહેતું પાણી
surface runoff

ક્રમિક પ્રસરણ
infiltration

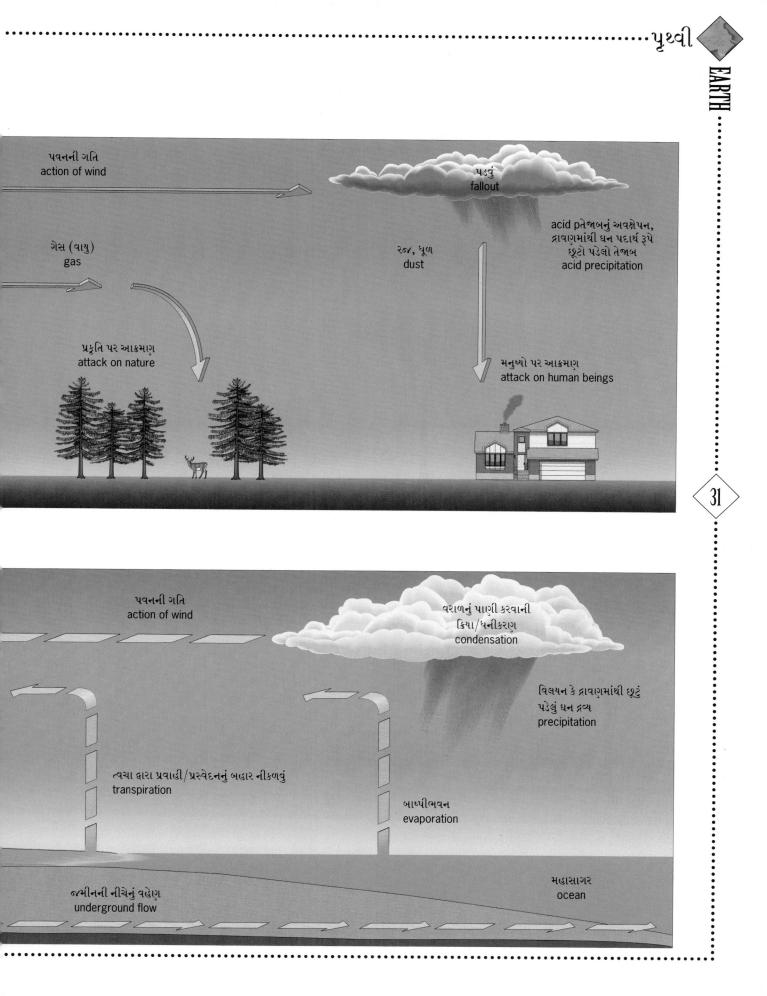

પવનની ગતિ
action of wind

પડવું
fallout

ગેસ (વાયુ)
gas

રજ, ધૂળ
dust

acid pતેજબનું અવક્ષેપન,
દ્રાવણમાંથી ઘન પદાર્થ રૂપે
છૂટો પડેલો તેજબ
acid precipitation

પ્રકૃતિ પર આક્રમણ
attack on nature

મનુષ્યો પર આક્રમણ
attack on human beings

પવનની ગતિ
action of wind

વરાળનું પાણી કરવાની
ક્રિયા/ઘનીકરણ
condensation

વિલયન કે દ્રાવણમાંથી છૂટું
પડેલું ઘન દ્રવ્ય
precipitation

ત્વચા દ્વારા પ્રવાહી/પ્રસ્વેદનનું બહાર નીકળવું
transpiration

બાષ્પીભવન
evaporation

જમીનની નીચેનું વહેણ
underground flow

મહાસાગર
ocean

જીવન પધ્ધતિઓ અને તેના વાતાવરણનું વિજ્ઞાન
ECOLOGY

જમીન પર ખોરાકનું પ્રદૂષણ
food pollution on ground

તેજાબનો વરસાદ
acid rain

ખેતરનું પ્રદૂષણ
farm pollution

ઔદ્યોગિક પ્રદૂષણ
industrial pollution

પાણીમાં ખોરાકનું પ્રદૂષણ
food pollution in water

ખાતર
fertilizers

જંતુનાશકો
pesticides

ખેતરનું પ્રદૂષણ
farm pollution

ઉપરના ભાગનું વહેતું પાણી
surface runoff

જમીનની નીચેનું વહેણ
underground flow

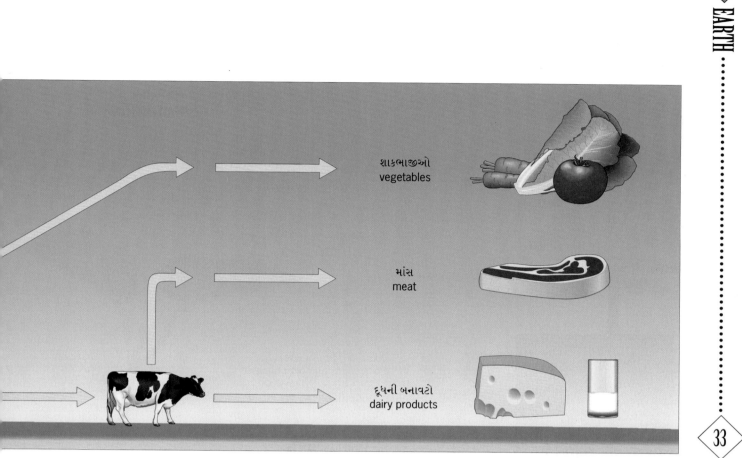

શાકભાજીઓ
vegetables

માંસ
meat

દૂધની બનાવટો
dairy products

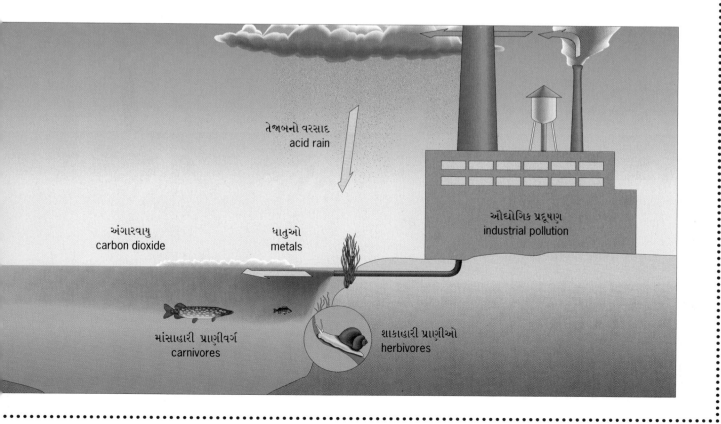

તેજબનો વરસાદ
acid rain

ઔદ્યોગિક પ્રદૂષણ
industrial pollution

અંગારવાયુ
carbon dioxide

ધાતુઓ
metals

માંસાહારી પ્રાણીવર્ગ
carnivores

શાકાહારી પ્રાણીઓ
herbivores

વનસ્પતિ અને માટી
PLANT AND SOIL

માટી/જમીનની રૂપરેખા
SOIL PROFILE

અંકુરોદ્ભવ
GERMINATION

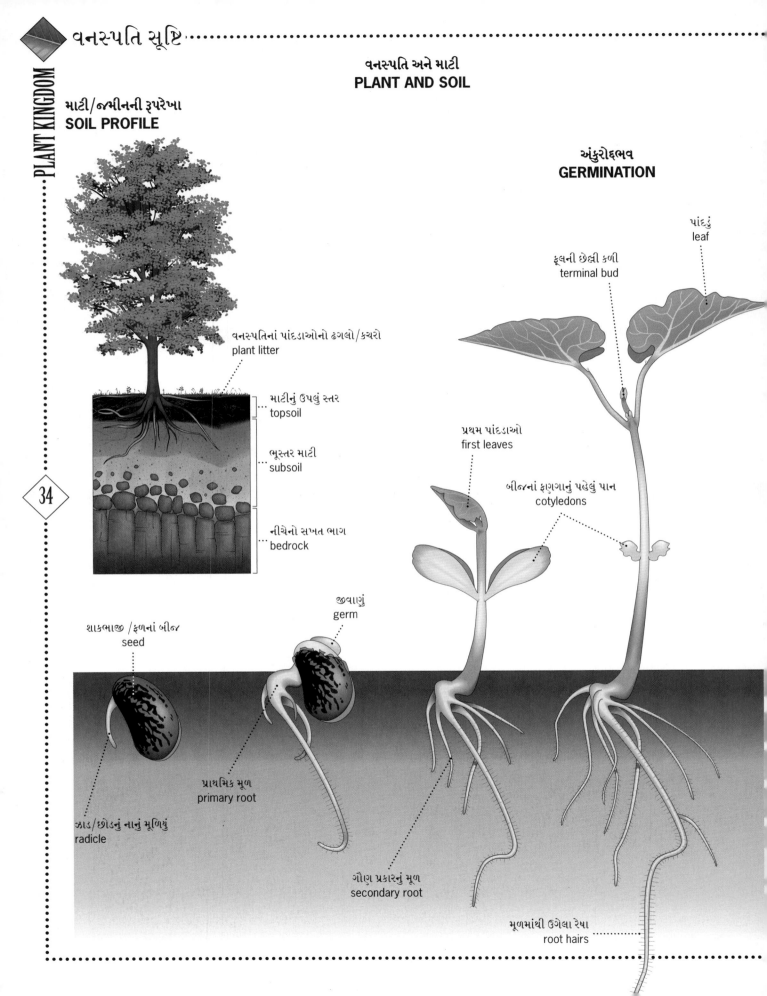

પાંદડું
leaf

ફૂલની છેલ્લી કળી
terminal bud

વનસ્પતિનાં પાંદડાઓનો ઢગલો/કચરો
plant litter

માટીનું ઉપલું સ્તર
topsoil

ભૂસ્તર માટી
subsoil

નીચેનો સખત ભાગ
bedrock

પ્રથમ પાંદડાઓ
first leaves

બીજનાં ફણગાનું પહેલું પાન
cotyledons

જીવાણું
germ

શાકભાજી /ફળનાં બીજ
seed

પ્રાથમિક મૂળ
primary root

ઝાડ/છોડનું નાનું મૂળિયું
radicle

ગૌણ પ્રકારનું મૂળ
secondary root

મૂળમાંથી ઉગેલા રેષા
root hairs

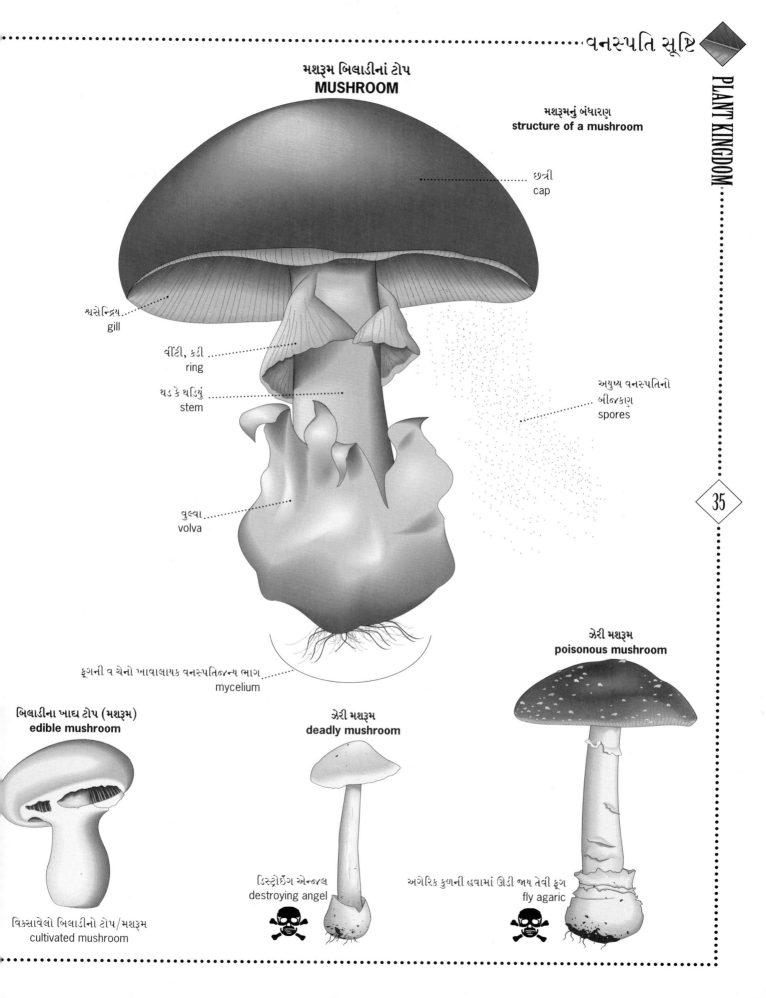

મશરૂમ બિલાડીનાં ટોપ
MUSHROOM

મશરૂમનું બંધારણ
structure of a mushroom

છત્રી
cap

શ્વસેન્દ્રિય
gill

વીંટી, કડી
ring

થડ કે થડિયું
stem

વુલ્વા
volva

અયુષ્ય વનસ્પતિનો બીજકણ
spores

ફૂગની વ ચેનો ખાવાલાયક વનસ્પતિજન્ય ભાગ
mycelium

બિલાડીના ખાદ્ય ટોપ (મશરૂમ)
edible mushroom

વિક્સાવેલો બિલાડીનો ટોપ/મશરૂમ
cultivated mushroom

ઝેરી મશરૂમ
deadly mushroom

ડિસ્ટ્રોઇંગ એન્જલ
destroying angel

ઝેરી મશરૂમ
poisonous mushroom

અગેરિક કુળની હવામાં ઊડી જાય તેવી ફૂગ
fly agaric

છોડની સંરચના
STRUCTURE OF A PLANT

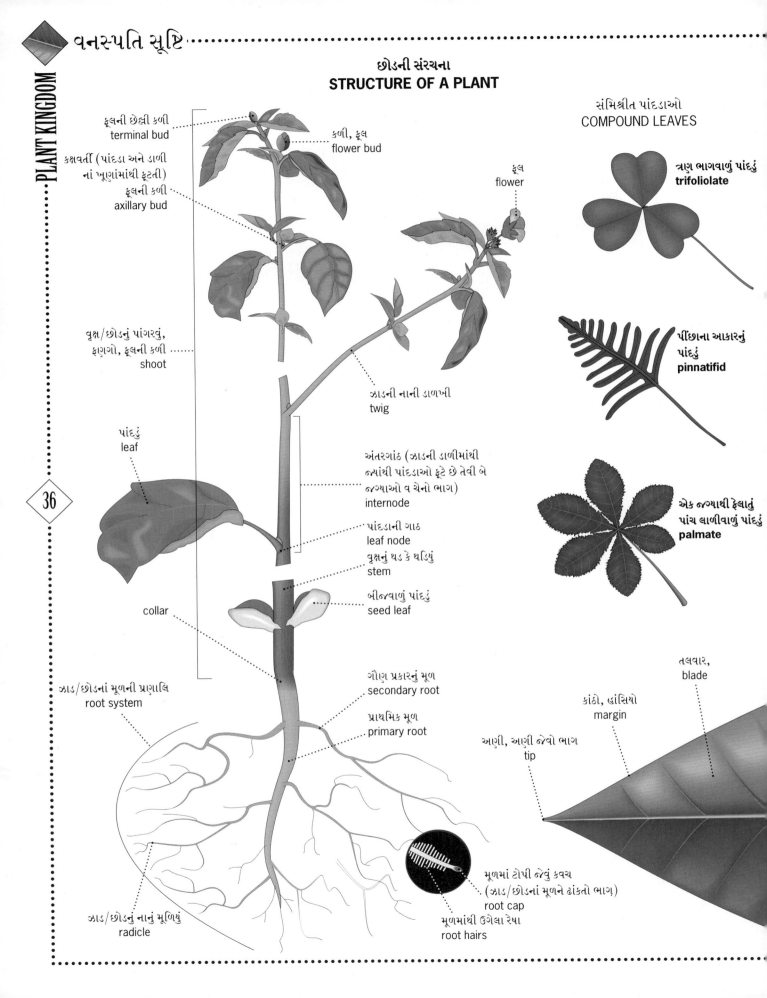

ફૂલની છેલ્લી કળી
terminal bud

કક્ષવર્તી (પાંદડા અને ડાળી
નાં ખૂણાંમાંથી ફૂટતી)
ફૂલની કળી
axillary bud

કળી, ફૂલ
flower bud

ફૂલ
flower

વૃક્ષ/છોડનું પાંગરવું,
ફણગો, ફૂલની કળી
shoot

ઝાડની નાની ડાળખી
twig

પાંદડું
leaf

અંતરગાંઠ (ઝાડની ડાળીમાંથી
જ્યાંથી પાંદડાઓ ફૂટે છે તેવી બે
જગ્યાઓ વ ચેનો ભાગ)
internode

પાંદડાની ગાંઠ
leaf node

વૃક્ષનું થડ કે થડિયું
stem

collar

બીજવાળું પાંદડું
seed leaf

ઝાડ/છોડનાં મૂળની પ્રણાલિ
root system

ગૌણ પ્રકારનું મૂળ
secondary root

પ્રાથમિક મૂળ
primary root

ઝાડ/છોડનું નાનું મૂળિયું
radicle

મૂળમાં ટોપી જેવું કવચ
(ઝાડ/છોડનાં મૂળને ઢાંકતો ભાગ)
root cap

મૂળમાંથી ઉગેલા રેષા
root hairs

સંમિશ્રીત પાંદડાઓ
COMPOUND LEAVES

ત્રણ ભાગવાળું પાંદડું
trifoliolate

પીંછાના આકારનું
પાંદડું
pinnatifid

એક જગ્યાથી ફેલાતું
પાંચ લાળીવાળું પાંદડું
palmate

તલવાર,
blade

કાંઠો, હાંસિયો
margin

આણી, આણી જેવો ભાગ
tip

36

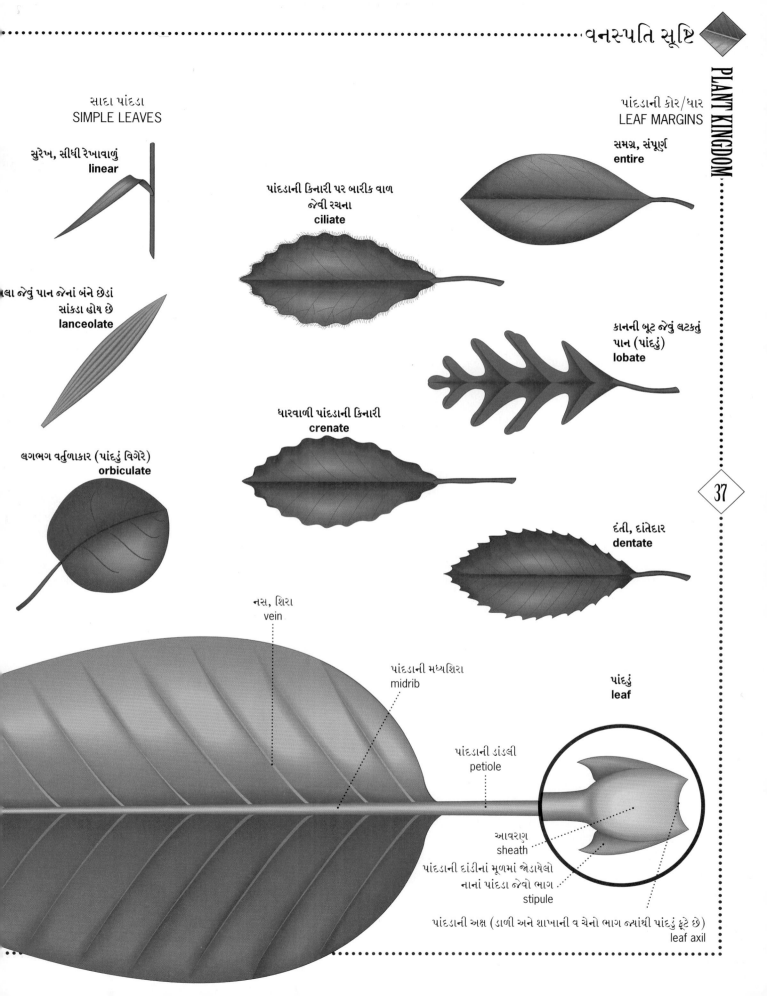

સાદા પાંદડા
SIMPLE LEAVES

સુરેખ, સીધી રેખાવાળું
linear

...લા જેવું પાન જેનાં બંને છેડાં સાંકડા હોય છે
lanceolate

લગભગ વર્તુળાકાર (પાંદડું વિગેરે)
orbiculate

પાંદડાની કિનારી પર બારીક વાળ જેવી રચના
ciliate

ધારવાળી પાંદડાની કિનારી
crenate

પાંદડાની કોર/ધાર
LEAF MARGINS

સમગ્ર, સંપૂર્ણ
entire

કાનની બૂટ જેવું લટકતું પાન (પાંદડું)
lobate

દંતી, દાંતેદાર
dentate

નસ, શિરા
vein

પાંદડાની મધ્યશિરા
midrib

પાંદડું
leaf

પાંદડાની ડાંડલી
petiole

આવરણ
sheath

પાંદડાની દાંડીનાં મૂળમાં જોડાયેલો નાનાં પાંદડા જેવો ભાગ
stipule

પાંદડાની અક્ષ (ડાળી અને શાખાની વ ચેનો ભાગ જ્યાંથી પાંદડું ફૂટે છે)
leaf axil

ફૂલો
FLOWERS

ફૂલનો ઢાંચો/સંરચના
structure of a flower

પુષ્પયોનિ
stigma

ફૂલનો પરાગ કોષ
anther

સ્ટાયલ
style

ફૂલ અથવા પ્રાણીમાં ફૂલની નાની દાંડી જેવું માળખું
pedicel

સૂક્ષ્મ તંતુ અથવા તાંતણો
filament

ફૂલની પાંખડી
petal

ફૂલનો પાંખડીવાળો ભાગ
sepal

ફળ/ફૂલ રાખવાનું પાત્ર
receptacle

નારીદેહની રજઃ પિંડ ગ્રન્થિ
ovary

બિનફળદ્રુપ બીજ
ovule

ફૂલની પાંદડીઓનું વર્તુલ
corolla

પુંકેસર, ફૂલની અંદરનું નરબીજ
stamen

ફૂલનો બીજકોશ
pistil

કાચા ફૂલ પર પાંદડાનું આછાદન
calyx

38

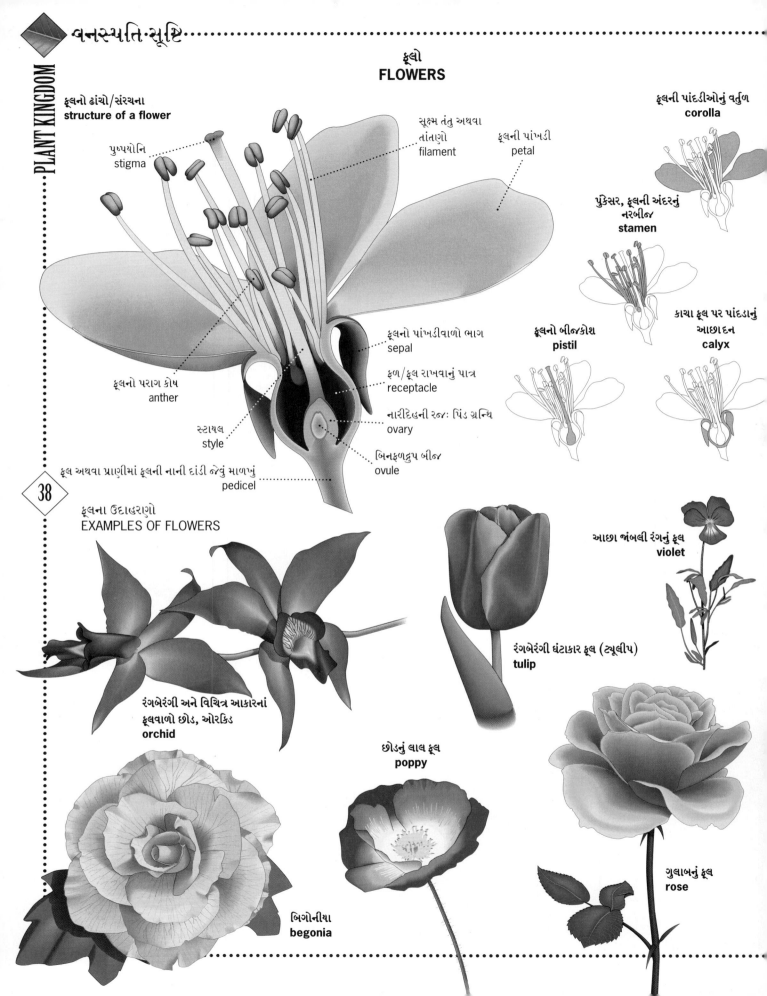

ફૂલના ઉદાહરણો
EXAMPLES OF FLOWERS

રંગબેરંગી અને વિચિત્ર આકારનાં ફૂલવાળો છોડ, ઓરકિડ
orchid

રંગબેરંગી ઘંટાકાર ફૂલ (ટ્યૂલીપ)
tulip

આછા જાંબલી રંગનું ફૂલ
violet

છોડનું લાલ ફૂલ
poppy

ગુલાબનું ફૂલ
rose

બિગોનીયા
begonia

ચમેલી, કુમુદ, રાત્રિકમલ
lily

ખીણનાં ખૂબસૂરત ચમેલીનાં ફૂલો
lily of the valley

સૂર્યમુખીનું ફૂલ
sunflower

જાંબલી, સફેદ ફૂલવાળું એક ફૂલઝાડ
crocus

ફૂલ કારનેશન
carnation

વસંતઋતુનું પીળા રંગનું ફૂલ ડેફોડિલ
daffodil

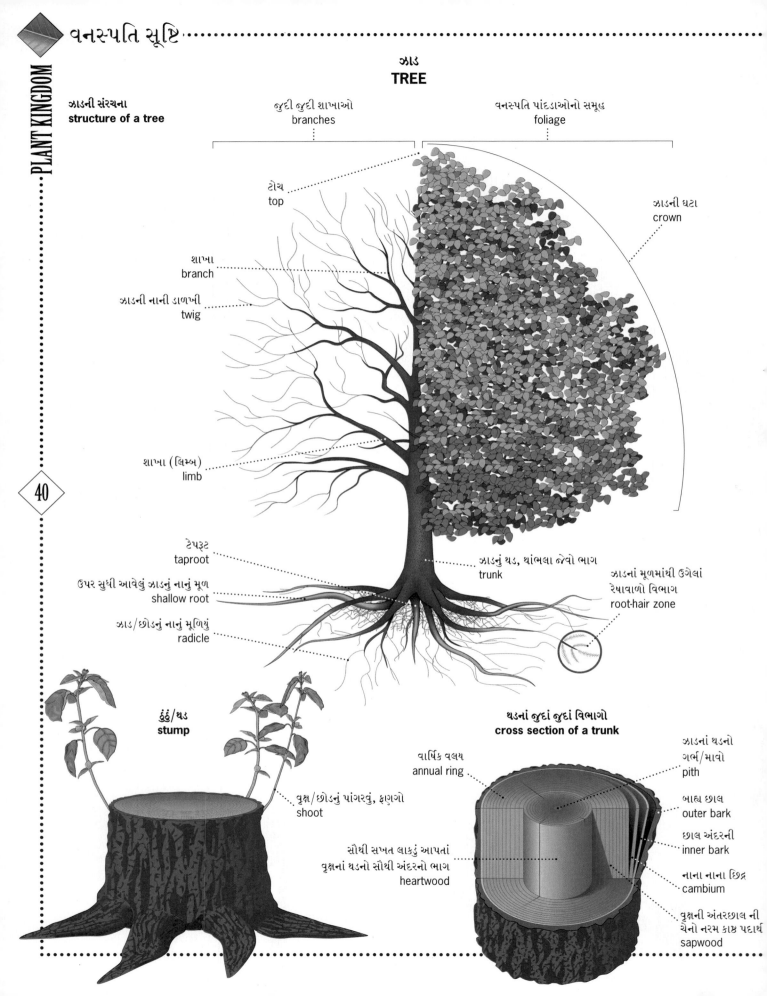

ઝાડ
TREE

ઝાડની સંરચના
structure of a tree

જુદી જુદી શાખાઓ
branches

વનસ્પતિ પાંદડાઓનો સમૂહ
foliage

ટોચ
top

ઝાડની ઘટા
crown

શાખા
branch

ઝાડની નાની ડાળખી
twig

શાખા (લિમ્બ)
limb

ટેપરૂટ
taproot

ઝાડનું થડ, થાંભલા જેવો ભાગ
trunk

ઝાડનાં મૂળમાંથી ઉગેલાં
રેષાવાળો વિભાગ
root-hair zone

ઉપર સુધી આવેલું ઝાડનું નાનું મૂળ
shallow root

ઝાડ/છોડનું નાનું મૂળિયું
radicle

ઠૂંઠું/થડ
stump

વૃક્ષ/છોડનું પાંગરવું, ફણગો
shoot

થડનાં જુદાં જુદાં વિભાગો
cross section of a trunk

વાર્ષિક વલય
annual ring

ઝાડનાં થડનો
ગર્ભ/માવો
pith

બાહ્ય છાલ
outer bark

છાલ અંદરની
inner bark

સૌથી સખત લાકડું આપતાં
વૃક્ષનાં થડનો સૌથી અંદરનો ભાગ
heartwood

નાના નાના છિદ્ર
cambium

વૃક્ષની અંતરછાલ ની
ચેનો નરમ કાષ્ઠ પદાર્થ
sapwood

ઝાડનાં ઉદાહરણો
EXAMPLES OF TREES

ઝડપથી ઊગી જતું એક ઝાડ (પોપલર)
poplar

ઓક વૃક્ષ
oak

એક જાતનું ઘટાદાર વૃક્ષ (મેપલ)
maple

તાડનું ઝાડ
palm tree

વિપીંગ વિલો (ઝાડ)
weeping willow

બર્ચ
birch

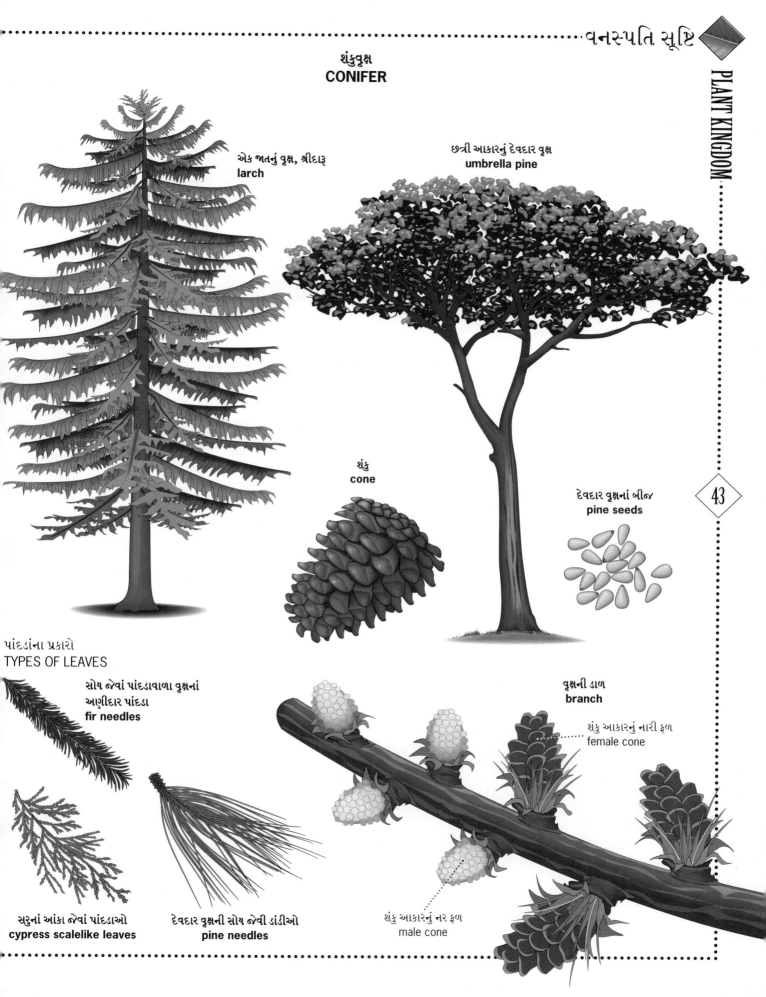

શંકુવૃક્ષ
CONIFER

એક જાતનું વૃક્ષ, શ્રીદાર
larch

છત્રી આકારનું દેવદાર વૃક્ષ
umbrella pine

શંકુ
cone

દેવદાર વૃક્ષનાં બીજ
pine seeds

પાંદડાંના પ્રકારો
TYPES OF LEAVES

સોય જેવાં પાંદડાવાળા વૃક્ષનાં
આણીદાર પાંદડા
fir needles

વૃક્ષની ડાળ
branch

શંકુ આકારનું નારી ફળ
female cone

સુરનાં આંકા જેવાં પાંદડાઓ
cypress scalelike leaves

દેવદાર વૃક્ષની સોય જેવી દાંડીઓ
pine needles

શંકુ આકારનું નર ફળ
male cone

ગર્ભવાળાં ફળો: બેરી ફળ
FLESHY FRUITS: BERRY FRUITS

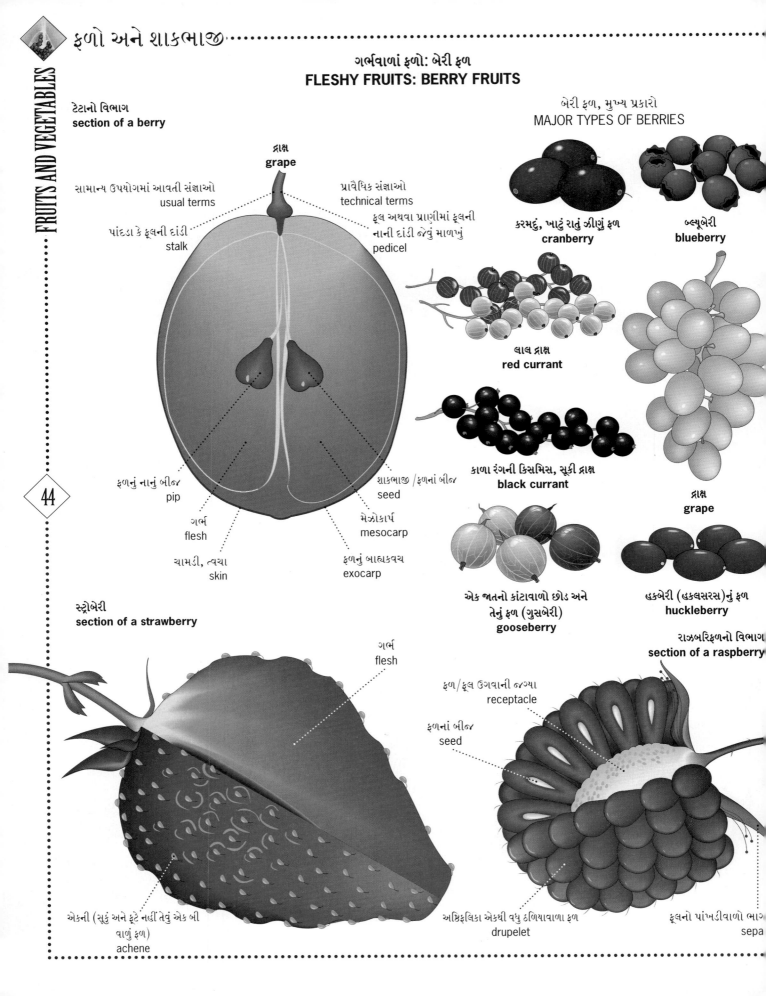

ટેટાનો વિભાગ
section of a berry

બેરી ફળ, મુખ્ય પ્રકારો
MAJOR TYPES OF BERRIES

દ્રાક્ષ
grape

સામાન્ય ઉપયોગમાં આવતી સંજ્ઞાઓ
usual terms

પ્રાવૈધિક સંજ્ઞાઓ
technical terms

ફૂલ અથવા પ્રાણીમાં ફૂલની
નાની દાંડી જેવું માળખું
pedicel

પાંદડા કે ફૂલની દાંડી
stalk

કરમદું, ખાટું રાતું ઝીણું ફળ
cranberry

બ્લ્યૂબેરી
blueberry

લાલ દ્રાક્ષ
red currant

ફળનું નાનું બીજ
pip

શાકભાજ઼ી/ફળનાં બીજ
seed

કાળા રંગની કિસમિસ, સૂકી દ્રાક્ષ
black currant

દ્રાક્ષ
grape

ગર્ભ
flesh

મેઝોકાર્પ
mesocarp

ચામડી, ત્વચા
skin

ફળનું બાહ્યકવચ
exocarp

એક જાતનો કાંટાવાળો છોડ અને
તેનું ફળ (ગુસબેરી)
gooseberry

હકબેરી (હકલસરસ)નું ફળ
huckleberry

સ્ટ્રોબેરી
section of a strawberry

ગર્ભ
flesh

રાઝબરિફળનો વિભાગ
section of a raspberry

ફળ/ફૂલ ઉગવાની જગ્યા
receptacle

ફળનાં બીજ
seed

એકની (સૂકું અને ફૂટે નહીં તેવું એક બી
વાળું ફળ)
achene

અષ્ટિફલિકા એકથી વધુ ઠળિયાવાળા ફળ
drupelet

ફૂલનો પાંખડીવાળો ભાગ
sepa

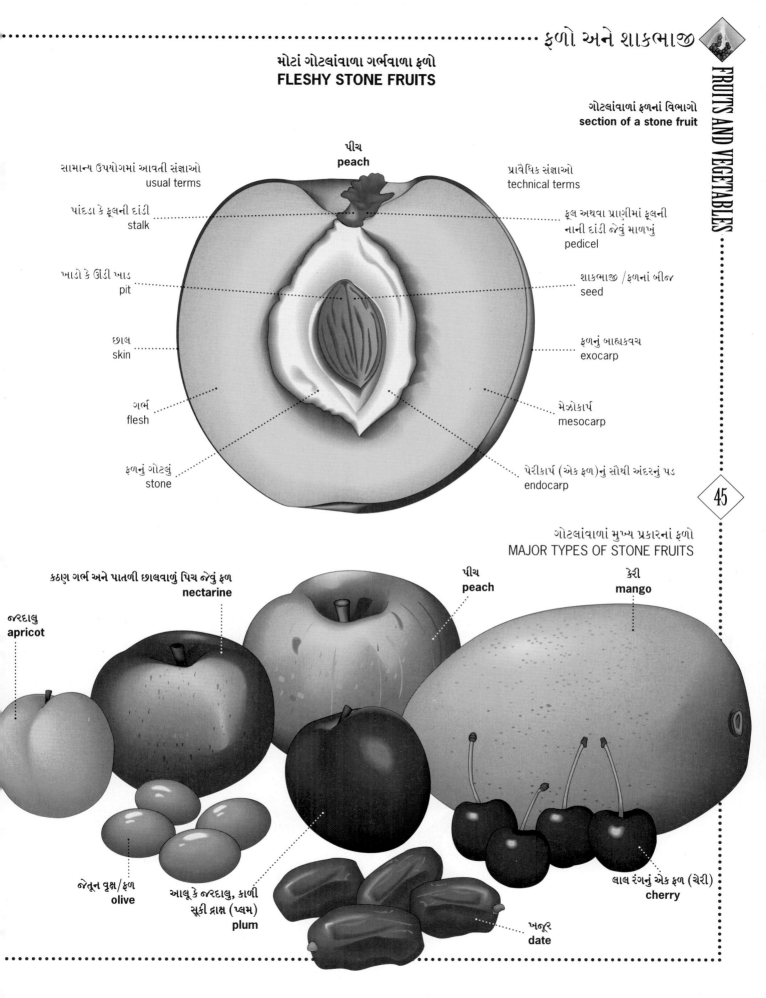

મોટાં ગોટલાંવાળા ગર્ભવાળા ફળો
FLESHY STONE FRUITS

ગોટલાંવાળાં ફળનાં વિભાગો
section of a stone fruit

પીચ
peach

સામાન્ય ઉપયોગમાં આવતી સંજ્ઞાઓ
usual terms

પ્રાવૈધિક સંજ્ઞાઓ
technical terms

પાંદડા કે ફૂલની દાંડી
stalk

ફૂલ અથવા પ્રાણીમાં ફૂલની
નાની દાંડી જેવું માળખું
pedicel

ખાડો કે ઊંડી ખાડ
pit

શાકભાજી /ફળનાં બીજ
seed

છાલ
skin

ફળનું બાહ્યકવચ
exocarp

ગર્ભ
flesh

મેઝોકાર્પ
mesocarp

ફળનું ગોટલું
stone

પેરીકાર્પ (એક ફળ)નું સૌથી અંદરનું પડ
endocarp

ગોટલાંવાળાં મુખ્ય પ્રકારનાં ફળો
MAJOR TYPES OF STONE FRUITS

કઠણ ગર્ભ અને પાતળી છાલવાળું પિચ જેવું ફળ
nectarine

પીચ
peach

કેરી
mango

જરદાલુ
apricot

જેતૂન વૃક્ષ/ફળ
olive

આલૂ કે જરદાલુ, કાળી
સૂકી દ્રાક્ષ (પ્લમ)
plum

લાલ રંગનું એક ફળ (ચેરી)
cherry

ખજૂર
date

ગર્ભવાળા સફરજન જેવાં ફળો
FLESHY POME FRUITS

સફરજન જેવાં ફળનાં, આડો છેદ
section of a pome fruit

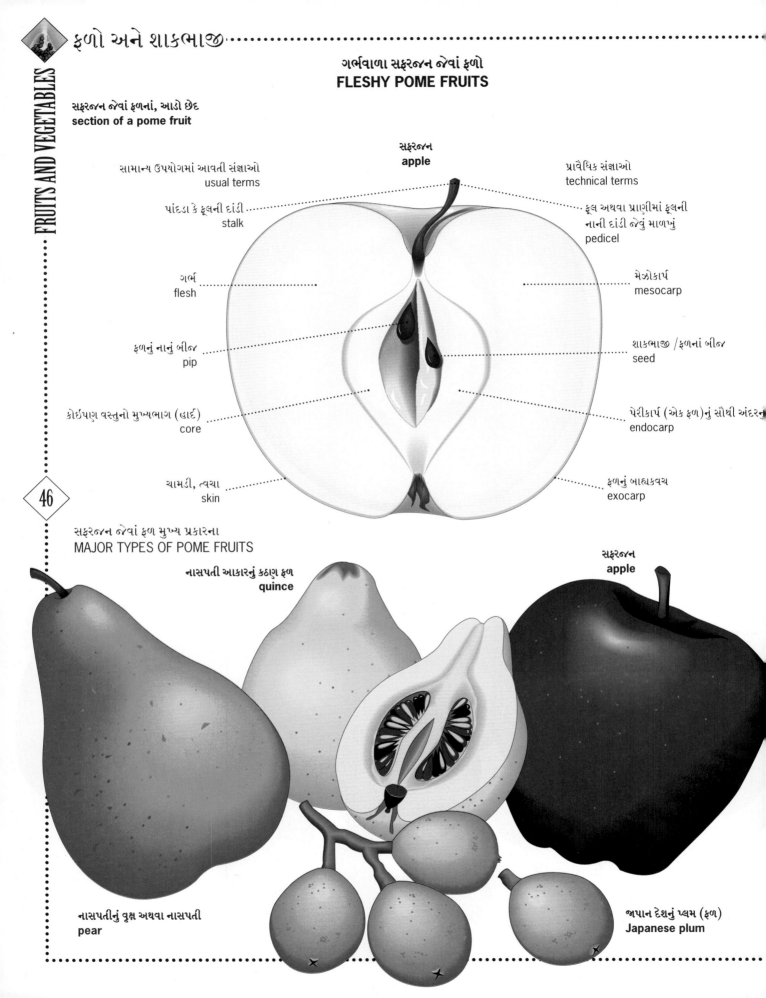

સામાન્ય ઉપયોગમાં આવતી સંજ્ઞાઓ
usual terms

પ્રાવૈધિક સંજ્ઞાઓ
technical terms

સફરજન
apple

પાંદડા કે ફૂલની દાંડી
stalk

ફૂલ અથવા પ્રાણીમાં ફૂલની
નાની દાંડી જેવું માળખું
pedicel

ગર્ભ
flesh

મેઝોકાર્પ
mesocarp

ફળનું નાનું બીજ
pip

શાકભાજી / ફળનાં બીજ
seed

કોઈપણ વસ્તુનો મુખ્યભાગ (હાર્દ)
core

પેરીકાર્પ (એક ફળ)નું સૌથી અંદરનું
endocarp

ચામડી, ત્વચા
skin

ફળનું બાહ્યકવચ
exocarp

સફરજન જેવાં ફળ મુખ્ય પ્રકારના
MAJOR TYPES OF POME FRUITS

નાસપતી આકારનું કઠણ ફળ
quince

સફરજન
apple

નાસપતીનું વૃક્ષ અથવા નાસપતી
pear

જપાન દેશનું પ્લમ (ફળ)
Japanese plum

ગર્ભવાળાં ફળો: ખટાશવાળા ફળ
FLESHY FRUITS: CITRUS FRUITS

ખટાશવાળા ફળનો વિભાગ
section of a citrus fruit

નારંગી, સંતરું
orange

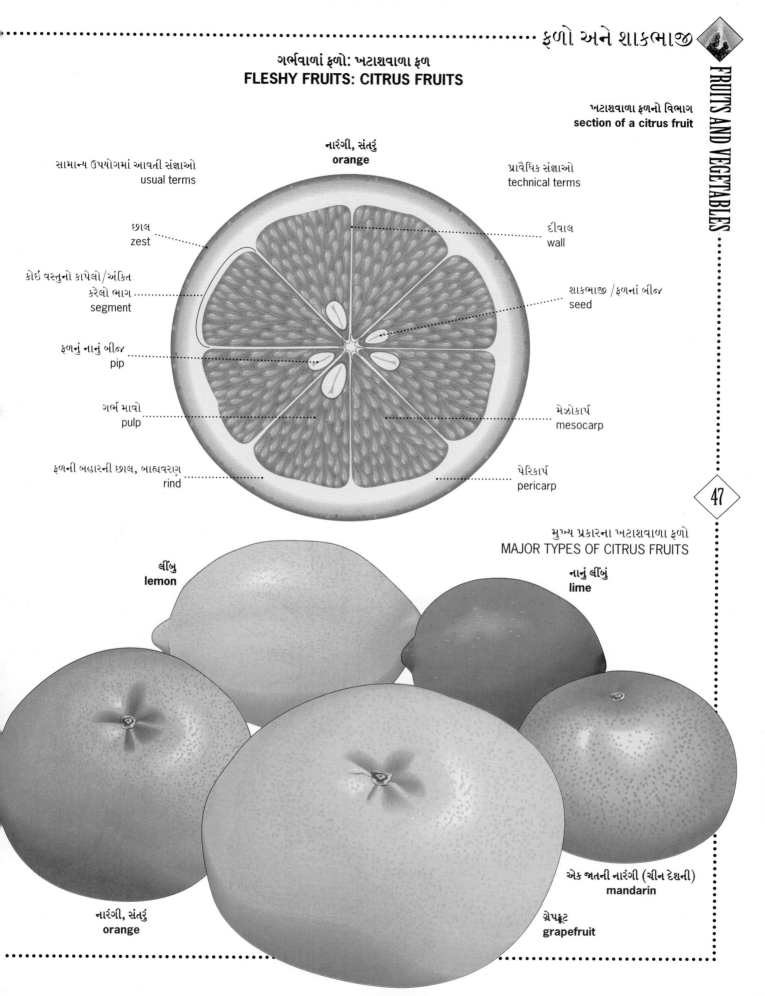

સામાન્ય ઉપયોગમાં આવતી સંજ્ઞાઓ
usual terms

પ્રાવૈધિક સંજ્ઞાઓ
technical terms

છાલ
zest

દીવાલ
wall

કોઈ વસ્તુનો કાપેલો/અંકિત
કરેલો ભાગ
segment

શાકભાજ /ફળનાં બીજ
seed

ફળનું નાનું બીજ
pip

ગર્ભ માવો
pulp

મેઝોકાર્પ
mesocarp

ફળની બહારની છાલ, બાહ્યવરાણ
rind

પેરિકાર્પ
pericarp

47

મુખ્ય પ્રકારના ખટાશવાળા ફળો
MAJOR TYPES OF CITRUS FRUITS

લીંબુ
lemon

નાનું લીંબું
lime

નારંગી, સંતરું
orange

એક જાતની નારંગી (ચીન દેશની)
mandarin

ગ્રેપફ્રૂટ
grapefruit

ઉષ્ણકટિબંધનાં ફળો
TROPICAL FRUITS

મુખ્ય પ્રકારનાં ઉષ્ણ કટિબંધનાં ફળો
MAJOR TYPES OF TROPICAL FRUITS

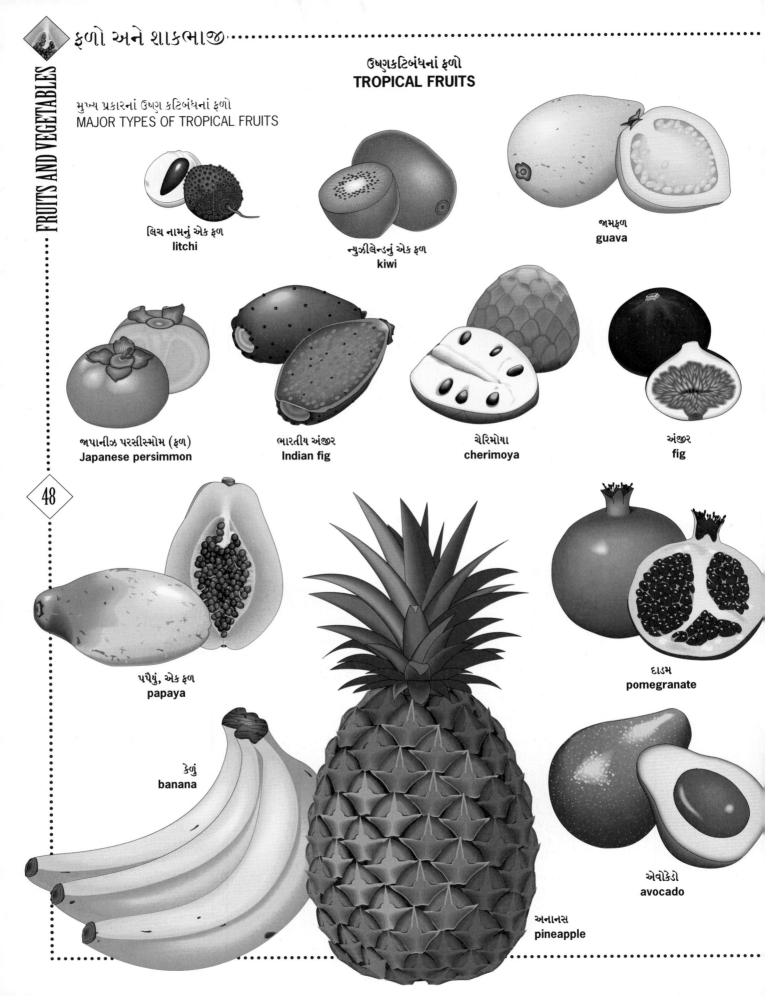

લિચ નામનું એક ફળ
litchi

ન્યુઝીલેન્ડનું એક ફળ
kiwi

જમફળ
guava

જાપાનીઝ પરસીસ્મોમ (ફળ)
Japanese persimmon

ભારતીય અંજીર
Indian fig

ચેરિમોયા
cherimoya

અંજીર
fig

પપૈયું, એક ફળ
papaya

દાડમ
pomegranate

કેળું
banana

એવોકેડો
avocado

અનાનસ
pineapple

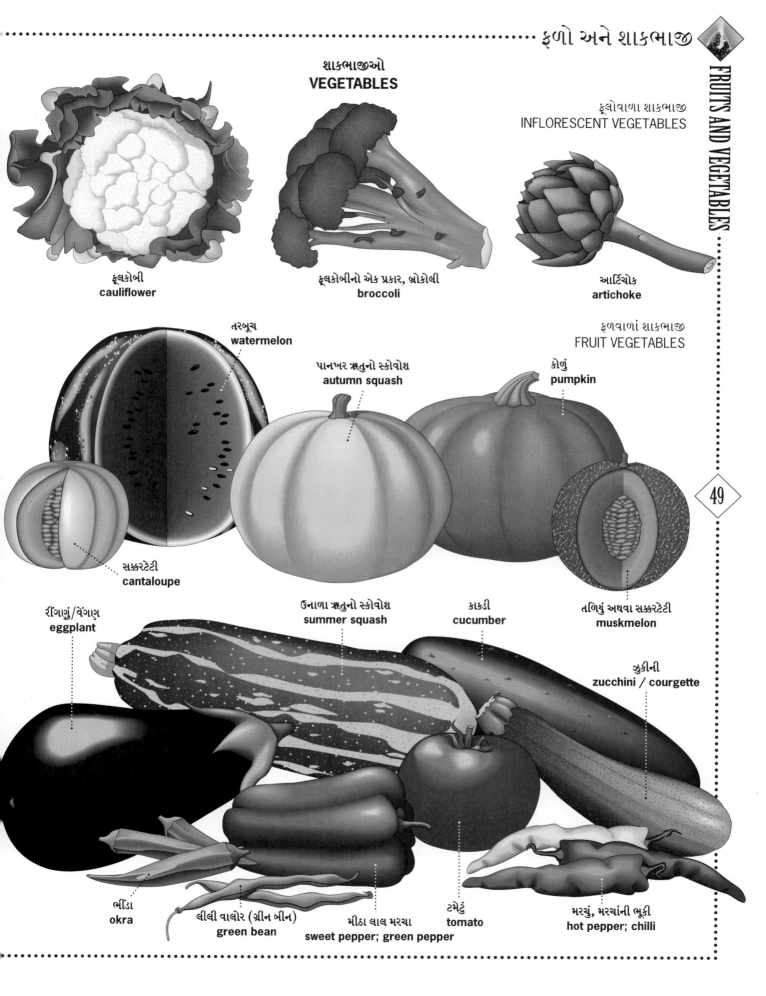

શાકભાજીઓ
VEGETABLES

ફૂલોવાળા શાકભાજ
INFLORESCENT VEGETABLES

ફૂલકોબી
cauliflower

ફૂલકોબીનો એક પ્રકાર, બ્રોકોલી
broccoli

આર્ટિચોક
artichoke

ફળવાળાં શાકભાજ
FRUIT VEGETABLES

તરબૂચ
watermelon

પાનખર ઋતુનો સ્કોવોશ
autumn squash

કોળું
pumpkin

સક્કરટેટી
cantaloupe

તળિયું અથવા સક્કરટેટી
muskmelon

રીંગણું/વેંગણ
eggplant

ઉનાળા ઋતુનો સ્કોવોશ
summer squash

કાકડી
cucumber

ઝુકીની
zucchini / courgette

ભીંડા
okra

લીલી વાલોર (ગ્રીન બીન)
green bean

મીઠા લાલ મરચા
sweet pepper; green pepper

ટમેટું
tomato

મરચું, મરચાંની ભૂકી
hot pepper; chilli

49

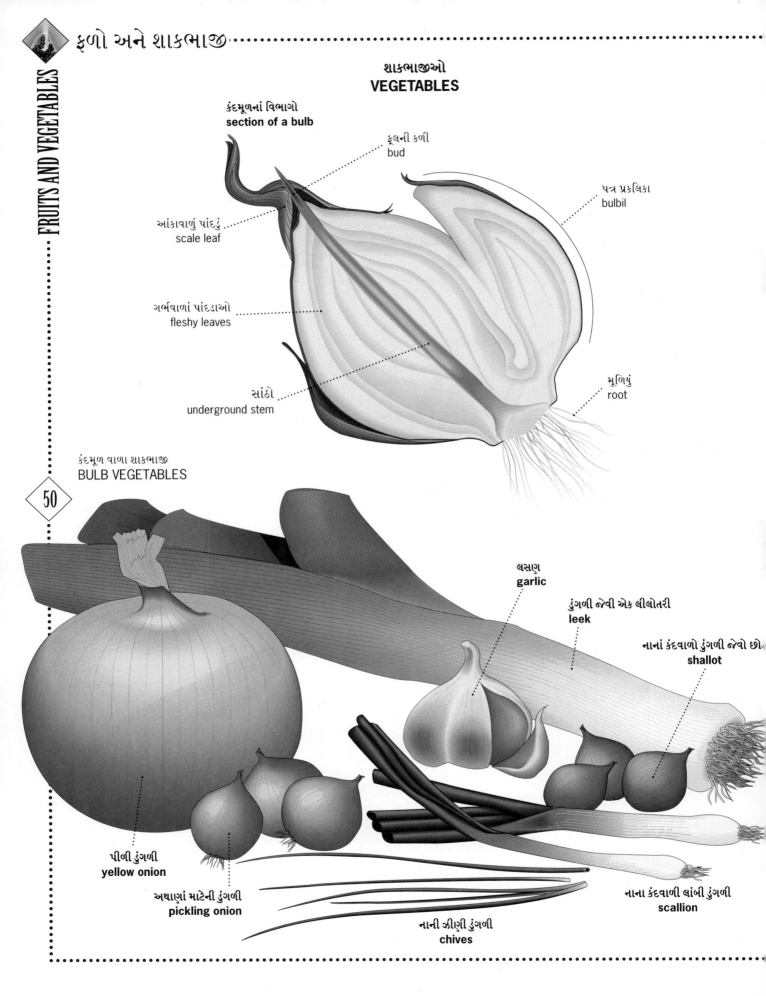

શાકભાજીઓ
VEGETABLES

કંદમૂળનાં વિભાગો
section of a bulb

ફૂલની કળી
bud

પત્ર પ્રકલિકા
bulbil

આંકાવાળું પાંદડું
scale leaf

ગર્ભવાળાં પાંદડાઓ
fleshy leaves

સાંઠો
underground stem

મૂળિયું
root

કંદમૂળ વાળા શાકભાજી
BULB VEGETABLES

લસણ
garlic

ડુંગળી જેવી એક લીલોતરી
leek

નાનાં કંદવાળો ડુંગળી જેવો છો
shallot

પીળી ડુંગળી
yellow onion

અથાણાં માટેની ડુંગળી
pickling onion

નાની ઝીણી ડુંગળી
chives

નાના કંદવાળી લાંબી ડુંગળી
scallion

50

બટેટું
potato

કંદ કે કંદમૂળવાળી શાકભાજ
TUBER VEGETABLES

જેરુસલેમ આર્ટીચોક
Jerusalem artichoke

મીઠાં બટેટાં
sweet potato

જડાં મૂળવાળી કોબીનો એક પ્રકાર (કોહલ્રાબી)
kohlrabi

મૂળવાળાં શાકભાજ
ROOT VEGETABLES

લાંબી પત્તીની લીલોતરી વાળું (ભાજી)
celeriac

સ્વીડ
swede

(બીટ) લાલ રંગનું કંદમૂળ
beet

કચુંબર
turnip

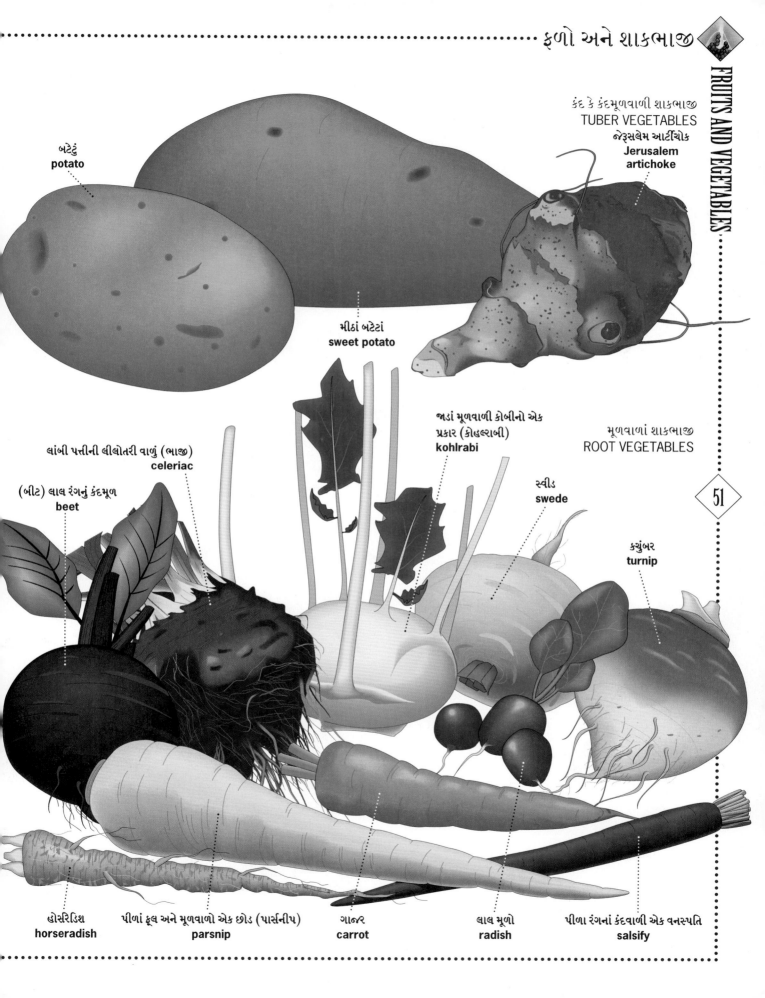

હોસરિડિશ
horseradish

પીળાં ફૂલ અને મૂળવાળો એક છોડ (પાર્સનીપ)
parsnip

ગાજર
carrot

લાલ મૂળો
radish

પીળા રંગનાં કંદવાળી એક વનસ્પતિ
salsify

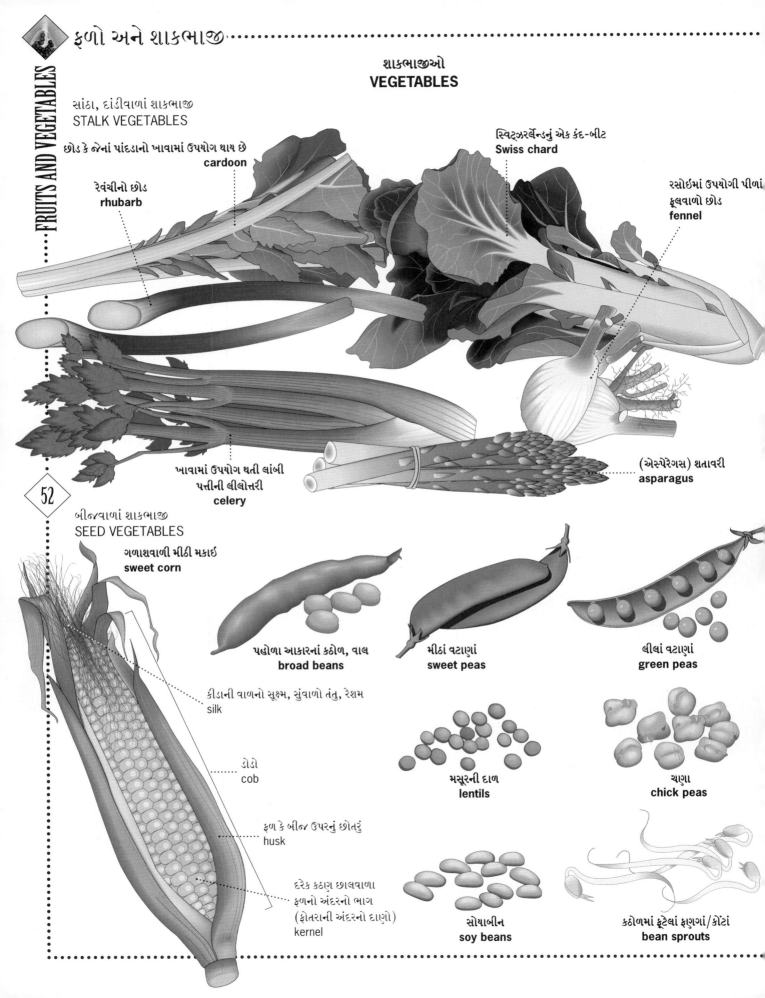

શાકભાજીઓ
VEGETABLES

સાંઠા, દાંડીવાળાં શાકભાજ
STALK VEGETABLES

છોડ કે જેનાં પાંદડાનો ખાવામાં ઉપયોગ થાય છે
cardoon

રેવંચીનો છોડ
rhubarb

સ્વિટ્ઝર્લેન્ડનું એક કંદ-બીટ
Swiss chard

રસોઈમાં ઉપયોગી પીળાં ફૂલવાળો છોડ
fennel

ખાવામાં ઉપયોગ થતી લાંબી પત્તીની લીલોત્તરી
celery

(એસ્પેરેગસ) શતાવરી
asparagus

બીજવાળાં શાકભાજ
SEED VEGETABLES

ગળાશવાળી મીઠી મકાઈ
sweet corn

કીડાની વાળનો સૂક્ષ્મ, સુંવાળો તંતુ, રેશમ
silk

ડોડો
cob

ફળ કે બીજ ઉપરનું છોતરું
husk

દરેક કઠણ છાલવાળા ફળનો અંદરનો ભાગ (છોતરાની અંદરનો દાણો)
kernel

પહોળા આકારનાં કઠોળ, વાલ
broad beans

મીઠાં વટાણાં
sweet peas

લીલાં વટાણાં
green peas

મસૂરની દાળ
lentils

ચણા
chick peas

સોયાબીન
soy beans

કઠોળમાં ફૂટેલાં ફણગાં/કોટાં
bean sprouts

52

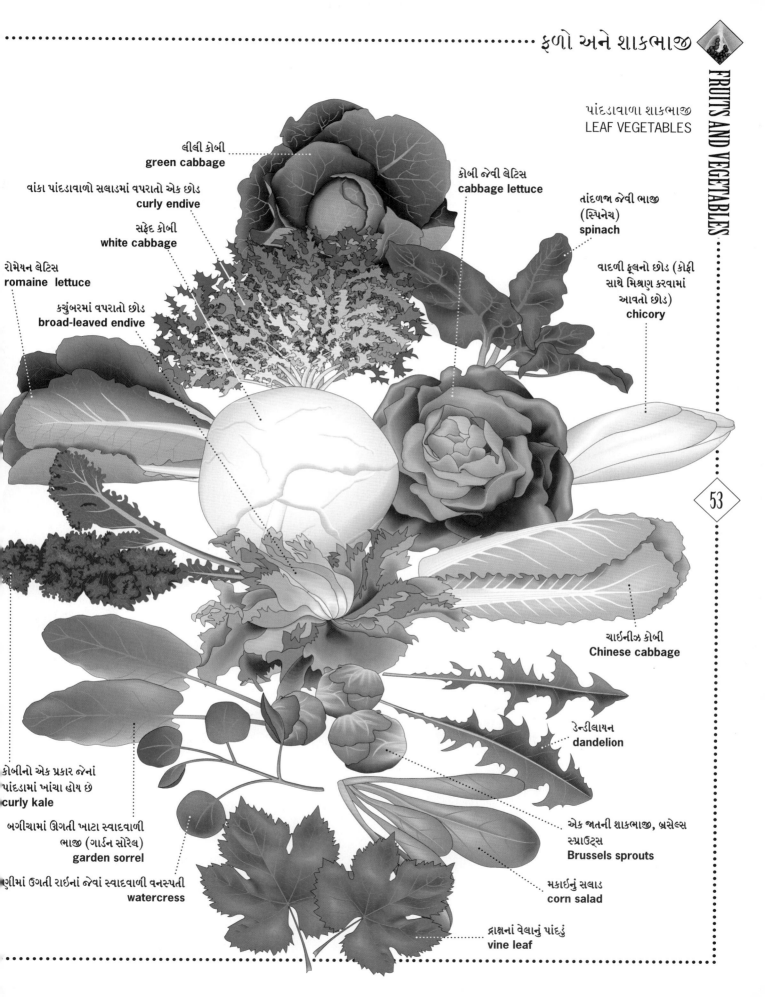

પાંદડાવાળા શાકભાજી
LEAF VEGETABLES

લીલી કોબી
green cabbage

વાંકા પાંદડાવાળો સલાડમાં વપરાતો એક છોડ
curly endive

સફેદ કોબી
white cabbage

રોમેયન લેટિસ
romaine lettuce

કચુંબરમાં વપરાતો છોડ
broad-leaved endive

કોબી જેવી લેટિસ
cabbage lettuce

તાંદળજા જેવી ભાજી
(સ્પિનચ)
spinach

વાદળી ફૂલનો છોડ (કોફી
સાથે મિશ્રણ કરવામાં
આવતો છોડ)
chicory

ચાઈનીઝ કોબી
Chinese cabbage

ડૅન્ડીલાયન
dandelion

કોબીનો એક પ્રકાર જેનાં
પાંદડામાં ખાંચા હોય છે
curly kale

બગીચામાં ઊગતી ખાટા સ્વાદવાળી
ભાજી (ગાર્ડન સોરેલ)
garden sorrel

ઝણીમાં ઉગતી રાઈનાં જેવાં સ્વાદવાળી વનસ્પતી
watercress

એક જાતની શાકભાજી, બ્રસેલ્સ
સ્પ્રાઉટ્સ
Brussels sprouts

મકાઈનું સલાડ
corn salad

દ્રાક્ષનાં વેલાનું પાંદડું
vine leaf

53

બાગ-કામ
GARDENING

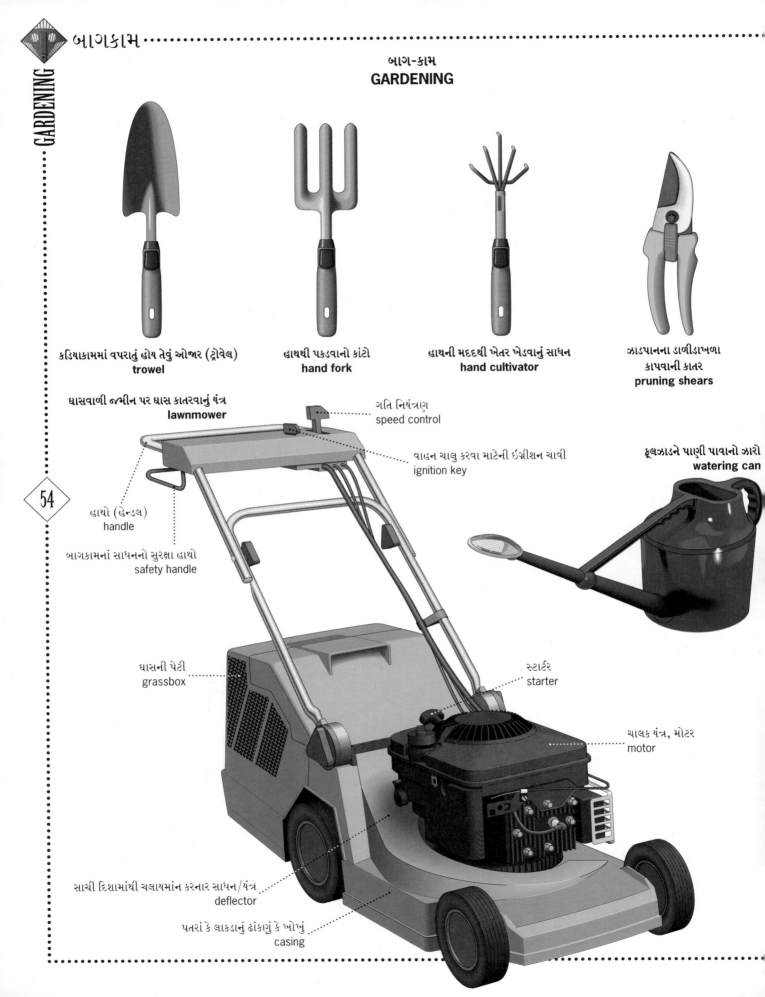

કડિયાકામમાં વપરાતું હોય તેવું ઓજાર (ટ્રોવેલ)
trowel

હાથથી પકડવાનો કાંટો
hand fork

હાથની મદદથી ખેતર ખેડવાનું સાધન
hand cultivator

ઝાડપાનના ડાળીડાખળા કાપવાની કાતર
pruning shears

ઘાસવાળી જમીન પર ઘાસ કાતરવાનું યંત્ર
lawnmower

ગતિ નિયંત્રણ
speed control

વાહન ચાલુ કરવા માટેની ઇગ્નીશન ચાવી
ignition key

ફૂલઝાડને પાણી પાવાનો ઝારો
watering can

હાથો (હેન્ડલ)
handle

બાગકામનાં સાધનનો સુરક્ષા હાથો
safety handle

ઘાસની પેટી
grassbox

સ્ટાર્ટર
starter

ચાલક યંત્ર, મોટર
motor

સાચી દિશામાંથી ચલાયમાન કરનાર સાધન/યંત્ર
deflector

પતરાં કે લાકડાનું ઢાંકણું કે ખોખું
casing

54

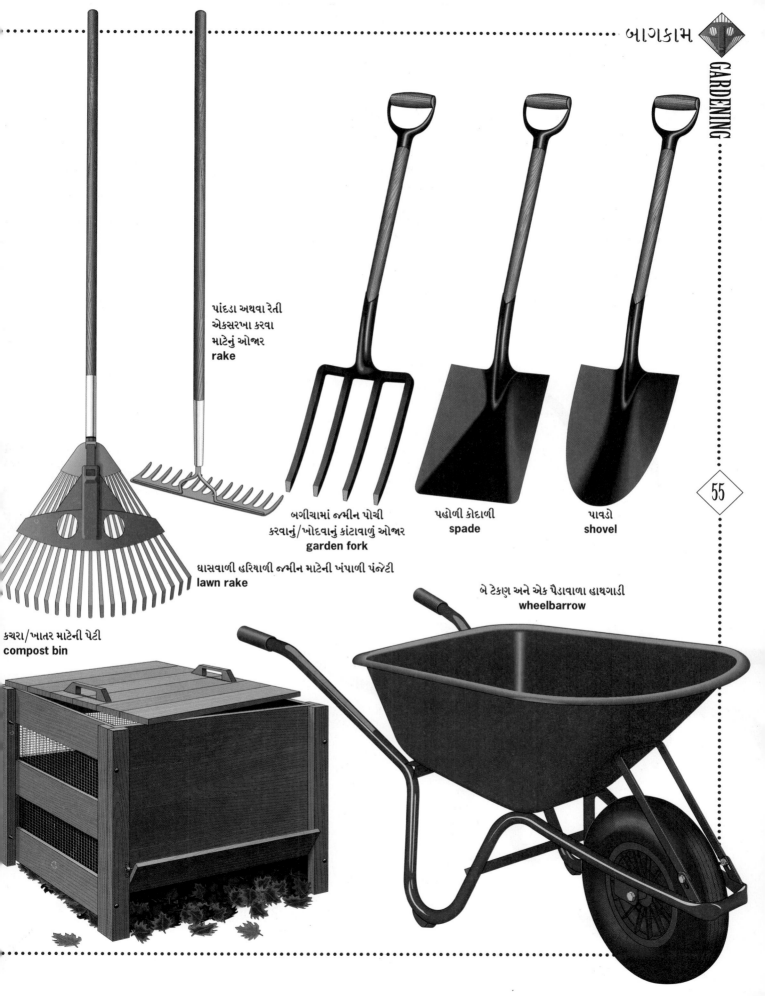

પાંદડા અથવા રેતી
એકસરખા કરવા
માટેનું ઓજાર
rake

બગીચામાં જમીન પોચી
કરવાનું/ખોદવાનું કાંટાવાળું ઓજાર
garden fork

ધાસવાળી હરિયાળી જમીન માટેની ખંપાળી પંજેટી
lawn rake

પહોળી કોદાળી
spade

પાવડો
shovel

55

કચરા/ખાતર માટેની પેટી
compost bin

બે ટેકણ અને એક પૈડાવાળા હાથગાડી
wheelbarrow

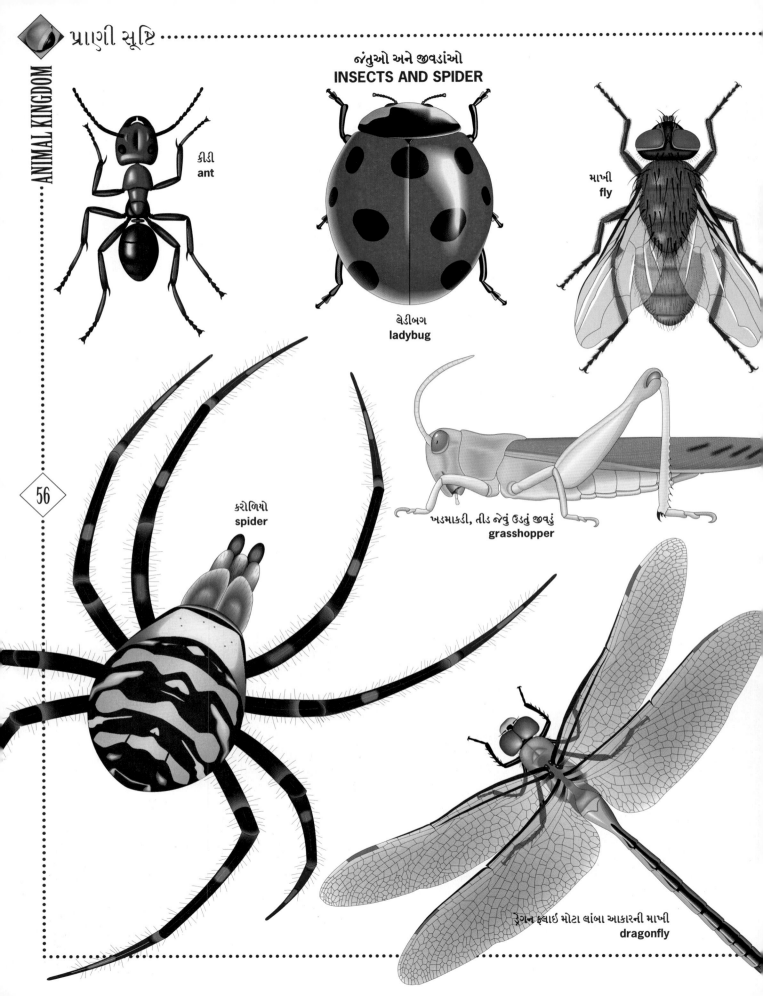

પ્રાણી સૃષ્ટિ

જંતુઓ અને જીવડાંઓ
INSECTS AND SPIDER

કીડી
ant

લેડીબગ
ladybug

માખી
fly

કરોળિયો
spider

ખડમાકડી, તીડ જેવું ઉડતું જીવડું
grasshopper

ડ્રેગન ફ્લાઈ મોટા લાંબા આકારની માખી
dragonfly

56

પતંગિયું
BUTTERFLY

ઈયળ
caterpillar

માથું, મસ્તક
head

સાદી આંખ
simple eye

નીચલું જડબું
mandible

ચાલવા માટેનો કૃત્રિમ પગ
walking leg

ઈયળ જેવાં જંતુઓનો પેટનો માંસલ ભાગ
proleg

પતંગિયાની પાંખની નસ
wing vein

ખાનું
cell

છાતી, વક્ષસ્થળ
thorax

માથું, મસ્તક, મુખ્યભાગ
head

એન્ટેના
antenna

હોઠ દ્વારાં કરેલો સ્પર્શ
labial palp

સંમિશ્રીત આંખ
compound eye

સૂંઢ (પતંગીયાની)
proboscis

આગલો પગ
foreleg

મધ્ય પગ
middle leg

પશુ કે પંખીનાં પગનો અણિયાળો નખ
claw

આગલી પાંખ
forewing

જંતુનાં વિકાસ ક્રમમાં તેની સુષુમાવસ્થાનું સ્વરૂપ
chrysalis

પાછલી પાંખ
hind wing

પેટનો નીચલો ભાગ, ઉદર, પેડુ
abdomen

પાછળના પગ
hind leg

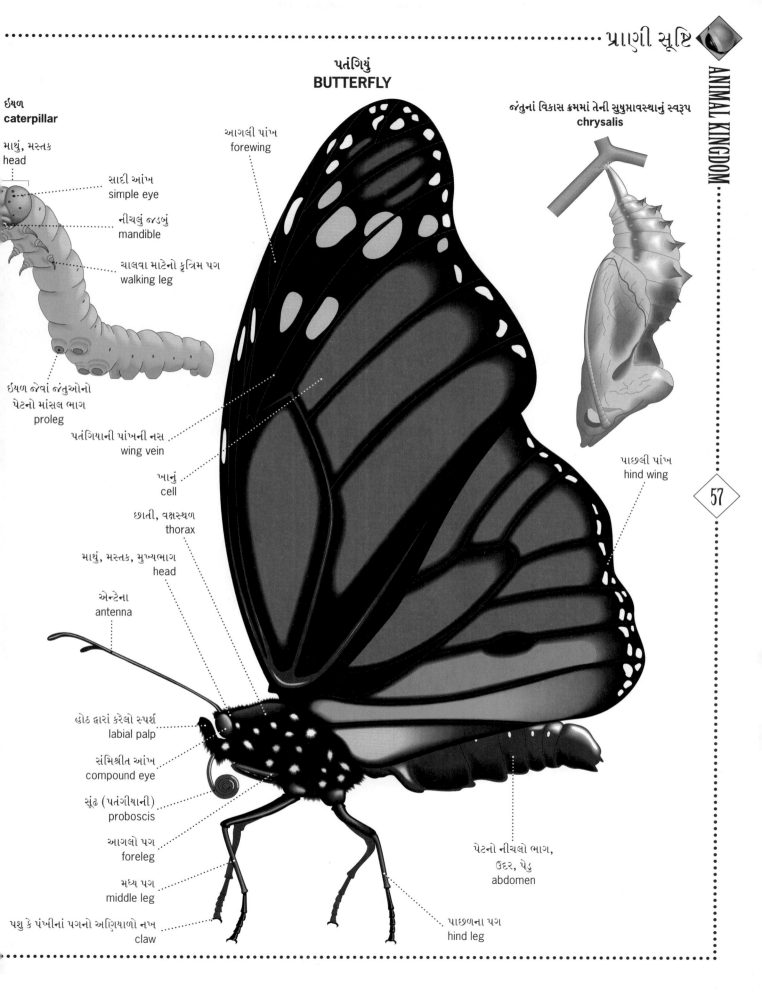

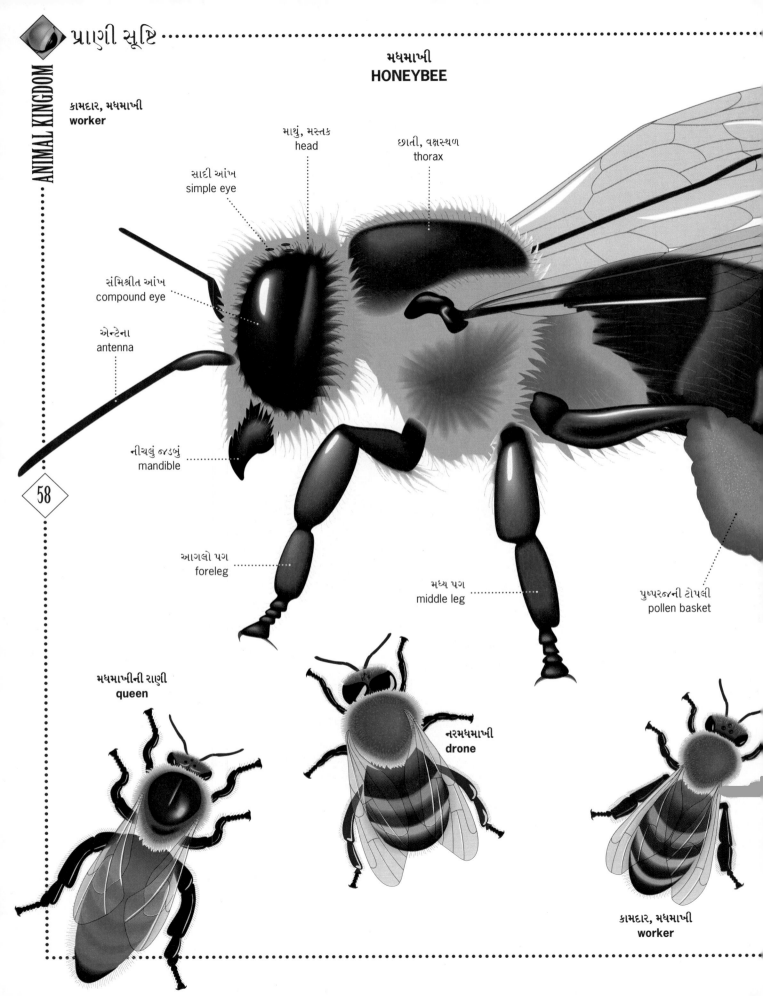

મધમાખી
HONEYBEE

કામદાર, મધમાખી
worker

સાદી આંખ
simple eye

માથું, મસ્તક
head

છાતી, વક્ષસ્થળ
thorax

સંમિશ્રીત આંખ
compound eye

એન્ટેના
antenna

નીચલું જડબું
mandible

આગલો પગ
foreleg

મધ્ય પગ
middle leg

પુષ્પરજની ટોપલી
pollen basket

મધમાખીની રાણી
queen

નરમધમાખી
drone

કામદાર, મધમાખી
worker

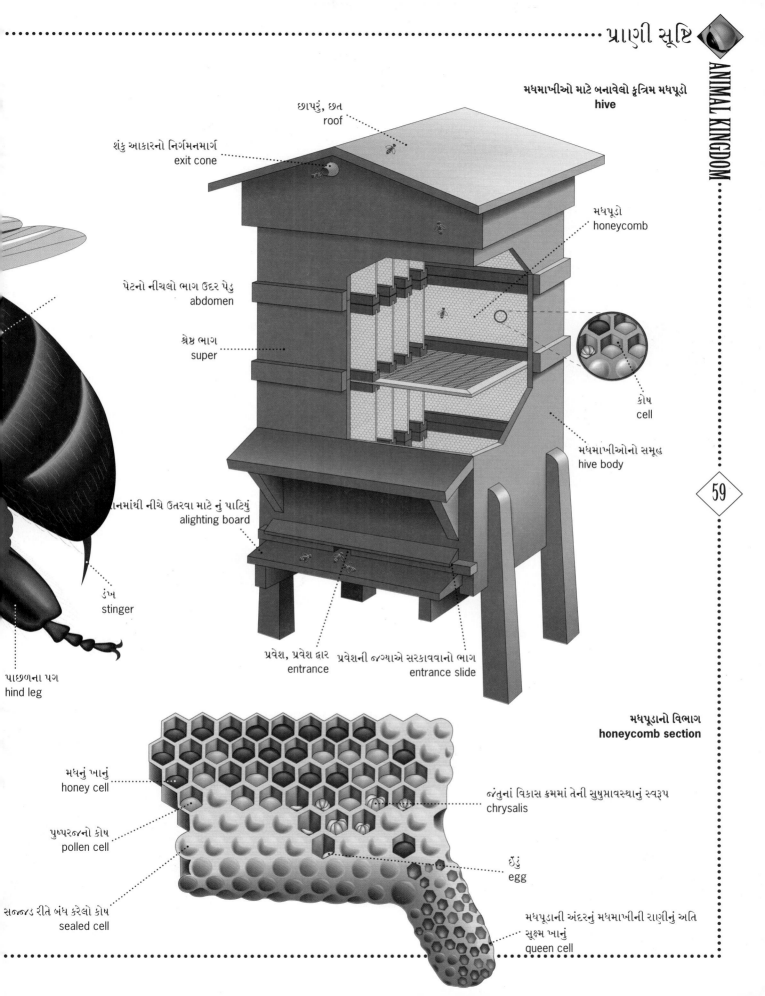

મધમાખીઓ માટે બનાવેલો કૃત્રિમ મધપૂડો
hive

છાપરું, છત
roof

શંકુ આકારનો નિર્ગમનમાર્ગ
exit cone

મધપૂડો
honeycomb

પેટનો નીચલો ભાગ ઉદર પેડુ
abdomen

શ્રેષ્ઠ ભાગ
super

કોષ
cell

મધમાખીઓનો સમૂહ
hive body

...નમાંથી નીચે ઉતરવા માટે નું પાટિયું
alighting board

ડંખ
stinger

પાછળના પગ
hind leg

પ્રવેશ, પ્રવેશ દ્વાર
entrance

પ્રવેશની જગ્યાએ સરકાવવાનો ભાગ
entrance slide

મધપૂડાનો વિભાગ
honeycomb section

મધનું ખાનું
honey cell

જંતુનાં વિકાસ ક્રમમાં તેની સુષુપ્તાવસ્થાનું સ્વરૂપ
chrysalis

પુષ્પરજનો કોષ
pollen cell

ઈંડું
egg

સજ્જડ રીતે બંધ કરેલો કોષ
sealed cell

મધપૂડાની અંદરનું મધમાખીની રાણીનું અતિ
સૂક્ષ્મ ખાનું
queen cell

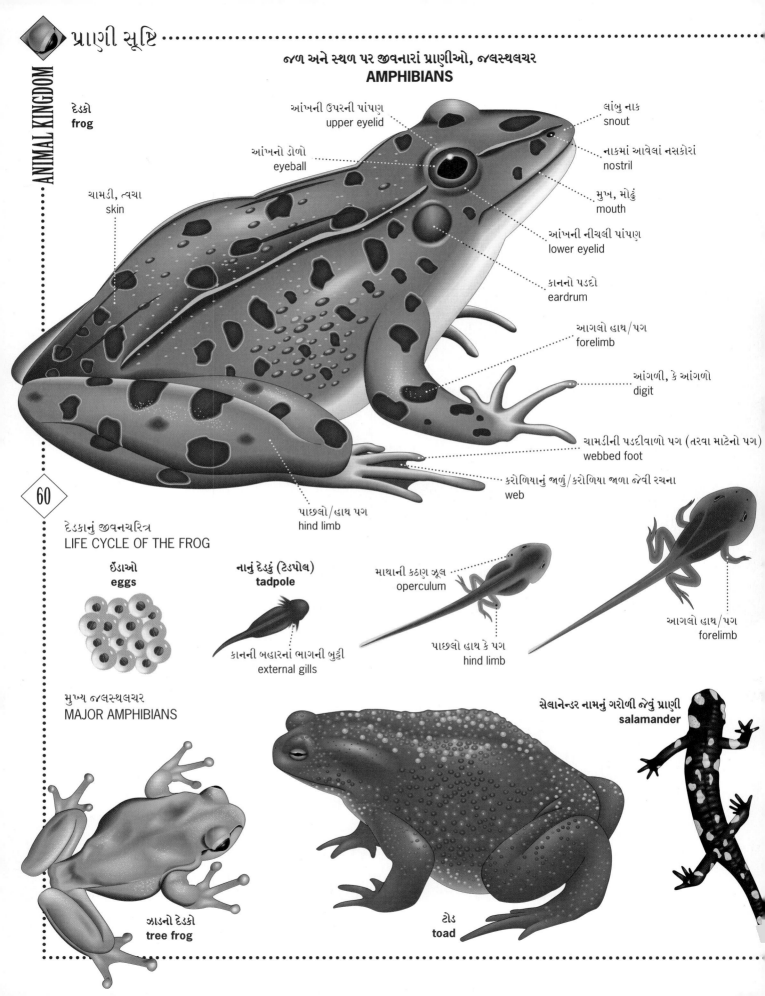

પ્રાણી સૃષ્ટિ

જળ અને સ્થળ પર જીવનારાં પ્રાણીઓ, જલસ્થલચર
AMPHIBIANS

દેડકો
frog

આંખની ઉપરની પાંપણ
upper eyelid

લાંબુ નાક
snout

આંખનો ડોળો
eyeball

નાકમાં આવેલાં નસકોરાં
nostril

મુખ, મોઢું
mouth

ચામડી, ત્વચા
skin

આંખની નીચલી પાંપણ
lower eyelid

કાનનો પડદો
eardrum

આગલો હાથ/પગ
forelimb

આંગળી, કે આંગળો
digit

ચામડીની પડદીવાળો પગ (તરવા માટેનો પગ)
webbed foot

કરોળિયાનું જાળું/કરોળિયા જાળા જેવી રચના
web

પાછલો/હાથ પગ
hind limb

60

દેડકાનું જીવનચરિત્ર
LIFE CYCLE OF THE FROG

ઈંડાઓ
eggs

નાનું દેડકું (ટેડપોલ)
tadpole

માથાની કઠણ ઝૂલ
operculum

કાનની બહારનાં ભાગની બુટ્ટી
external gills

પાછલો હાથ કે પગ
hind limb

આગલો હાથ/પગ
forelimb

મુખ્ય જલસ્થલચર
MAJOR AMPHIBIANS

સેલાનેન્ડર નામનું ગરોળી જેવું પ્રાણી
salamander

ઝાડનો દેડકો
tree frog

ટોડ
toad

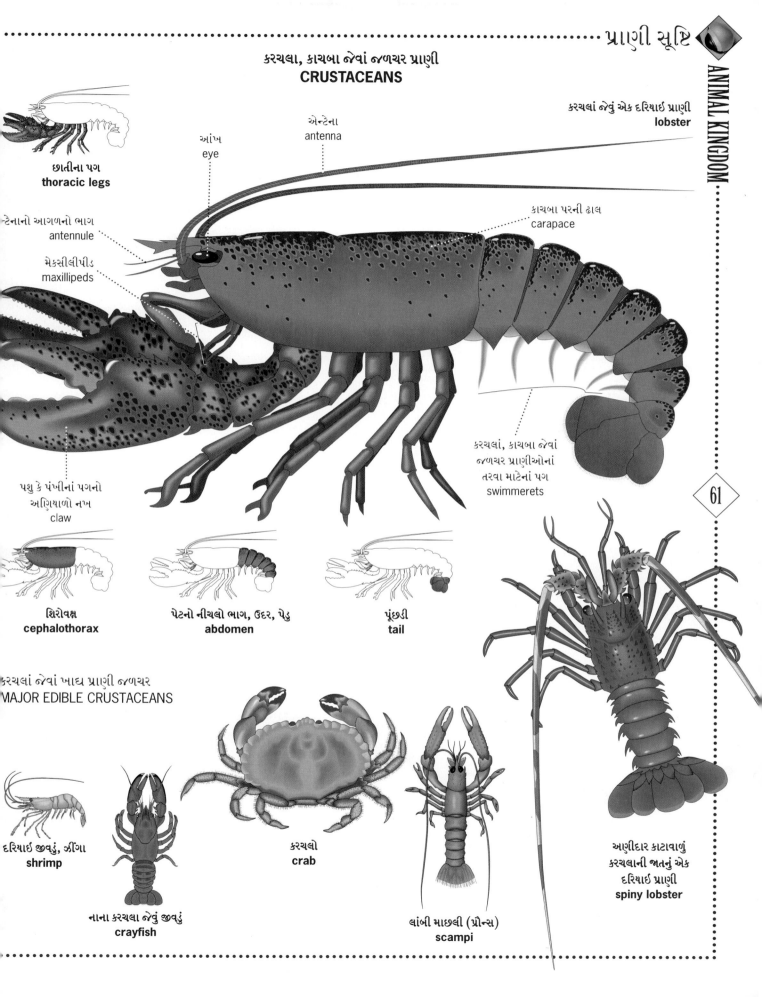

કરચલા, કાચબા જેવાં જળચર પ્રાણી
CRUSTACEANS

કરચલાં જેવું એક દરિયાઈ પ્રાણી
lobster

છાતીના પગ
thoracic legs

આંખ
eye

એન્ટેના
antenna

ટેનાનો આગળનો ભાગ
antennule

મેક્સીલીપીડ
maxillipeds

કાચબા પરની ઢાલ
carapace

પશુ કે પંખીનાં પગનો
અણિયાળો નખ
claw

કરચલાં, કાચબા જેવાં
જળચર પ્રાણીઓનાં
તરવા માટેનાં પગ
swimmerets

શિરોવક્ષ
cephalothorax

પેટનો નીચલો ભાગ, ઉદર, પેડુ
abdomen

પૂંછડી
tail

કરચલાં જેવાં ખાદ્ય પ્રાણી જળચર
MAJOR EDIBLE CRUSTACEANS

દરિયાઈ જીવડું, જીંગા
shrimp

નાના કરચલા જેવું જીવડું
crayfish

કરચલો
crab

લાંબી માછલી (પ્રૉન્સ)
scampi

અણીદાર કાટાવાળું
કરચલાની જાતનું એક
દરિયાઈ પ્રાણી
spiny lobster

પ્રાણી સૃષ્ટિ

માછલીઓ
FISHES

મત્સ્યવિજ્ઞાન
MORPHOLOGY

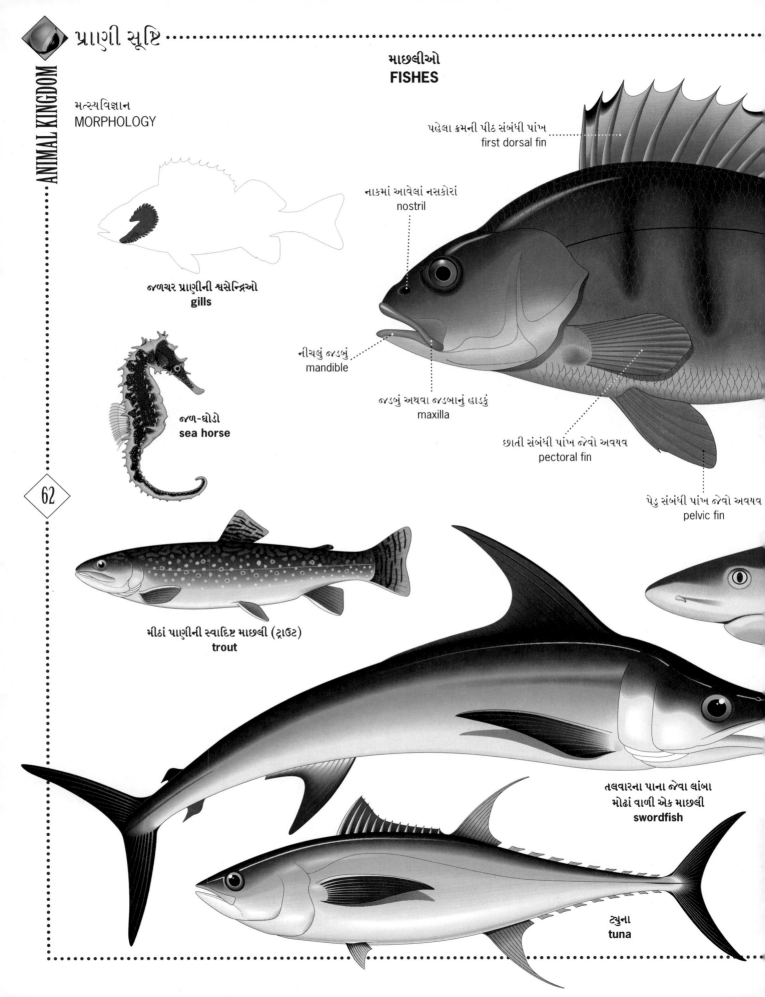

પહેલા ક્રમની પીઠ સંબંધી પાંખ
first dorsal fin

નાકમાં આવેલાં નસકોરાં
nostril

જળચર પ્રાણીની શ્વસેન્દ્રિઓ
gills

નીચલું જડબું
mandible

જડબું અથવા જડબાનું હાડકું
maxilla

છાતી સંબંધી પાંખ જેવો અવયવ
pectoral fin

પેડુ સંબંધી પાંખ જેવો અવયવ
pelvic fin

જળ-ઘોડો
sea horse

મીઠાં પાણીની સ્વાદિષ્ટ માછલી (ટ્રાઉટ)
trout

તલવારના પાના જેવા લાંબા
મોઢાં વાળી એક માછલી
swordfish

ટ્યુના
tuna

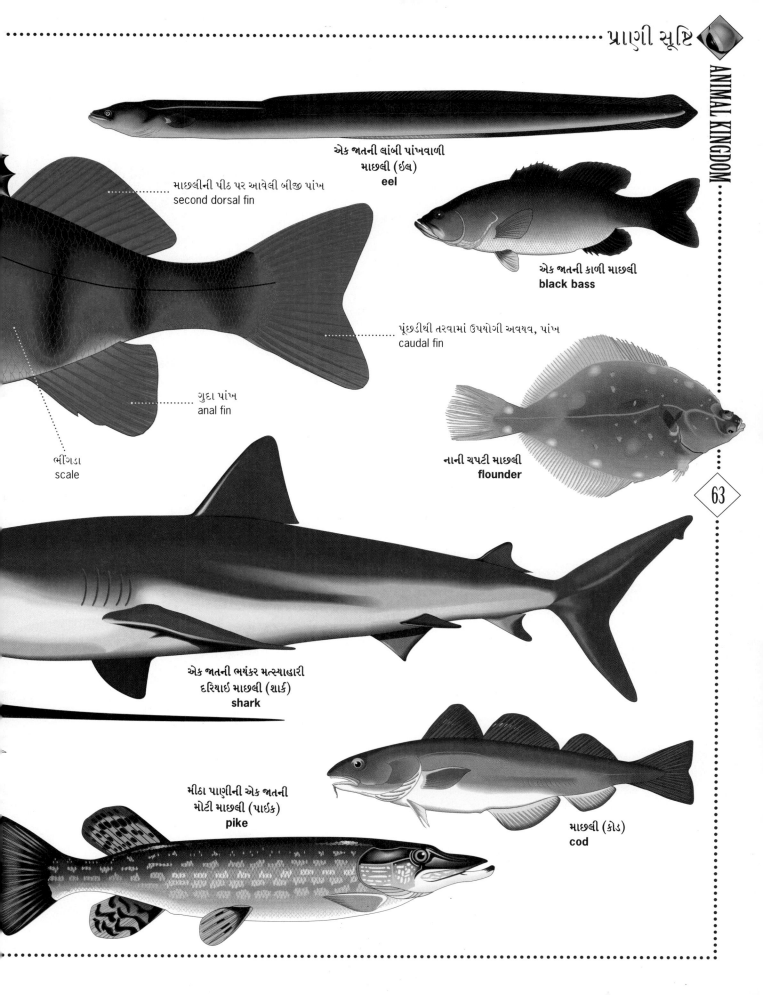

એક જાતની લાંબી પાંખવાળી
માછલી (ઈલ)
eel

માછલીની પીઠ પર આવેલી બીજી પાંખ
second dorsal fin

એક જાતની કાળી માછલી
black bass

પૂંછડીથી તરવામાં ઉપયોગી અવયવ, પાંખ
caudal fin

ગુદા પાંખ
anal fin

ભીંગડા
scale

નાની ચપટી માછલી
flounder

63

એક જાતની ભયંકર મત્સ્યાહારી
દરિયાઈ માછલી (શાર્ક)
shark

મીઠા પાણીની એક જાતની
મોટી માછલી (પાઇક)
pike

માછલી (કોડ)
cod

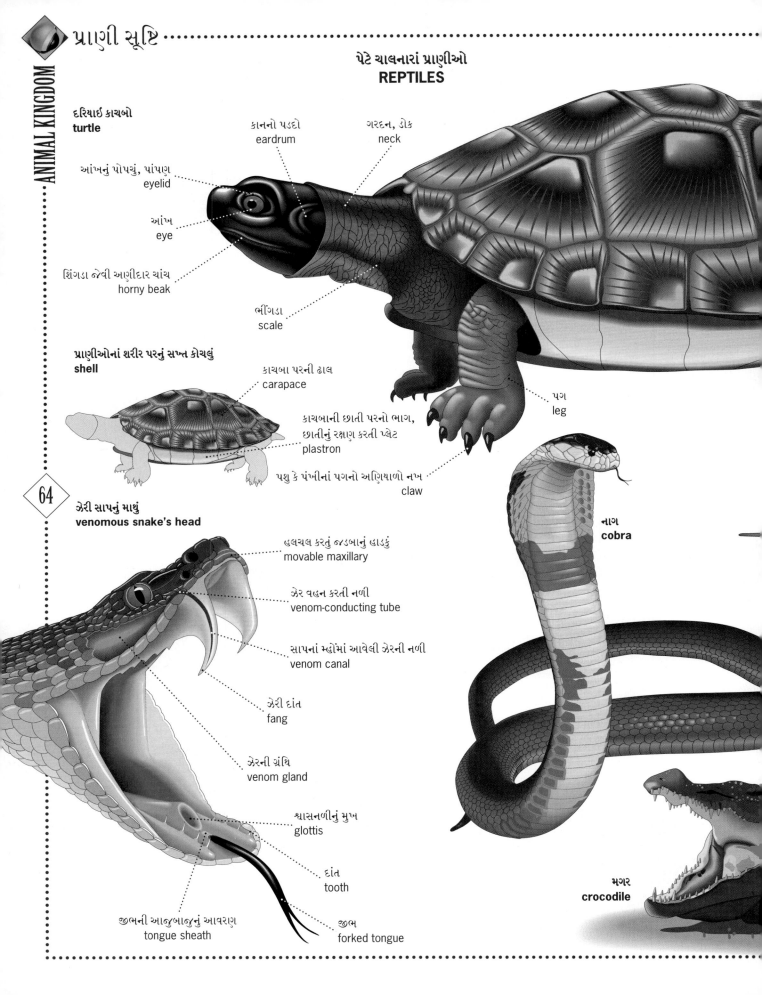

ANIMAL KINGDOM

પેટે ચાલનારાં પ્રાણીઓ
REPTILES

દરિયાઈ કાચબો
turtle

કાનનો પડદો
eardrum

ગરદન, ડોક
neck

આંખનું પોપચું, પાંપણ
eyelid

આંખ
eye

શિંગડા જેવી આણીદાર ચાંચ
horny beak

ભીંગડા
scale

પ્રાણીઓનાં શરીર પરનું સખ્ત કોચલું
shell

કાચબા પરની ઢાલ
carapace

કાચબાની છાતી પરનો ભાગ,
છાતીનું રક્ષાણ કરતી પ્લેટ
plastron

પશુ કે પંખીનાં પગનો અણિયાળો નખ
claw

પગ
leg

ઝેરી સાપનું માથું
venomous snake's head

હલચલ કરતું જડબાનું હાડકું
movable maxillary

ઝેર વહન કરતી નળી
venom-conducting tube

સાપનાં મ્હોંમાં આવેલી ઝેરની નળી
venom canal

ઝેરી દાંત
fang

ઝેરની ગ્રંથિ
venom gland

શ્વાસનળીનું મુખ
glottis

દાંત
tooth

જીભની આજુબાજુનું આવરણ
tongue sheath

જીભ
forked tongue

નાગ
cobra

મગર
crocodile

64

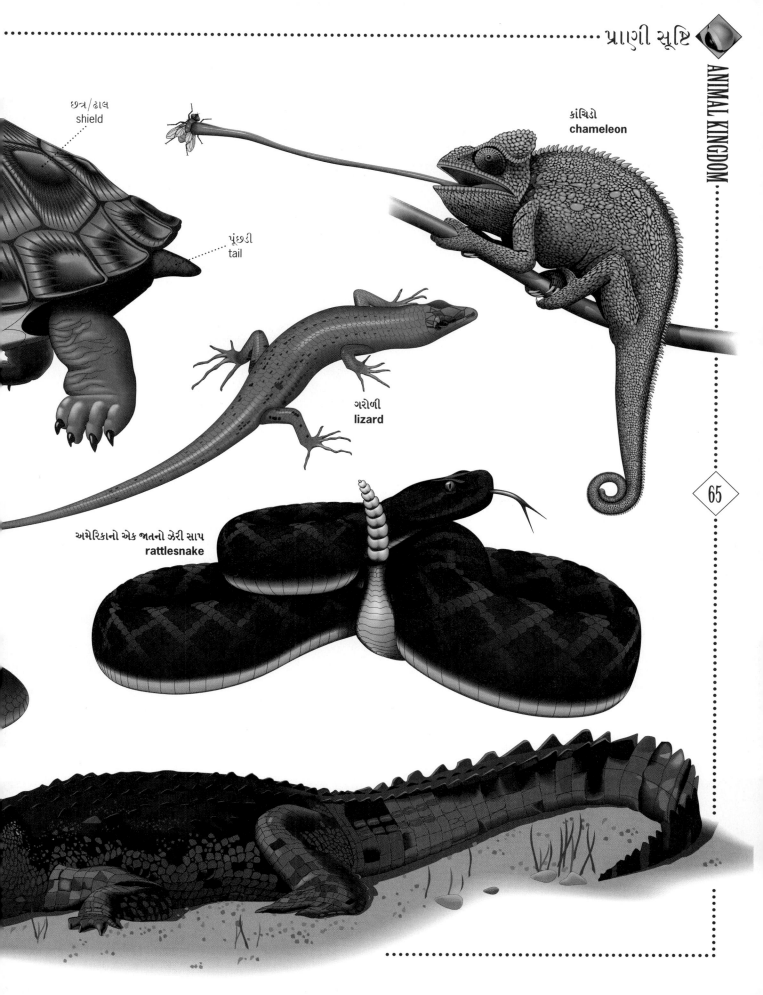

છત્ર/ઢાલ
shield

કાંચિડો
chameleon

પૂંછડી
tail

ગરોળી
lizard

અમેરિકાનો એક જાતનો ઝેરી સાપ
rattlesnake

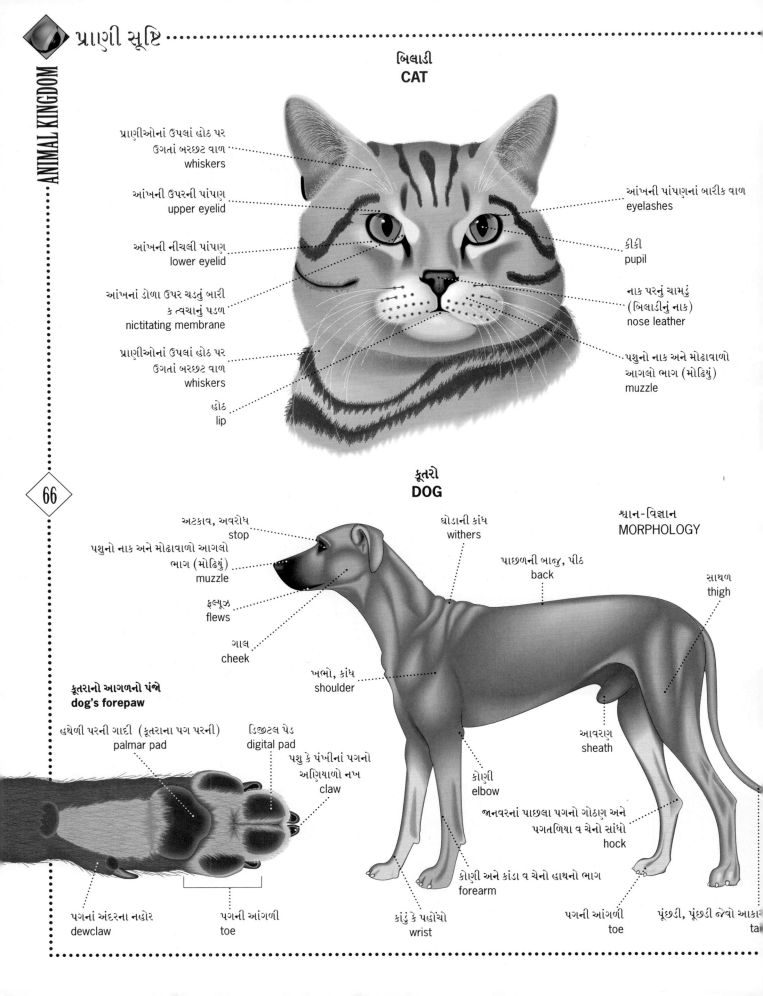

બિલાડી
CAT

પ્રાણીઓનાં ઉપલાં હોઠ પર ઉગતાં બરછટ વાળ
whiskers

આંખની ઉપરની પાંપણ
upper eyelid

આંખની નીચલી પાંપણ
lower eyelid

આંખનાં ડોળા ઉપર ચડતું બારીક ત્વચાનું પડળ
nictitating membrane

પ્રાણીઓનાં ઉપલાં હોઠ પર ઉગતાં બરછટ વાળ
whiskers

હોઠ
lip

આંખની પાંપણનાં બારીક વાળ
eyelashes

કીકી
pupil

નાક પરનું ચામડું (બિલાડીનું નાક)
nose leather

પશુનો નાક અને મોઢાવાળો આગલો ભાગ (મોઢિયું)
muzzle

કૂતરો
DOG

અટકાવ, અવરોધ
stop

પશુનો નાક અને મોઢાવાળો આગલો ભાગ (મોઢિયું)
muzzle

ફ્લ્યૂઝ
flews

ગાલ
cheek

ઘોડાની ક્રાંધ
withers

પાછળની બાજુ, પીઠ
back

શ્વાન-વિજ્ઞાન
MORPHOLOGY

સાથળ
thigh

ખભો, ક્રાંધ
shoulder

આવરણ
sheath

કોણી
elbow

જાનવરનાં પાછલા પગનો ગોઠણ અને પગતળિયા વ ચેનો સાંધો
hock

કોણી અને કાંડા વ ચેનો હાથનો ભાગ
forearm

કાંડું કે પહોંચો
wrist

પગની આંગળી
toe

પૂંછડી, પૂંછડી જેવો આકાર
tail

કૂતરાનો આગળનો પંજો
dog's forepaw

હથેળી પરની ગાદી (કૂતરાના પગ પરની)
palmar pad

ડિજિટલ પેડ
digital pad

પશુ કે પંખીનાં પગનો અણિયાળો નખ
claw

પગનાં અંદરના નહોર
dewclaw

પગની આંગળી
toe

ધોડો
HORSE

માથાનાં વાળનો ગુચ્છો
forelock

નાક
nose

નાકમાં આવેલાં નસકોરાં
nostril

પશુનો નાક અને મોઢાવાળો આગલો ભાગ (મોઢિયું)
muzzle

હોઠ
lip

ધોડાની કેશવાળી
mane

ધોડાની કાંધ
withers

પાછલની બાજુ, પીઠ
back

કમર કે કટિપ્રદેશ
loin

પૂંછડી
tail

કમર, કટિ
flank

ધોડાનો પાછલો પગ
croup

ગરદન, ડોક
neck

ખભો, કાંધ
shoulder

છાતી
chest

આર્મ
arm

કોણી
elbow

ઢીંચણ, ઘૂંટણ, ગોઠણ
knee

ચેસ્ટનટ
chestnut

ધોડાનાં ડાબલાથી ઉપરનાં પગનાં
હાડકાંનો સાંધો
fetlock joint

કોરોનેટ
coronet

ધોડાના ડાબલાથી ઉપરના
પગનો ભાગ જેના પર
લાંબા વાળ ઊગે છે
fetlock

પેટ
belly

આવરણ
sheath

સાથળ
thigh

સાથળનો પાછલનો ભાગ
gaskin

પગનો ગોઠણ અને ખરી વચેનો ભાગ
pastern

હુક
hoof

પાછલા પગનો ગોઠણ અને
પગતળિયા વચેનો સાંધો
hock

કેનન
cannon

67

પ્રાણી સૃષ્ટિ

ખેતરનાં પ્રાણીઓ
FARM ANIMALS

મરઘી
hen

મરઘીનું બચ્ચું
chick

કૂકડો
rooster; cock

બતક
duck

કલહંસ
goose

બતક જેવું મોઢું પંખી (ટર્કી)
turkey

ગાય
cow

વાછરડું
calf

પ્રાણી સૃષ્ટિ

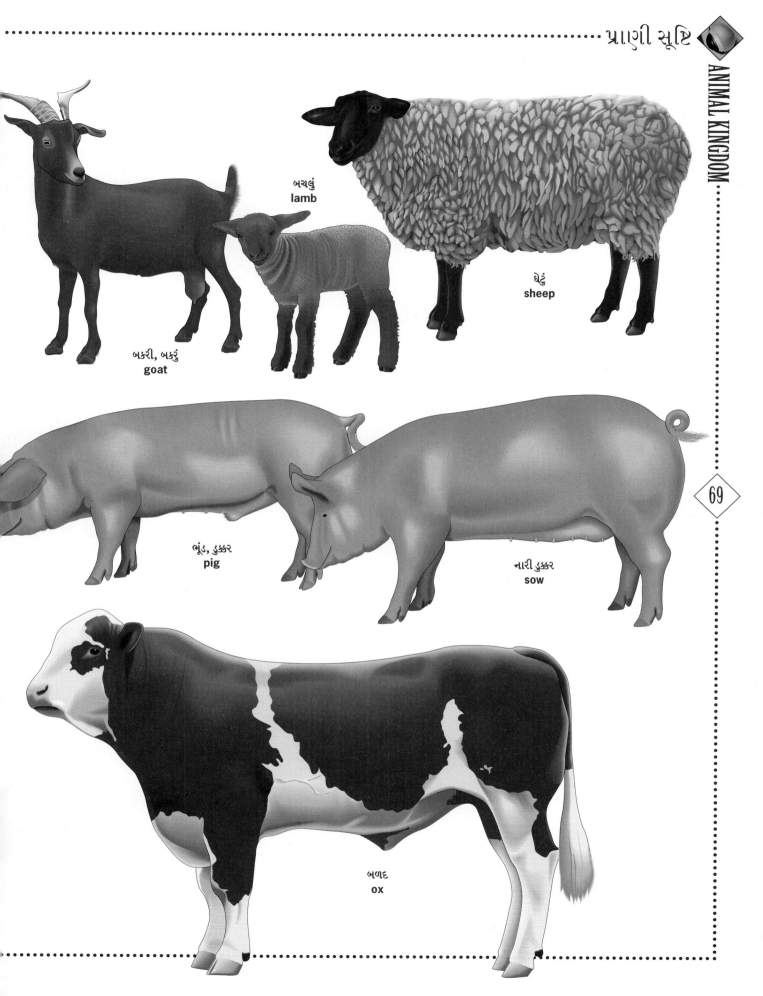

બચ્ચું
lamb

ઘેટું
sheep

બકરી, બકરું
goat

ભૂંડ, ડુક્કર
pig

નારી ડુક્કર
sow

બળદ
ox

જડબાના પ્રકારો
TYPES OF JAWS

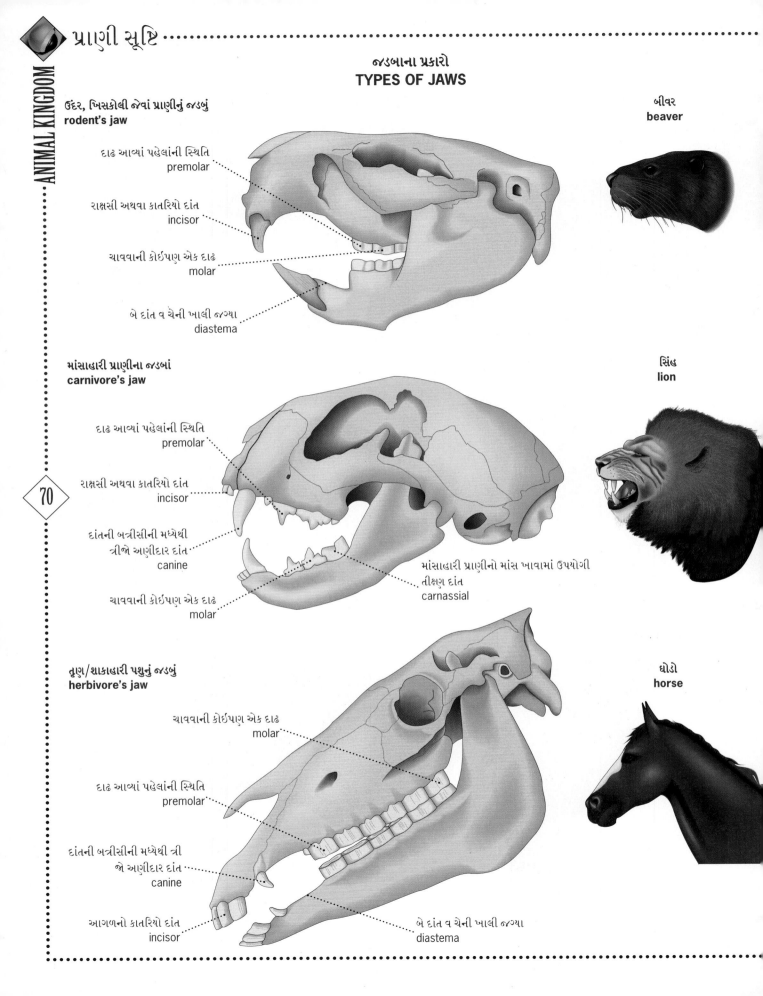

ઉંદર, ખિસકોલી જેવાં પ્રાણીનું જડબું
rodent's jaw

દાઢ આવ્યાં પહેલાંની સ્થિતિ
premolar

રાક્ષસી અથવા કાતરિયો દાંત
incisor

ચાવવાની કોઈપણ એક દાઢ
molar

બે દાંત વ ચેની ખાલી જગ્યા
diastema

બીવર
beaver

માંસાહારી પ્રાણીના જડબાં
carnivore's jaw

દાઢ આવ્યાં પહેલાંની સ્થિતિ
premolar

રાક્ષસી અથવા કાતરિયો દાંત
incisor

દાંતની બત્રીસીની મધ્યેથી
ત્રીજે આણીદાર દાંત
canine

ચાવવાની કોઈપણ એક દાઢ
molar

માંસાહારી પ્રાણીનો માંસ ખાવામાં ઉપયોગી
તીક્ષ્ણ દાંત
carnassial

સિંહ
lion

તૃણ/શાકાહારી પશુનું જડબું
herbivore's jaw

ચાવવાની કોઈપણ એક દાઢ
molar

દાઢ આવ્યાં પહેલાંની સ્થિતિ
premolar

દાંતની બત્રીસીની મધ્યેથી ત્રી
જે આણીદાર દાંત
canine

આગળનો કાતરિયો દાંત
incisor

બે દાંત વ ચેની ખાલી જગ્યા
diastema

ઘોડો
horse

શિંગડાના મુખ્ય પ્રકારો
MAJOR TYPES OF HORNS

પહાડી ઘેટાંનાં શિંગડા
horns of mouflon

જિરાફનાં શિંગડા
horns of giraffe

ગેંડાના શિંગડા
horns of rhinoceros

હાથી દાંતનાં મુખ્ય પ્રકારો
MAJOR TYPES OF TUSKS

રિયાઈ ઘોડા જેવાં પ્રાણીનાં દંતશૂળ
tusks of walrus

હાથી-દાંત
tusks of elephant

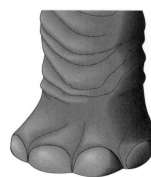

આફ્રિકન ભૂંડનાં દંતશૂળ
tusks of wart hog

ખરીના પ્રકારો
TYPES OF HOOFS

ઘરનાં પગની એક આંગળાવાળી ખરી
one-toe hoof

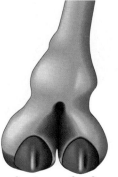

બે આંગળાવાળી ખરી
two-toed hoof

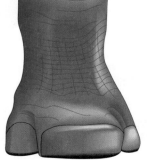

ત્રણ આંગળાવાળી જાનવરનાં પગની ખરી
three-toed hoof

ચાર આંગળાવાળી ખરી
four-toed hoof

ANIMAL KINGDOM

જંગલી પ્રાણીઓ
WILD ANIMALS

જિરાફ
giraffe

ઉત્તર/દક્ષિણ ધ્રુવનું રીંછ
polar bear

વાંદરો
monkey

સિંહ
lion

72

ડોલ્ફિન
dolphin

વ્હેલ
whale

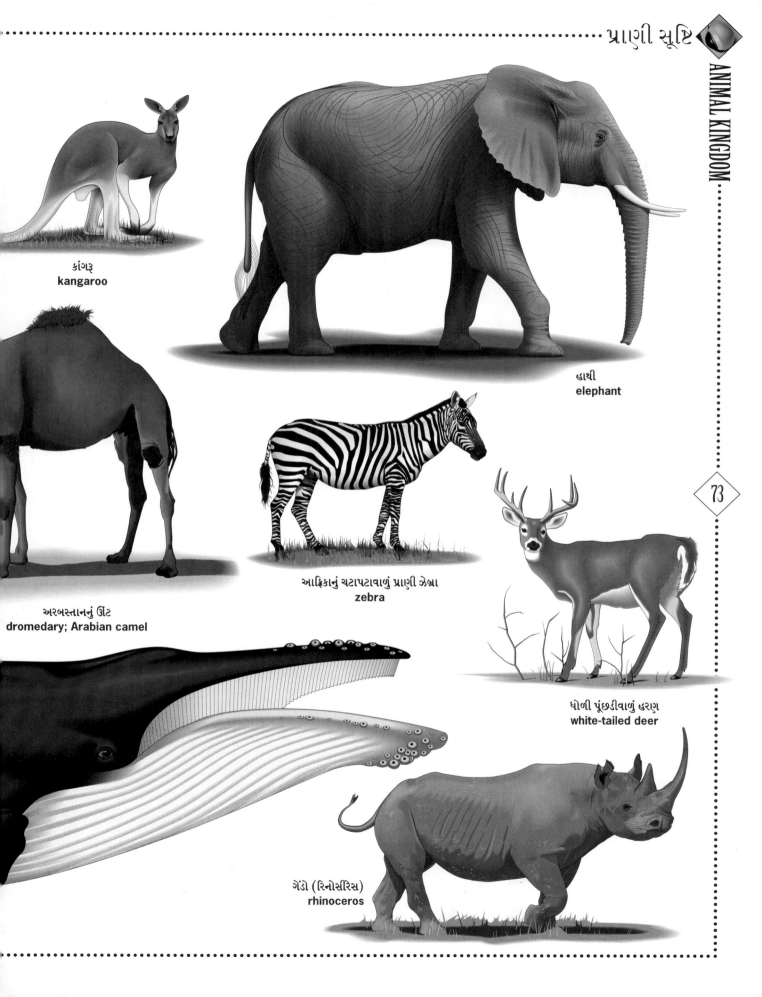

કાંગરુ
kangaroo

હાથી
elephant

આફ્રિકાનું ચટાપટાવાળું પ્રાણી ઝેબ્રા
zebra

અરબસ્તાનનું ઊંટ
dromedary; Arabian camel

ધોળી પૂંછડીવાળું હરણ
white-tailed deer

ગેંડો (રિનોસરિસ)
rhinoceros

પક્ષી
BIRD

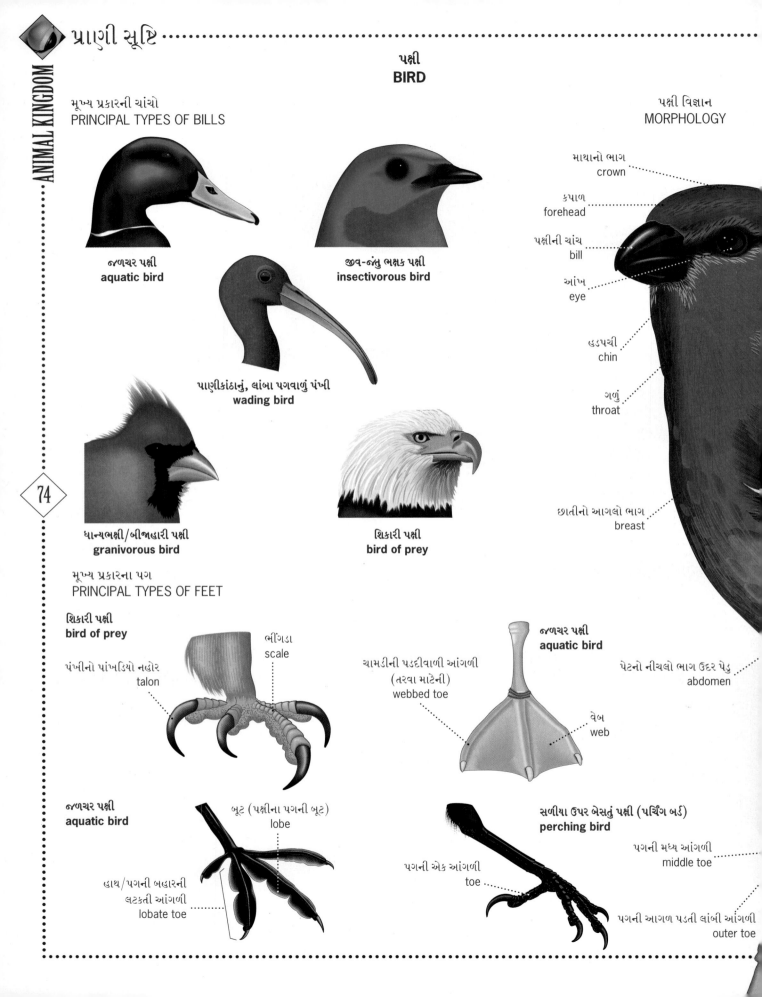

મૂખ્ય પ્રકારની ચાંચો
PRINCIPAL TYPES OF BILLS

જળચર પક્ષી
aquatic bird

જીવ-જંતુ ભક્ષક પક્ષી
insectivorous bird

પાણીકાંઠાનું, લાંબા પગવાળું પંખી
wading bird

ધાન્યભક્ષી/બીજાહારી પક્ષી
granivorous bird

શિકારી પક્ષી
bird of prey

પક્ષી વિજ્ઞાન
MORPHOLOGY

માથાનો ભાગ
crown

કપાળ
forehead

પક્ષીની ચાંચ
bill

આંખ
eye

હડપચી
chin

ગળું
throat

છાતીનો આગલો ભાગ
breast

પેટનો નીચલો ભાગ ઉદર પેટ
abdomen

મૂખ્ય પ્રકારના પગ
PRINCIPAL TYPES OF FEET

શિકારી પક્ષી
bird of prey

પંખીનો પાંખડિયો નહોર
talon

ભીંગડા
scale

જળચર પક્ષી
aquatic bird

ચામડીની પડડીવાળી આંગળી
(તરવા માટેની)
webbed toe

વેબ
web

જળચર પક્ષી
aquatic bird

હાથ/પગની બહારની
લટકતી આંગળી
lobate toe

બૂટ (પક્ષીના પગની બૂટ)
lobe

સળીયા ઉપર બેસતું પક્ષી (પર્ચિંગ બર્ડ)
perching bird

પગની એક આંગળી
toe

પગની મધ્ય આંગળી
middle toe

પગની આગળ પડતી લાંબી આંગળી
outer toe

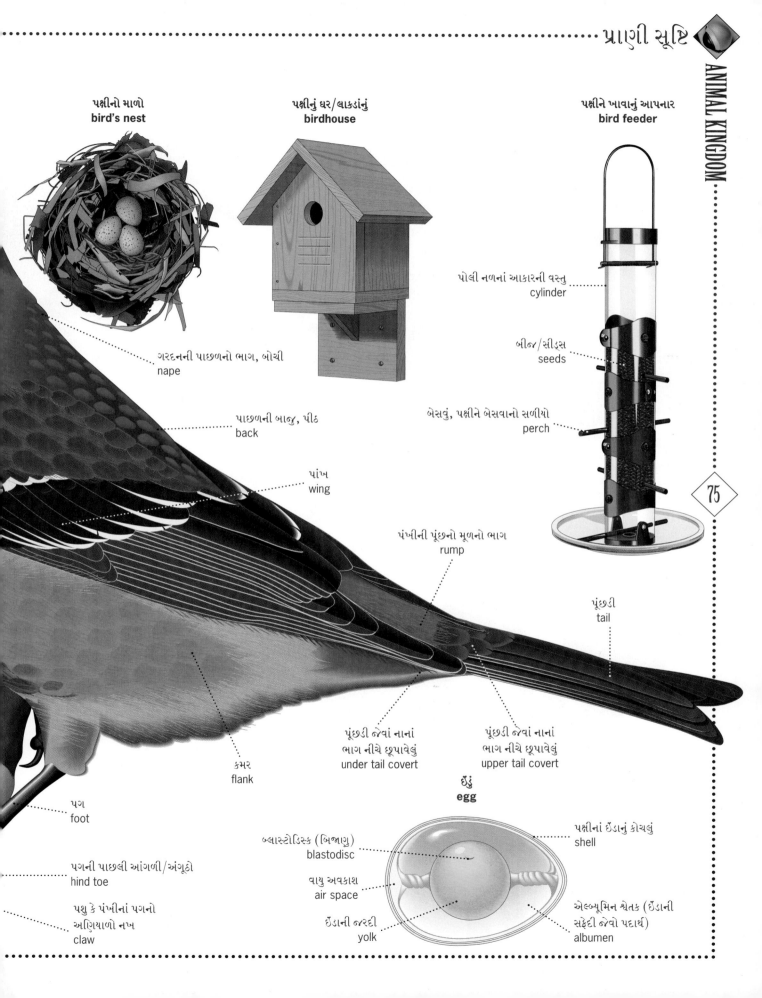

પક્ષીનો માળો
bird's nest

પક્ષીનું ઘર/લાકડાંનું
birdhouse

પક્ષીને ખાવાનું આપનાર
bird feeder

ગરદનની પાછળનો ભાગ, બોચી
nape

પાછલની બાજુ, પીઠ
back

પાંખ
wing

પોલી નળનાં આકારની વસ્તુ
cylinder

બીજ/સીડ્સ
seeds

બેસવું, પક્ષીને બેસવાનો સળીયો
perch

પંખીની પૂંછનો મૂળનો ભાગ
rump

પૂંછડી
tail

કમર
flank

પૂંછડી જેવાં નાનાં
ભાગ નીચે છૂપાવેલું
under tail covert

પૂંછડી જેવાં નાનાં
ભાગ નીચે છૂપાવેલું
upper tail covert

પગ
foot

પગની પાછલી આંગળી/અંગૂઠો
hind toe

પશુ કે પંખીનાં પગનો
અણિયાળો નખ
claw

ઈંડું
egg

બ્લાસ્ટોડિસ્ક (બિજાણુ)
blastodisc

વાયુ અવકાશ
air space

ઈંડાની જરદી
yolk

પક્ષીનાં ઈંડાનું કોચલું
shell

એલ્બ્યૂમિન શ્વેતક (ઈંડાની
સફેદી જેવો પદાર્થ)
albumen

પ્રાણી સૃષ્ટિ

પક્ષીના દાખલા
EXAMPLES OF BIRDS

કાગડો
crow

પોપટ
parrot

લાંલ ચાંચવાળો બગલો
stork

અબાબિલ, કાળી ચકલી
swallow

સુરખાબ
flamingo

શાહમૃગ
ostrich

76

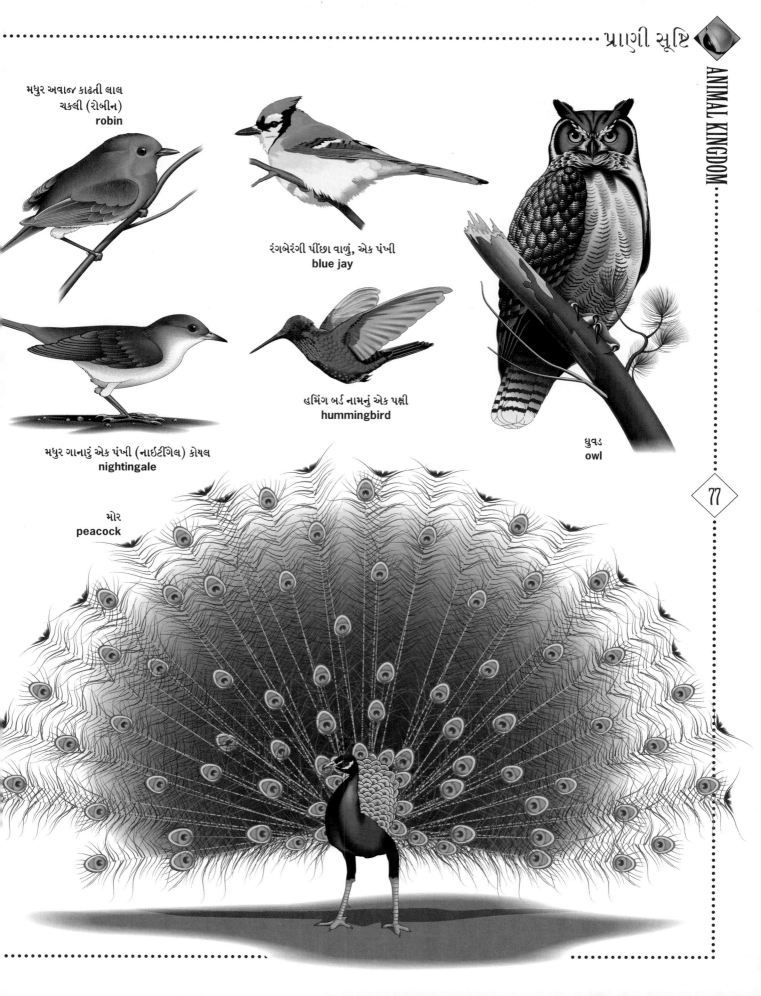

મધુર અવાજ કાઢતી લાલ
ચકલી (રોબીન)
robin

રંગબેરંગી પીંછા વાળું, એક પંખી
blue jay

હમિંગ બર્ડ નામનું એક પક્ષી
hummingbird

ધુવડ
owl

મધુર ગાનારું એક પંખી (નાઇટીંગેલ) કોયલ
nightingale

મોર
peacock

માનવ શરીર, આગળનું અભિપ્રાય
HUMAN BODY, ANTERIOR VIEW

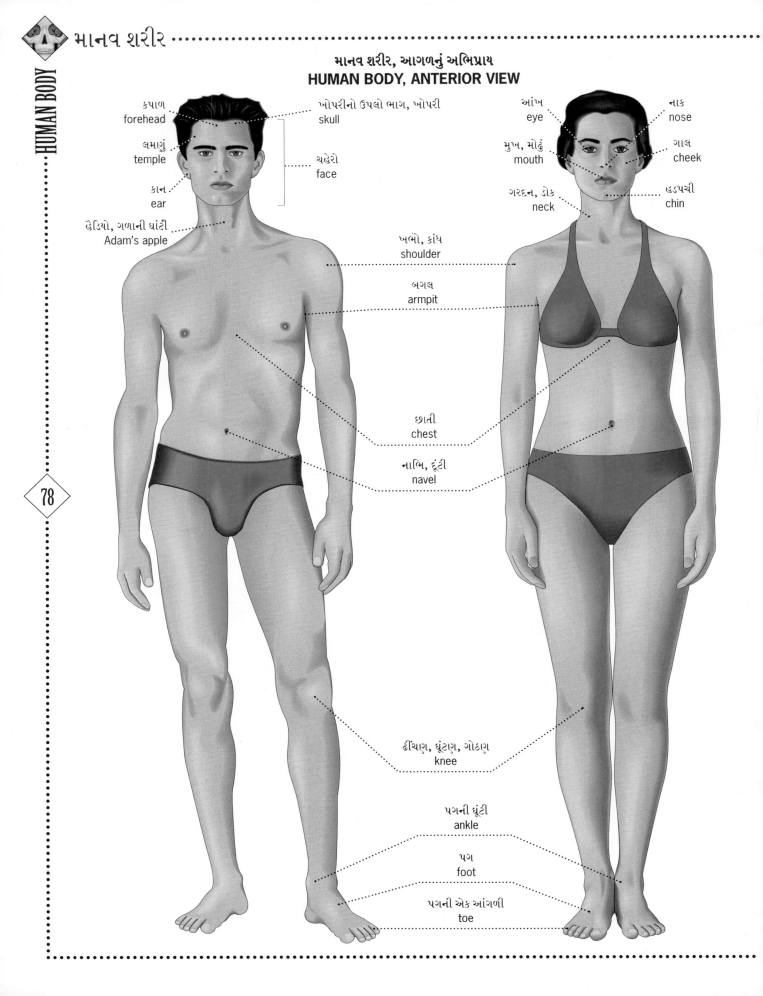

કપાળ
forehead

ખોપરીનો ઉપલો ભાગ, ખોપરી
skull

લમાણું
temple

ચહેરો
face

કાન
ear

હૈડિયો, ગળાની ઘાંટી
Adam's apple

આંખ
eye

નાક
nose

મુખ, મોઢું
mouth

ગાલ
cheek

ગરદન, ડોક
neck

હડપચી
chin

ખભો, કાંધ
shoulder

બગલ
armpit

છાતી
chest

નાભિ, ડૂંટી
navel

ઢીંચણ, ઘૂંટણ, ગોઠણ
knee

પગની ઘૂંટી
ankle

પગ
foot

પગની એક આંગળી
toe

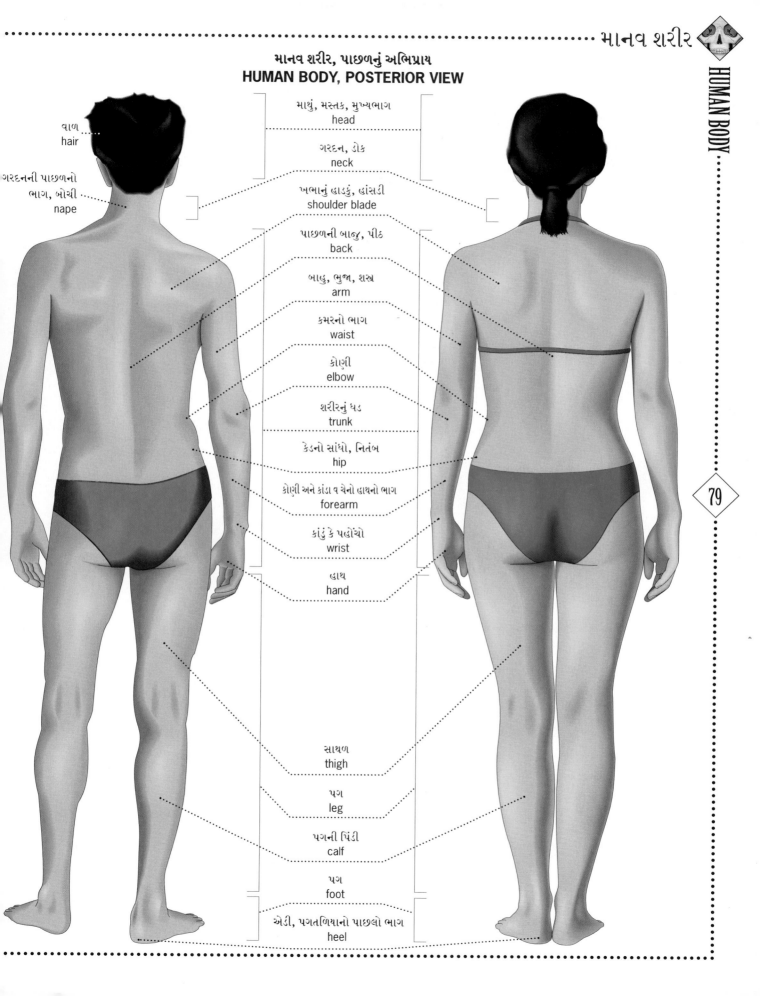

માનવ શરીર, પાછળનું અભિપ્રાય
HUMAN BODY, POSTERIOR VIEW

વાળ
hair

ગરદનની પાછળનો
ભાગ, બોચી
nape

માથું, મસ્તક, મુખ્યભાગ
head

ગરદન, ડોક
neck

ખભાનું હાડકું, હાંસડી
shoulder blade

પાછળની બાજુ, પીઠ
back

બાહુ, ભુજા, શસ્ર
arm

કમરનો ભાગ
waist

કોણી
elbow

શરીરનું ધડ
trunk

કેડનો સાંધો, નિતંબ
hip

કોણી અને કાંડા વ ચેનો હાથનો ભાગ
forearm

કાંડું કે પહોંચો
wrist

હાથ
hand

સાથળ
thigh

પગ
leg

પગની પિંડી
calf

પગ
foot

એડી, પગતળિયાનો પાછલો ભાગ
heel

હાડપિંજર
SKELETON

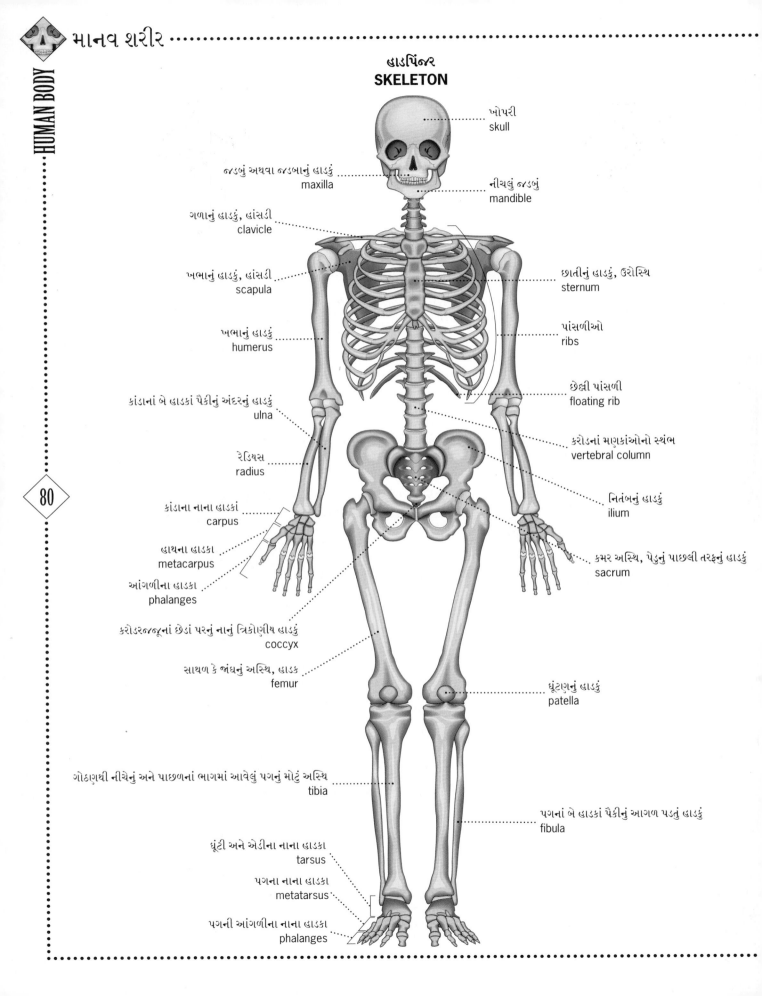

ખોપરી
skull

જડબું અથવા જડબાનું હાડકું
maxilla

નીચલું જડબું
mandible

ગળાનું હાડકું, હાંસડી
clavicle

છાતીનું હાડકું, ઉરોસ્થિ
sternum

ખભાનું હાડકું, હાંસડી
scapula

પાંસળીઓ
ribs

ખભાનું હાડકું
humerus

છેલ્લી પાંસળી
floating rib

કાંડાનાં બે હાડકાં પૈકીનું અંદરનું હાડકું
ulna

કરોડનાં માણકાંઓનો સ્થંભ
vertebral column

રેડિયસ
radius

નિતંબનું હાડકું
ilium

કાંડાના નાના હાડકાં
carpus

હાથના હાડકા
metacarpus

કમર અસ્થિ, પેડુનું પાછલી તરફનું હાડકું
sacrum

આંગળીના હાડકા
phalanges

કરોડરજ્જૂનાં છેડાં પરનું નાનું ત્રિકોણીય હાડકું
coccyx

સાથળ કે જાંઘનું અસ્થિ, હાડક
femur

ઘૂંટણનું હાડકું
patella

ગોઠણથી નીચેનું અને પાછળનાં ભાગમાં આવેલું પગનું મોટું અસ્થિ
tibia

પગનાં બે હાડકાં પૈકીનું આગળ પડતું હાડકું
fibula

ઘૂંટી અને એડીના નાના હાડકા
tarsus

પગના નાના હાડકા
metatarsus

પગની આંગળીના નાના હાડકા
phalanges

માનવીના શરીરની રચના
HUMAN ANATOMY

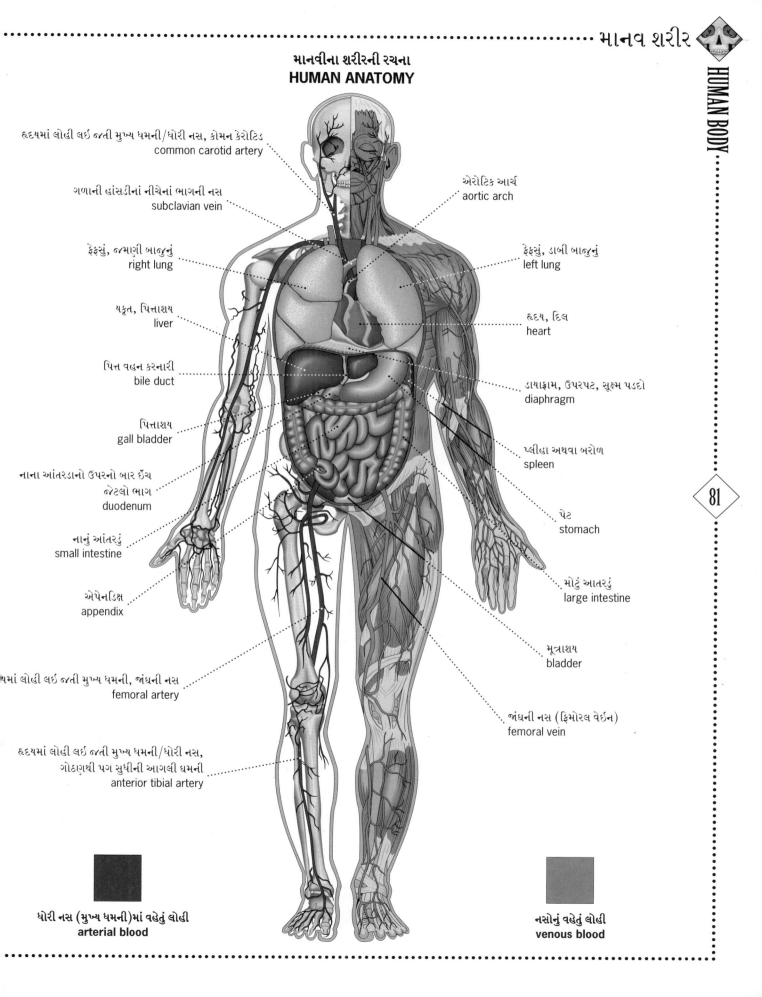

હૃદયમાં લોહી લઈ જતી મુખ્ય ધમની/ધોરી નસ, કોમન કેરોટિડ
common carotid artery

ગળાની હાંસડીનાં નીચેનાં ભાગની નસ
subclavian vein

ફેફસું, જમણી બાજુનું
right lung

યકૃત, પિત્તાશય
liver

પિત્ત વહન કરનારી
bile duct

પિત્તાશય
gall bladder

નાના આંતરડાનો ઉપરનો બાર ઈંચ જેટલો ભાગ
duodenum

નાનું આંતરડું
small intestine

એપેનડિક્ષ
appendix

...માં લોહી લઈ જતી મુખ્ય ધમની, જાંઘની નસ
femoral artery

હૃદયમાં લોહી લઈ જતી મુખ્ય ધમની/ધોરી નસ,
ગોઠણથી પગ સુધીની આગલી ધમની
anterior tibial artery

એરોટિક આર્ચ
aortic arch

ફેફસું, ડાબી બાજુનું
left lung

હૃદય, દિલ
heart

ડાયાફ્રામ, ઉપરપટ, સૂક્ષ્મ પડદો
diaphragm

પ્લીહા અથવા બરોળ
spleen

પેટ
stomach

મોટું આતરડું
large intestine

મૂત્રાશય
bladder

જાંઘની નસ (ફિમોરલ વેઈન)
femoral vein

ધોરી નસ (મુખ્ય ધમની)માં વહેતું લોહી
arterial blood

નસોનું વહેતું લોહી
venous blood

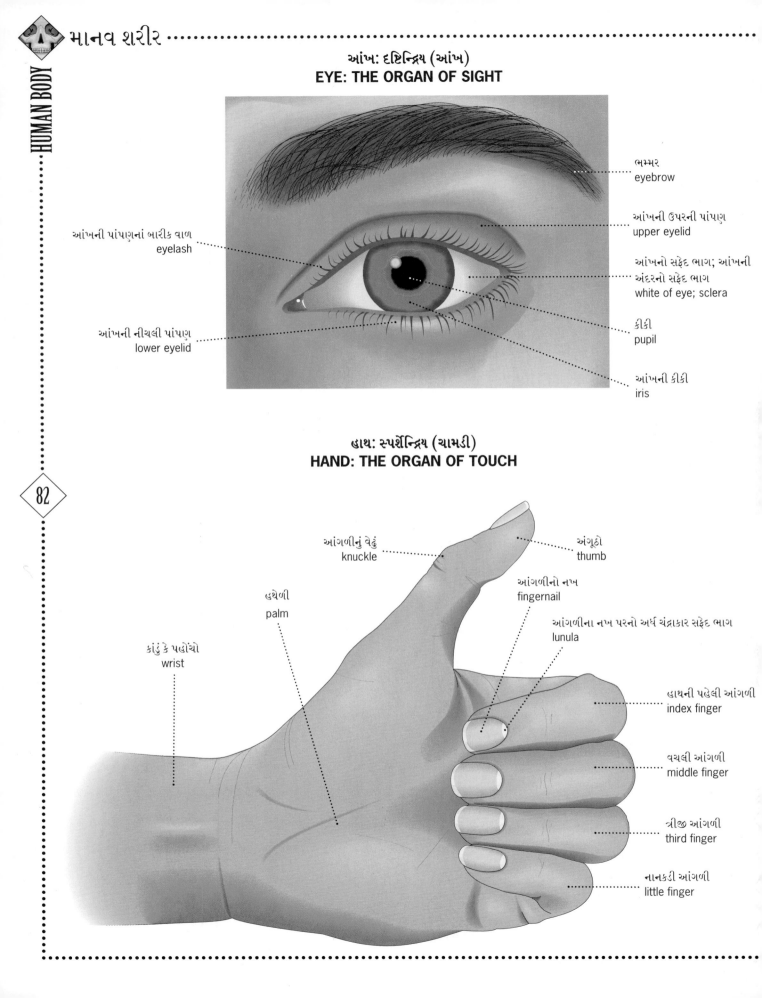

આંખ: દૃષ્ટિન્દ્રિય (આંખ)
EYE: THE ORGAN OF SIGHT

ભમ્મર
eyebrow

આંખની ઉપરની પાંપણ
upper eyelid

આંખની પાંપણનાં બારીક વાળ
eyelash

આંખનો સફેદ ભાગ; આંખની અંદરનો સફેદ ભાગ
white of eye; sclera

કીકી
pupil

આંખની નીચલી પાંપણ
lower eyelid

આંખની કીકી
iris

હાથ: સ્પર્શેન્દ્રિય (ચામડી)
HAND: THE ORGAN OF TOUCH

આંગળીનું વેઢું
knuckle

અંગૂઠો
thumb

આંગળીનો નખ
fingernail

આંગળીના નખ પરનો અર્ધ ચંદ્રાકાર સફેદ ભાગ
lunula

હથેળી
palm

કાંડું કે પહોંચો
wrist

હાથની પહેલી આંગળી
index finger

વચલી આંગળી
middle finger

ત્રીજી આંગળી
third finger

નાનકડી આંગળી
little finger

82

કાન: શ્રવણેન્દ્રિય (કાન)
EAR: THE ORGAN OF HEARING

કાનનો બાહ્ય ભાગ
auricle

કાનમાં અવાજનાં તરંગો
લઈ જતાં જ્ઞાનતંતુઓ
auditory nerve

શ્રવણ સંબંધી અસ્થિકા/
નાનું હાડકું
auditory ossicles

કાનની અંદરની અર્ધવર્તુળાકાર
કેનાલ/નળી
semicircular canals

શ્રવણેન્દ્રિય નળી
(કાનમાં અવાજનાં
તરંગો લઈ જતી નળી)
auditory canal

કાનનો પડદો
ear drum

કાનનું અંદરનું ગોળ પોલાણ
cochlea

ગળામાંથી પસાર થતી કાનની નળી (યૂસ્ટેચિયન ટ્યૂ)
Eustachian tube

બહારનાં કાનની ધાર,
કિનારી
helix

બૂટ
lobe

કાનના ભાગો
PARTS OF THE EAR

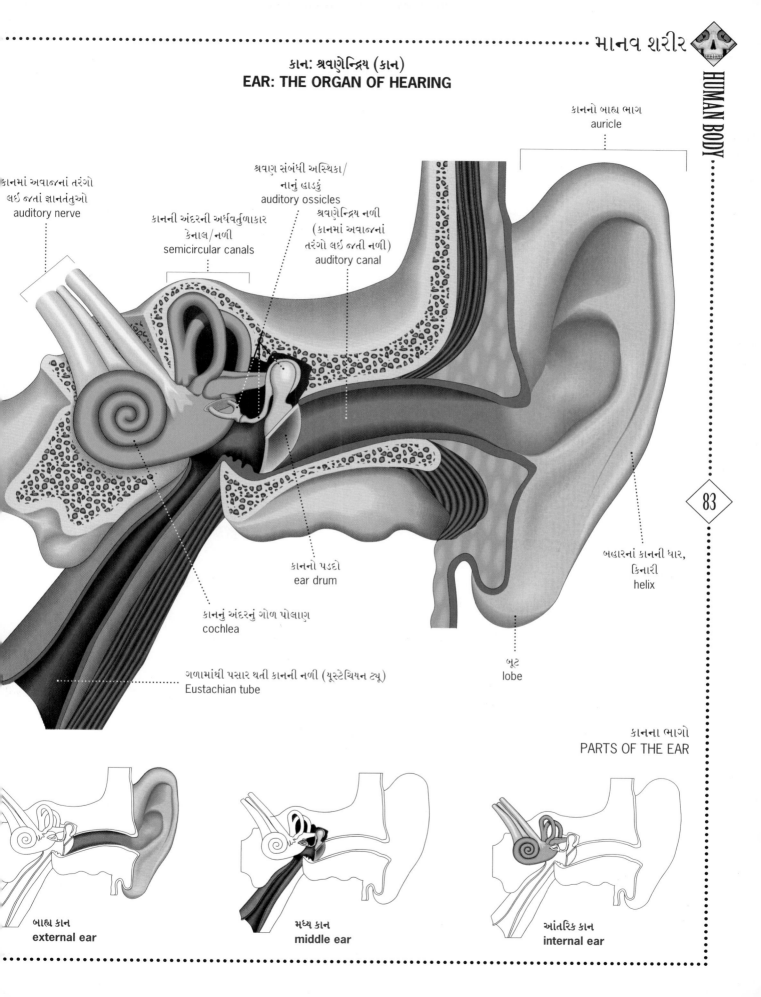

બાહ્ય કાન
external ear

મધ્ય કાન
middle ear

આંતરિક કાન
internal ear

નાક, ઘ્રાણેન્દ્રિય: ઘ્રાણેન્દ્રિય (નાક)
NOSE: THE ORGAN OF SMELL

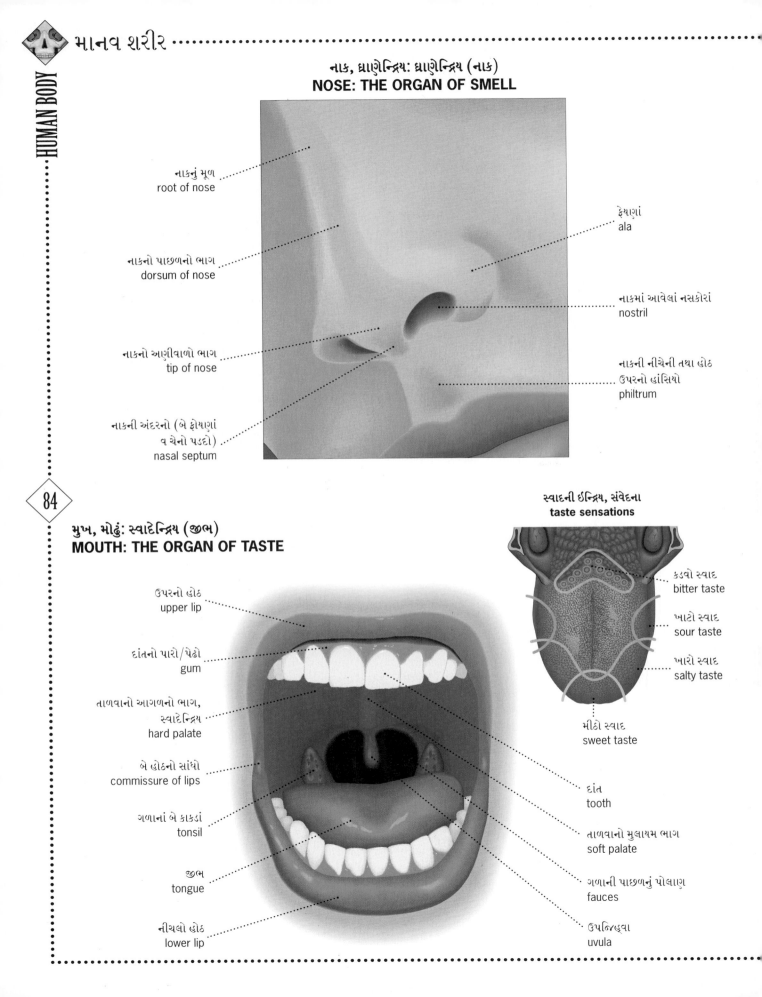

નાકનું મૂળ
root of nose

ફેણાં
ala

નાકનો પાછળનો ભાગ
dorsum of nose

નાકમાં આવેલાં નસકોરાં
nostril

નાકનો અણીવાળો ભાગ
tip of nose

નાકની નીચેની તથા હોઠ
ઉપરનો હાંસિયો
philtrum

નાકની અંદરનો (બે ફોયાણાં
વ ચેનો પડદો)
nasal septum

મુખ, મોઢું: સ્વાદેન્દ્રિય (જીભ)
MOUTH: THE ORGAN OF TASTE

સ્વાદની ઇન્દ્રિય, સંવેદના
taste sensations

કડવો સ્વાદ
bitter taste

ખાટો સ્વાદ
sour taste

ખારો સ્વાદ
salty taste

મીઠો સ્વાદ
sweet taste

ઉપરનો હોઠ
upper lip

દાંતનો પારો/પેઢો
gum

તાળવાનો આગળનો ભાગ,
સ્વાદેન્દ્રિય
hard palate

બે હોઠનો સાંધો
commissure of lips

ગળાનાં બે કાકડાં
tonsil

જીભ
tongue

નીચલો હોઠ
lower lip

દાંત
tooth

તાળવાનો મુલાયમ ભાગ
soft palate

ગળાની પાછળનું પોલાણ
fauces

ઉપજિહ્વા
uvula

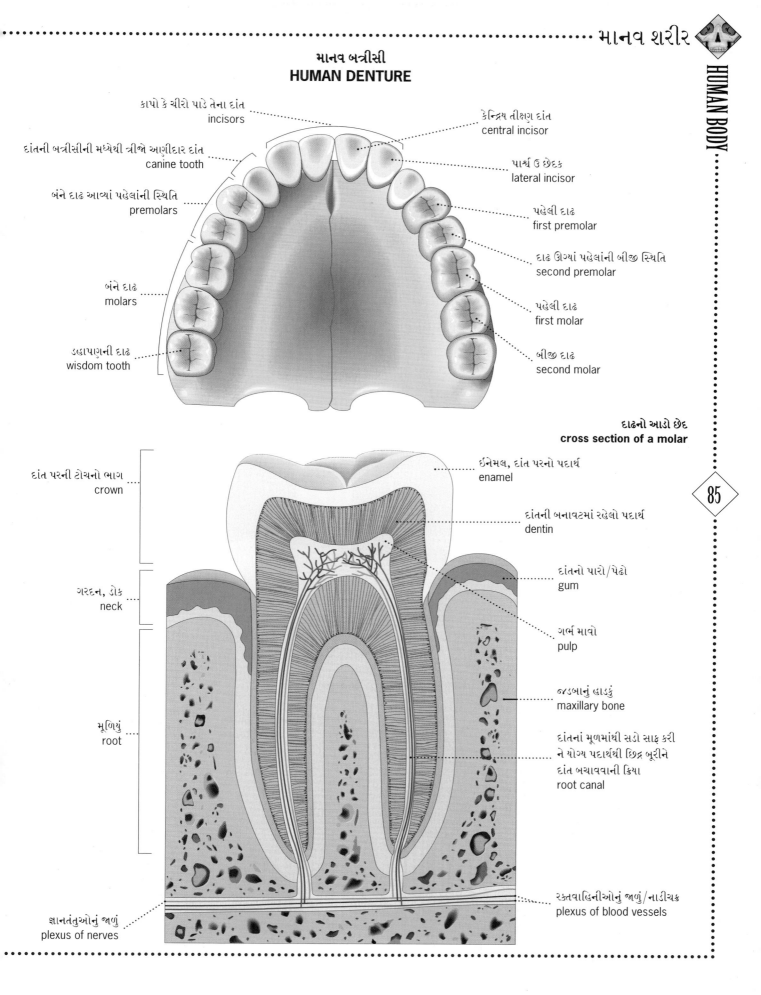

માનવ બત્રીસી
HUMAN DENTURE

કાપો કે ચીરો પાડે તેના દાંત
incisors

દાંતની બત્રીસીની મધ્યેથી ત્રીજો આગીદાર દાંત
canine tooth

બંને દાઢ આવ્યાં પહેલાંની સ્થિતિ
premolars

બંને દાઢ
molars

ડહાપણની દાઢ
wisdom tooth

કેન્દ્રિય તીક્ષ્ણ દાંત
central incisor

પાર્શ્વ ઉ છેદક
lateral incisor

પહેલી દાઢ
first premolar

દાઢ ઊગ્યાં પહેલાંની બીજી સ્થિતિ
second premolar

પહેલી દાઢ
first molar

બીજી દાઢ
second molar

દાઢનો આડો છેદ
cross section of a molar

દાંત પરની ટોચનો ભાગ
crown

ગરદન, ડોક
neck

મૂળિયું
root

જ્ઞાનતંતુઓનું જાળું
plexus of nerves

ઈનેમલ, દાંત પરનો પદાર્થ
enamel

દાંતની બનાવટમાં રહેલો પદાર્થ
dentin

દાંતનો પારો/પેઢો
gum

ગર્ભ માવો
pulp

જડબાનું હાડકું
maxillary bone

દાંતનાં મૂળમાંથી સડો સાફ કરી
ને યોગ્ય પદાર્થથી છિદ્ર બૂરીને
દાંત બચાવવાની ક્રિયા
root canal

રક્તવાહિનીઓનું જાળું/નાડીચક્ર
plexus of blood vessels

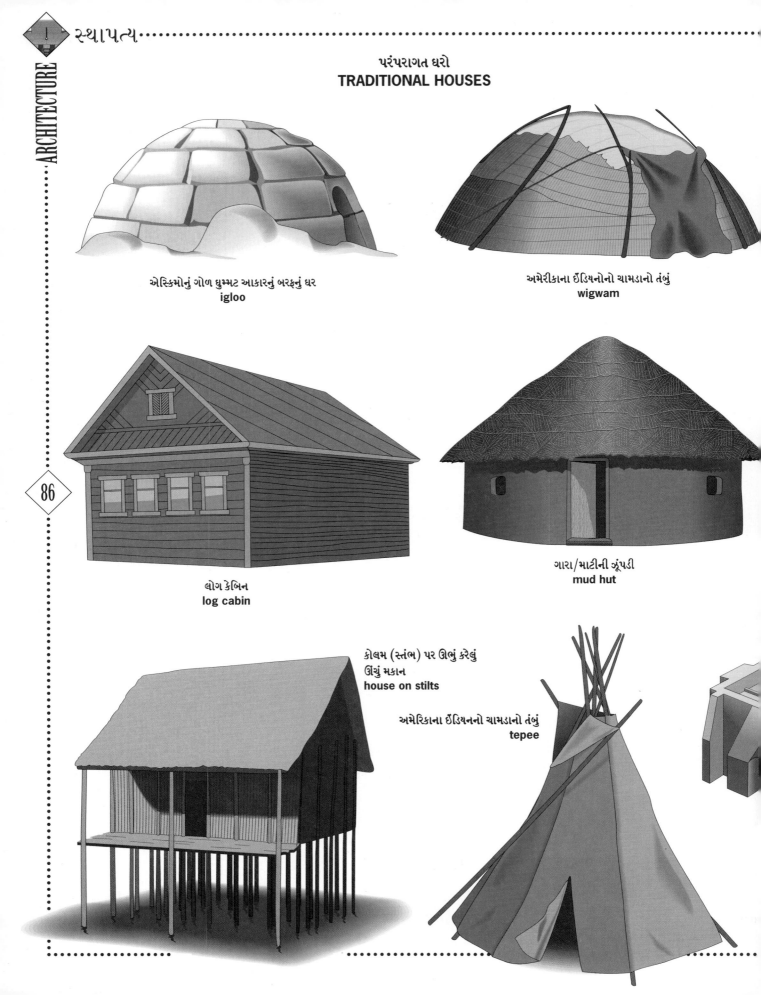

પરંપરાગત ઘરો
TRADITIONAL HOUSES

એસ્કિમોનું ગોળ ઘુમ્મટ આકારનું બરફનું ઘર
igloo

અમેરીકાના ઈડિયનોનો ચામડાનો તંબુ
wigwam

લોગ કેબિન
log cabin

ગારા/માટીની ઝૂંપડી
mud hut

કોલમ (સ્તંભ) પર ઊભું કરેલું
ઊંચું મકાન
house on stilts

અમેરિકાના ઈડિયનનો ચામડાનો તંબુ
tepee

ઝૂંપડું
hut

ચામડાનો તંબુ (યુર્ટ)
yurt

મસ્જિદ
MOSQUE

કેન્દ્રિય નાભિ, મસ્જિદનો
મધ્યભાગ
central nave

પ્રાર્થના ખંડ
prayer hall

મસ્જિદમાં મક્કા તરફની દિશા
દર્શાવતા ભાગ પરનો ઘુમ્મટ
Mihrab dome

મક્કા તરફની દિશા
direction of Mecca

છાંયાવાળો વૃક્ષોથી આ છાદિત માર્ગ
shady arcades

મક્કાનાં પવિત્ર 'કબ્બા'ની દીવાલ
Qibla wall

મસ્જિદનો મિનારો
minaret

87

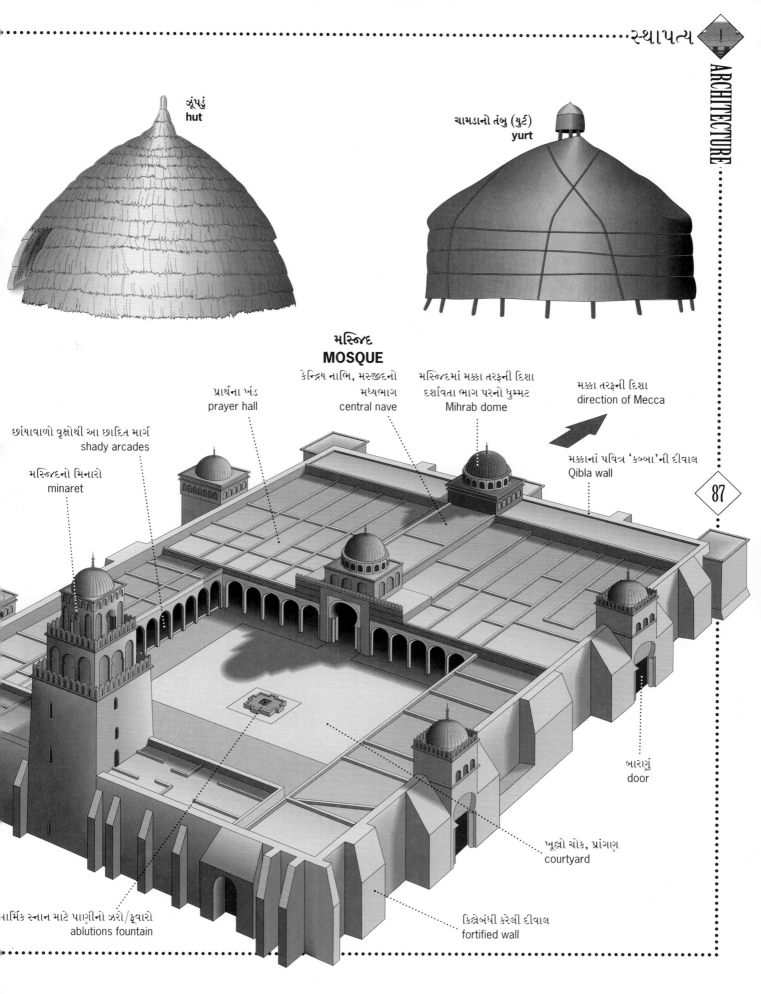

બારણું
door

ખુલ્લો ચોક, પ્રાંગણ
courtyard

ધાર્મિક સ્નાન માટે પાણીનો ઝરો/ફૂવારો
ablutions fountain

કિલ્લેબંધી કરેલી દીવાલ
fortified wall

સ્થાપત્ય

કિલ્લો
CASTLE

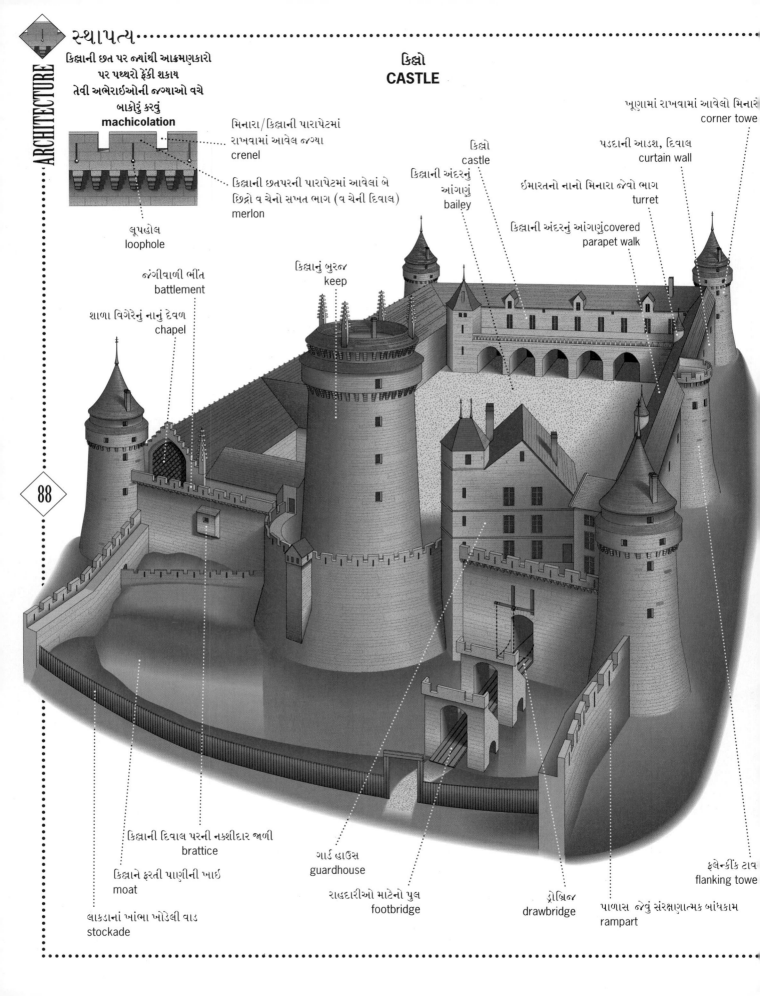

કિલ્લાની છત પર જ્યાંથી આક્રમણકારો પર પથ્થરો ફેંકી શકાય તેવી અભરાઈઓની જગ્યાઓ વચે બાકોરું કરવું
machicolation

લૂપહોલ
loophole

મિનારા/કિલ્લાની પારાપેટમાં રાખવામાં આવેલ જગ્યા
crenel

કિલ્લાની છતપરની પારાપેટમાં આવેલાં બે છિદ્રો વ ચેનો સખત ભાગ (વ ચેની દિવાલ)
merlon

જંગીવાળી ભીંત
battlement

શાળા વિગેરેનું નાનું દેવળ
chapel

કિલ્લાનું બુરજ
keep

કિલ્લો
castle

કિલ્લાની અંદરનું આંગણું
bailey

કિલ્લાની અંદરનું આંગણું covered parapet walk

ખૂણામાં રાખવામાં આવેલો મિનાર
corner towe

પડદાની આડશ, દિવાલ
curtain wall

ઈમારતનો નાનો મિનારા જેવો ભાગ
turret

કિલ્લાની દિવાલ પરની નક્શીદાર જાળી
brattice

કિલ્લાને ફરતી પાણીની ખાઈ
moat

લાકડાનાં ખાંભા ખોડેલી વાડ
stockade

ગાર્ડ હાઉસ
guardhouse

રાહદારીઓ માટેનો પુલ
footbridge

ડ્રોબ્રિજ
drawbridge

પાળાસ જેવું સંરક્ષણાત્મક બાંધકામ
rampart

ફ્લેન્કીંક ટાવ
flanking towe

88

ગોથિક દેવળ/મઢ
GOTHIC CATHEDRAL

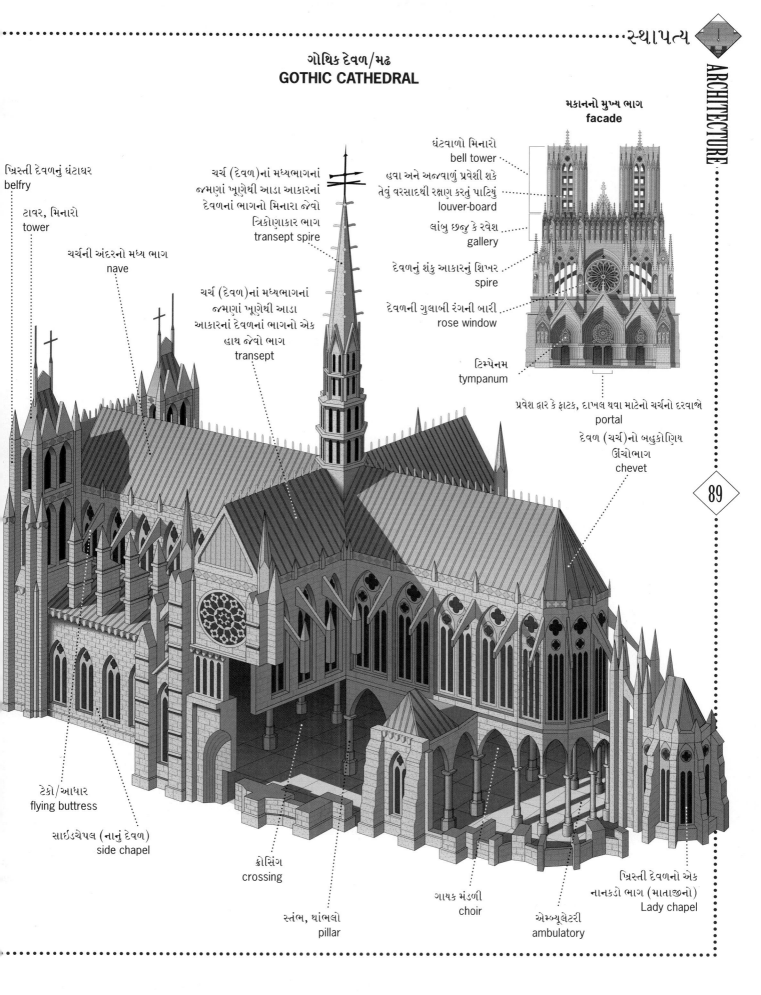

ખ્રિસ્તી દેવળનું ઘંટાઘર
belfry

ટાવર, મિનારો
tower

ચર્ચની અંદરનો મધ્ય ભાગ
nave

ચર્ચ (દેવળ)નાં મધ્યભાગનાં
જમાણાં ખૂણેથી આડા આકારનાં
દેવળનાં ભાગનો મિનારા જેવો
ત્રિકોણાકાર ભાગ
transept spire

ચર્ચ (દેવળ)નાં મધ્યભાગનાં
જમાણાં ખૂણેથી આડા
આકારનાં દેવળનાં ભાગનો એક
હાથ જેવો ભાગ
transept

મકાનનો મુખ્ય ભાગ
facade

ઘંટવાળો મિનારો
bell tower

હવા અને અજવાળું પ્રવેશી શકે
તેવું વરસાદથી રક્ષાણ કરતું પાટિયું
louver-board

લાંબુ છજ્જુ કે રવેશ
gallery

દેવળનું શંકુ આકારનું શિખર
spire

દેવળની ગુલાબી રંગની બારી
rose window

ટિમ્પેનમ
tympanum

પ્રવેશ દ્વાર કે ફાટક, દાખલ થવા માટેનો ચર્ચનો દરવાજો
portal

દેવળ (ચર્ચ)નો બહુકોણિય
ઊંચોભાગ
chevet

ટેકો/આધાર
flying buttress

સાઈડચેપલ (નાનું દેવળ)
side chapel

ક્રોસિંગ
crossing

સ્તંભ, થાંભલો
pillar

ગાયક મંડળી
choir

એમ્બ્યુલેટરી
ambulatory

ખ્રિસ્તી દેવળનો એક
નાનકડો ભાગ (માતાજીનો)
Lady chapel

89

શહેરમાં વેપારનું મુખ્ય કેન્દ્ર
DOWNTOWN

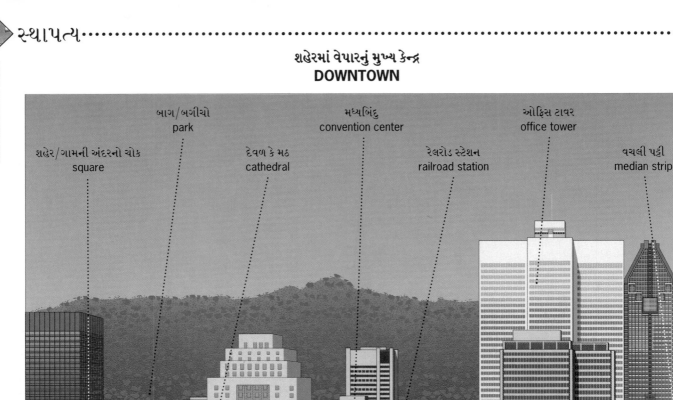

બાગ/બગીચો
park

મધ્યબિંદુ
convention center

ઓફિસ ટાવર
office tower

શહેર/ગામની અંદરનો ચોક
square

દેવળ કે મઠ
cathedral

રેલરોડ સ્ટેશન
railroad station

વચલી પટ્ટી
median strip

તારામંડળ (તારાંઓ અને
ગ્રહોનું દર્શન કરાવતું સ્થાન)
planetarium

લોખંડની સડકવાળો માર્ગ (રેલરોડ)
railroad

ટ્રાફિક આઇલેન્ડ
traffic island

બંને બાજુ વૃક્ષોવાળો પહોળો રસ્તો
boulevard / high street

શેરી
street

કોઈ વસ્તુ પહોંચાડવા/વહેંચણી કરવા માટેનો રસ્તો
delivery ramp

મુક્તમાર્ગ
freeway / dual carriageway

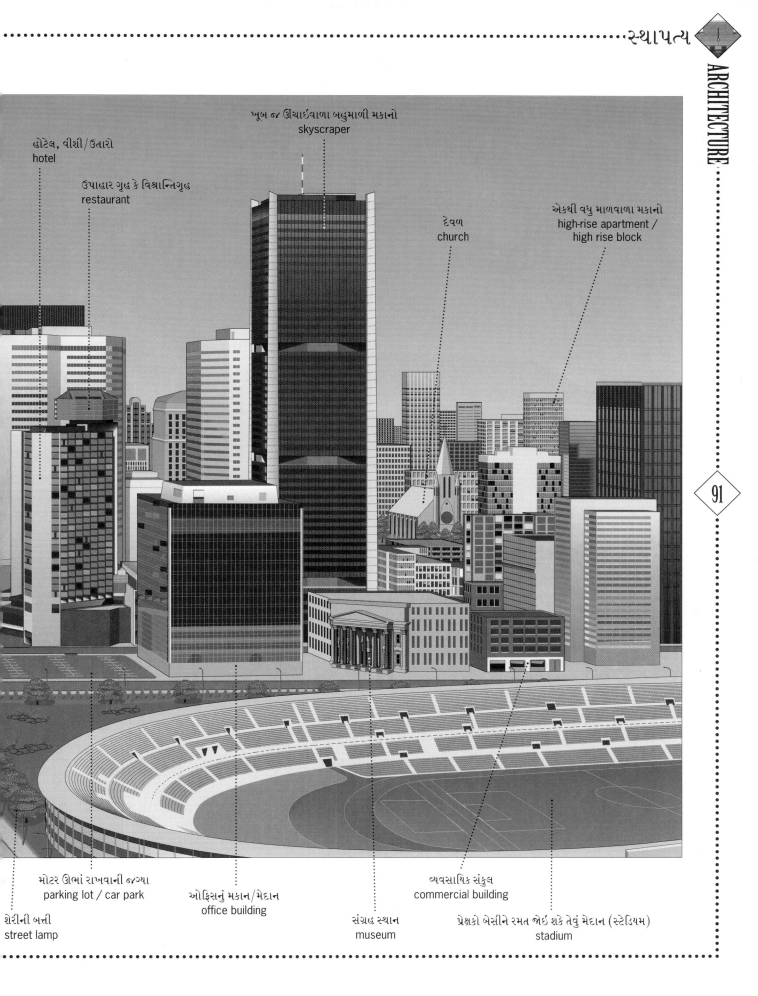

ખૂબ જ ઊંચાઈવાળા બહુમાળી મકાનો
skyscraper

હોટેલ, વીશી/ઉતારો
hotel

ઉપાહાર ગૃહ કે વિશ્રાન્તિગૃહ
restaurant

દેવળ
church

એકથી વધુ માળવાળા મકાનો
high-rise apartment /
high rise block

મોટર ઊભાં રાખવાની જગ્યા
parking lot / car park

ઓફિસનું મકાન/મેદાન
office building

વ્યવસાયિક સંકુલ
commercial building

શેરીની બત્તી
street lamp

સંગ્રહ સ્થાન
museum

પ્રેક્ષકો બેસીને રમત જોઈ શકે તેવું મેદાન (સ્ટેડિયમ)
stadium

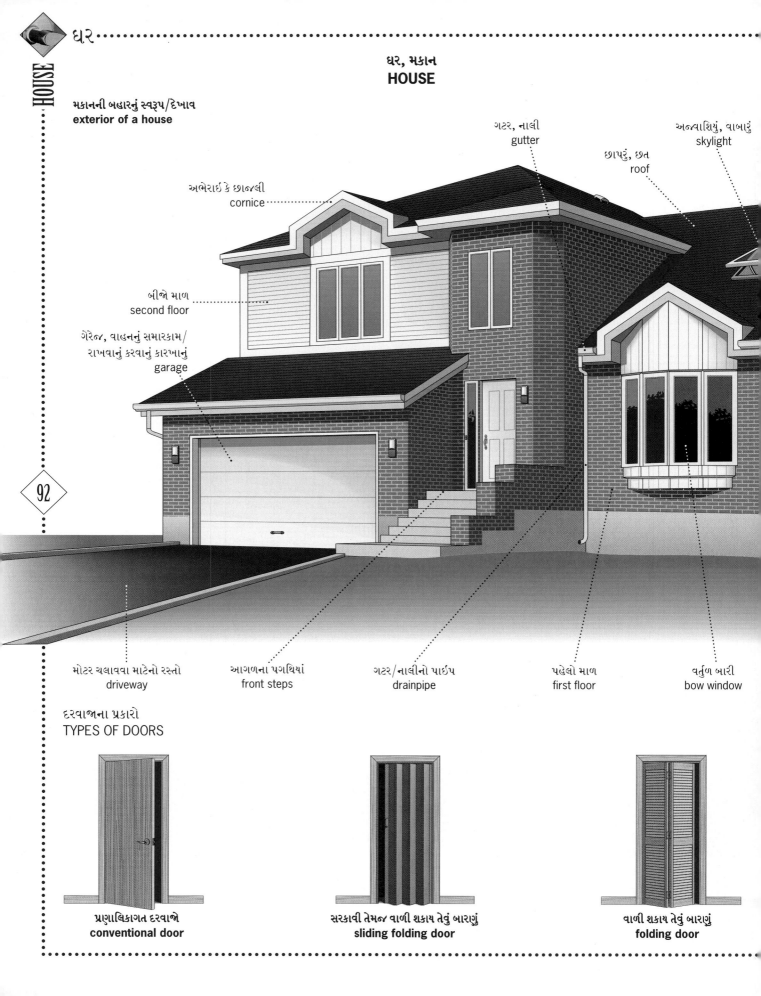

ઘર, મકાન
HOUSE

મકાનની બહારનું સ્વરૂપ/દેખાવ
exterior of a house

ગટર, નાળી
gutter

અન્નવાશિયું, વાબારું
skylight

છાપરું, છત
roof

અભેરાઈ કે છાજલી
cornice

બીજો માળ
second floor

ગેરેજ, વાહનનું સમારકામ/
રાખવાનું કરવાનું કારખાનું
garage

મોટર ચલાવવા માટેનો રસ્તો
driveway

આગળના પગથિયાં
front steps

ગટર/નાળીનો પાઈપ
drainpipe

પહેલો માળ
first floor

વર્તુળ બારી
bow window

દરવાજાના પ્રકારો
TYPES OF DOORS

પ્રણાલિકાગત દરવાજો
conventional door

સરકાવી તેમજ વાળી શકાય તેવું બારણું
sliding folding door

વાળી શકાય તેવું બારણું
folding door

92

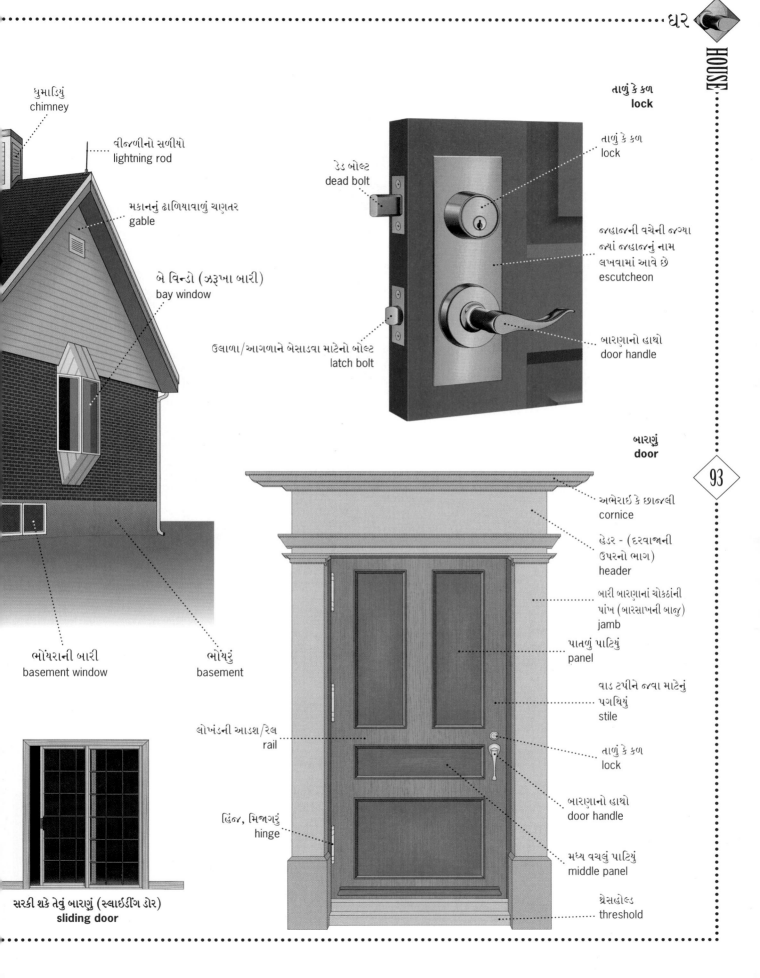

ધુમાડિયું
chimney

વીજળીનો સળીયો
lightning rod

મકાનનું ઢાળિયાવાળું ચણતર
gable

બે વિન્ડો (ઝરૂખા બારી)
bay window

ભોંયરાની બારી
basement window

ભોંયરું
basement

ડેડ બોલ્ટ
dead bolt

ઉલાળા/આગળાને બેસાડવા માટેનો બોલ્ટ
latch bolt

તાળું કે કળ
lock

તાળું કે કળ
lock

જહાજની વચેની જગ્યા જ્યાં જહાજનું નામ લખવામાં આવે છે
escutcheon

બારણાનો હાથો
door handle

બારણું
door

અભેરાઈ કે છાજલી
cornice

હેડર - (દરવાજાની ઉપરનો ભાગ)
header

બારી બારણાનાં ચોકઠાંની પાંખ (બારસાખની બાજુ)
jamb

પાતળું પાટિયું
panel

વાડ ટપીને જવા માટેનું પગથિયું
stile

તાળું કે કળ
lock

બારણાનો હાથો
door handle

મધ્ય વચલું પાટિયું
middle panel

થ્રેસહોલ્ડ
threshold

લોખંડની આડશ/રેલ
rail

હિંજ, મિજાગરું
hinge

સરકી શકે તેવું બારણું (સ્લાઈડીંગ ડોર)
sliding door

બારી
WINDOW

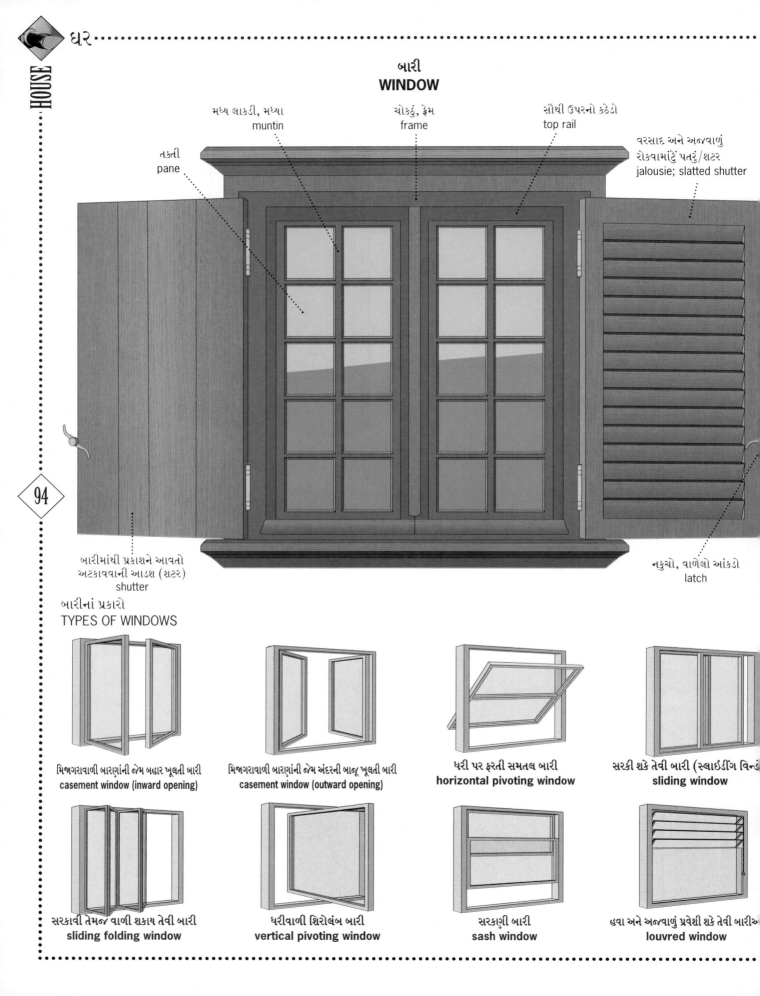

મધ્ય લાકડી, મધ્યા
muntin

ચોકઠું, ફ્રેમ
frame

સૌથી ઉપરનો કઠેડો
top rail

વરસાદ અને અજવાળું
રોકવામાટેં પતરું/શટર
jalousie; slatted shutter

તક્તી
pane

બારીમાંથી પ્રકાશને આવતો
અટકાવવાની આડશ (શટર)
shutter

નકુચો, વાળેલો આંકડો
latch

બારીનાં પ્રકારો
TYPES OF WINDOWS

મિજાગરાવાળી બારાણાંની જેમ બહાર ખૂલતી બારી
casement window (inward opening)

મિજાગરાવાળી બારાણાંની જેમ અંદરની બાજૂ ખૂલતી બારી
casement window (outward opening)

ધરી પર ફરતી સમતલ બારી
horizontal pivoting window

સરકી શકે તેવી બારી (સ્લાઈડીંગ વિન્ડ
sliding window

સરકાવી તેમજ વાળી શકાય તેવી બારી
sliding folding window

ધરીવાળી શિરોલંબ બારી
vertical pivoting window

સરકણી બારી
sash window

હવા અને અજવાળું પ્રવેશી શકે તેવી બારીઅ
louvred window

94

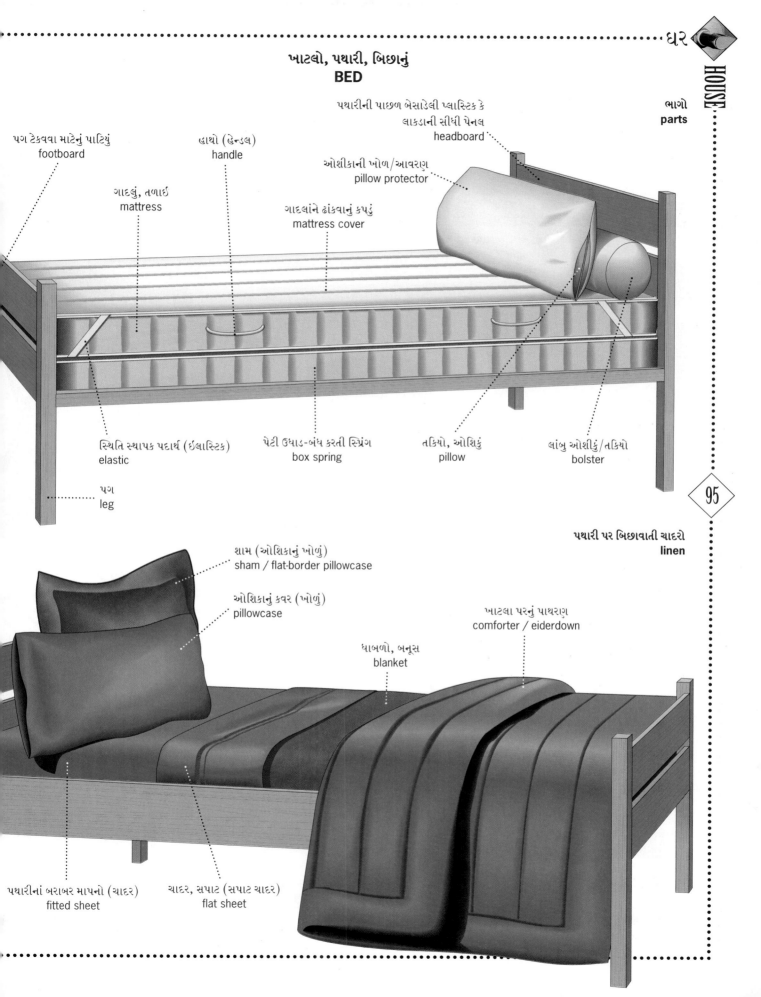

ખાટલો, પથારી, બિછાનું
BED

પથારીની પાછળ બેસાડેલી પ્લાસ્ટિક કે
લાકડાની સીધી પેનલ
headboard

પગ ટેકવવા માટેનું પાટિયું
footboard

હાથો (હેન્ડલ)
handle

ઓશીકાની ખોળ/આવરણ
pillow protector

ગાદલું, તબાઈ
mattress

ગાદલાંને ઢાંકવાનું કપડું
mattress cover

સ્થિતિ સ્થાપક પદાર્થ (ઇલાસ્ટિક)
elastic

પેટી ઉઘાડ-બંધ કરતી સ્પ્રિંગ
box spring

તકિયો, ઓશિકું
pillow

લાંબુ ઓશીકું/તકિયો
bolster

પગ
leg

95

શામ (ઓશિકાનું ખોળું)
sham / flat-border pillowcase

ઓશિકાનું કવર (ખોળું)
pillowcase

ખાટલા પરનું પાથરણ
comforter / eiderdown

ધાબળો, બનૂસ
blanket

પથારીનાં બરાબર માપનો (ચાદર)
fitted sheet

ચાદર, સપાટ (સપાટ ચાદર)
flat sheet

મેજ અને ખુરશી
SEATS

સોફા, લાંબી આરામદાયક બેઠક
sofa / settee

બે જણાં બેસી શકે તેવો નાનો સોફો અથવા ખુરશી
loveseat / settee

આરામ ખુરશી
armchair

પગ ટેકવવાનું ઢાળિયું, મેજ
footstool

બેઠક, બાંકડો
bench

બાર સ્ટૂલ
bar stool

સ્ટૂલ, બેઠક
stool

એક જ હાથાવાળો સોફો
chaise longue

ગોઠવીને મૂકવી તેવી ખુરશી
stacking chairs

વાળી શકાય તેવી ખુરશી
folding chair

ઝૂલતી ખુરશી
rocking chair

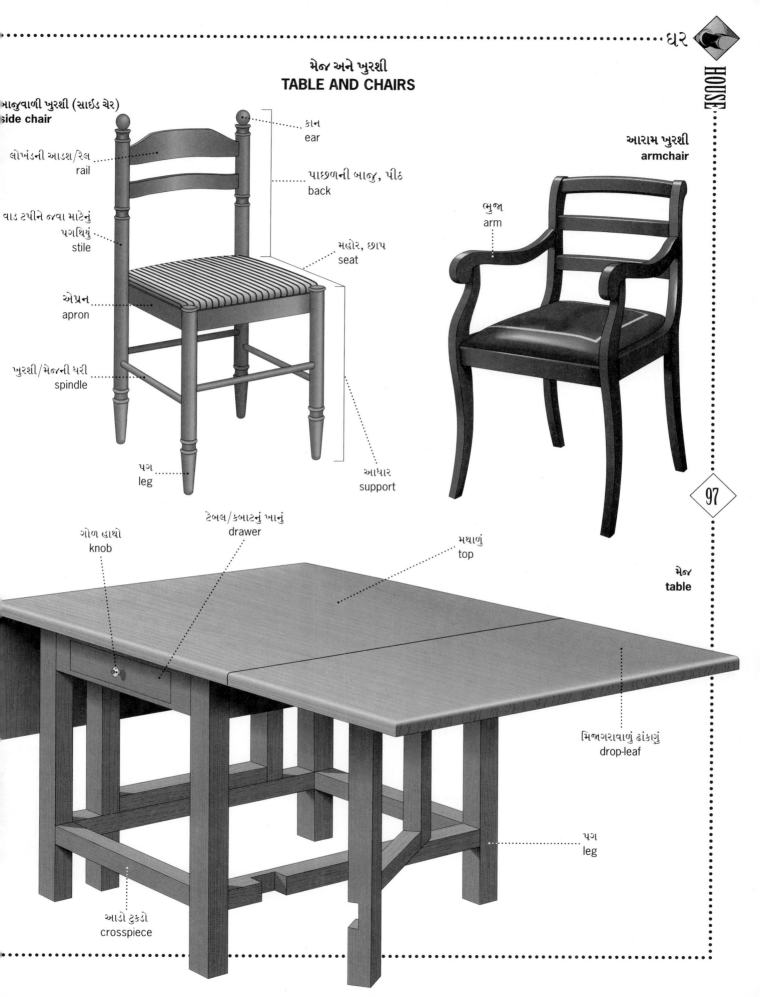

મેજ અને ખુરશી
TABLE AND CHAIRS

બાજુવાળી ખુરશી (સાઇડ ચેર)
side chair

કાન
ear

લોખંડની આડશ/રેલ
rail

પાછળની બાજુ, પીઠ
back

વાડ ટપીને જવા માટેનું પગથિયું
stile

મહોર, છાપ
seat

એપ્રન
apron

ખુરશી/મેજની ધરી
spindle

પગ
leg

આધાર
support

આરામ ખુરશી
armchair

ભુજ
arm

ગોળ હાથો
knob

ટેબલ/કબાટનું ખાનું
drawer

મથાળું
top

મેજ
table

મિજગરાવાળું ઢાંકણું
drop-leaf

પગ
leg

આડો ટુકડો
crosspiece

બત્તીઓ
LIGHTS

માર્ગ પરની બત્તીઓ (ટ્રેક લાઇટિંગ)
track lighting

ફ્લોર લેમ્પ
floor lamp

પથ, કેડી
track

વીજળીના પ્રવાહનું વૉલ્ટેજ
transformer

છતમાં બેસાડવામાં આવતી લાઇટો
ceiling fixture

મેજ પરનો દીવો
table lamp

પ્રકાશનો પડછાયો
shade

લટકતું પેન્ડન્ટ
hanging pendant

ચીજવસ્તુનો ઘોડો
stand

દીવાલમાં બેસાડેલી ઉપસ્કરની વસ્તુઓ (ફિક્સ્ચર્સ
wall fixture

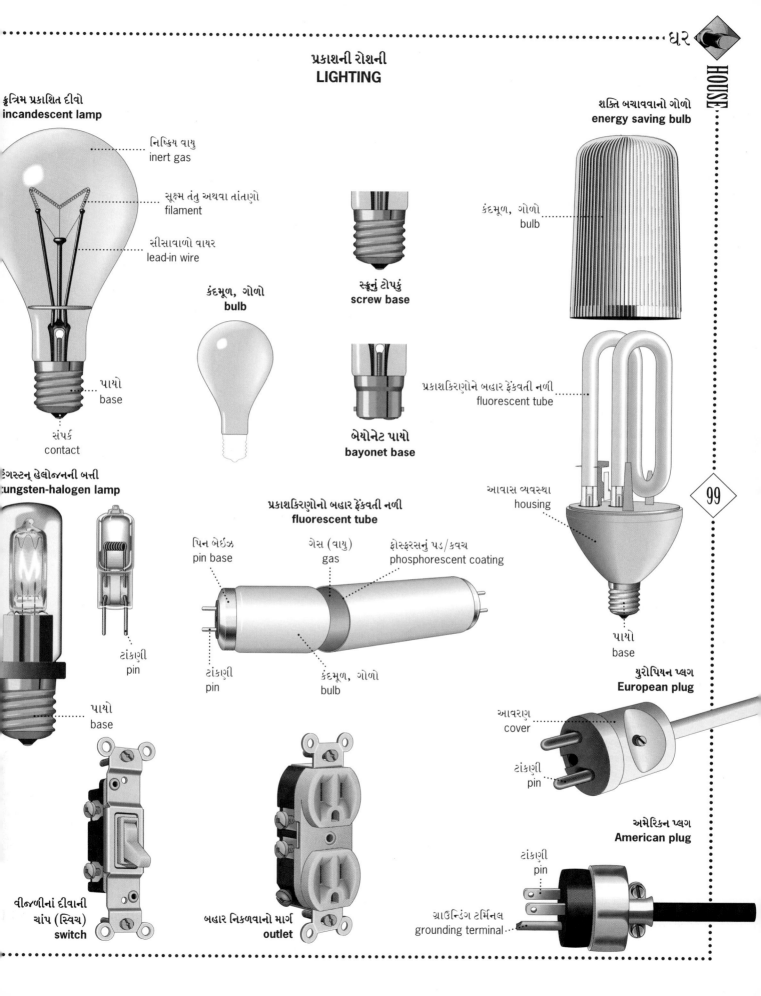

પ્રકાશની રોશની
LIGHTING

ફ્રુત્રિમ પ્રકાશિત દીવો
incandescent lamp

નિષ્ક્રિય વાયુ
inert gas

સૂક્ષ્મ તંતુ અથવા તાંતાણો
filament

સીસાવાળો વાયર
lead-in wire

પાયો
base

સંપર્ક
contact

કંદમૂળ, ગોળો
bulb

સ્ક્રૂનું ટોપકું
screw base

બેયોનેટ પાયો
bayonet base

શક્તિ બચાવવાનો ગોળો
energy saving bulb

કંદમૂળ, ગોળો
bulb

પ્રકાશકિરણોને બહાર ફેંકવતી નળી
fluorescent tube

આવાસ વ્યવસ્થા
housing

પાયો
base

ંગસ્ટન હેલોજનની બત્તી
ungsten-halogen lamp

ટાંકણી
pin

પાયો
base

પ્રકાશકિરણોનો બહાર ફેંકવતી નળી
fluorescent tube

પિન બેઈઝ
pin base

ગેસ (વાયુ)
gas

ફોસ્ફરસનું પડ/કવચ
phosphorescent coating

ટાંકણી
pin

કંદમૂળ, ગોળો
bulb

યુરોપિયન પ્લગ
European plug

આવરણ
cover

ટાંકણી
pin

અમેરિકન પ્લગ
American plug

ટાંકણી
pin

ગ્રાઉન્ડિંગ ટર્મિનલ
grounding terminal

વીજળીનાં દીવાની ચાંપ (સ્વિચ)
switch

બહાર નિકળવાનો માર્ગ
outlet

કાચનાં વાસણો
GLASSWARE

શેમ્પેઈનનો પ્યાલા
champagne glass

સફેદ દારૂનો પ્યાલો
white wine glass

લાલ રંગના દારૂનો પ્યાલો
red wine glass

શેમ્પેઈન ફ્લ્યૂટ
champagne flute

કાંઠા વિનાનો કાચનો પ્યાલો
tumbler; glass

બીયર પીવા માટેનો પ્યાલો
beer mug

ટેબલ અથવા પથારી પાસે રાખવામાં આવેલો ચંબુ
carafe

દારૂ ભરવાનું પાત્ર
decanter

ભોજન માટેનાં વાસણોનો સમૂહ
DINNERWARE

કોફીનો પ્યાલો
coffee cup

પ્યાલો
cup

સીધા ઘાટનો પ્યાલો
mug

દૂધની મલાઈ કાઢતું મશીન
creamer

ખાંડ રાખવાનો વાટકો
sugar bowl

મરીનો ભૂકો કરનાર સાધન
pepper shaker

મીઠાને હલાવનાર સાધન/શીશી
salt shaker

માખણ રાખવા માટેની રકાબી
butter dish

નાસ્તા માટેનું પાત્ર
cereal bowl

સૂપ પીવા માટેનો વાટકો
soup bowl

કચુંબર રાખવાની થાળી
salad dish

ભોજન સમયે ઉપયોગમાં આવતી થાળી
dinner plate

કચુંબર રાખવાની રકાબી
salad plate

બ્રેડ અને માખણ માટેની પ્લેટ; સાઈડ પ્લેટ
bread and butter plate; side plate

કચુંબર રાખવાનો વાટકો
salad bowl

ચા રાખવા માટેનું પાત્ર (કિટલી)
teapot

કોફી દબાવવાનો દાંડો
coffee plunger

સૂપ રાખવા માટેનું મોટું પાત્ર
soup tureen

પાણી રેડવાનું એક મોટું પાત્ર
water pitcher

ચાંદીનાં વાસણો
SILVERWARE

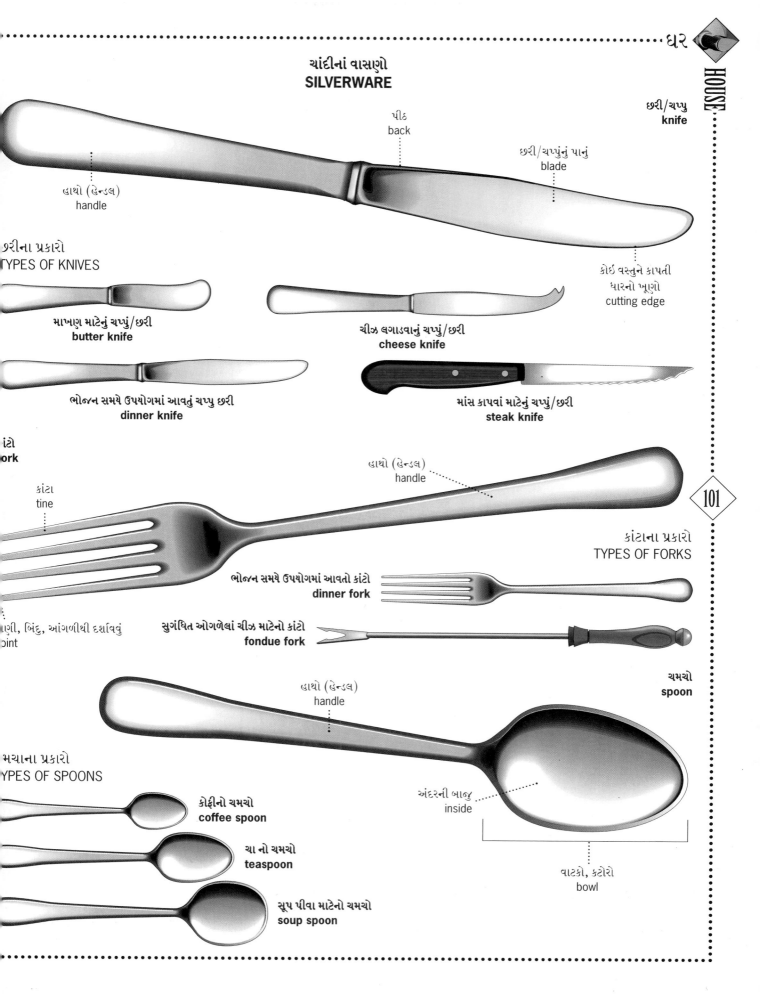

પીઠ
back

છરી/ચપ્પુ
knife

છરી/ચપ્પુંનું પાનું
blade

હાથો (હેન્ડલ)
handle

કોઈ વસ્તુને કાપતી
ધારનો ખૂણો
cutting edge

છરીના પ્રકારો
TYPES OF KNIVES

માખણ માટેનું ચપ્પું/છરી
butter knife

ચીઝ લગાડવાનું ચપ્પું/છરી
cheese knife

ભોજન સમયે ઉપયોગમાં આવતું ચપ્પુ છરી
dinner knife

માંસ કાપવાં માટેનું ચપ્પું/છરી
steak knife

કાંટો
fork

કાંટા
tine

હાથો (હેન્ડલ)
handle

કાંટાના પ્રકારો
TYPES OF FORKS

ભોજન સમયે ઉપયોગમાં આવતો કાંટો
dinner fork

રેખા, બિંદુ, આંગળીથી દર્શાવવું
point

સુગંધિત ઓગળેલાં ચીઝ માટેનો કાંટો
fondue fork

ચમચો
spoon

હાથો (હેન્ડલ)
handle

ચમચાના પ્રકારો
TYPES OF SPOONS

કોફીનો ચમચો
coffee spoon

ચા નો ચમચો
teaspoon

સૂપ પીવા માટેનો ચમચો
soup spoon

અંદરની બાજુ
inside

વાટકો, કટોરો
bowl

રસોડામાં વપરાતાં વાસણો
KITCHEN UTENSILS

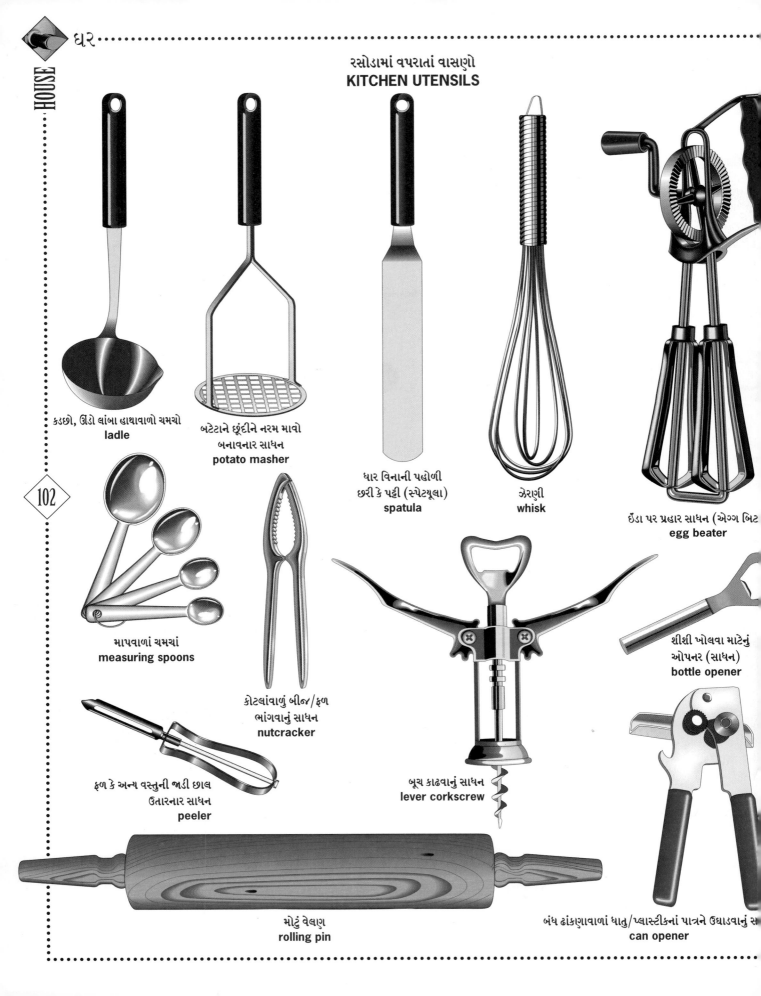

કડછો, ઊંડો લાંબા હાથાવાળો ચમચો
ladle

બટેટાને છૂંદીને નરમ માવો
બનાવનાર સાધન
potato masher

ધાર વિનાની પહોળી
છરી કે પટ્ટી (સ્પેટ્યૂલા)
spatula

ઝેરણી
whisk

ઇંડા પર પ્રહાર સાધન (એગ્ગ બિટ
egg beater

માપવાળાં ચમચાં
measuring spoons

કોટલાંવાળું બીજ/ફળ
ભાંગવાનું સાધન
nutcracker

શીશી ખોલવા માટેનું
ઓપનર (સાધન)
bottle opener

ફળ કે અન્ય વસ્તુની જાડી છાલ
ઉતારનાર સાધન
peeler

બૂચ કાઢવાનું સાધન
lever corkscrew

મોટું વેલણ
rolling pin

બંધ ઢાંકણાવાળાં ધાતુ/પ્લાસ્ટીકનાં પાત્રને ઉઘાડવાનું સ
can opener

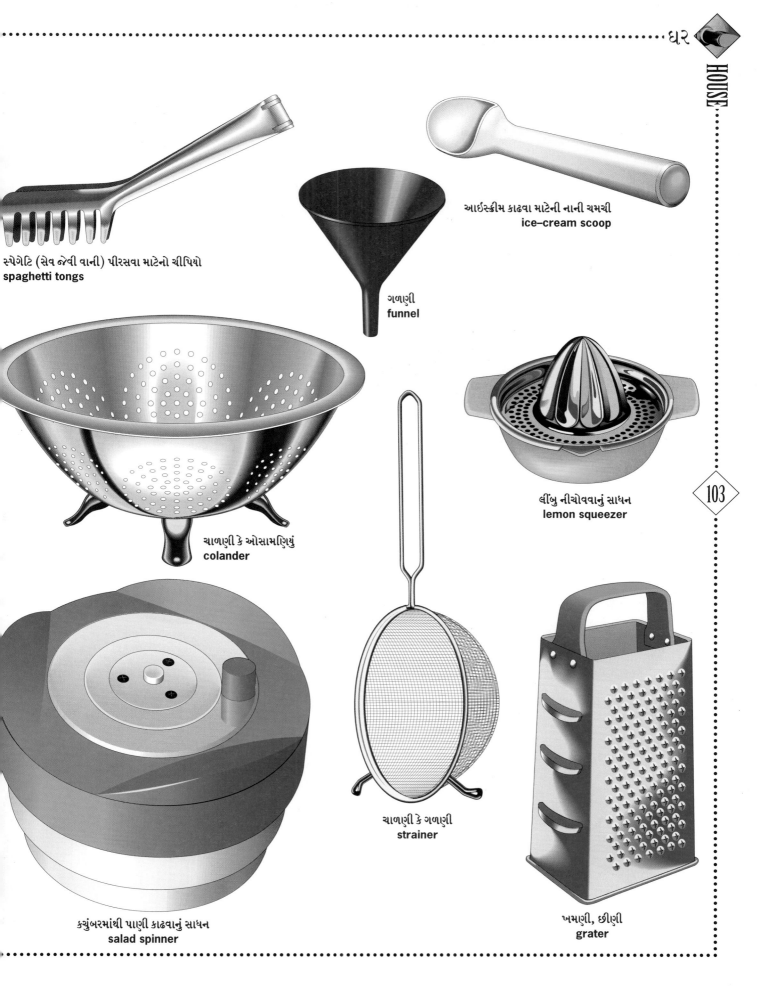

આઈસ્ક્રીમ કાઢવા માટેની નાની ચમચી
ice–cream scoop

સ્પેગેટિ (સેવ જેવી વાની) પીરસવા માટેનો ચીપિયો
spaghetti tongs

ગળણી
funnel

લીંબુ નીચોવવાનું સાધન
lemon squeezer

ચાળણી કે ઓસામણિયું
colander

ચાળણી કે ગળણી
strainer

કચુંબરમાંથી પાણી કાઢવાનું સાધન
salad spinner

ખમણી, છીણી
grater

રાંધવાનાં વાસણો
COOKING UTENSILS

ચીજવસ્તુ તળવા
માટેની કડાઈ
frying pan

ઝડપથી તળવા માટે
(ખાસ કરીને બટેટા
વિગેરે)નો તવો
sauté pan

ફ્રોન્ડયૂ સેટ
fondue set

રાંધવાનું, પીરસવાનું વાસણ
stockpot; casserole

ચાઈનીઝ પ્રકારની નાનાં વાટકા
જેવી તળવા માટેની તવી/તવો
wok

ફ્રોન્ડયૂ પાત્ર
fondue pot

(બર્નર) મોઢીયું, સાધનના જે ભાગમાંથી
જ્વાળા નીકળતી હોય તે ભાગ
burner

પાણીની વરાળથી રાંધવામાં
ઉપયોગી બે ખાનાવાળી તપેલી
double boiler

શાકભાજીને વરાળથી બાફતું
vegetable steamer

હાથાવાળી તપેલી/પોટ
saucepan

ખાવાની વસ્તુ
શેકવાનો તવો
roasting pans

વરાળનાં દબાણથી રાંધવાનું બનાવતું સાધન (કૂકર)
pressure cooker

સુરક્ષા માટે વાયુ કે પ્રવાહીનું
નિયંત્રાણ કરવાનો વાલ્વ
safety valve

દબાણનું નિયંત્રાણ કરતું સાધન
pressure regulator

રસોડામાં વપરાતાં સાધનો
KITCHEN APPLIANCES

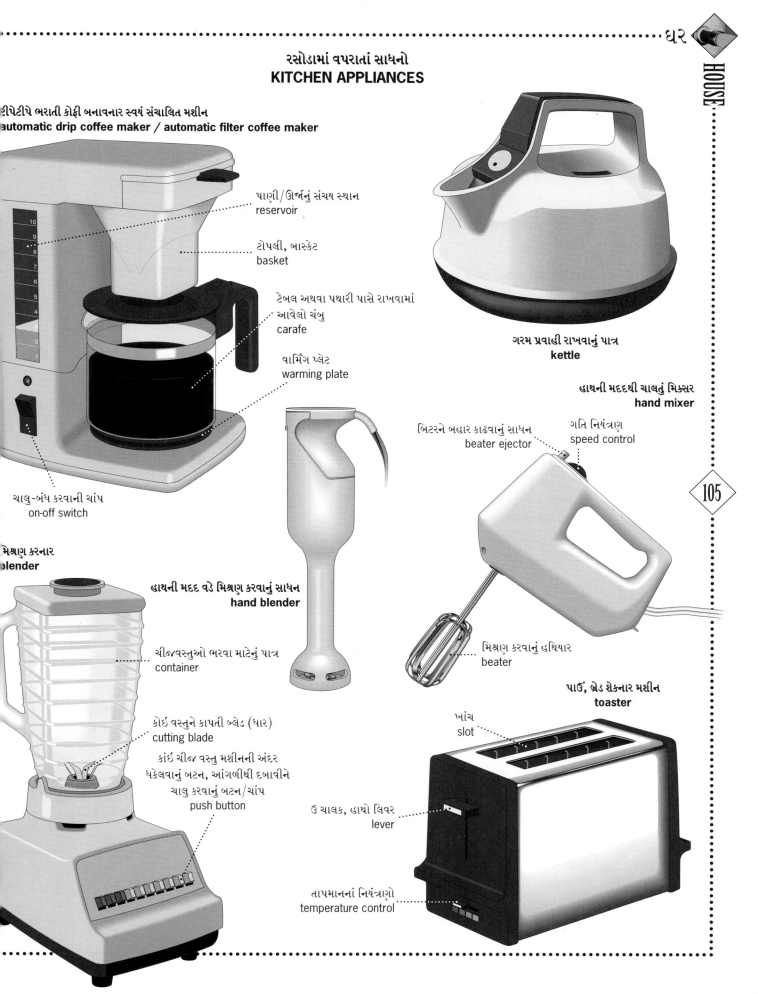

ડ્રીપેટીપે ભરાતી કોફી બનાવનાર સ્વયં સંચાલિત મશીન
automatic drip coffee maker / automatic filter coffee maker

પાણી/ઊર્જાનું સંચય સ્થાન
reservoir

ટોપલી, બાસ્કેટ
basket

ટેબલ અથવા પથારી પાસે રાખવામાં આવેલો ચંબુ
carafe

વાર્મિંગ પ્લેટ
warming plate

ચાલુ-બંધ કરવાની ચાંપ
on-off switch

મિશ્રણ કરનાર
blender

ચીજવસ્તુઓ ભરવા માટેનું પાત્ર
container

કોઈ વસ્તુને કાપતી બ્લેડ (ધાર)
cutting blade

કાંઈ ચીજ વસ્તુ મશીનની અંદર ધકેલવાનું બટન, આંગળીથી દબાવીને ચાલુ કરવાનું બટન/ચાંપ
push button

હાથની મદદ વડે મિશ્રણ કરવાનું સાધન
hand blender

ગરમ પ્રવાહી રાખવાનું પાત્ર
kettle

હાથની મદદથી ચાલતું મિક્સર
hand mixer

બિટરને બહાર કાઢવાનું સાધન
beater ejector

ગતિ નિયંત્રણ
speed control

મિશ્રણ કરવાનું હથિયાર
beater

પાઉં, બ્રેડ શેકનાર મશીન
toaster

ખાંચ
slot

ઉ ચાલક, હાથો લિવર
lever

તાપમાનનાં નિયંત્રણો
temperature control

HOUSE

ચીજવસ્તુને ઠંડી રાખવાનું યંત્ર
REFRIGERATOR

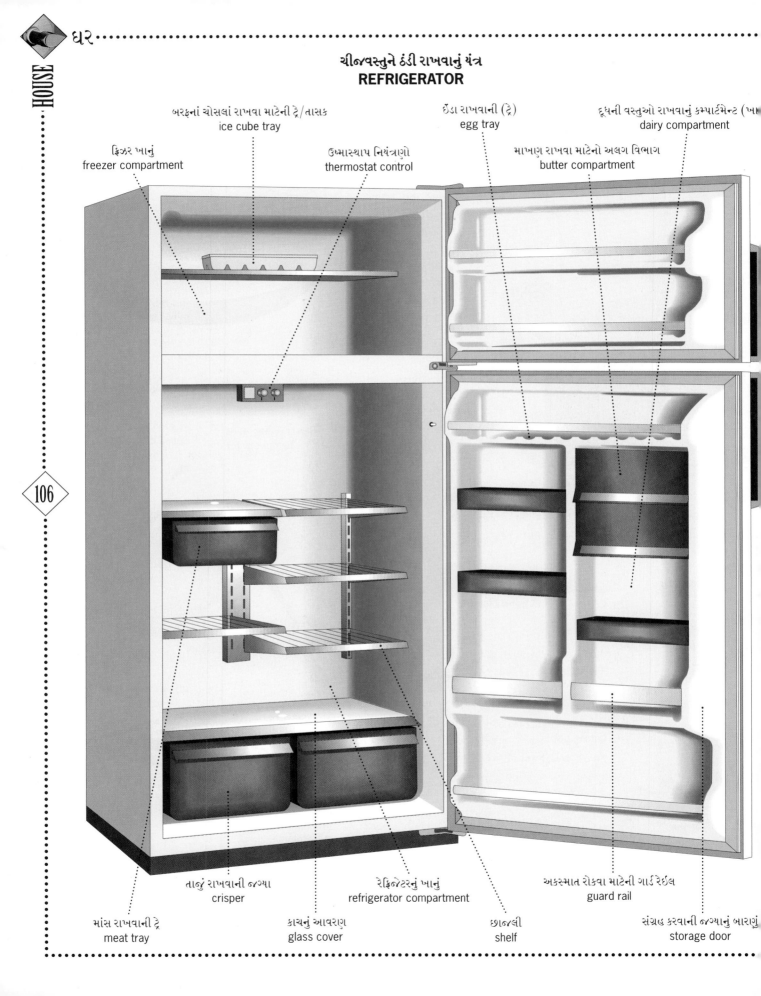

બરફનાં ચોસલાં રાખવા માટેની ટ્રે/તાસક
ice cube tray

ઇંડા રાખવાની (ટ્રે)
egg tray

દૂધની વસ્તુઓ રાખવાનું કમ્પાર્ટમેન્ટ (ખ
dairy compartment

ફ્રિઝર ખાનું
freezer compartment

ઉષ્માસ્થાપ નિયંત્રાણો
thermostat control

માખણ રાખવા માટેનો અલગ વિભાગ
butter compartment

તાજું રાખવાની જગ્યા
crisper

રેફ્રિજેટરનું ખાનું
refrigerator compartment

અકસ્માત રોકવા માટેની ગાર્ડ રેઇલ
guard rail

માંસ રાખવાની ટ્રે
meat tray

કાચનું આવરણ
glass cover

છાજલી
shelf

સંગ્રહ કરવાની જગ્યાનું બારાણું
storage door

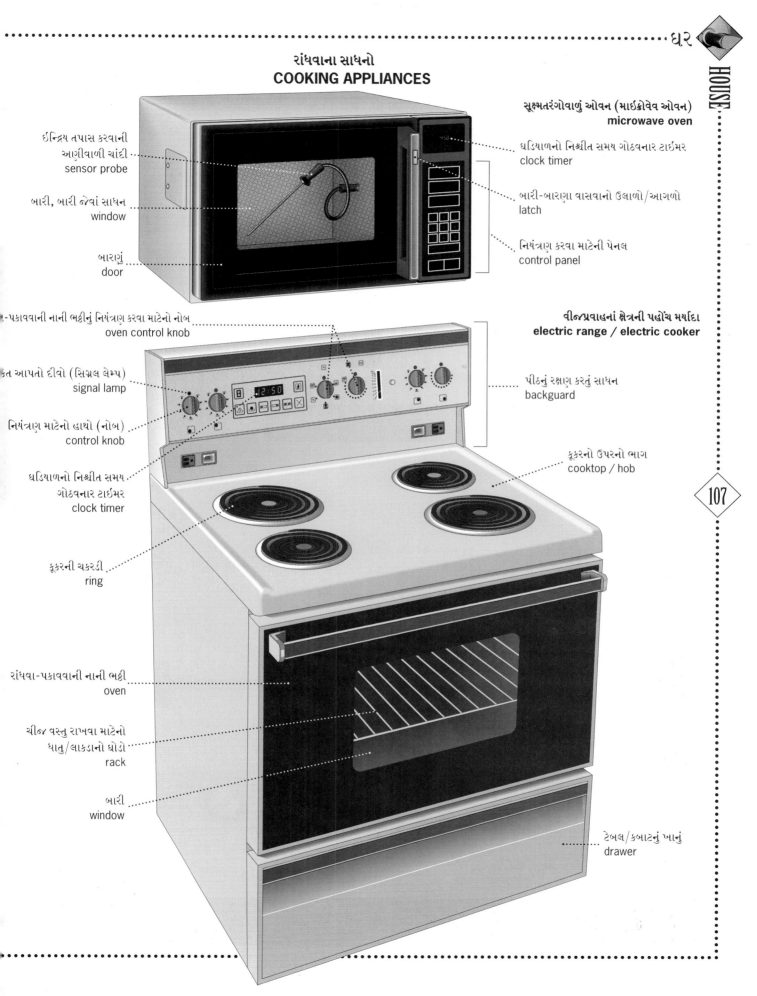

રાંધવાના સાધનો
COOKING APPLIANCES

સૂક્ષ્મતરંગોવાળું ઓવન (માઈક્રોવેવ ઓવન)
microwave oven

ઈન્દ્રિય તપાસ કરવાની
અણીવાળી ચાંદી
sensor probe

બારી, બારી જેવાં સાધન
window

બારણું
door

ઘડિયાળનો નિશ્ચીત સમય ગોઠવનાર ટાઈમર
clock timer

બારી-બારણા વાસવાનો ઉલાળો/આગળો
latch

નિયંત્રણ કરવા માટેની પેનલ
control panel

-પકાવવાની નાની ભઠ્ઠીનું નિયંત્રણ કરવા માટેનો નોબ
oven control knob

ત આપતો દીવો (સિગ્નલ લેમ્પ)
signal lamp

નિયંત્રણ માટેનો હાથો (નોબ)
control knob

ઘડિયાળનો નિશ્ચીત સમય
ગોઠવનાર ટાઈમર
clock timer

ફૂકરની ચકરડી
ring

વીજપ્રવાહનાં ક્ષેત્રની પહોંચ મર્યાદા
electric range / electric cooker

પીઠનું રક્ષણ કરતું સાધન
backguard

ફૂકરનો ઉપરનો ભાગ
cooktop / hob

રાંધવા-પકાવવાની નાની ભઠ્ઠી
oven

ચીજ વસ્તુ રાખવા માટેનો
ધાતુ/લાકડાનો ઘોડો
rack

બારી
window

ટેબલ/કબાટનું ખાનું
drawer

સુથારીકામના ઓજરો
CARPENTRY TOOLS

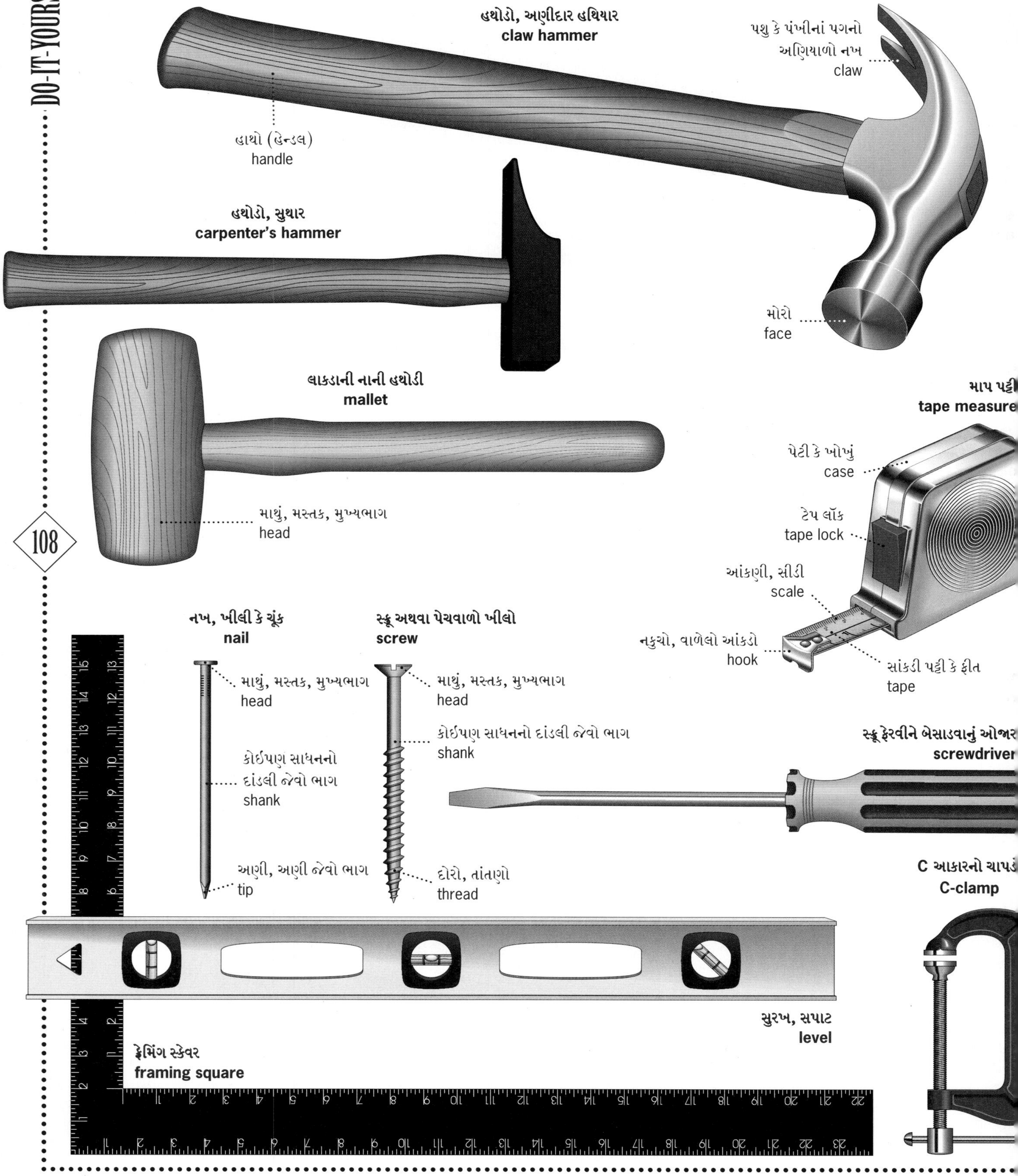

હથોડો, અણીદાર હથિયાર
claw hammer

પશુ કે પંખીનાં પગનો
અણિયાળો નખ
claw

હાથો (હેન્ડલ)
handle

હથોડો, સુથાર
carpenter's hammer

મોરો
face

લાકડાની નાની હથોડી
mallet

માથું, મસ્તક, મુખ્યભાગ
head

માપ પટ્ટી
tape measure

પેટી કે ખોખું
case

ટેપ લૉક
tape lock

આંકણી, સીડી
scale

નકુચો, વાળેલો આંકડો
hook

સાંકડી પટ્ટી કે ફીત
tape

નખ, ખીલી કે ચૂંક
nail

માથું, મસ્તક, મુખ્યભાગ
head

કોઈપણ સાધનનો
દાંડલી જેવો ભાગ
shank

આણી, આણી જેવો ભાગ
tip

સ્ક્રૂ અથવા પેચવાળો ખીલો
screw

માથું, મસ્તક, મુખ્યભાગ
head

કોઈપણ સાધનનો દાંડલી જેવો ભાગ
shank

દોરો, તાંતણો
thread

સ્ક્રૂ ફેરવીને બેસાડવાનું ઓજાર
screwdriver

C આકારનો ચાપડ
C-clamp

ફ્રેમિંગ સ્કેવર
framing square

સુરખ, સપાટ
level

108

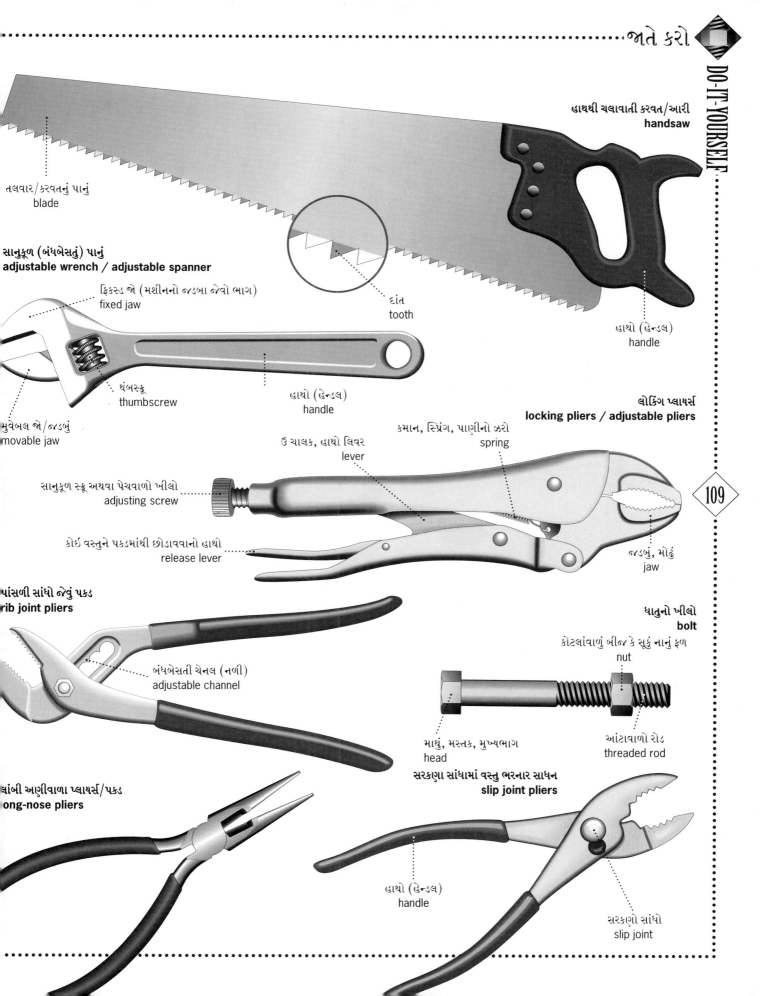

હાથથી ચલાવાતી કરવત/આરી
handsaw

તલવાર/કરવતનું પાનું
blade

સાનુકૂળ (બંધબેસતું) પાનું
adjustable wrench / adjustable spanner

ફ્રિકસ્ડ જૉ (મશીનનો જડબા જેવો ભાગ)
fixed jaw

દાંત
tooth

થંબસ્ક્રૂ
thumbscrew

હાથો (હેન્ડલ)
handle

મુવેબલ જૉ/જડબું
movable jaw

હાથો (હેન્ડલ)
handle

લૉકિંગ પ્લાયર્સ
locking pliers / adjustable pliers

ઉ ચાલક, હાથો લિવર
lever

કમાન, સ્પ્રિંગ, પાણીનો ઝરો
spring

સાનુકૂળ સ્ક્રૂ અથવા પેચવાળો ખીલો
adjusting screw

કોઈ વસ્તુને પકડમાંથી છોડાવવાનો હાથો
release lever

જડબું, મોઢું
jaw

પાંસળી સાંધો જેવું પકડ
rib joint pliers

ધાતુનો ખીલો
bolt

કોટલાંવાળું બીજ કે સૂકું નાનું ફળ
nut

બંધબેસતી ચેનલ (નળી)
adjustable channel

માથું, મસ્તક, મુખ્યભાગ
head

આંટાવાળો રોડ
threaded rod

લાંબી અણીવાળા પ્લાયર્સ/પકડ
long-nose pliers

સરકણ સાંધામાં વસ્તુ ભરનાર સાધન
slip joint pliers

હાથો (હેન્ડલ)
handle

સરકણો સાંધો
slip joint

109

જાતે કરો

વીજપ્રવાહથી ચાલતાં સાધનો
ELECTRIC TOOLS

વીજળીથી ચાલતી શારડી
electric drill

આવાસ વ્યવસ્થા
housing

લેથની પકડ કે ચાંપ
chuck

ચાંપને બંધ કરવાની કળ (સ્વિચ લોક)
switch lock

જડબું, મોઢું
jaw

મદદકર્તા હાથો (હેન્ડલ)
auxiliary handle

વીજળીનાં દીવાની ચાંપ (સ્વિચ)
switch

હેન્ડલ
pistol grip handle

લેથની પકડની ચાવી
chuck key

જાડી સાંકળ, તારનું દોરડું
cable

વિદ્યુત પ્રવાહનું જોડાણ કરનારું
સાધન (પ્લગ)
plug

લાકડામાં ખાડા કરવાનો ભાગ
auger bit

ટવીસ્ટ ડ્રીલ
twist drill

110

વર્તુળાકાર કરવત
circular saw

ધારનું રક્ષણ કરતું સાધન
blade guard

હાથો (હેન્ડલ)
handle

ટ્રિગર સ્વિચ
trigger switch

ધારને ત્રાંસી/કરવા માટેની યંત્ર પ્રણાલિ
blade tilting mechanism

ચાલક યંત્ર, મોટર
motor

હાથો પકડવાનું હેન્ડલ
knob handle

વર્તુળાકાર કરવત/આરીની ધાર
circular saw blade

આણી, આણી જેવો ભાગ
tip

તલવાર/પાનું
blade

આધાર પડી
base plate

દાંત
tooth

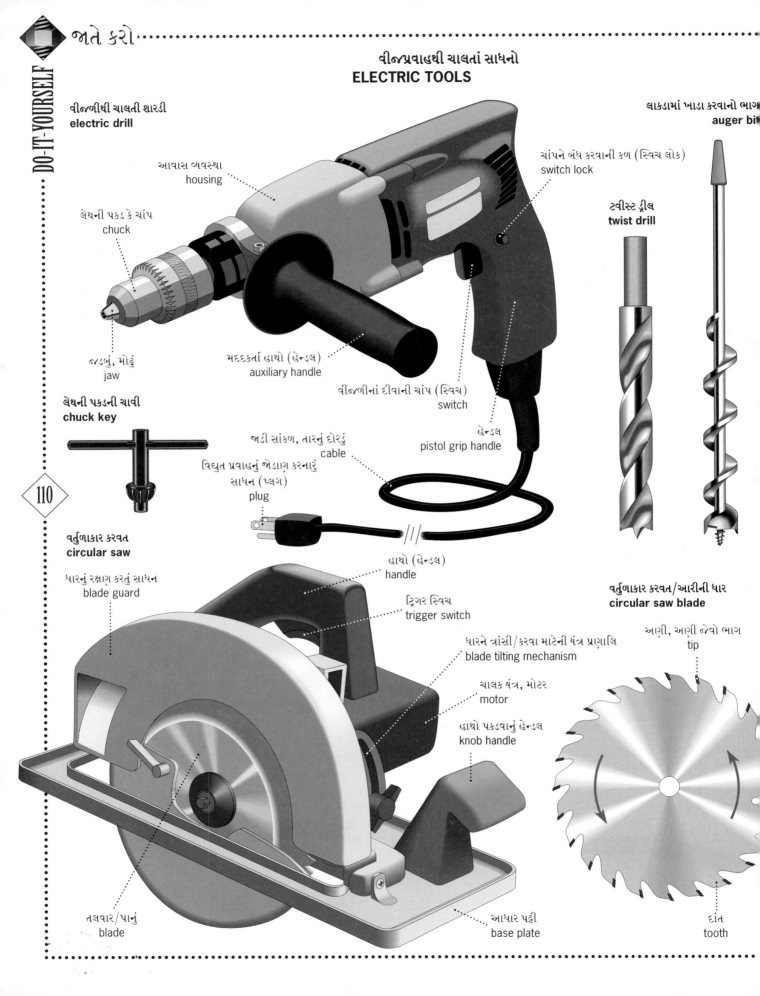

રંગકામની જળવણીનો અર્થ
PAINTING UPKEEP

રંગ કરવા માટેનો ગોળ આકારનો દાંડાવાળો ભાગ
paint roller

તાસક અથવા થાળ
tray

રોલરનું ચોકઠું
roller frame

ચિત્રકામ માટેનાં ગોળ
ઘાટનાં વીંટાનું આવરણ
roller cover

પગથિયાંવાળી સીડી
stepladder

તવેથો, ઉખેડિયું (સ્ક્રેપર)
scraper

તલવાર, ખભાનું સપાટ હાડકું
blade

વિસ્તરીત સીડી
extension ladder

ચિત્રકામ કરવાનું એક
સાધન, પીછી
brush

હાથો (હેન્ડલ)
handle

ટૂંકા, બરછટ રેસા/વાળ
bristles

સાઈડ રેલ
side rail

ગરગડી, ગરેડી
pulley

તાળું વાસી દે તેવું સાધન
locking device

સીડીનું પગથિયું
rung

મંચ પર ચઢવાની સીડી
platform ladder

લપસી ન જવાય તેવાં જૂતાં
anti-slip shoe

કોઈ સાધન વડે ઊંચે ઉઠાવેલું
દોરડું
hoisting rope

**Library Resource Center
Renton Technical College
3000 N.E. 4th St.
Renton, WA 98056**

માણસોનાં વસ્ત્રો/કપડાં
MEN'S CLOTHING

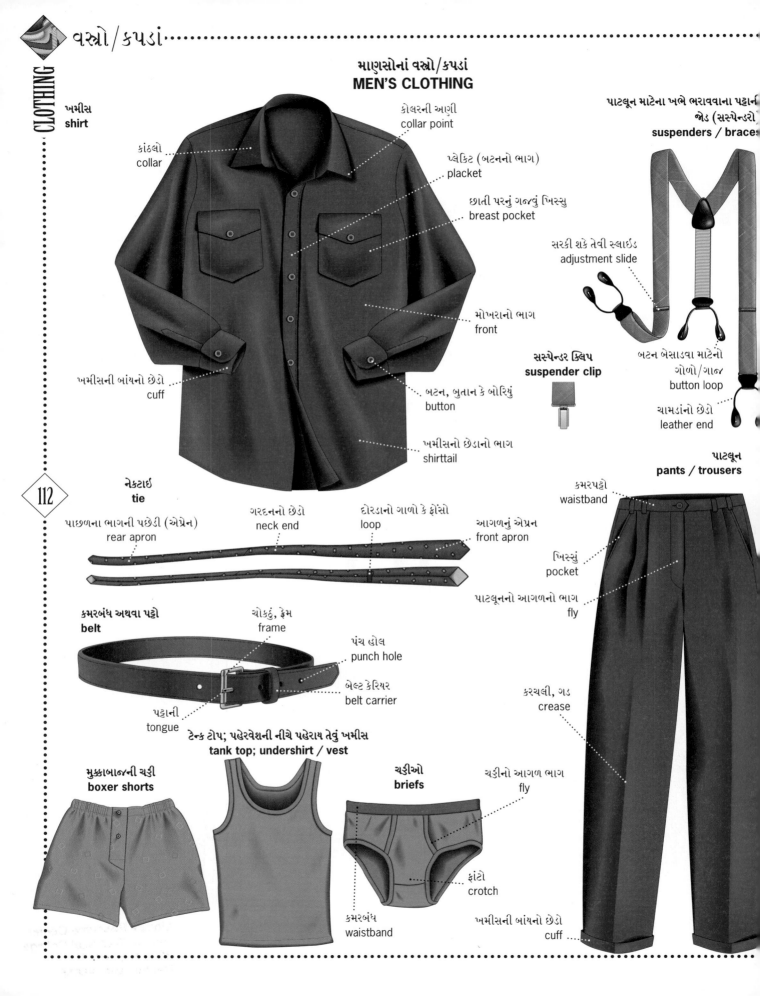

ખમીસ
shirt

કોલરની અણી
collar point

કાંઠલો
collar

પ્લેકિટ (બટનનો ભાગ)
placket

છાતી પરનું ગજવું ખિસ્સુ
breast pocket

મોખરનો ભાગ
front

ખમીસની બાંયનો છેડો
cuff

બટન, બુતાન કે બોરિયું
button

ખમીસનો છેડાનો ભાગ
shirttail

પાટલૂન માટેના ખભે ભરાવવાના પટ્ટાન
જોડ (સસ્પેન્ડરો)
suspenders / braces

સરકી શકે તેવી સ્લાઈડ
adjustment slide

સસ્પેન્ડર ક્લિપ
suspender clip

બટન બેસાડવા માટેનો
ગોળો/ગાન
button loop

ચામડાંનો છેડો
leather end

નેકટાઈ
tie

પાછળના ભાગની પછેડી (એપ્રન)
rear apron

ગરદનનો છેડો
neck end

દોરડાનો ગાળો કે ફાંસો
loop

આગળનું એપ્રન
front apron

કમરબંધ અથવા પટ્ટો
belt

ચોકઠું, ફ્રેમ
frame

પંચ હોલ
punch hole

બેલ્ટ કેરિયર
belt carrier

પટ્ટાની
tongue

પાટલૂન
pants / trousers

કમરપટ્ટો
waistband

ખિસ્સું
pocket

પાટલૂનનો આગળનો ભાગ
fly

કરચલી, ગડ
crease

ટેન્ક ટોપ; પહેરવેશની નીચે પહેરાય તેવું ખમીસ
tank top; undershirt / vest

મુક્કાબાજીની ચડી
boxer shorts

ચડીઓ
briefs

ચડીનો આગળ ભાગ
fly

ફાંટો
crotch

કમરબંધ
waistband

ખમીસની બાંયનો છેડો
cuff

વ ચેથી બે ભાગમાં ખૂલતું જેકેટ
double-breasted jacket

ગળા પડ્ડી/કૉલર
collar

આછી રેખા, લીટી
lining

ખિસ્સું
breast welt pocket

કપડાંની બાંય
sleeve

છૂપાવેલું ખિસ્સું
concealed pocket

મોટાં મોજ઼
patch pocket

ફ્લેપ
flap

ઉનનો મોટો કોટ (રમતમાં ઉપયોગી)
duffle coat

હૂડ
hood

દેડકો
frog

કોઇ વસ્તુ બાંધવા માટેની પીન/ખીલી (ટોગલ ફ઼ાસ્ટનીંગ)
toggle fastening

ટોપી
cap

રીનો આગલો ભાગ
crown

ટોચ, શિખર
peak

જેવી ટોપી
stocking cap / bobble hat

શિકારીની ટોપી
hunting cap

કાનનો લટકતો ભાગ /
કાનની બુટ્ટી
ear flap

ટૂંકો કોટ કે જકીટ
jacket

સ્પેન ફ઼ાસ્ચનર
snap fastener

લવચીક કમરપટ્ટો
elastic waistband

વિન્ડબ્રેકર
windbreaker

કમર પટ્ટો ખેંચવાની
waistband

દોરી
drawstring

સ્ત્રીનાં વસ્ત્ર/કપડાં
WOMEN'S CLOTHING

ચેહરાનાં ભાગ સિવાય માથું
અને ગરદન ઢાંકી દેતી ટોપી
balaclava

ટોચ, શિખર
peak

સ્ત્રીઓ માટેની નાનો
છાજલી વગરનો ટોપા
toque

ગૂંથણ કામ કરેલી ટોપી
knitted hat

નરમ મુલાયમ ટોપી
beret

બ્લાઉસ
blouse

વ ચેથી બે ભાગમાં ખૂલતું જેકેટ
double-breasted jacket

સ્યૂટ
suit

ટૂંકો કોટ કે જકીટ
jacket

પહેરવાનો મોટો ઉગલો (ઓવરકોટ)
overcoat

ગળાની ખાંચવાળું ખભા અને શરીરને
ઢાંકતું પહોળું વસ્ત્ર (પોંચો)
poncho

સ્કર્ટ ટૂંકો ચણિયો
skirt

પહેરવેશ, પહેરવાનું વસ્ત્ર
dress

ભૂરા જાડા સુતરાઉ કાપડનું પાટલૂન
jeans

સ્કીની રમત વખતે પહેરવામાં
આવતું પાટલૂન (સ્કી પેન્ટ)
ski pants

ચડીઓ
shorts

બર્મુડા ચડી
Bermuda shorts

પગ પર બાંધવાનો પટ્ટો
footstrap

સ્કર્ટ (ઘેર કે ધાધરો)
straight skirt

સ્ત્રીઓ માટેની ઘૂટણ સુધીની સ્કર્ટ જેવી
દેખાતી ચડી/પાટલૂન
culottes

પાટલી કરેલું સ્કર્ટ
pleated skirt

સ્ત્રીનાં વસ્ત્ર
WOMEN'S CLOTHING

પાયજામો
pajamas

કાંચળી કમખી
bra

ખભા પર બાંધવાનો પટ્ટો
shoulder strap

સ્ત્રીની ચોળીનો પ્યાલા
આકારનો સ્તનને ઢાંકતો
પોલાણ જેવો ભાગ
cup

ચડ્ડી
pants / briefs

હાફ સ્લીપ
half-slip / waist slip

ગાઉન/નહાવાના સમયે પહેરવામાં આવતું વસ્ત્ર
bathrobe / dressing gowns

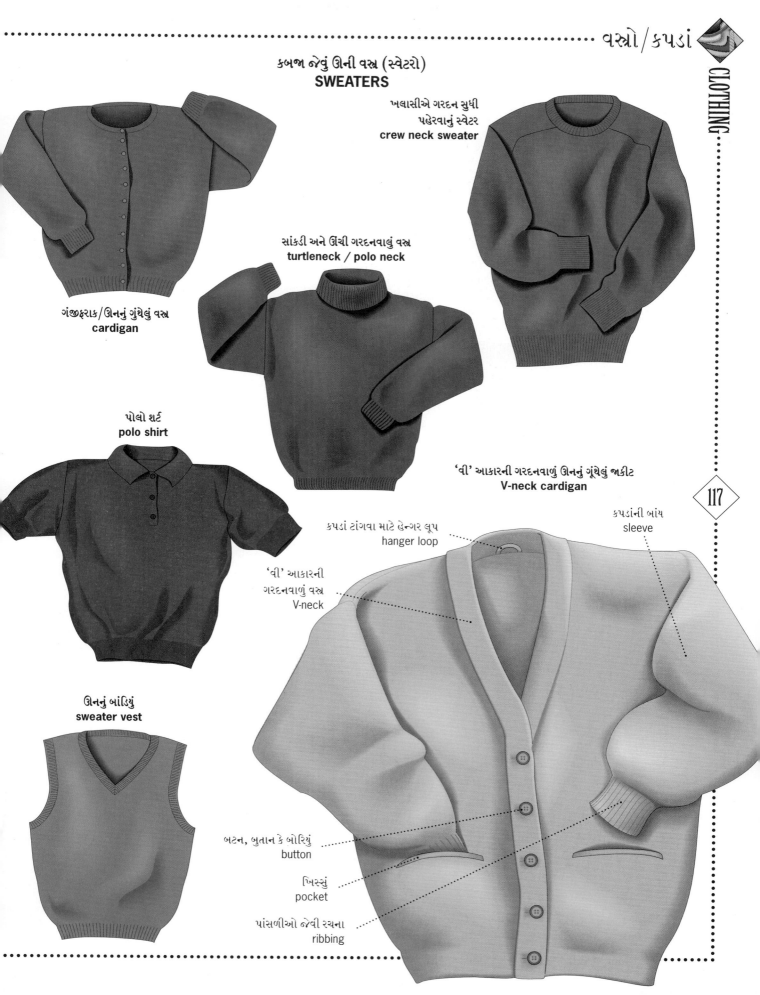

કબજા જેવું ઊની વસ્ત્ર (સ્વેટરો)
SWEATERS

ખલાસીએ ગરદન સુધી
પહેરવાનું સ્વેટર
crew neck sweater

સાંકડી અને ઊંચી ગરદનવાળું વસ્ત્ર
turtleneck / polo neck

ગંજીફ્રાક/ઊનનું ગૂંથેલું વસ્ત્ર
cardigan

પોલો શર્ટ
polo shirt

'વી' આકારની ગરદનવાળું ઊનનું ગૂંથેલું જકીટ
V-neck cardigan

117

કપડાં ટાંગવા માટે હેન્ગર લૂપ
hanger loop

કપડાંની બાંય
sleeve

'વી' આકારની
ગરદનવાળું વસ્ત્ર
V-neck

ઊનનું બાંડિયું
sweater vest

બટન, બુતાન કે બોરિયું
button

ખિસ્સું
pocket

પાંસળીઓ જેવી રચના
ribbing

હાથમોજાઓ, અને ગોઠણ સુધીનાં મોજાની જોડ
GLOVES AND STOCKINGS

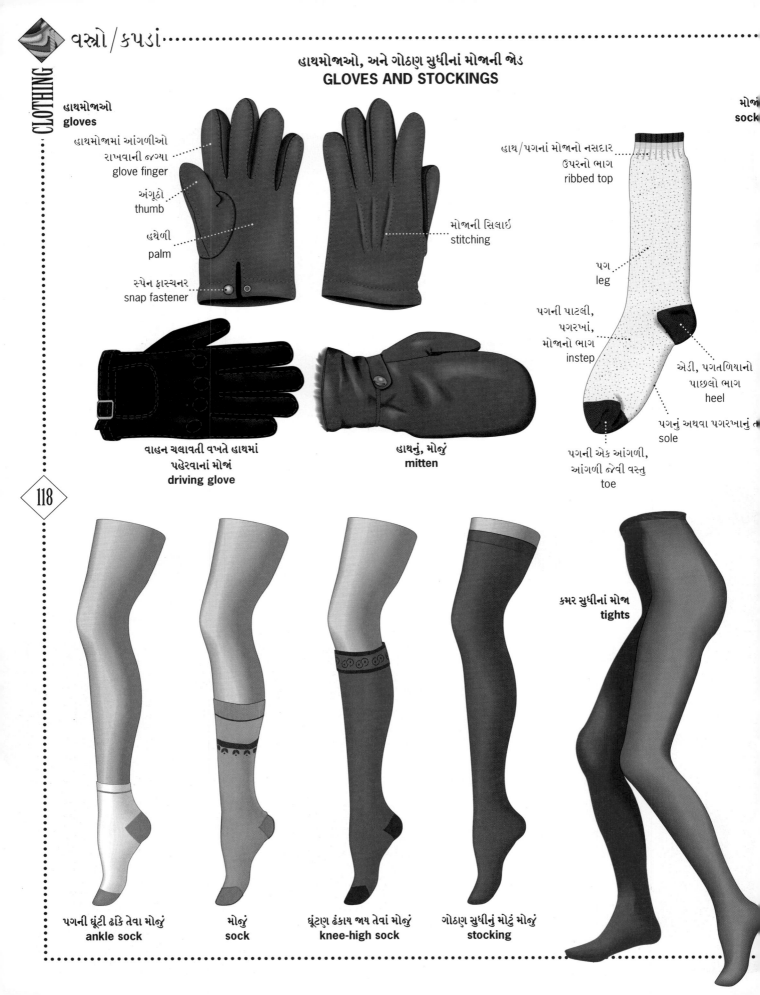

હાથમોજાઓ
gloves

હાથમોજામાં આંગળીઓ
રાખવાની જગ્યા
glove finger

અંગૂઠો
thumb

હથેળી
palm

સ્પેન ફાસ્ચનર
snap fastener

મોજાની સિલાઈ
stitching

મોજ
sock

હાથ/પગનાં મોજનો નસદાર
ઉપરનો ભાગ
ribbed top

પગ
leg

પગની પાટલી,
પગરખાં,
મોજાનો ભાગ
instep

એડી, પગતળિયાનો
પાછલો ભાગ
heel

પગનું અથવા પગરખાનું ત
sole

પગની એક આંગળી,
આંગળી જેવી વસ્તુ
toe

વાહન ચલાવતી વખતે હાથમાં
પહેરવાનાં મોજાં
driving glove

હાથનું, મોજું
mitten

કમર સુધીનાં મોજ
tights

પગની ઘૂંટી ઢંકે તેવા મોજું
ankle sock

મોજું
sock

ઘૂંટણ ઢંકાય જાય તેવાં મોજું
knee-high sock

ગોઠણ સુધીનું મોટું મોજું
stocking

જૂતાંઓ
SHOES

ભારે વજન વાળા બૂટ
heavy duty boot / walking boot

છોકરીના જુતાં
ballerina / pump

પાછળની પટ્ટીવાળા જુતાં
slingback

સાથળ સુધીનાં જૂતાં
thigh-boot

ઊંચી એડીના જુતાં
pump / court

ટેનિસ રમતી વખતે પહેરવાનાં જૂતાં
tennis shoe

ફાઇબર સોલ વાળાં હલવા
કેનવાસનાં જૂતાં
espadrille

દરરોજ સાદા પહેરવાના જુતાં
loafer

ચંપલ/સેન્ડલ
sandal

ઉત્તર અમેરિકાનાં ઇન્ડિયન હરણનાં ચામડાનું પગરખું
moccasin

બૂટ/જેઓ
boot

પગની ઘૂંટી ઢકેિ તેવાં જૂતાં
ankle boot

રમતવીરનાં પહેરવેશ
SPORTSWEAR

કસરત કરતી વખતે પહેરવાનાં વસ્ત્રો
EXERCISE WEAR

ટેન્ક ટોપ
tank top

તરવાનો પોશાક
swimsuit

બેલેટ નૃત્યકો/રમતવીરો દ્વારા પહેરવામાં આવ
સળંગ ચૂસ્ત વસ્ત્ર
leotard

ટ્રેક સૂટ
TRACK SUIT

ઊની શર્ટ
sweatshirt

હલકો કોટ
windbreaker /anorak

પરસેવો ન થાય તેવું કપડાં પર
પહેરવાનું ગડીદાર વસ્ત્ર
hooded sweatshirt

પાટલૂન
**pants /
waterproof
trousers**

ઊનું પાટલૂન
sweatpants / jogging bottoms

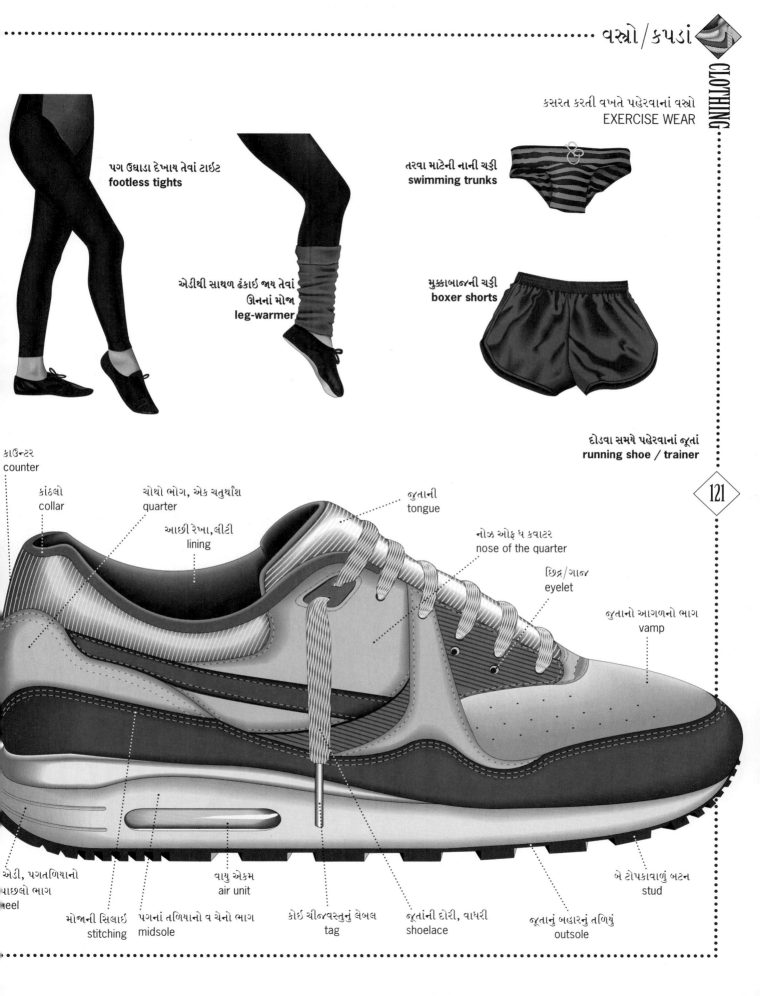

કસરત કરતી વખતે પહેરવાનાં વસ્ત્રો
EXERCISE WEAR

પગ ઉઘાડા દેખાય તેવાં ટાઇટ
footless tights

એડીથી સાથળ ઢંકાઈ જાય તેવાં
ઊનનાં મોજ
leg-warmer

તરવા માટેની નાની ચડી
swimming trunks

મુક્કાબાજની ચડી
boxer shorts

દોડવા સમયે પહેરવાનાં જૂતાં
running shoe / trainer

121

કાઉન્ટર
counter

કાંઠલો
collar

ચોથો ભોગ, એક ચતુર્થાંશ
quarter

આછી રેખા, લીટી
lining

જુતાની
tongue

નોઝ ઓફ્ ધ કવાટર
nose of the quarter

છિદ્ર/ગાળ
eyelet

જુતાનો આગળનો ભાગ
vamp

એડી, પગતળિયાનો
પાછલો ભાગ
heel

મોજની સિલાઈ
stitching

પગનાં તળિયાનો વ ચેનો ભાગ
midsole

વાયુ એકમ
air unit

કોઇ ચીજવસ્તુનું લેબલ
tag

જૂતાંની દોરી, વાધરી
shoelace

જૂતાનું બહારનું તળિયું
outsole

બે ટોપકાવાળું બટન
stud

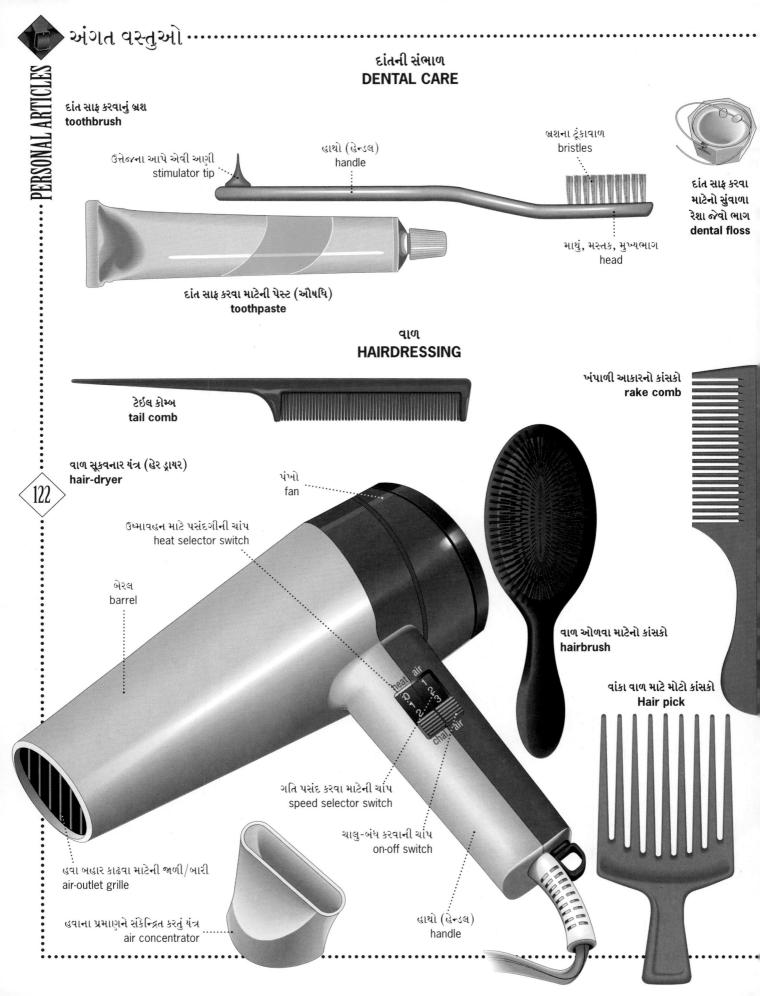

દાંતની સંભાળ
DENTAL CARE

દાંત સાફ કરવાનું બ્રશ
toothbrush

ઉત્તેજના આપે એવી અણી
stimulator tip

હાથો (હેન્ડલ)
handle

બ્રશના ટૂંકાવાળ
bristles

દાંત સાફ કરવા માટેનો સુંવાળા રેશા જેવો ભાગ
dental floss

માથું, મસ્તક, મુખ્યભાગ
head

દાંત સાફ કરવા માટેની પેસ્ટ (ઔષધિ)
toothpaste

વાળ
HAIRDRESSING

ખંપાળી આકારનો કાંસકો
rake comb

ટેઇલ કોમ્બ
tail comb

વાળ સૂકવનાર યંત્ર (હેર ડ્રાયર)
hair-dryer

પંખો
fan

ઉષ્માવહન માટે પસંદગીની ચાંપ
heat selector switch

બેરલ
barrel

વાળ ઓળવા માટેનો કાંસકો
hairbrush

વાંકા વાળ માટે મોટો કાંસકો
Hair pick

ગતિ પસંદ કરવા માટેની ચાંપ
speed selector switch

ચાલુ-બંધ કરવાની ચાંપ
on-off switch

હવા બહાર કાઢવા માટેની જાળી/બારી
air-outlet grille

હવાના પ્રમાણને સંકેન્દ્રિત કરતું યંત્ર
air concentrator

હાથો (હેન્ડલ)
handle

ચામડાંની ચીજવસ્તુઓ
LEATHER GOODS

દોરી વાળી બેગ
drawstring bag

તાણવાની દોરી
drawstring

પીઠ પર બાંધવાનો થેલો
knapsack

ચાવીઓની પેટી
key case

ખિસ્સામાં રાખવાનો નાનો બટવો
wallet

ખભા પર બાંધવાનો પટ્ટો
shoulder strap

થેલી, પૈસા માટેની
થેલી, બટવો
purse

આગળનું ખિસ્સું
front pocket

કાચ
GLASSES

કાચનાં લેન્સ
glass lens

પૂલ, સેતુ
bridge

સળિયો
bar

કોઈપણ વસ્તુ/સાધનની
ધાર કે કિનારી
rim

નાક પરની ગાદી
nose pad

લમણું, મંદિર
temple

છત્રી
UMBRELLA

છત્ર, ચંદની કે ચંદરવો
canopy

આણી, આણી જેવો ભાગ
tip

સ્પ્રેડર
spreader

ચકરડી
ring

બાંધવું
tie

દૂરબીનથી જોઈ શકાય તેવી છત્રી
(ટેલિસ્કોપિક અમ્બ્રેલા)
telescopic umbrella

છત્રીનો સળિયો
rib

કોઈ ચીજવસ્તુને પકડવા માટે લગાડેલી
કપડા/ચામડાની પટ્ટી
tab

કોઈપણ સાધનનો દાંડલી જેવો ભાગ
shank

હાથો (હેન્ડલ)
handle

આવરણ
cover

COMMUNICATIONS

ટેલિફોન દ્વારા સંવાદ
COMMUNICATION BY TELEPHONE

ટેલિફોનનો સેટ (સાધન)
telephone set

ટેલિફોનનું એક એકમ
(હેન્ડ સેટ)
handset

ઇયરપિસ
earpiece

નિદર્શન
display

માઉથ પિસ
mouthpiece

નિશ્ચીત કામગીરીની પસંદગી કરનાર
function selectors

ટેલિફોનનું દોરડું
handset cord

કોઈ ચીજ વસ્તુ મશીનની અંદર ધકેલવાના બટનો,
આંગળીથી દબાવીને ચાલુ કરવાનું બટન/ચાંપો
push buttons

ટેલિફોનની અનુક્રમણિકા
telephone index

સ્વયં સંચાલિત ટેલિફોનનો નંબર
જોડનારો ભાગ
automatic dialer

ટેલિફોન દ્વારા જવાબ આપતું સાધન
telephone answering machine

આઉટગોઇંગ એનાઉન્સમેન્ટ કેસેટ
outgoing announcement cassette

બહારથી આવતો સંદેશો આપતી કેસેટ
incoming message cassette

ધ્વનિ પ્રસારણ યંત્ર (સ્પીકર)
speaker

ધ્વનિ સાંભળવા માટેનું બટન
listen button

રેકર્ડ એનાઉન્સમેન્ટ બટન
record announcement button

વધ-ઘટનાં નિયંત્રણો
volume control

કેસેટ વગાડનાર સાધનનાં નિયંત્રણ
cassette player control

પૈસા મશીનમાં નાખીને કરવામાં આવતો ફોન (પે ફોન)
pay phone

મશીનમાં સિક્કા નાખવાની
ખાંચ કે ફાંટ
coin slot

નિદર્શન
display

કોઈ ચીજ વસ્તુ મશીનની અંદર
ધકેલવાના બટનો, આંગળીથી
દબાવીને ચાલુ કરવાનું બટન/ચાંપો
push buttons

ટેલિફોનનું એક એકમ (હેન્ડ સેટ)
handset

પત્તા પરથી ભવિષ્ય કહેનાર
card reader

સિક્કા પરત કરવાની ટ્રે
coin return tray

બટન/ચાંપ દબાવીને ડાયલ કરવામાં આવતો ટેલિફોન
push-button telephone

સુવાહ્ય સેલ્યુલર ટેલિફોન
portable cellular telephone

વાયર (તાર) વગરનો ટેલિફોન
cordless telephone

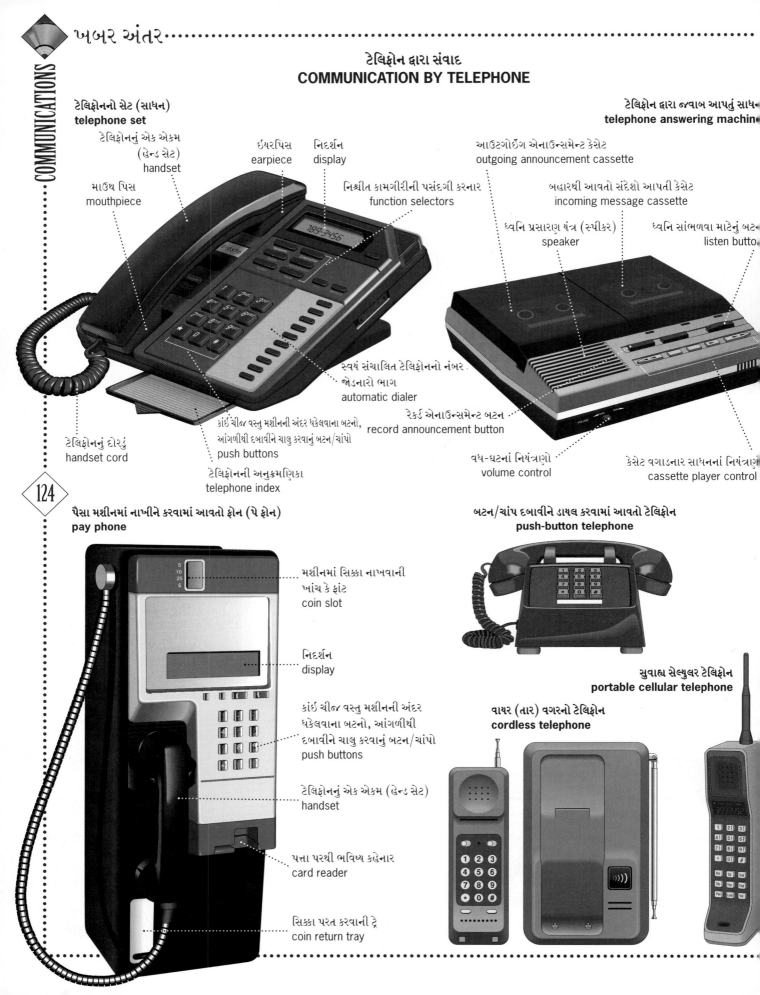

છબી પાડવાની કળા, ફોટોગ્રાફી - છબીકલા
PHOTOGRAPHY

વધારાની ઉપયોગી સાધન સામગ્રી રાખવાની થેલી/સાધન
accessory shoe

એક જ લેન્સથી પ્રકાશનાં કિરણો પરાવર્તિત કરતો કેમેરો
single lens reflex (slr) camera

ફિલ્મ રિવાઇન્ડ બટન
film rewind button

હોટ-શૂ કોન્ટેકટ
hot-shoe contact

ફિલ્મ એડવાન્સ બટન
film advance button

નિયંત્રણ કરવા માટેની પેનલ
control panel

કંટ્રોલ ડાયલ
control dial

કોઈપણ વસ્તુને ખૂલ્લી કરવા
માટેની ચાંપ (બટન)
exposure button

ફિલ્મ ગતિ
film speed

રિમોટ કન્ટ્રોલનું ટર્મિનલ
remote control terminal

કેમેરાનો સંપૂર્ણ ભાગ
camera body

ફોકસ સેટીંગ રીંગ
focus setting ring

શટર ખૂલ્લું કરવાની ચાંપ
shutter release button

ઇલેક્ટ્રોનિક ફ્લેશ
electronic flash

વાસ્તવિક (નિરીક્ષણકર્તા) કાચ
objective lens

ફ્લેશ ટ્યૂબ
flashtube

કોમ્પેક્ટ કેમેરા
compact camera

છિદ્ર, કાણું
perforation

કેસેટ ફિલ્મ
cassette film

ફિલ્મમાં લાગેલી ધાતુની પટ્ટી
film leader

પ્રકાશ-વિદ્યુત કોષ
photoelectric cell

પોલેરાઇડ લેન્ડ કેમેરો
Polaroid® Land camera

કેમેરાની ઉપર ફ્લેશ
રાખવા માટેનો સંપર્ક આધાર
mounting foot

ખસ્સામાં સમાય જાય તેવો કેમેરો
pocket camera

કાર્ટ્રીજ ફિલ્મ
cartridge film

ફિલ્મ પેક
film pack

125

COMMUNICATIONS

દૂરદર્શન (ટેલિવિઝન)
TELEVISION

ટેલિવિઝન સેટ (કેબિનેટ)
television set

ખાના અભેરાઈવાળી કેબિનેટ
cabinet

પડદો/આદશ કે આંતરો
screen

દૂરથી નિયંત્રણ કરવા માટેનાં
સાધન (રિમોટ કન્ટ્રોલ) માંથી
કળતાં કિરણોને પારખનારું સેન્
remote control sensor

ટી.વી. ચાલુ/બંધ કરવાની ચાંપ
on/off button

નિર્દેશકો
indicators

સૂર મેળવવાની વ્યવસ્થાનાં નિયંત્રણો
tuning controls

દૂરથી નિયંત્રણ કરવા માટેનું સાધન (રિમોટ કન્ટ્રોલ)
remote control

ટી.વી. ચાલુ કરવાનો મોડ (પ્રકાર)
TV mode

વધ-ઘટનાં નિયંત્રણો
volume control

ટી.વી./વિડીયોની ચાંપ
TV/video button

ટી.વી. ચાલુ/બંધ કરવાની ચાંપ
TV on/off button

ચેનલો ઝડપથી જોવા માટેનાં બ
channel scan buttons

વી.સી.આર. ચાલુ/બંધ કરવાની ચાંપ
VCR on/off button

વી.સી.આર.નો મોડ/પસંદગીકર્તા પોઇન્ટ
VCR mode

ચેનલો પસંદ કરવા માટેનાં નિયંત્રણો
channel selector controls

પહેલાંથી ગોઠવણ કરેલાં બટન/ચાંપ
preset buttons

વી.સી.આર.નાં નિયંત્રણો
VCR controls

ધીમી ગતિ
slow-motion

રેકોર્ડ
record

વિરામ, સ્થિર ચિત્ર (ટી.વી. માટે)
pause

ટેલિવિઝનનું દશ્ય પાછળની તરફ ફેરવવું
rewind

કેસેટની ગતિ ઝડપથી આગળ વધારવી
fast forward

ચાલુ કરો
play

અટકાવ, અવરોધ
stop

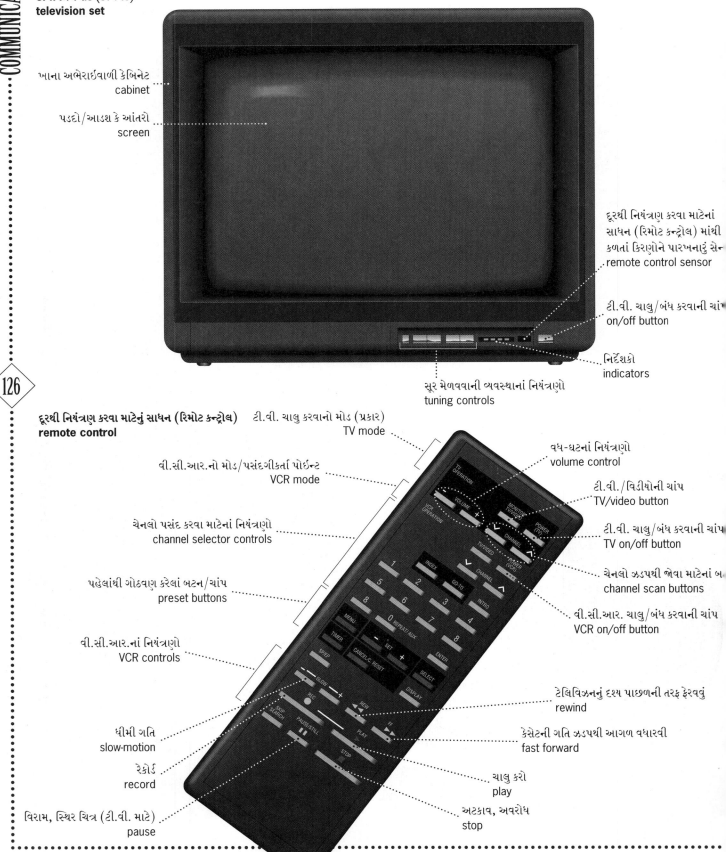

વિડિયો
VIDEO

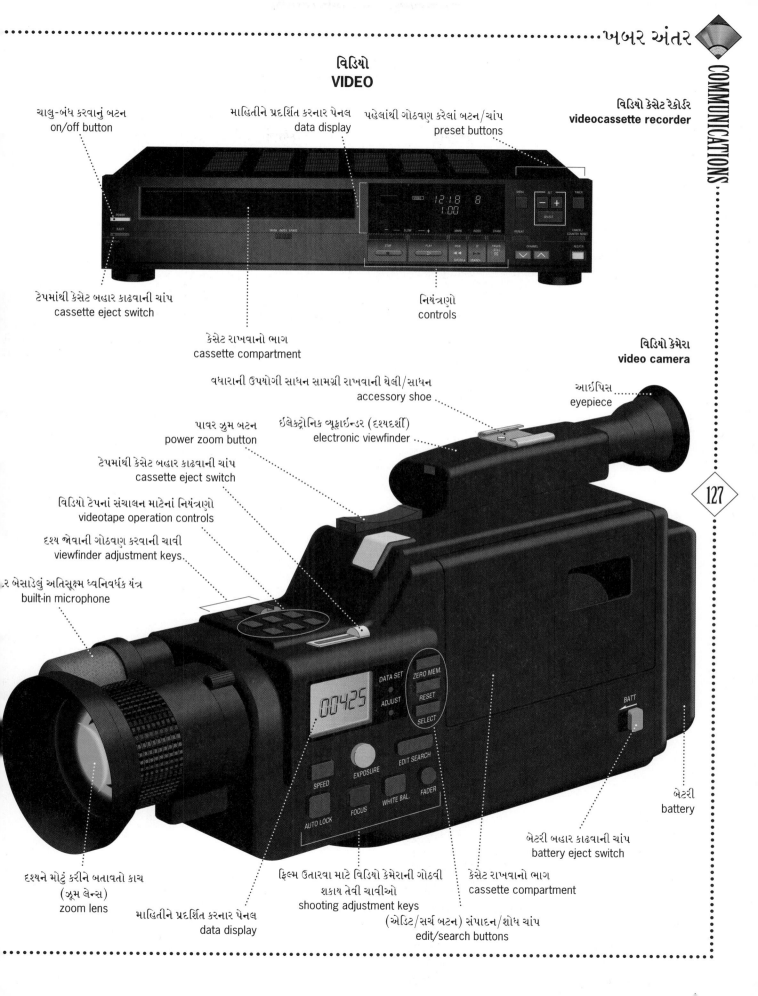

ચાલુ-બંધ કરવાનું બટન
on/off button

માહિતીને પ્રદર્શિત કરનાર પેનલ
data display

પહેલાંથી ગોઠવણ કરેલાં બટન/ચાંપ
preset buttons

વિડિયો કેસેટ રેકોર્ડર
videocassette recorder

ટેપમાંથી કેસેટ બહાર કાઢવાની ચાંપ
cassette eject switch

નિયંત્રાણો
controls

કેસેટ રાખવાનો ભાગ
cassette compartment

વિડિયો કેમેરા
video camera

વધારાની ઉપયોગી સાધન સામગ્રી રાખવાની થેલી/સાધન
accessory shoe

આઈપિસ
eyepiece

પાવર ઝુમ બટન
power zoom button

ઈલેક્ટ્રોનિક વ્યૂફાઈન્ડર (દશ્યદર્શી)
electronic viewfinder

ટેપમાંથી કેસેટ બહાર કાઢવાની ચાંપ
cassette eject switch

વિડિયો ટેપનાં સંચાલન માટેનાં નિયંત્રાણો
videotape operation controls

દશ્ય જોવાની ગોઠવણ કરવાની ચાવી
viewfinder adjustment keys

ર બેસાડેલું અતિસૂક્ષ્મ ધ્વનિવર્ધક યંત્ર
built-in microphone

બેટરી
battery

દશ્યને મોટું કરીને બતાવતો કાચ
(ઝૂમ લેન્સ)
zoom lens

ફિલ્મ ઉતારવા માટે વિડિયો કેમેરાની ગોઠવી
શકાય તેવી ચાવીઓ
shooting adjustment keys

કેસેટ રાખવાનો ભાગ
cassette compartment

બેટરી બહાર કાઢવાની ચાંપ
battery eject switch

માહિતીને પ્રદર્શિત કરનાર પેનલ
data display

(એડિટ/સર્ચ બટન) સંપાદન/શોધ ચાંપ
edit/search buttons

સ્ટિરિયો પ્રણાલિ
STEREO SYSTEM / HI-FI SYSTEM

ઘડકોનાં બનેલા તંત્ર
SYSTEM COMPONENTS

સૂર મેળવવા માટેની ચાંપ/કળ (ટ્યુનર)
tuner

એફ.એમ. તરંગો ઝડપવા માટેનું
એન્ટેના
FM antenna

એ.એમ. રેડિયો તરંગો ઝડપવા
માટેનું એરિયલ
AM antenna

89.9

ગ્રામોફોનમાં વગાડવાની થાળી મૂકવાનું ચક્કર
turntable

કોમ્પેક્ટ ડિસ્ક પ્લેયર
compact disc player

ધ્વનિવર્ધક
amplifier

કેસેટ ટેપ રેક
cassette tape deck

સંગીતને સમાન લયમાં ગોઠવતી ધ્વનિ-વ્યવસ્થા
graphic equalizer

રેડિયોનું ધ્વનિ વિસ્તારક યંત્ર
loudspeakers

ડાબીબાજુની ચેનલ
left channel

રાઇટ ચેનલ
right channel

ટ્વીટર (તીવ્રતાવાળો અવાજ કાઢાં લાઉડસ્પીકર)
tweeter

વચલો અવાજ
midrange

વૂફર
woofer

ડાયાફ્રામ, ઉપરપટ,
સૂક્ષ્મ પડદો
diaphragm; cone

ધ્વનિ પ્રસારણ યંત્રનું
આવરણ (સ્પીકર કવર)
speaker cover

હેડફોન્સ
headphone

કાનની ગાદી
ear cushion

મસ્તક પર બાંધવાનો પટ્ટો
headband

સાનુકૂળ (ગોઠવી શકાય તેવો)
પાટો અથવા પટ્ટો
adjusting band

અવાજ સાંભળવા માટે કાનમાં
પહેરવાનું યંત્ર
earphone

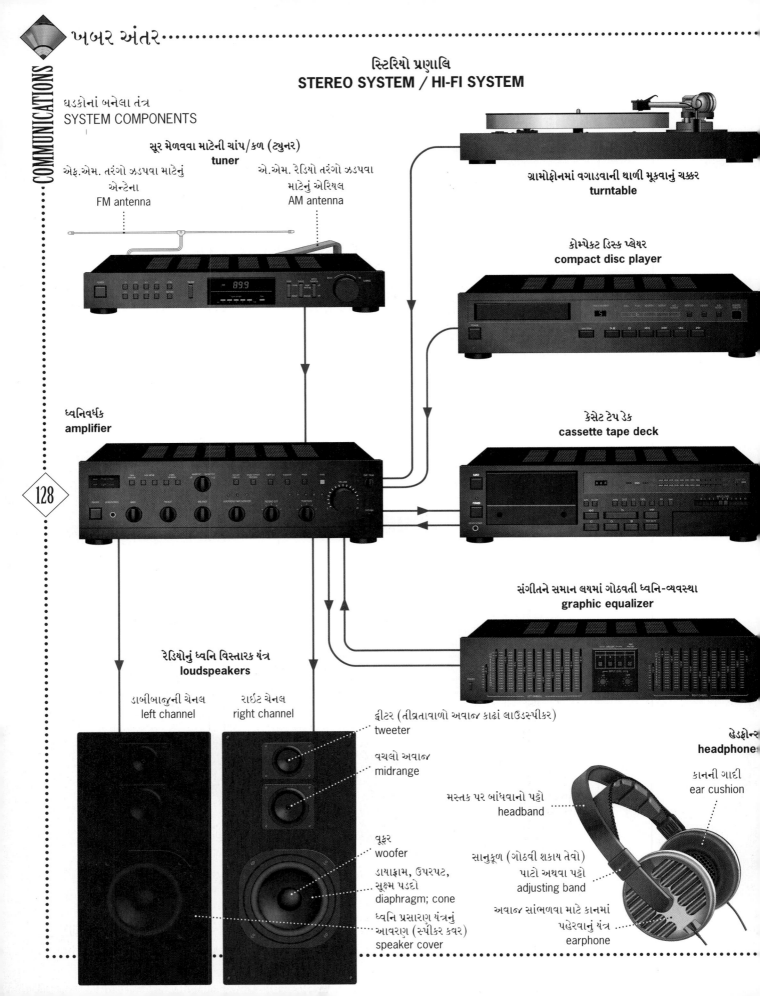

સુવાહ્ય ધ્વનિ પ્રણાલિ
PORTABLE SOUND SYSTEMS

તીવ્રતામાં વધ-ઘટ કરવાનું નિયંત્રણ
on/off/volume control

એ.એમ./એફ.એમ. બેન્ડ સાથેનું સુવાહ્ય/હલકું કોમ્પેક્ટ ડિસ્ક અને કેસેટ રેકોર્ડ
portable CD AM/FM cassette recorder

એન્ટેના
antenna

કોઈ વસ્તુનો આકાર/પ્રકાર
પસંદ કરવાવાળું
mode selectors

કોમ્પેક્ટ ડિસ્ક પ્લેયર
compact disc player

હાથો (હેન્ડલ)
handle

કોમ્પેક્ટ ડિસ્ક
compact disc

આપતાં યંત્રનાં નિયંત્રણ (સ્ટિરિયો કન્ટ્રોલ)
stereo control

ડિસ્ક પ્લેયર કંટ્રોલ
disc player controls

હેડફોન પ્લગ
headphone jack

સૂર મેળવવા માટેની ચાંપ/કળ
tuner

સૂર મેળવવાની વ્યવસ્થાનાં નિયંત્રણો
tuning control

ધ્વનિ પ્રસારણ યંત્ર (સ્પીકર)
speaker

કેસેટ / અવાજ સંગ્રહ
કરતી પડ્ઢીવાળી ડબ્બી
cassette

કેસેટ પ્લેયર
cassette player

કેસેટ વગાડનાર સાધનનાં નિયંત્રણો
cassette player controls

એ.એમ.,એફ.એમ. બેન્ડ સાથેનું અંગત કેસેટ પ્લેયર
personal AM/FM cassette player; Walkman®

ચપટો (કોમ્પેક્ટ ડિસ્ક) વિસ્તાર
pressed area

કોમ્પેક્ટ ડિસ્ક
compact disc

જાડી સાંકળ, તારનું દોરડું
cable

હેડફોન પ્લગ
headphone plug

મસ્તક પર બાંધવાનો પટ્ટો
headband

રીડિંગ સ્ટાર્ટ
reading start

ચાલુ-બંધ કરવાનું બટન
on/off button

વધ-ઘટનાં નિયંત્રણો
volume control

કસેટની પડ્ઢી પાછળની તરફ ફેરવવા
માટેની ચાંપ (બટન)
rewind button

સૂર મેળવવાની વ્યવસ્થાના નિયંત્રણ
tuning control

પ્રાવૈધિક ઓળખ પટ્ટો
technical identification band

વગાડવા માટેનું બટન
play button

કાન પર ગોઠવી શકાયે તેવો
ટેલિફોનનો ભાગ (હેડ ફોન)
headphones

રેકર્ડ
record

ટેની ગતિ જડપથી આગળની
તરફ વધારવાનું બટન
fast-forward button

કેસેટ / અવાજ સંગ્રહ કરતી પડ્ઢી
વાળી ડબ્બી
cassette

આપ ઊલટી દિશામાં ફરી જાય તેવું
auto reverse

કેસેટ પ્લેયર
cassette player

સર્પાકાર કે આવર્ત ધ્વની
spiral-in groove

સેટ / અવાજ સંગ્રહ
રતી પડ્ઢીવાળી ડબ્બી
cassette

આવાસ વ્યવસ્થા
housing

સૂર મેળવવા માટેની ચાંપ/કળ
tuner

સર્પાકાર કે આવર્ત ધ્વની
spiral

ટેક-અપ રીલ
take-up reel

પડ્ઢો અથવા પડ્ઢી
band

રેકર્ડ કરવા માટેની પડ્ઢી/ટેપ
recording tape

સ્ક્રૂના પાછળના ભાગનાં ખવાઈ
ગયેલાં આંટા/ખાંચા
tail-out groove

ટેપ ગાઈડ
tape guide

લેબલ
label

ગાઈડ રોલર
guide roller

રમવાની બારી
playing window

કેન્દ્રિય છિદ્ર
center hole

129

મોટરગાડી
CAR

બોડી
body

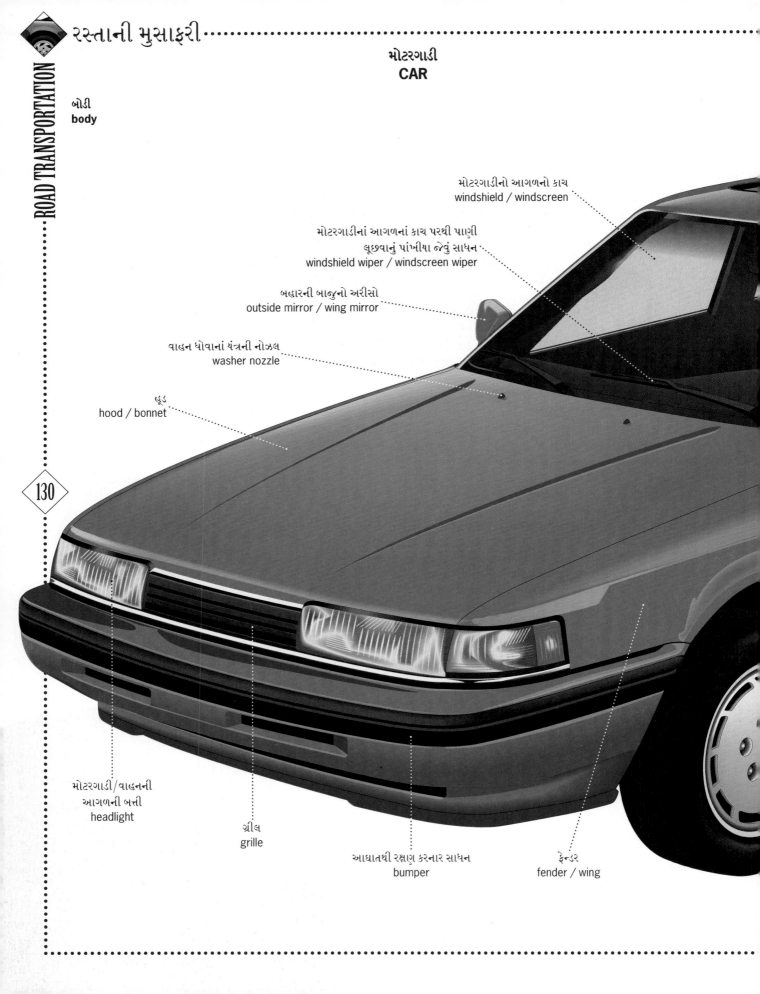

મોટરગાડીનો આગળનો કાચ
windshield / windscreen

મોટરગાડીનાં આગળનાં કાચ પરથી પાણી
લૂછવાનું પાંખીયા જેવું સાધન
windshield wiper / windscreen wiper

બહારની બાજુનો અરીસો
outside mirror / wing mirror

વાહન ધોવાનાં યંત્રની નોઝલ
washer nozzle

હૂડ
hood / bonnet

130

મોટરગાડી/વાહનની
આગળની બત્તી
headlight

ગ્રીલ
grille

આઘાતથી રક્ષણ કરનાર સાધન
bumper

ફેન્ડર
fender / wing

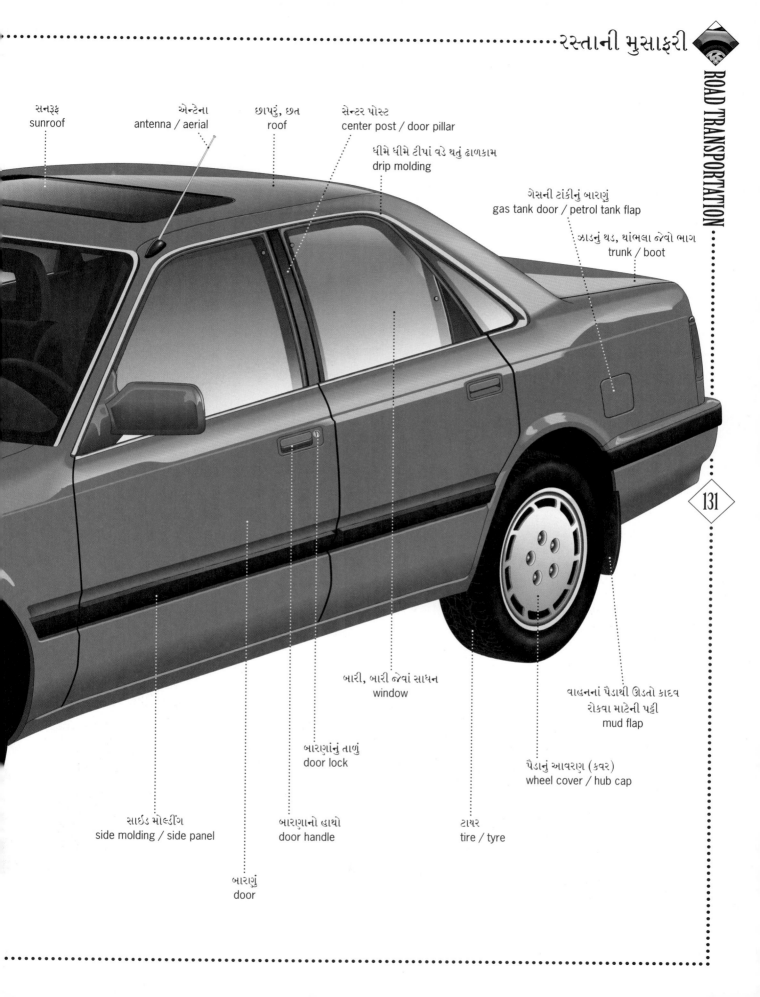

સનરૂફ
sunroof

એન્ટેના
antenna / aerial

છાપરું, છત
roof

સેન્ટર પોસ્ટ
center post / door pillar

ધીમે ધીમે ટીપાં વડે થતું ઢાળકામ
drip molding

ગેસની ટાંકીનું બારણું
gas tank door / petrol tank flap

ઝાડનું થડ, થાંભલા જેવો ભાગ
trunk / boot

બારી, બારી જેવાં સાધન
window

વાહનનાં પૈડાથી ઊડતો કાદવ
રોકવા માટેની પટ્ટી
mud flap

બારણાંનું તાળું
door lock

પૈડાનું આવરણ (કવર)
wheel cover / hub cap

સાઇડ મોલ્ડીંગ
side molding / side panel

બારણાનો હાથો
door handle

ટાયર
tire / tyre

બારણું
door

મોટરગાડી
CAR

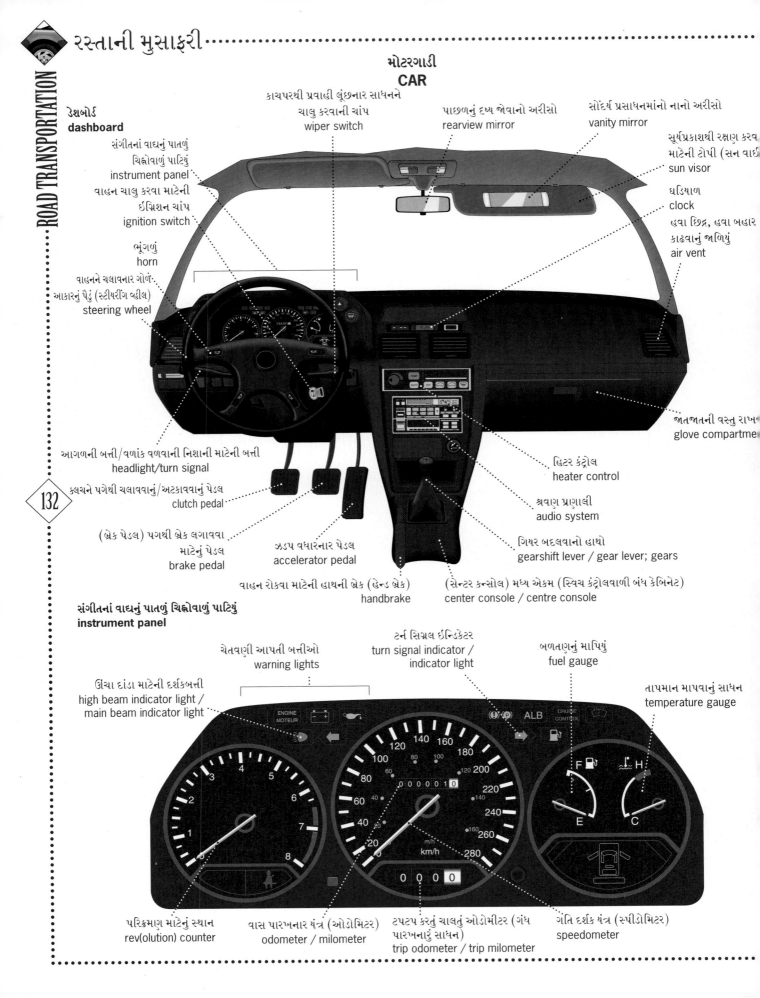

કાચપરથી પ્રવાહી લૂંછનાર સાધનને
ચાલુ કરવાની ચાંપ
wiper switch

પાછળનું દ્રશ્ય જોવાનો અરીસો
rearview mirror

સૌંદર્ય પ્રસાધનમાંનો નાનો અરીસો
vanity mirror

ડેશબોર્ડ
dashboard

સંગીતનાં વાઘનું પાતળું
ચિહ્નોવાળું પાટિયું
instrument panel

વાહન ચાલુ કરવા માટેની
ઇગ્નિશન ચાંપ
ignition switch

ભૂંગળું
horn

વાહનને ચલાવનાર ગોળ
આકારનું પૈડું (સ્ટીયરીંગ વ્હીલ)
steering wheel

સૂર્યપ્રકાશથી રક્ષણ કરવ
માટેની ટોપી (સન વાઈ
sun visor

ઘડિયાળ
clock

હવા છિદ્ર, હવા બહાર
કાઢવાનું જાળિયું
air vent

આગળની બત્તી/વળાંક વળવાની નિશાની માટેની બત્તી
headlight/turn signal

ક્લચને પગેથી ચલાવવાનું/અટકાવવાનું પેડલ
clutch pedal

(બ્રેક પેડલ) પગથી બ્રેક લગાવવા
માટેનું પેડલ
brake pedal

ઝડપ વધારનાર પેડલ
accelerator pedal

જાતજાતની વસ્તુ રાખ
glove compartme

હિટર કંટ્રોલ
heater control

શ્રવણ પ્રણાલી
audio system

ગિયર બદલવાનો હાથો
gearshift lever / gear lever; gears

વાહન રોકવા માટેની હાથની બ્રેક (હેન્ડ બ્રેક)
handbrake

(સેન્ટર કન્સોલ) મધ્ય એકમ (સ્વિચ કંટ્રોલવાળી બંધ કેબિનેટ)
center console / centre console

સંગીતનાં વાઘનું પાતળું ચિહ્નોવાળું પાટિયું
instrument panel

ચેતવણી આપતી બત્તીઓ
warning lights

ટર્ન સિગ્નલ ઇન્ડિકેટર
turn signal indicator /
indicator light

બળતણનું માપિયું
fuel gauge

ઊંચા દાંડા માટેની દર્શકબત્તી
high beam indicator light /
main beam indicator light

તાપમાન માપવાનું સાધન
temperature gauge

પરિક્રમણ માટેનું સ્થાન
rev(olution) counter

વાસ પારખનાર યંત્ર (ઓડોમિટર)
odometer / milometer

ટપટપ કરતું ચાલતું ઓડોમિટર (ગંધ
પારખનારું સાધન)
trip odometer / trip milometer

ગતિ દર્શક યંત્ર (સ્પીડોમિટર)
speedometer

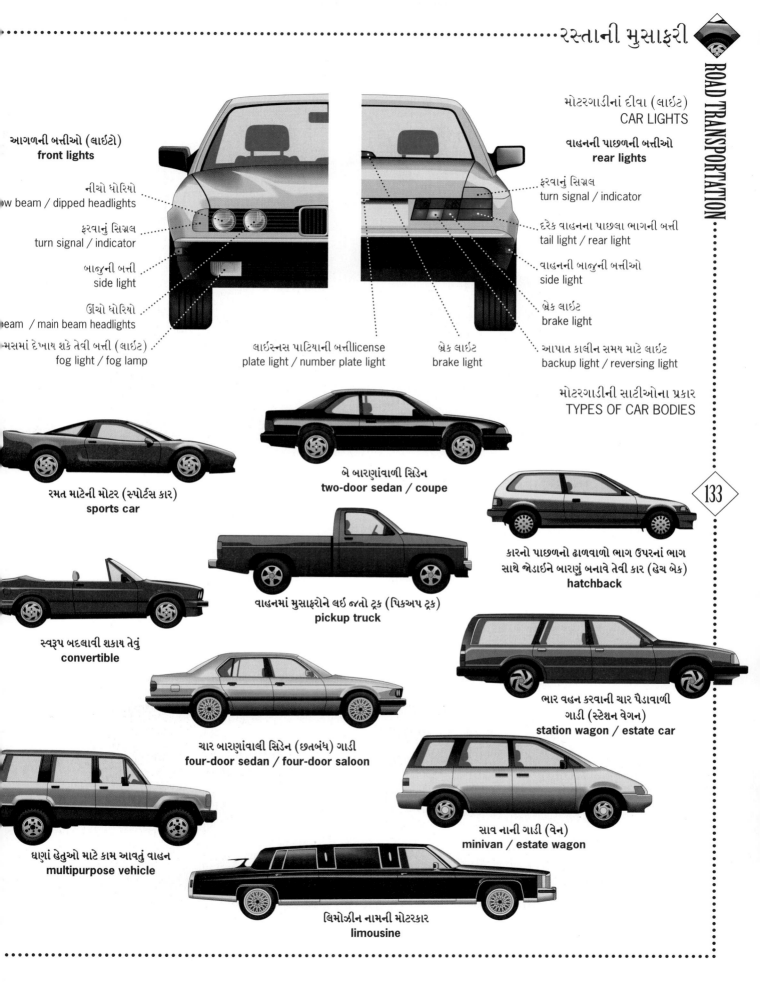

આગળની બત્તીઓ (લાઇટો)
front lights

નીચો ધોરિયો
w beam / dipped headlights

ફરવાનું સિગ્નલ
turn signal / indicator

બાજુની બત્તી
side light

ઊંચો ધોરિયો
beam / main beam headlights

મસમાં દેખાય શકે તેવી બત્તી (લાઇટ)
fog light / fog lamp

લાઇસન્સ પાટિયાની બત્તીlicense
plate light / number plate light

બ્રેક લાઇટ
brake light

મોટરગાડીનાં દીવા (લાઇટ)
CAR LIGHTS

વાહનની પાછળની બત્તીઓ
rear lights

ફરવાનું સિગ્નલ
turn signal / indicator

દરેક વાહનના પાછલા ભાગની બત્તી
tail light / rear light

વાહનની બાજુની બત્તીઓ
side light

બ્રેક લાઇટ
brake light

આપાત કાલીન સમય માટે લાઇટ
backup light / reversing light

મોટરગાડીની સાટીઓના પ્રકાર
TYPES OF CAR BODIES

રમત માટેની મોટર (સ્પોર્ટ્સ કાર)
sports car

બે બારણાંવાળી સિડેન
two-door sedan / coupe

કારનો પાછળનો ઢાળવાળો ભાગ ઉપરનાં ભાગ
સાથે જોડાઈને બારણું બનાવે તેવી કાર (હેચ બેક)
hatchback

વાહનમાં મુસાફરોને લઈ જતો ટ્રક (પિકઅપ ટ્રક)
pickup truck

સ્વરૂપ બદલાવી શકાય તેવું
convertible

ભાર વહન કરવાની ચાર પૈડાવાળી
ગાડી (સ્ટેશન વેગન)
station wagon / estate car

ચાર બારણાંવાળી સિડેન (છતબંધ) ગાડી
four-door sedan / four-door saloon

સાવ નાની ગાડી (વેન)
minivan / estate wagon

ઘણાં હેતુઓ માટે કામ આવતું વાહન
multipurpose vehicle

લિમોઝીન નામની મોટરકાર
limousine

133

અમેરિકા અને કેનેડામાં માલ લઈ જવા માટેનું વાહન/ખટારો
TRUCK / LORRY

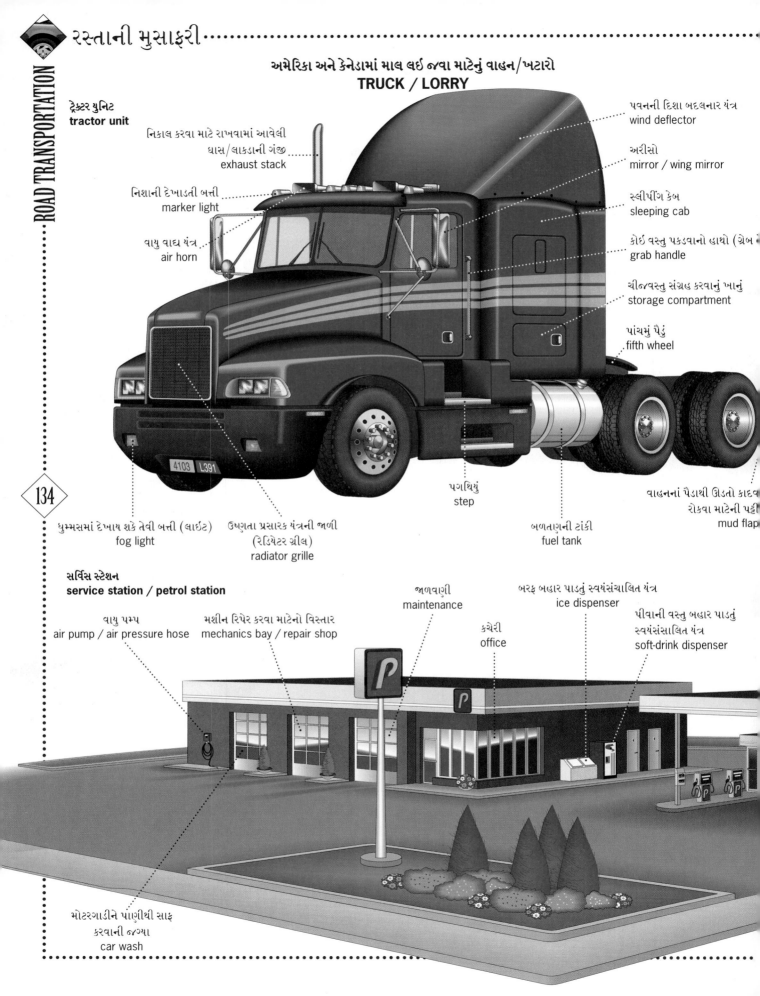

ટ્રેક્ટર યુનિટ
tractor unit

નિકાલ કરવા માટે રાખવામાં આવેલી
ઘાસ/લાકડાની ગંજી
exhaust stack

નિશાની દેખાડતી બત્તી
marker light

વાયુ વાઘ યંત્ર
air horn

પવનની દિશા બદલનાર યંત્ર
wind deflector

અરીસો
mirror / wing mirror

સ્લીપીંગ કેબ
sleeping cab

કોઈ વસ્તુ પકડવાનો હાથો (ગ્રેબ)
grab handle

ચીજવસ્તુ સંગ્રહ કરવાનું ખાનું
storage compartment

પાંચમું પૈડું
fifth wheel

પગથિયું
step

વાહનનાં પૈડાથી ઊડતો કાદવ
રોકવા માટેની પટ્ટી
mud flap

ધુમ્મસમાં દેખાય શકે તેવી બત્તી (લાઈટ)
fog light

ઉષ્ણતા પ્રસારક યંત્રની જાળી
(રેડિયેટર ગ્રીલ)
radiator grille

બળતણની ટાંકી
fuel tank

4103 L391

સર્વિસ સ્ટેશન
service station / petrol station

વાયુ પમ્પ
air pump / air pressure hose

મશીન રિપેર કરવા માટેનો વિસ્તાર
mechanics bay / repair shop

જાળવણી
maintenance

કચેરી
office

બરફ બહાર પાડતું સ્વયંસંચાલિત યંત્ર
ice dispenser

પીવાની વસ્તુ બહાર પાડતું
સ્વયંસંચાલિત યંત્ર
soft-drink dispenser

મોટરગાડીને પાણીથી સાફ
કરવાની જગ્યા
car wash

મોટર સાયકલ
MOTORCYCLE

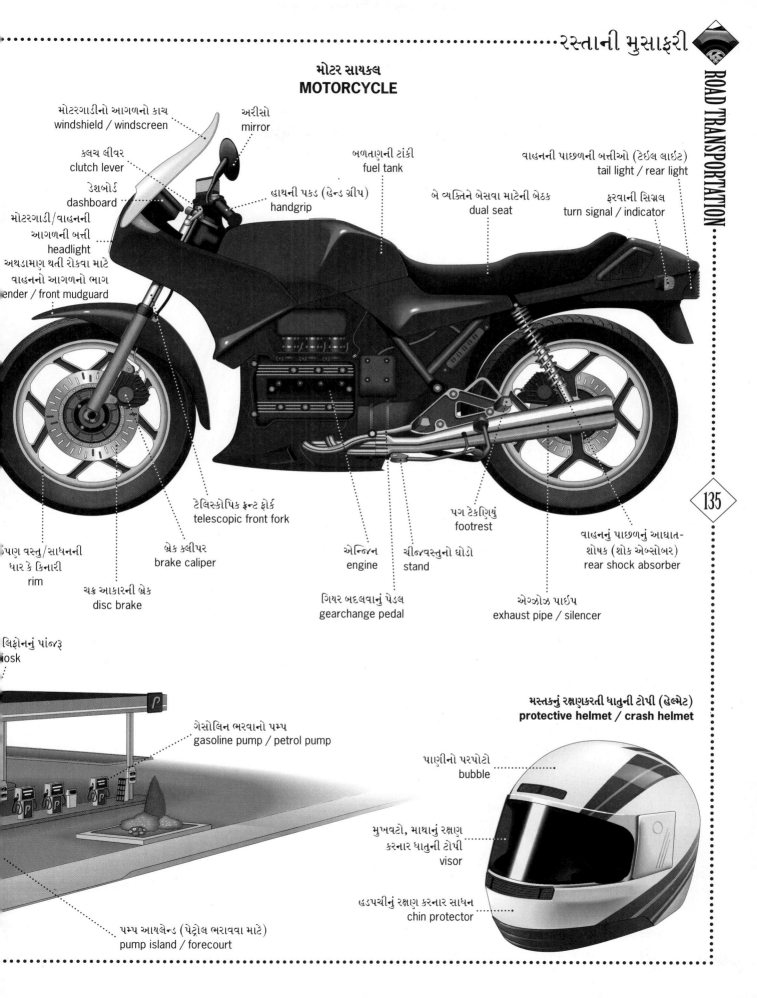

મોટરગાડીનો આગળનો કાચ
windshield / windscreen

અરીસો
mirror

બળતણની ટાંકી
fuel tank

વાહનની પાછળની બત્તીઓ (ટેઈલ લાઈટ)
tail light / rear light

ક્લચ લીવર
clutch lever

બે વ્યક્તિને બેસવા માટેની બેઠક
dual seat

ફરવાની સિગ્નલ
turn signal / indicator

ડેશબોર્ડ
dashboard

હાથની પકડ (હેન્ડ ગ્રીપ)
handgrip

મોટરગાડી/વાહનની
આગળની બત્તી
headlight

અથડામણ થતી રોકવા માટે
વાહનનો આગળનો ભાગ
ender / front mudguard

ટેલિસ્કોપિક ફ્રન્ટ ફોર્ક
telescopic front fork

બ્રેક ક્લીપર
brake caliper

એન્જિન
engine

ચીજવસ્તુનો ઘોડો
stand

પગ ટેકણિયું
footrest

વાહનનું પાછળનું આઘાત-
શોષક (શોક એબ્સોબર)
rear shock absorber

ક્પણ વસ્તુ/સાધનની
ધાર કે કિનારી
rim

ચક્ર આકારની બ્રેક
disc brake

ગિયર બદલવાનું પેડલ
gearchange pedal

એગ્ઝોઝ પાઈપ
exhaust pipe / silencer

135

લિફોનનું પાંજરું
iosk

ગેસોલિન ભરવાનો પમ્પ
gasoline pump / petrol pump

મસ્તકનું રક્ષણકરતી ધાતુની ટોપી (હેલ્મેટ)
protective helmet / crash helmet

પાણીનો પરપોટો
bubble

મુખવટો, માથાનું રક્ષણ
કરનાર ધાતુની ટોપી
visor

હડપચીનું રક્ષણ કરનાર સાધન
chin protector

પમ્પ આયલેન્ડ (પેટ્રોલ ભરાવવા માટે)
pump island / forecourt

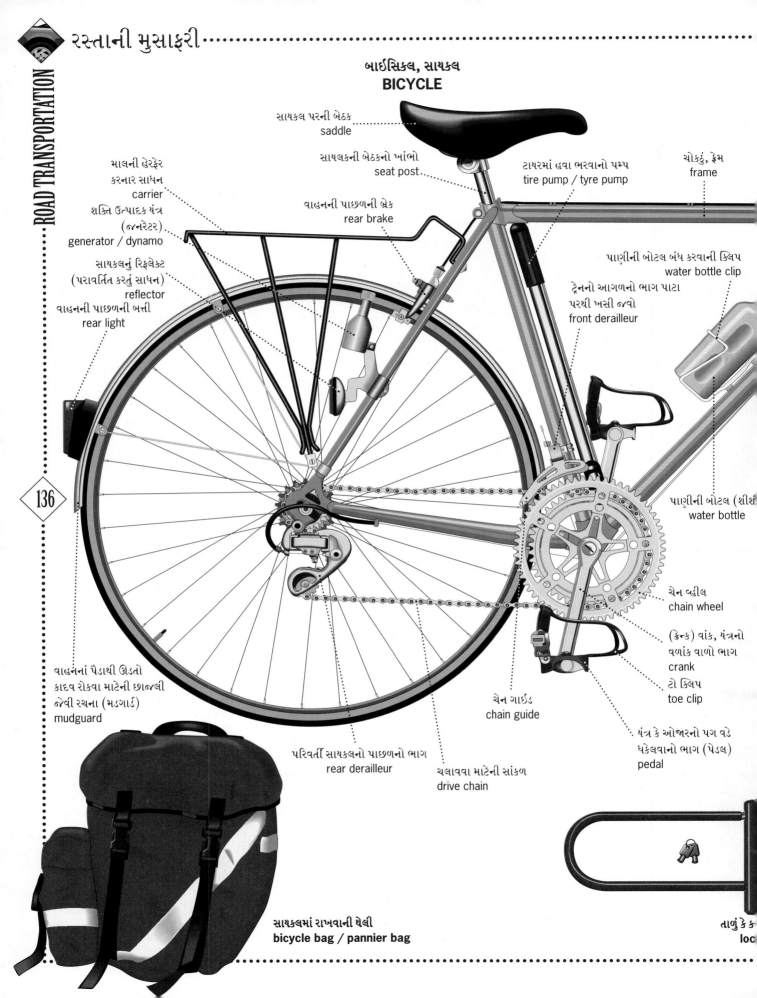

બાઇસિકલ, સાયકલ
BICYCLE

સાયકલ પરની બેઠક
saddle

સાયકલની બેઠકનો ખાંભો
seat post

વાહનની પાછળની બ્રેક
rear brake

માલની હેરફેર
કરનાર સાધન
carrier

શક્તિ ઉત્પાદક યંત્ર
(જનરેટર)
generator / dynamo

સાયકલનું રિફ્લેકટ
(પરાવર્તિત કરતું સાધન)
reflector

વાહનની પાછળની બત્તી
rear light

ટાયરમાં હવા ભરવાનો પમ્પ
tire pump / tyre pump

ચોકઠું, ફ્રેમ
frame

પાણીની બોટલ બંધ કરવાની ક્લિપ
water bottle clip

ટ્રેનનો આગળનો ભાગ પાટા
પરથી ખસી જવો
front derailleur

પાણીની બોટલ (શીશ
water bottle

ચેન વ્હીલ
chain wheel

(ક્રેન્ક) વાંક, યંત્રનો
વળાંક વાળો ભાગ
crank

ટો ક્લિપ
toe clip

યંત્ર કે ઓજારનો પગ વડે
ધકેલવાનો ભાગ (પેડલ)
pedal

ચેન ગાઇડ
chain guide

વાહનનાં પૈડાંથી ઊડતો
કાદવ રોકવા માટેની છાજલી
જેવી રચના (મડગાર્ડ)
mudguard

પરિવર્તી સાયકલનો પાછળનો ભાગ
rear derailleur

ચલાવવા માટેની સાંકળ
drive chain

સાયકલમાં રાખવાની થેલી
bicycle bag / pannier bag

તાળું કે ક

loc

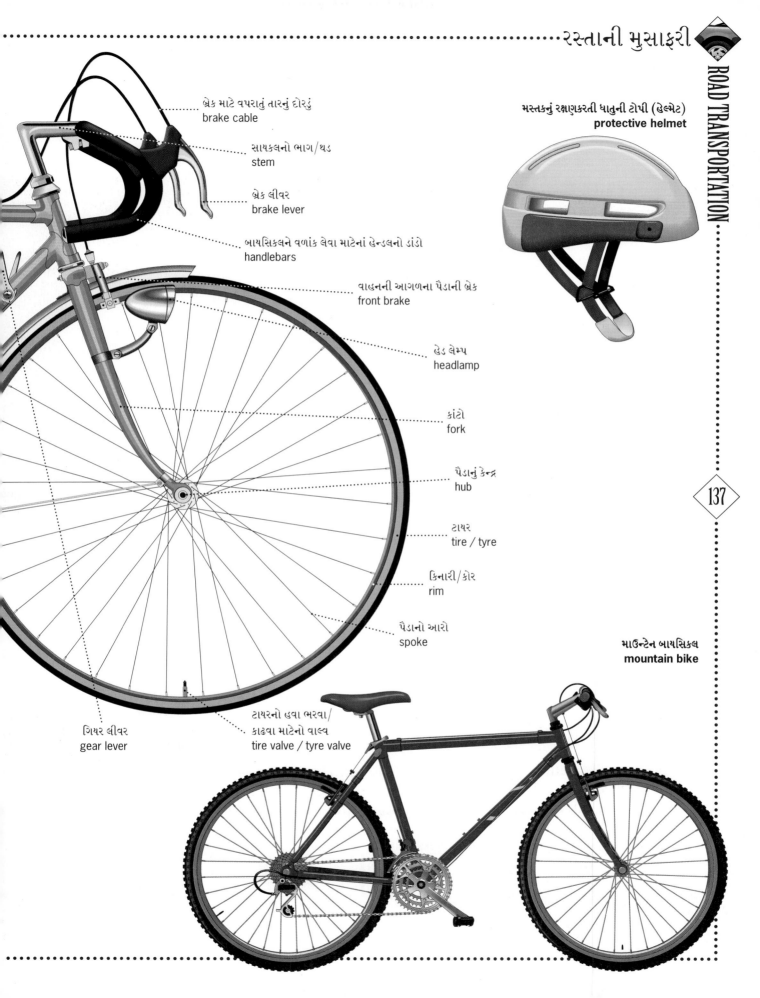

બ્રેક માટે વપરાતું તારનું દોરડું
brake cable

સાયકલનો ભાગ/થડ
stem

બ્રેક લીવર
brake lever

બાયસિકલને વળાંક લેવા માટેનાં હેન્ડલનો દાંડો
handlebars

વાહનની આગળના પૈડાની બ્રેક
front brake

હેડ લેમ્પ
headlamp

કાંટો
fork

પૈડાનું કેન્દ્ર
hub

ટાયર
tire / tyre

કિનારી/કોર
rim

પૈડાનો આરો
spoke

ગિયર લીવર
gear lever

ટાયરનો હવા ભરવા/
કાઢવા માટેનો વાલ્વ
tire valve / tyre valve

મસ્તકનું રક્ષણકરતી ધાતુની ટોપી (હેલ્મેટ)
protective helmet

માઉન્ટેન બાયસિકલ
mountain bike

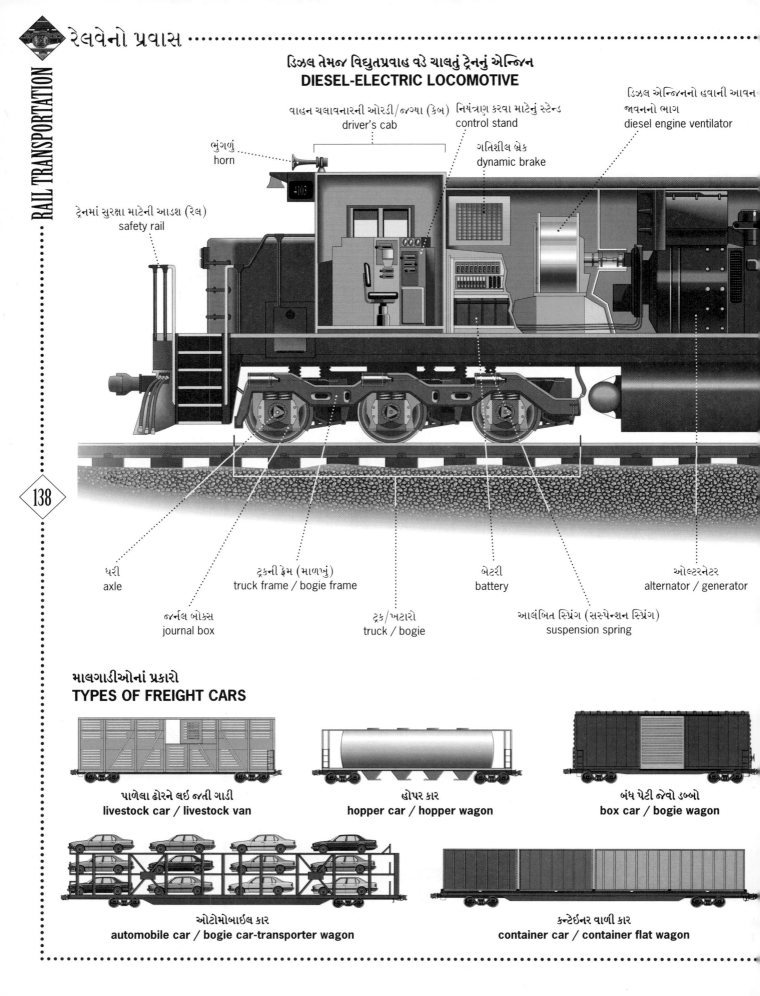

ડિઝલ તેમજ વિદ્યુતપ્રવાહ વડે ચાલતું ટ્રેનનું એન્જિન
DIESEL-ELECTRIC LOCOMOTIVE

વાહન ચલાવનારની ઓરડી/જગ્યા (કેબ)
driver's cab

નિયંત્રણ કરવા માટેનું સ્ટેન્ડ
control stand

ડિઝલ એન્જિનનો હવાની આવન
જવનનો ભાગ
diesel engine ventilator

ભુંગળું
horn

ગતિશીલ બ્રેક
dynamic brake

ટ્રેનમાં સુરક્ષા માટેની આડશ (રેલ)
safety rail

4103

ઘરી
axle

ટ્રકની ફ્રેમ (માળખું)
truck frame / bogie frame

બેટરી
battery

ઓલ્ટરનેટર
alternator / generator

જર્નલ બોક્સ
journal box

ટ્રક/ખટારો
truck / bogie

આલંબિત સ્પ્રિંગ (સસ્પેન્શન સ્પ્રિંગ)
suspension spring

માલગાડીઓનાં પ્રકારો
TYPES OF FREIGHT CARS

પાળેલા ઢોરને લઈ જતી ગાડી
livestock car / livestock van

હોપર કાર
hopper car / hopper wagon

બંધ પેટી જેવો ડબ્બો
box car / bogie wagon

ઓટોમોબાઇલ કાર
automobile car / bogie car-transporter wagon

કન્ટેઇનર વાળી કાર
container car / container flat wagon

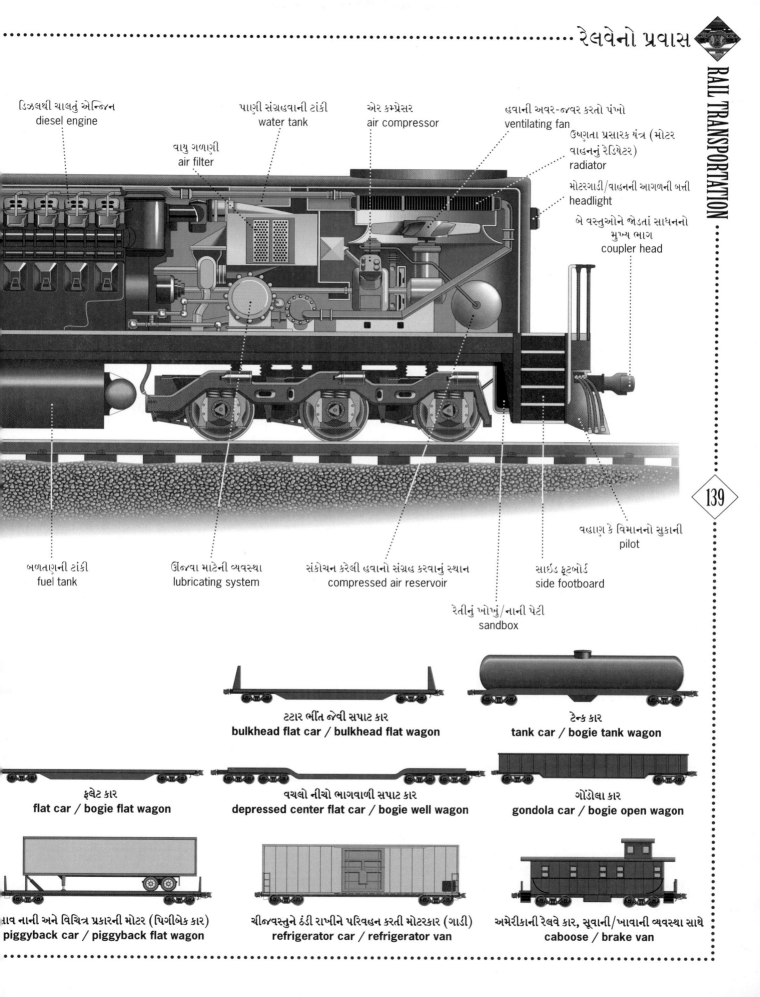

ડિઝલથી ચાલતું એન્જિન
diesel engine

પાણી સંગ્રહવાની ટાંકી
water tank

એર કમ્પ્રેસર
air compressor

હવાની અવર-જવર કરતો પંખો
ventilating fan

વાયુ ગળાણી
air filter

ઉષ્ણતા પ્રસારક યંત્ર (મોટર વાહનનું રેડિએટર)
radiator

મોટરગાડી/વાહનની આગળની બત્તી
headlight

બે વસ્તુઓને જોડતાં સાધનનો મુખ્ય ભાગ
coupler head

બળતણની ટાંકી
fuel tank

ઊંજવા માટેની વ્યવસ્થા
lubricating system

સંકોચન કરેલી હવાનો સંગ્રહ કરવાનું સ્થાન
compressed air reservoir

સાઇડ ફૂટબોર્ડ
side footboard

વહાણ કે વિમાનનો સુકાની
pilot

રેતીનું ખોખું/નાની પેટી
sandbox

139

ટટાર ભીંત જેવી સપાટ કાર
bulkhead flat car / bulkhead flat wagon

ટેન્ક કાર
tank car / bogie tank wagon

ફ્લેટ કાર
flat car / bogie flat wagon

વચલો નીચો ભાગવાળી સપાટ કાર
depressed center flat car / bogie well wagon

ગોંડોલા કાર
gondola car / bogie open wagon

...ાવ નાની અને વિચિત્ર પ્રકારની મોટર (પિગીબેક કાર)
piggyback car / piggyback flat wagon

ચીજવસ્તુને ઠંડી રાખીને પરિવહન કરતી મોટરકાર (ગાડી)
refrigerator car / refrigerator van

અમેરીકાની રેલવે કાર, સૂવાની/ખાવાની વ્યવસ્થા સાથે
caboose / brake van

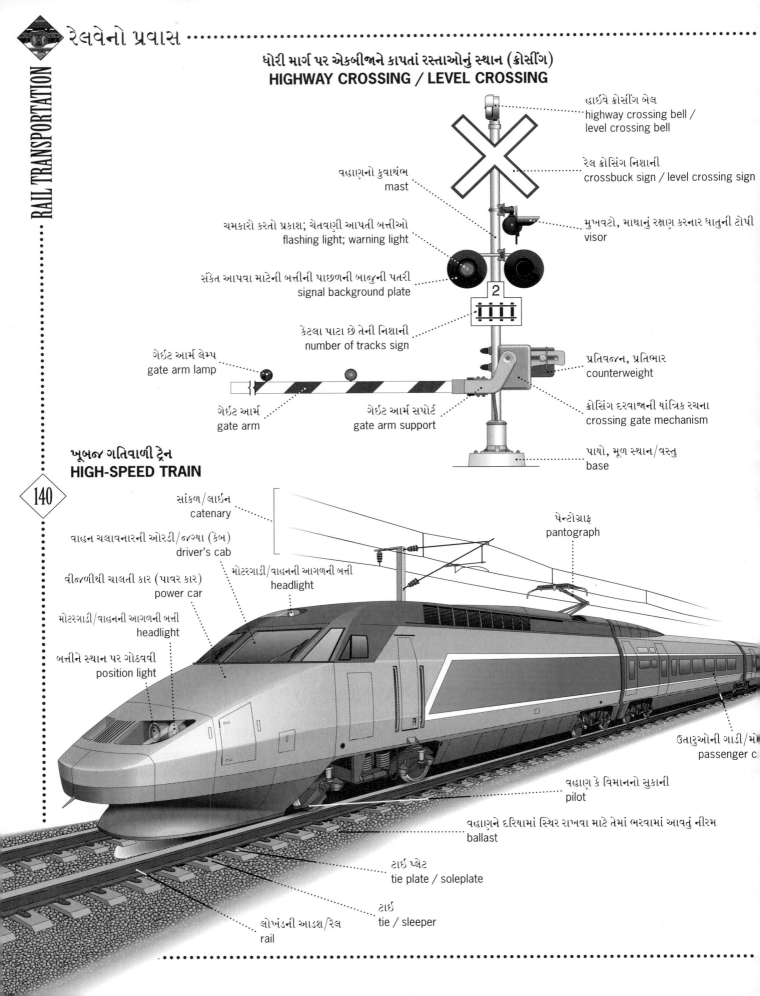

ધોરી માર્ગ પર એકબીજાને કાપતાં રસ્તાઓનું સ્થાન (ક્રોસીંગ)
HIGHWAY CROSSING / LEVEL CROSSING

હાઈવે ક્રોસીંગ બેલ
highway crossing bell /
level crossing bell

રેલ ક્રોસિંગ નિશાની
crossbuck sign / level crossing sign

વહાણનો કુવાથંભ
mast

મુખવટો, માથાનું રક્ષણ કરનાર ધાતુની ટોપી
visor

ચમકારો કરતો પ્રકાશ; ચેતવાણી આપતી બત્તીઓ
flashing light; warning light

સંકેત આપવા માટેની બત્તીની પાછળની બાજુની પતરી
signal background plate

કેટલા પાટા છે તેની નિશાની
number of tracks sign

પ્રતિવજન, પ્રતિભાર
counterweight

ગેઇટ આર્મ લેમ્પ
gate arm lamp

ક્રોસિંગ દરવાજાની યાંત્રિક રચના
crossing gate mechanism

ગેઇટ આર્મ
gate arm

ગેઇટ આર્મ સપોર્ટ
gate arm support

પાયો, મૂળ સ્થાન/વસ્તુ
base

ખૂબજ ગતિવાળી ટ્રેન
HIGH-SPEED TRAIN

140

સાંકળ/લાઈન
catenary

પેન્ટોગ્રાફ
pantograph

વાહન ચલાવનારની ઓરડી/જગ્યા (કેબ)
driver's cab

મોટરગાડી/વાહનની આગળની બત્તી
headlight

વીજળીથી ચાલતી કાર (પાવર કાર)
power car

મોટરગાડી/વાહનની આગળની બત્તી
headlight

બત્તીને સ્થાન પર ગોઠવવી
position light

ઉતારુઓની ગાડી/મે
passenger c

વહાણ કે વિમાનનો સુકાની
pilot

વહાણને દરિયામાં સ્થિર રાખવા માટે તેમાં ભરવામાં આવતું નીરમ
ballast

ટાઈ પ્લેટ
tie plate / soleplate

ટાઈ
tie / sleeper

લોખંડની આડશ/રેલ
rail

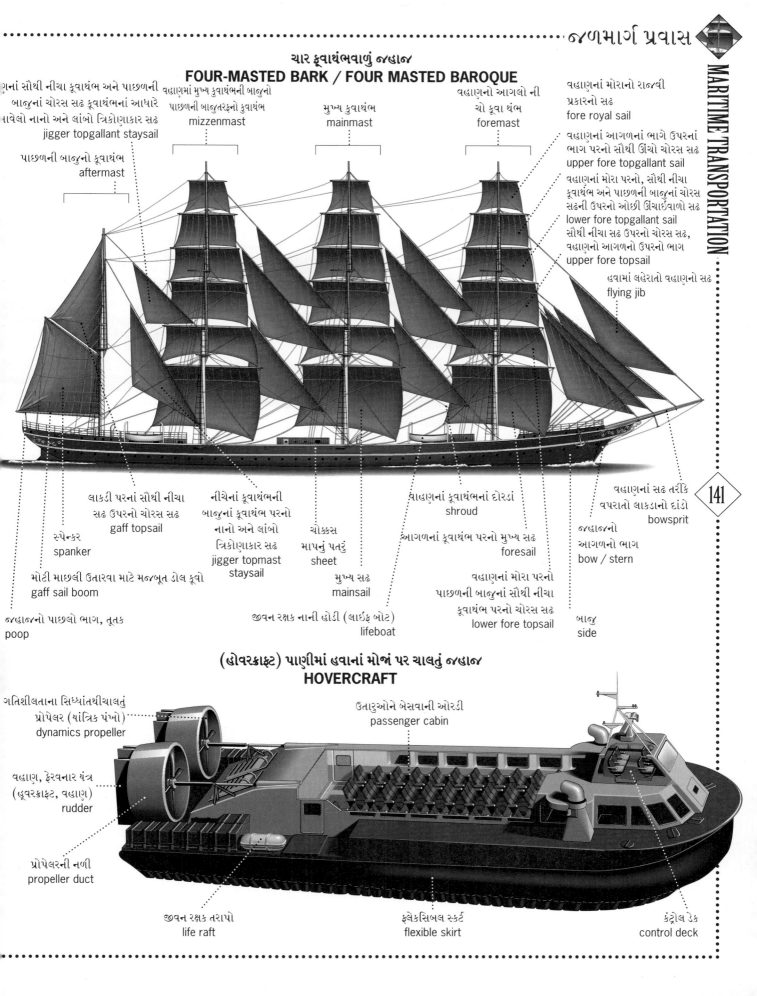

ચાર ફૂવાથંભવાળું જહાજ
FOUR-MASTED BARK / FOUR MASTED BAROQUE

ગુનાં સૌથી નીચા ફૂવાથંભ અને પાછળની
બાજુનાં ચોરસ સઢ ફૂવાથંભનાં આધારે
રાવેલો નાનો અને લાંબો ત્રિકોણાકાર સઢ
jigger topgallant staysail

વહાણમાં મુખ્ય કુવાથંભની બાજુનો
પાછળની બાજુતરફનો કુવાથંભ
mizzenmast

મુખ્ય કુવાથંભ
mainmast

વહાણનો આગલો ની
ચો કુવા થંભ
foremast

વહાણનાં મોરાનો રાજવી
પ્રકારનો સઢ
fore royal sail

પાછળની બાજુનો ફૂવાથંભ
aftermast

વહાણનાં આગળનાં ભાગે ઉપરનાં
ભાગ પરનો સૌથી ઊંચો ચોરસ સઢ
upper fore topgallant sail

વહાણનાં મોરા પરનો, સૌથી નીચા
ફૂવાથંભ અને પાછળની બાજુનાં ચોરસ
સઢની ઉપરનો ઓછી ઊંચાઈવાળો સઢ
lower fore topgallant sail

સૌથી નીચા સઢ ઉપરનો ચોરસ સઢ,
વહાણનો આગળનો ઉપરનો ભાગ
upper fore topsail

હવામાં લહેરાતો વહાણનો સઢ
flying jib

લાકડી પરનાં સૌથી નીચા
સઢ ઉપરનો ચોરસ સઢ
gaff topsail

નીચેનાં કુવાથંભની
બાજુનાં કુવાથંભ પરનો
નાનો અને લાંબો
ત્રિકોણાકાર સઢ
jigger topmast
staysail

ચોક્કસ
માપનું પતરું
sheet

મુખ્ય સઢ
mainsail

વહાણનાં કુવાથંભનાં દોરડાં
shroud

આગળનાં કુવાથંભ પરનો મુખ્ય સઢ
foresail

વહાણનાં સઢ તરીકે
વપરાતો લાકડાનો દાંડો
bowsprit

૧૪૧

141

સ્પેન્કર
spanker

મોટી માછલી ઉતારવા માટે મજબૂત ડોલ કૂવો
gaff sail boom

જહાજનો પાછલો ભાગ, તૂતક
poop

જીવન રક્ષક નાની હોડી (લાઈફ બોટ)
lifeboat

વહાણનાં મોરા પરનો
પાછળની બાજુનાં સૌથી નીચા
ફૂવાથંભ પરનો ચોરસ સઢ
lower fore topsail

જહાજનો
આગળનો ભાગ
bow / stern

બાજુ
side

(હોવરક્રાફ્ટ) પાણીમાં હવાનાં મોજાં પર ચાલતું જહાજ
HOVERCRAFT

ગતિશીલતાના સિધ્ધાંતથીચાલતું
પ્રોપેલર (યાંત્રિક પંખો)
dynamics propeller

ઉતારુઓને બેસવાની ઓરડી
passenger cabin

વહાણ, ફેરવનાર યંત્ર
(હૂવરક્રાફ્ટ, વહાણ)
rudder

પ્રોપેલરની નળી
propeller duct

જીવન રક્ષક તરાપો
life raft

ફ્લેકસિબલ સ્કર્ટ
flexible skirt

કંટ્રોલ ડેક
control deck

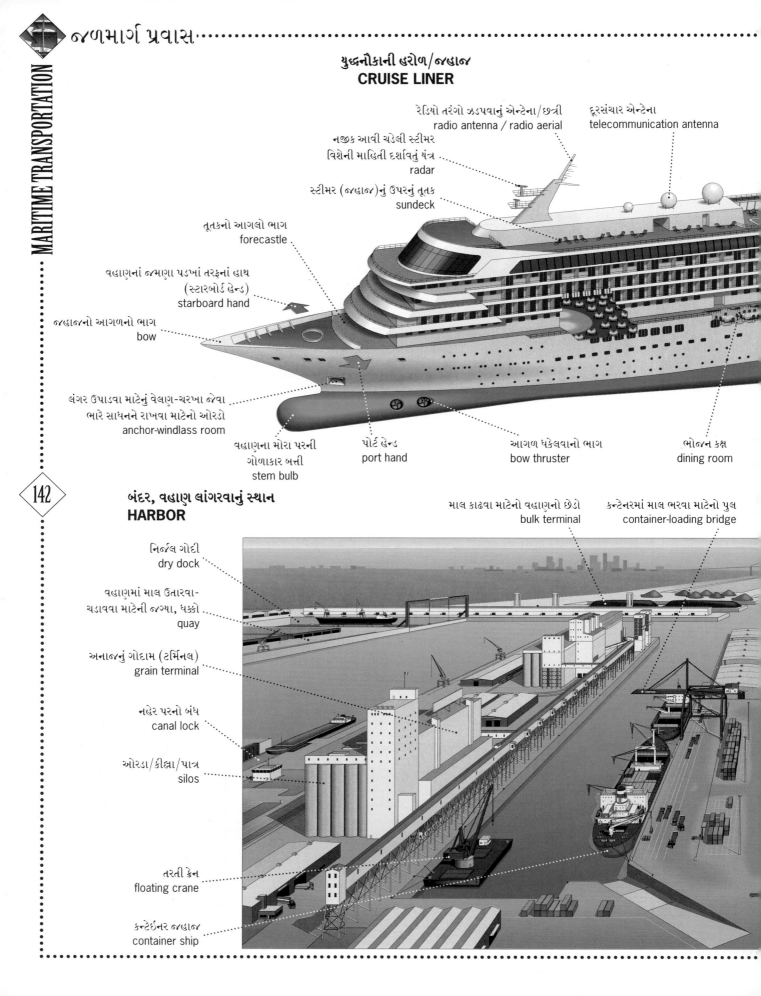

યુદ્ધનૌકાની હરોળ/જહાજ
CRUISE LINER

રેડિયો તરંગો ઝડપવાનું એન્ટેના/છત્રી
radio antenna / radio aerial

દૂરસંચાર એન્ટેના
telecommunication antenna

નજીક આવી ચઢેલી સ્ટીમર
વિશેની માહિતી દર્શાવતું યંત્ર
radar

સ્ટીમર (જહાજ)નું ઉપરનું તૂતક
sundeck

તૂતકનો આગલો ભાગ
forecastle

વહાણનાં જમાણા પડખાં તરફનાં હાથ
(સ્ટારબોર્ડ હેન્ડ)
starboard hand

જહાજનો આગળનો ભાગ
bow

લંગર ઉપાડવા માટેનું વેલણ-ચરખા જેવા
ભારે સાધનને રાખવા માટેનો ઓરડો
anchor-windlass room

વહાણના મોરા પરની
ગોળાકાર બત્તી
stem bulb

પોર્ટ હેન્ડ
port hand

આગળ ધકેલવાનો ભાગ
bow thruster

ભોજન કક્ષ
dining room

બંદર, વહાણ લાંગરવાનું સ્થાન
HARBOR

માલ કાઢવા માટેનો વહાણનો છેડો
bulk terminal

કન્ટેનરમાં માલ ભરવા માટેનો પુલ
container-loading bridge

નિર્જલ ગોદી
dry dock

વહાણમાં માલ ઉતારવા-
ચઢાવવા માટેની જગ્યા, ધક્કો
quay

અનાજનું ગોદામ (ટર્મિનલ)
grain terminal

નહેર પરનો બંધ
canal lock

ઓરડા/કીલ્લા/પાત્ર
silos

તરતી ક્રેન
floating crane

કન્ટેઈનર જહાજ
container ship

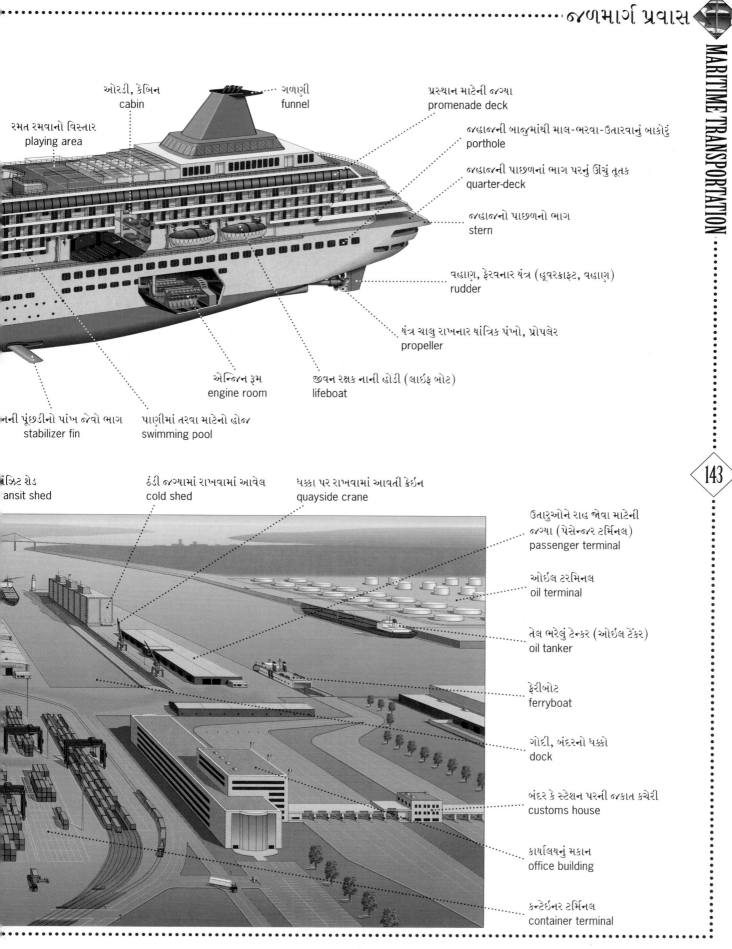

ઓરડી, કેબિન
cabin

ગળણી
funnel

રમત રમવાનો વિસ્તાર
playing area

પ્રસ્થાન માટેની જગ્યા
promenade deck

જહાજની બાજુમાંથી માલ-ભરવા-ઉતારવાનું બાકોરું
porthole

જહાજની પાછળનાં ભાગ પરનું ઊંચું તૂતક
quarter-deck

જહાજનો પાછલનો ભાગ
stern

વહાણ, ફેરવનાર યંત્ર (હૂવરક્રાફ્ટ, વહાણ)
rudder

યંત્ર ચાલુ રાખનાર યાંત્રિક પંખો, પ્રોપલેર
propeller

એન્જિન રૂમ
engine room

જીવન રક્ષક નાની હોડી (લાઈફ બોટ)
lifeboat

નની પૂંછડીનો પાંખ જેવો ભાગ
stabilizer fin

પાણીમાં તરવા માટેનો હોજ
swimming pool

ઝિટ શેડ
ansit shed

ઠંડી જગ્યામાં રાખવામાં આવેલ
cold shed

ધક્કા પર રાખવામાં આવતી ક્રેઈન
quayside crane

ઉતારુઓને રાહ જોવા માટેની જગ્યા (પેસેન્જર ટર્મિનલ)
passenger terminal

ઓઈલ ટરમિનલ
oil terminal

તેલ ભરેલું ટેન્કર (ઓઈલ ટેંકર)
oil tanker

ફેરીબોટ
ferryboat

ગોદી, બંદરનો ધક્કો
dock

બંદર કે સ્ટેશન પરની જકાત કચેરી
customs house

કાર્યાલયનું મકાન
office building

કન્ટેઈનર ટર્મિનલ
container terminal

વિમાન
PLANE

પાંખનાં આકારો અને પ્રકારો
TYPES OF WING SHAPES

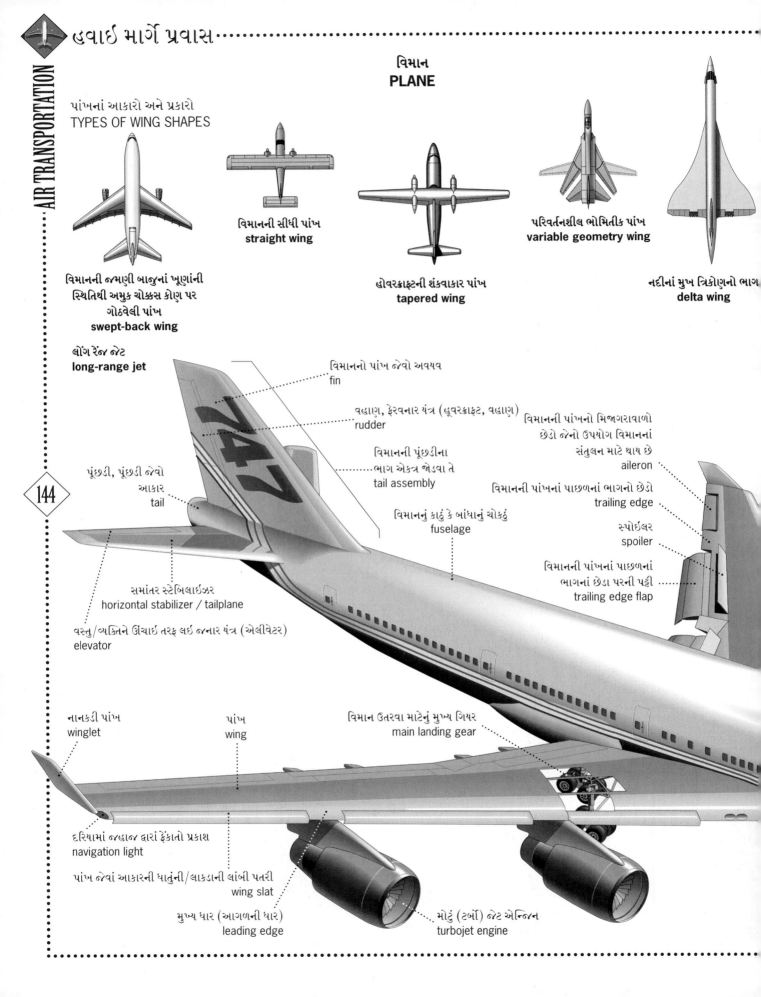

વિમાનની સીધી પાંખ
straight wing

પરિવર્તનશીલ ભૌમિતીક પાંખ
variable geometry wing

વિમાનની જમણી બાજુનાં ખૂણાંની
સ્થિતિથી અમુક ચોક્કસ કોણ પર
ગોઠવેલી પાંખ
swept-back wing

હોવરક્રાફ્ટની શંકવાકાર પાંખ
tapered wing

નદીનાં મુખ ત્રિકોણનો ભાગ
delta wing

લોંગ રેંજ જેટ
long-range jet

વિમાનનો પાંખ જેવો અવયવ
fin

વહાણ, ફેરવનાર યંત્ર (હૂવરક્રાફ્ટ, વહાણ)
rudder

વિમાનની પૂંછડીના
ભાગ એકત્ર જોડવા તે
tail assembly

વિમાનની પાંખનો મિજગરાવાળો
છેડો જેનો ઉપયોગ વિમાનનાં
સંતુલન માટે થાય છે
aileron

વિમાનની પાંખનાં પાછળનાં ભાગનો છેડો
trailing edge

પૂંછડી, પૂંછડી જેવો
આકાર
tail

વિમાનનું કાઠું કે બાંધાનું ચોકઠું
fuselage

સ્પોઈલર
spoiler

વિમાનની પાંખનાં પાછળનાં
ભાગનાં છેડા પરની પટ્ટી
trailing edge flap

સમાંતર સ્ટેબિલાઈઝર
horizontal stabilizer / tailplane

વસ્તુ/વ્યક્તિને ઊંચાઈ તરફ લઈ જનાર યંત્ર (એલીવેટર)
elevator

નાનકડી પાંખ
winglet

પાંખ
wing

વિમાન ઉતરવા માટેનું મુખ્ય ગિયર
main landing gear

દરિયામાં જહાજ દ્વારા ફેંકાતો પ્રકાશ
navigation light

પાંખ જેવાં આકારની ધાતુની/લાકડાની લાંબી પતરી
wing slat

મુખ્ય ધાર (આગળની ધાર)
leading edge

મોટું (ટર્બો) જેટ એન્જિન
turbojet engine

હેલિકોપ્ટર
HELICOPTER

રોટર બ્લેડ (ધાર)
rotor blade

રોટરની ધરી
rotor hub

હેલિકોપ્ટરનો કુવાથંભ
mast

પાછળનું ગોળ ફરતું રોટર
anti-torque tail rotor

હેલિકોપ્ટરનો
પાંખ જેવો અવયવ
fin

સમાંતર સ્ટેબિલાઈઝર
horizontal stabilizer / tailplane

હેલીકોપ્ટરનાં પાછળનાં
ભાગનાં થાંભલાનો
છેડાનો ભાગ
tail boom

રોટર હેડ
rotor head

વિમાન નિયંત્રણ માટેની
પાયલટની કેબીન
cockpit

બત્તી સ્થાન પર ગોઠવવી
position light

કોઈ વસ્તુને લપસતાં અટકાવવા
માટેનાં અટકાણનો પાછલો ભાગ
tail skid

એગ્ઝોઝ પાઈપ
exhaust pipe

માલ-સામાન રાખવાનો વિભાગ
baggage compartment / luggage compartment

હવાનો પ્રવેશ માર્ગ
air inlet

એન્ટેના
antenna / aerial

નિયંત્રણ માટેની લાકડી
control stick

ઉતરાણ માટેની બારી
landing window

હેલિકોપ્ટરનાં પૈડાને
અટકાવતું અટકાણ
skid

બળતણની ટાંકી
fuel tank

ઉતારુઓને બેસવાની ઓરડી
passenger cabin

ચઢવા માટેનું પગથિયું
boarding step

વિમાનનાં ઉતરાણ માટેની
નિર્દેશક બત્તીઓ
landing light

145

પૂંછડી ના આકારો અને તેનાં પ્રકારો
TYPES OF TAIL SHAPES

વિમાનનાં માળખાં પર મઢેલું ઊંચું એકમ
fuselage mounted tail unit

પાંખ જેવું મઢેલું ઊંચું એકમ (યુનિટ)
fin-mounted tail unit

ટી આકારનું એકમ/યુનિટ
T-tail unit

હેલિકોપ્ટરનું સાવ નાનું ત્રિગુણિત એકમ
triple tail unit

એન્ટેના
antenna / aerial

વિમાનનાં ઉડ્ડયન અને ઉતરાણ
માટે ઉપયોગમાં આવતું ડેક
flight deck

નાક
nose

હવામાન વિશેની જાણકારી
આપતું રડાર
weather radar

window

ર...નું
or

વિમાનની ચાંચ બાજુથી ઉતરાણ કરવાનું ગિયર
nose landing gear

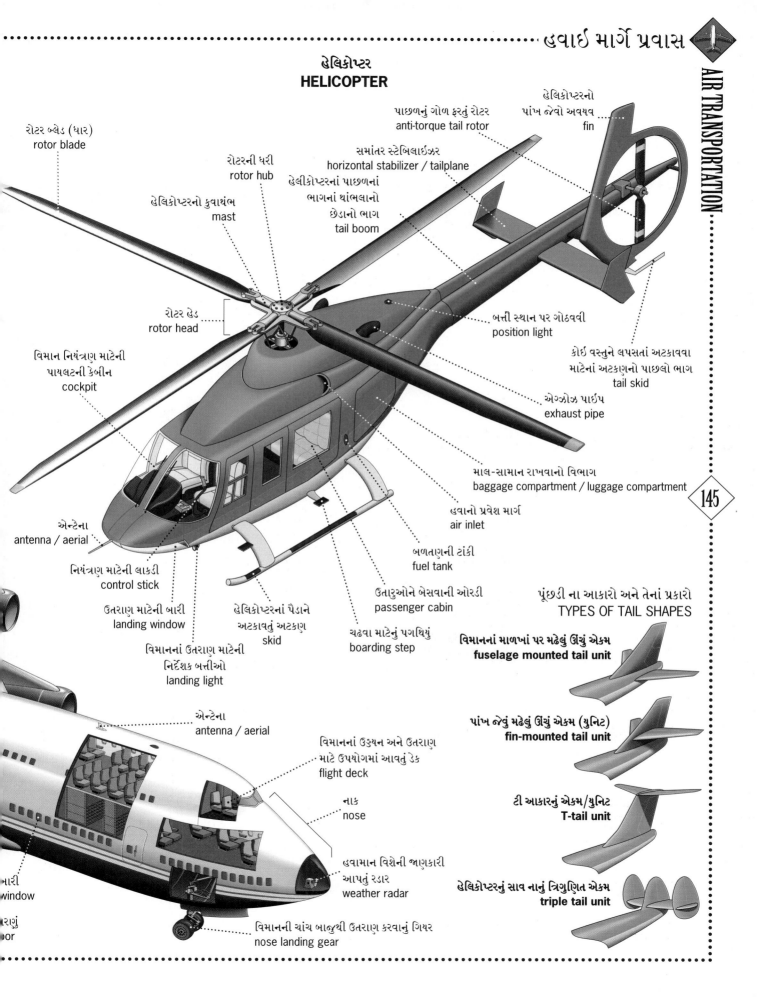

વિમાન મથક, વિમાન ઘર
AIRPORT

નિયંત્રણ માટેનો મિનારો (કંટ્રોલ ટાવર)
control tower

કંટ્રોલ ટાવર કેબ
control tower cab

પ્રવેશ માર્ગ/આવવા-જવાનો રસ
access road

વધુ ગતિએ વાહન બહાર કાઢવા માટેનો માર્ગ
high-speed exit runway

બાય પાસ હવાઈ પટ્ટી
by-pass runway

કઠણ સપાટી જગ્યા
apron

કઠણ સપાટી જગ્યા
apron

વિમાનની અવરજવર માટેનો રસ્તો (સર્વિસ રોડ)
service road

હવાઈ પટ્ટી
runway

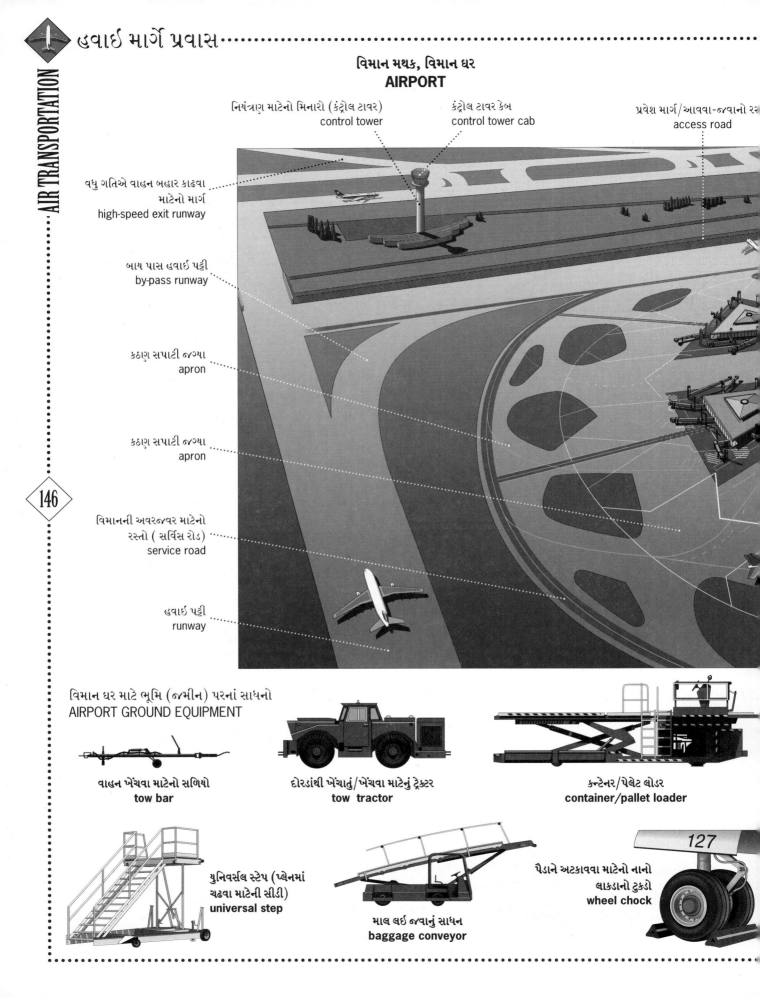

વિમાન ઘર માટે ભૂમિ (જમીન) પરનાં સાધનો
AIRPORT GROUND EQUIPMENT

વાહન ખેંચવા માટેનો સળિયો
tow bar

દોરડાંથી ખેંચાતું/ખેંચવા માટેનું ટ્રેક્ટર
tow tractor

કન્ટેનર/પેલેટ લોડર
container/pallet loader

યુનિવર્સલ સ્ટેપ (પ્લેનમાં ચઢવા માટેની સીડી)
universal step

માલ લઈ જવાનું સાધન
baggage conveyor

પૈડાને અટકાવવા માટેનો નાનો લાકડાનો ટુકડો
wheel chock

127

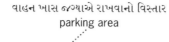

વિમાનની જળવાણી માટેનું સ્થાન (હેન્ગર)
maintenance hangar

વાહન ખાસ જગ્યાએ રાખવાનો વિસ્તાર
parking area

ઉતારુઓને રાહ જોવા માટેની જગ્યા (પેસેન્જર ટર્મિનલ)
passenger terminal

વાહનમાં ઉપર ચઢવા માટેનો ચાલવાનો રસ્તો
boarding walkway

યાત્રીઓને સ્ટીમરમાં અર્ધવર્તુળાકાર ચઢાવવાનો વિસ્તાર
radial passenger loading area

ટેલિસ્કોપિક કોરિડોર
telescopic corridor

સર્વિસ એરીયા
service area

હવાઇ પટ્ટી નિર્દેશીત કરતી રેખા
runway line

માલ સામાનની હેરફેર કરનાર નાનું ટ્રેલર (વાહન)
baggage trailer

દોરડાંથી ખેંચાતું/ખેંચવા માટેનું ટ્રેક્ટર
tow tractor

189 189

ખાન-પાનની વસ્તુઓ પહોંચાડનાર વાહન
catering vehicle

ઉતારુઓને એક જગ્યાએથી બીજી જગ્યાએ લઇ જતી ગાડી/વાહન
passenger transfer vehicle

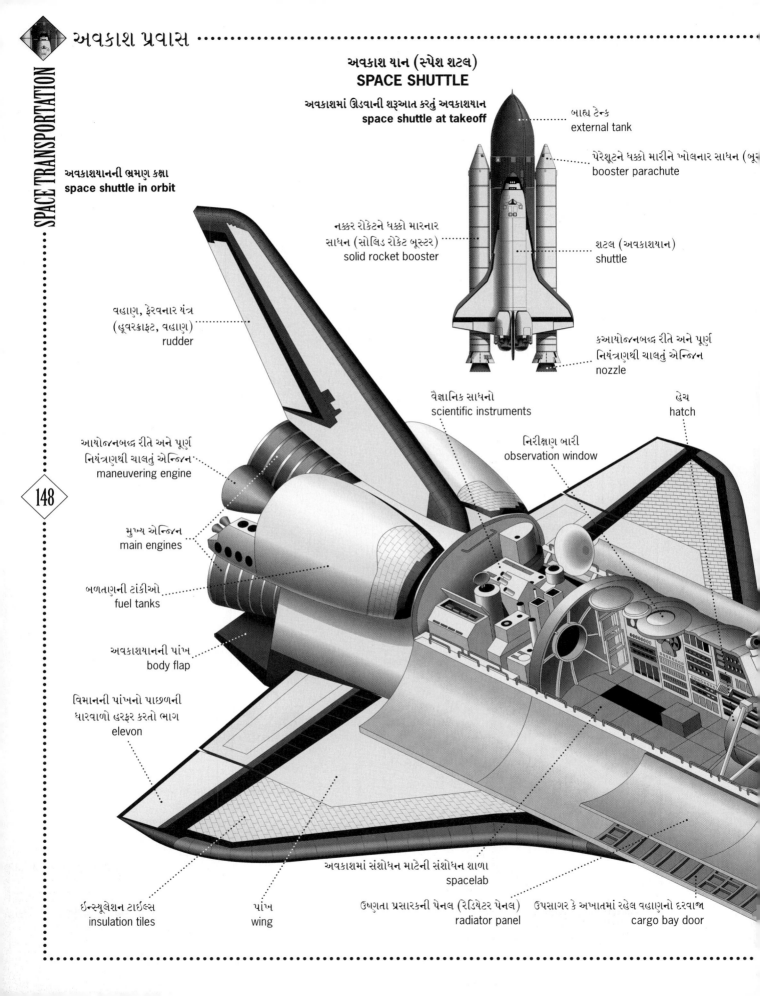

અવકાશ યાન (સ્પેશ શટલ)
SPACE SHUTTLE

અવકાશમાં ઊડવાની શરૂઆત કરતું અવકાશયાન
space shuttle at takeoff

બાહ્ય ટેન્ક
external tank

પેરેશૂટને ધક્કો મારીને ખોલનાર સાધન (બૂ
booster parachute

અવકાશયાનની ભ્રમણ કક્ષા
space shuttle in orbit

નક્કર રોકેટને ધક્કો મારનાર
સાધન (સોલિડ રોકેટ બૂસ્ટર)
solid rocket booster

શટલ (અવકાશયાન)
shuttle

વહાણ, ફેરવનાર યંત્ર
(હ્યુવરક્રાફ્ટ, વહાણ)
rudder

કઆયોજનબદ્ધ રીતે અને પૂર્ણ
નિયંત્રાણથી ચાલતું એન્જિન
nozzle

વૈજ્ઞાનિક સાધનો
scientific instruments

હેચ
hatch

નિરીક્ષાણ બારી
observation window

આયોજનબદ્ધ રીતે અને પૂર્ણ
નિયંત્રાણથી ચાલતું એન્જિન
maneuvering engine

મુખ્ય એન્જિન
main engines

બળતાણની ટાંકીઓ
fuel tanks

અવકાશયાનની પાંખ
body flap

વિમાનની પાંખનો પાછળની
ધારવાળો હરફર કરતો ભાગ
elevon

ઇન્સ્યુલેશન ટાઇલ્સ
insulation tiles

પાંખ
wing

અવકાશમાં સંશોધન માટેની સંશોધન શાળા
spacelab

ઉષ્ણતા પ્રસારકની પેનલ (રેડિયેટર પેનલ)
radiator panel

ઉપસાગર કે અભાતમાં રહેલ વહાણનો દરવાજ
cargo bay door

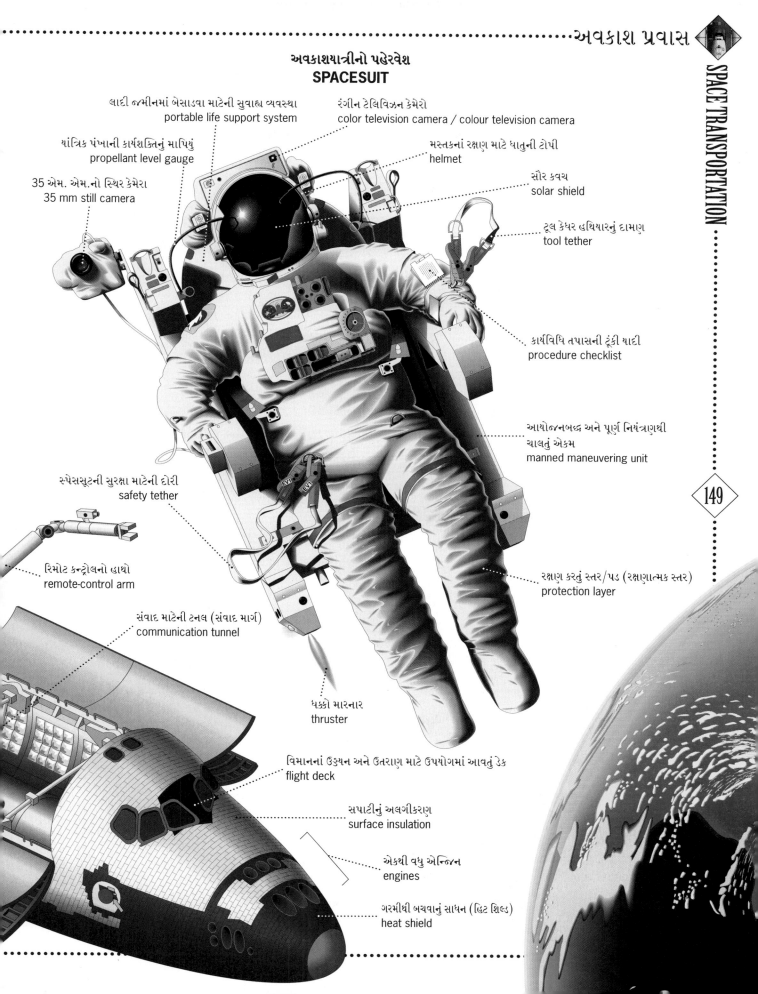

અવકાશયાત્રીનો પહેરવેશ
SPACESUIT

લાદી જમીનમાં બેસાડવા માટેની સુવાહ્ય વ્યવસ્થા
portable life support system

યાંત્રિક પંખાની કાર્યશક્તિનું માપિયું
propellant level gauge

35 એમ. એમ.નો સ્થિર કેમેરા
35 mm still camera

રંગીન ટેલિવિઝન કેમેરો
color television camera / colour television camera

મસ્તકનાં રક્ષાણ માટે ધાતુની ટોપી
helmet

સૌર કવચ
solar shield

ટૂલ કેધર હથિયારનું દામાણ
tool tether

કાર્યવિધિ તપાસની ટૂંકી યાદી
procedure checklist

આયોજનબદ્ધ અને પૂર્ણ નિયંત્રાણથી ચાલતું એકમ
manned maneuvering unit

સ્પેસસૂટની સુરક્ષા માટેની દોરી
safety tether

રિમોટ કન્ટ્રોલનો હાથો
remote-control arm

સંવાદ માટેની ટનલ (સંવાદ માર્ગ)
communication tunnel

રક્ષાણ કરતું સ્તર/પડ (રક્ષાણાત્મક સ્તર)
protection layer

ધક્કો મારનાર
thruster

વિમાનનાં ઉડ્ડયન અને ઉતરાણ માટે ઉપયોગમાં આવતું ડેક
flight deck

સપાટીનું અલગીકરણ
surface insulation

એકથી વધુ એન્જિન
engines

ગરમીથી બચવાનું સાધન (હિટ શિલ્ડ)
heat shield

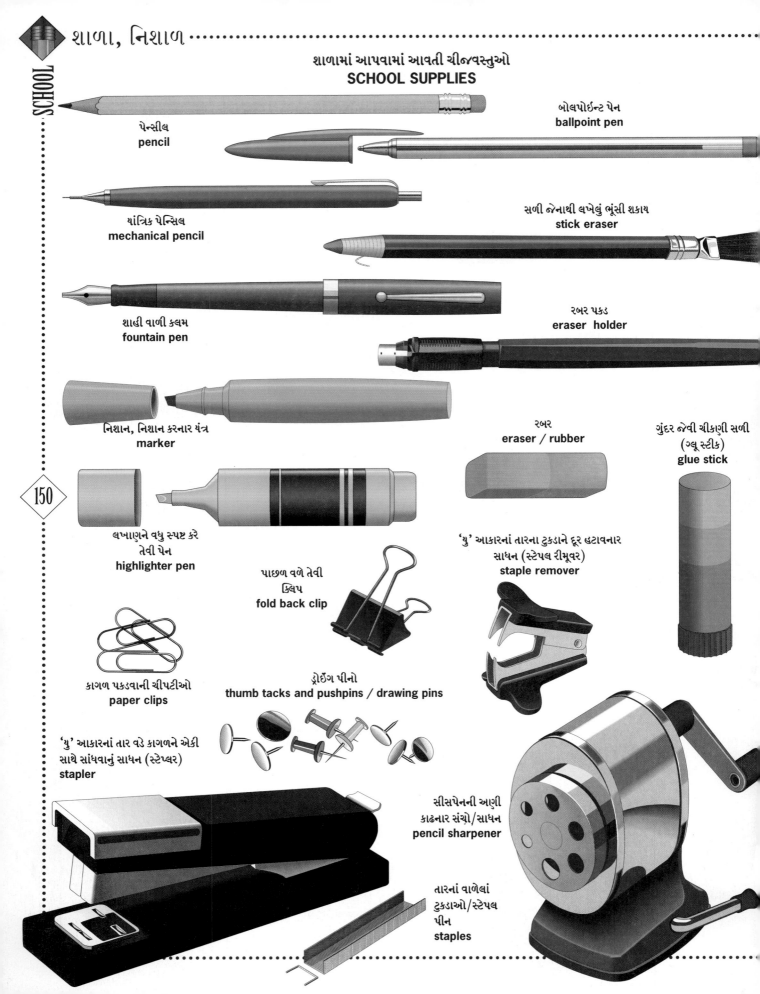

શાળામાં આપવામાં આવતી ચીજવસ્તુઓ
SCHOOL SUPPLIES

પેન્સીલ
pencil

બોલપોઈન્ટ પેન
ballpoint pen

યાંત્રિક પેન્સિલ
mechanical pencil

સળી જેનાથી લખેલું ભૂંસી શકાય
stick eraser

શાહી વાળી કલમ
fountain pen

રબર પકડ
eraser holder

નિશાન, નિશાન કરનાર યંત્ર
marker

રબર
eraser / rubber

ગુંદર જેવી ચીકણી સળી
(ગ્લૂ સ્ટીક)
glue stick

150

લખાણને વધુ સ્પષ્ટ કરે
તેવી પેન
highlighter pen

'યુ' આકારનાં તારના ટુકડાને દૂર હટાવનાર
સાધન (સ્ટેપલ રીમૂવર)
staple remover

પાછળ વળે તેવી
ક્લિપ
fold back clip

ડ્રોઈંગ પીનો
thumb tacks and pushpins / drawing pins

કાગળ પકડવાની ચીપટીઓ
paper clips

'યુ' આકારનાં તાર વડે કાગળને એકી
સાથે સાંધવાનું સાધન (સ્ટેપ્લર)
stapler

સીસપેનની આણી
કાઢનાર સંચો/સાધન
pencil sharpener

તારનાં વાળેલાં
ટુકડાઓ/સ્ટેપલ
પીન
staples

આંકણી
ruler

કોણમાપક
protractor

કાગળ બાંધનાર
ring binder

સેટ સ્કેવર
set square

ટેપ ડિસ્પેન્સર
tape dispenser

પ્લાસ્ટિકનાં તારનાં
સર્પાકાર ગૂંચળાથી બાંધેલી
નોટબૂક
**spiral bound
notebook**

છૂટા પાના
loose-leaf paper

નોંધપોથી
notebook

નોંધપોથી રાખવાનું પેડ/પાટીયું
notepad

નાની બેગ/પેટી
briefcase

છળ બાંધવાની/પેટી
ckpack / satchel

શાળાનાં સાધનો
SCHOOL EQUIPMENT

કાળું પાટીયું
blackboard

ઓવરહેડ પ્રોજેક્ટર
overhead projector

અરીસો
mirror

પ્રોજેક્શન હેડ
projection head

દૃષ્ટિ સંબંધી
optical lens

દૃષ્ટિ સંબંધી બેઠક
optical stage

પૃથ્વીનો ગોળો
globe of Earth

યામ્યોત્તર રેખાનો પટ્ટો
meridian band

ગોળો
globe

પાયો, મૂળ સ્થાન/વસ્તુ
base

ચક્રાકાર ગતિ કરતાં યંત્રની ધ
axis of rotation

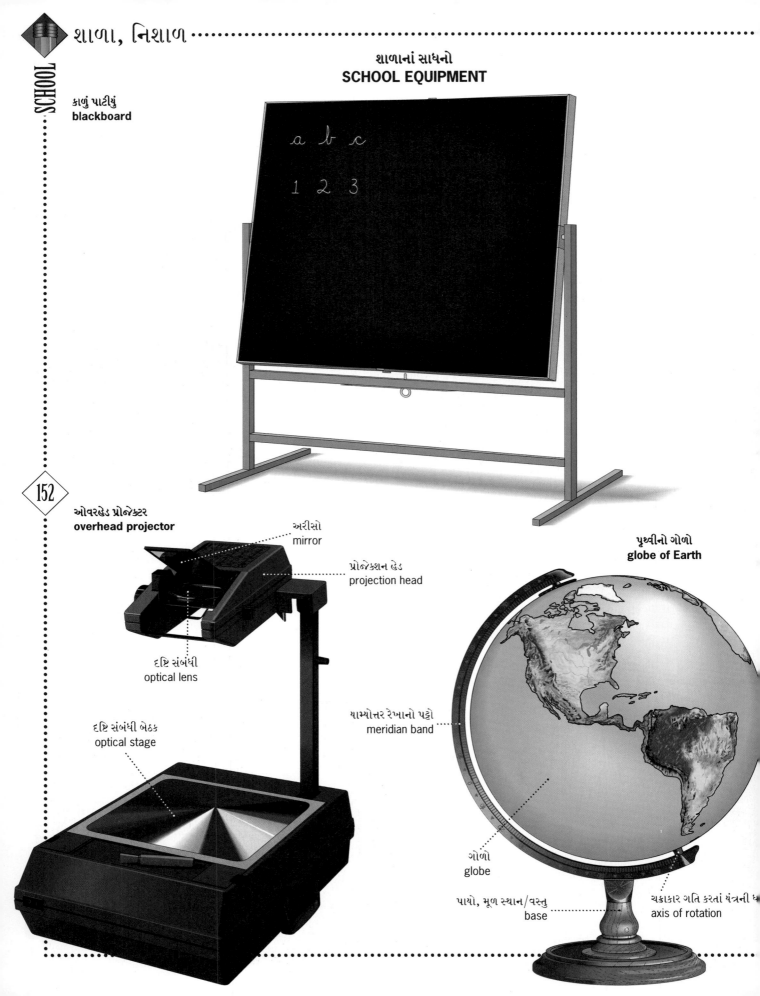

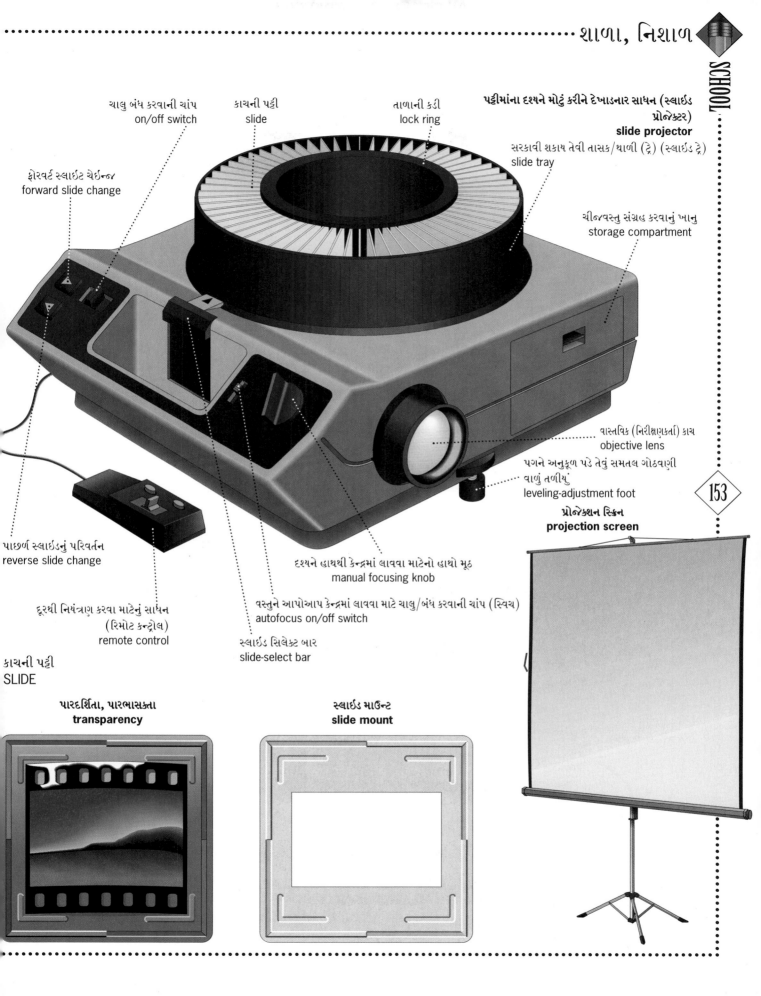

ચાલુ બંધ કરવાની ચાંપ
on/off switch

કાચની પટ્ટી
slide

તાળાની કડી
lock ring

પડ્ડીમાંના દશ્યને મોટું કરીને દેખાડનાર સાધન (સ્લાઇડ પ્રોજેક્ટર)
slide projector

ફોરવર્ડ સ્લાઇડ ચેઇન્જ
forward slide change

સરકાવી શકાય તેવી તાસક/થાળી (ટ્રે) (સ્લાઇડ ટ્રે)
slide tray

ચીજવસ્તુ સંગ્રહ કરવાનું ખાનુ
storage compartment

વાસ્તવિક (નિરીક્ષણકર્તા) કાચ
objective lens

પગને અનુકૂળ પડે તેવું સમતલ ગોઠવણી
વાળું તળીયું
leveling-adjustment foot

પાછળ સ્લાઇડનું પરિવર્તન
reverse slide change

દૂરથી નિયંત્રણ કરવા માટેનું સાધન
(રિમોટ કન્ટ્રોલ)
remote control

કાચની પટ્ટી
SLIDE

દશ્યને હાથથી કેન્દ્રમાં લાવવા માટેનો હાથો મૂઠ
manual focusing knob

વસ્તુને આપોઆપ કેન્દ્રમાં લાવવા માટે ચાલુ/બંધ કરવાની ચાંપ (સ્વિચ)
autofocus on/off switch

સ્લાઇડ સિલેક્ટ બાર
slide-select bar

પ્રોજેક્શન સ્ક્રિન
projection screen

પારદર્શિતા, પારભાસક્તા
transparency

સ્લાઇડ માઉન્ટ
slide mount

153

શાળાનાં સાધનો
SCHOOL EQUIPMENT

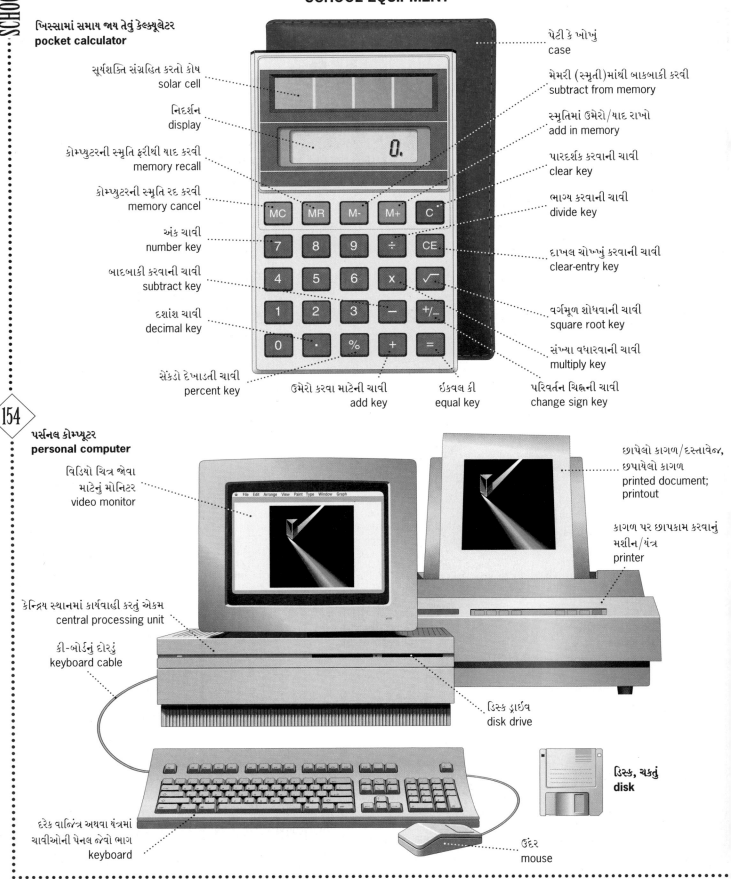

ખિસ્સામાં સમાય જાય તેવું કેલ્ક્યૂલેટર
pocket calculator

સૂર્યશક્તિ સંગ્રહિત કરતો કોષ
solar cell

નિદર્શન
display

કોમ્પ્યુટરની સ્મૃતિ ફરીથી યાદ કરવી
memory recall

કોમ્પ્યુટરની સ્મૃતિ રદ કરવી
memory cancel

અંક ચાવી
number key

બાદબાકી કરવાની ચાવી
subtract key

દશાંશ ચાવી
decimal key

સેંકડો દેખાડતી ચાવી
percent key

ઉમેરો કરવા માટેની ચાવી
add key

ઈકવલ કી
equal key

પેટી કે ખોખું
case

મેમરી (સ્મૃતી)માંથી બાકબાકી કરવી
subtract from memory

સ્મૃતિમાં ઉમેરો/યાદ રાખો
add in memory

પારદર્શક કરવાની ચાવી
clear key

ભાગ્ય કરવાની ચાવી
divide key

દાખલ ચોખ્ખું કરવાની ચાવી
clear-entry key

વર્ગમૂળ શોધવાની ચાવી
square root key

સંખ્યા વધારવાની ચાવી
multiply key

પરિવર્તન ચિહ્નની ચાવી
change sign key

154

પર્સનલ કોમ્પ્યુટર
personal computer

વિડિઓ ચિત્ર જોવા
માટેનું મોનિટર
video monitor

કેન્દ્રિય સ્થાનમાં કાર્યવાહી કરતું એકમ
central processing unit

કી-બોર્ડનું દોરડું
keyboard cable

દરેક વાજિંત્ર અથવા યંત્રમાં
ચાવીઓની પેનલ જેવો ભાગ
keyboard

છાપેલો કાગળ/દસ્તાવેજ,
છપાયેલો કાગળ
printed document;
printout

કાગળ પર છાપકામ કરવાનું
મશીન/યંત્ર
printer

ડિસ્ક ડ્રાઇવ
disk drive

ડિસ્ક, ચકતું
disk

ઉંદર
mouse

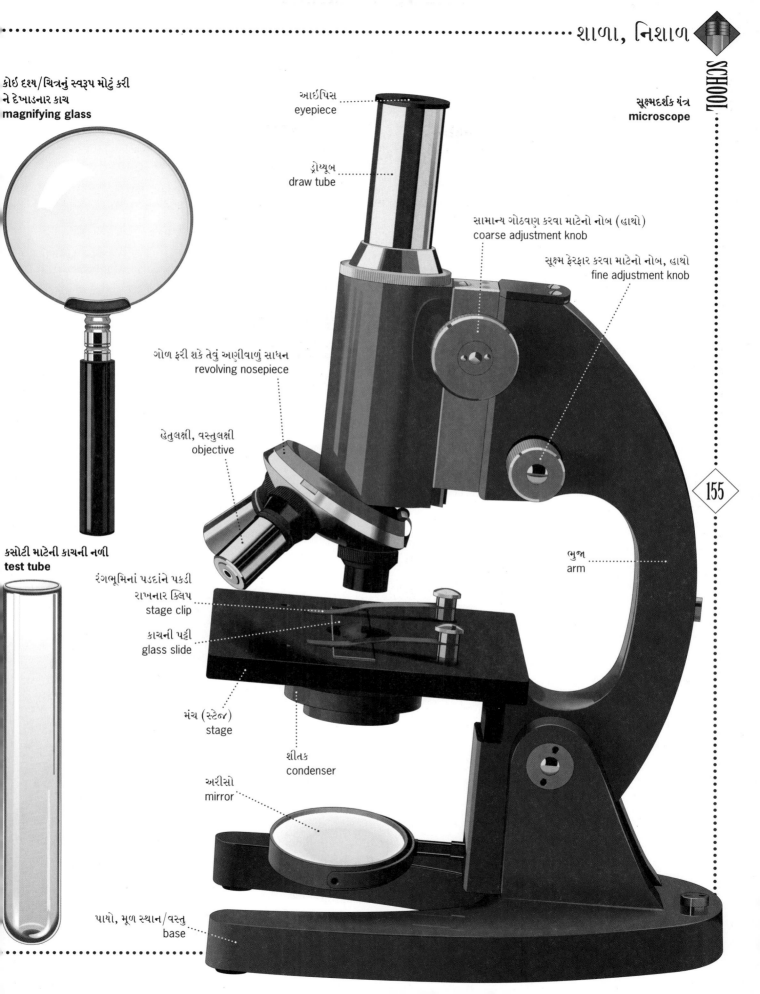

કોઈ દશ્ય/ચિત્રનું સ્વરૂપ મોટું કરી
ને દેખાડનાર કાચ
magnifying glass

સૂક્ષ્મદર્શક યંત્ર
microscope

આઈપિસ
eyepiece

ડ્રોય્યૂબ
draw tube

સામાન્ય ગોઠવણ કરવા માટેનો નોબ (હાથો)
coarse adjustment knob

સૂક્ષ્મ ફેરફાર કરવા માટેનો નોબ, હાથો
fine adjustment knob

ગોળ ફરી શકે તેવું આણીવાળું સાધન
revolving nosepiece

હેતુલક્ષી, વસ્તુલક્ષી
objective

રંગભૂમિના પડદાંને પકડી
રાખનાર ક્લિપ
stage clip

કાચની પટ્ટી
glass slide

ભુજા
arm

મંચ (સ્ટેજ)
stage

શીતક
condenser

કસોટી માટેની કાચની નળી
test tube

અરીસો
mirror

પાયો, મૂળ સ્થાન/વસ્તુ
base

ભૂમિતિ
GEOMETRY

સપાટી પદાર્થો
PLANE SURFACES

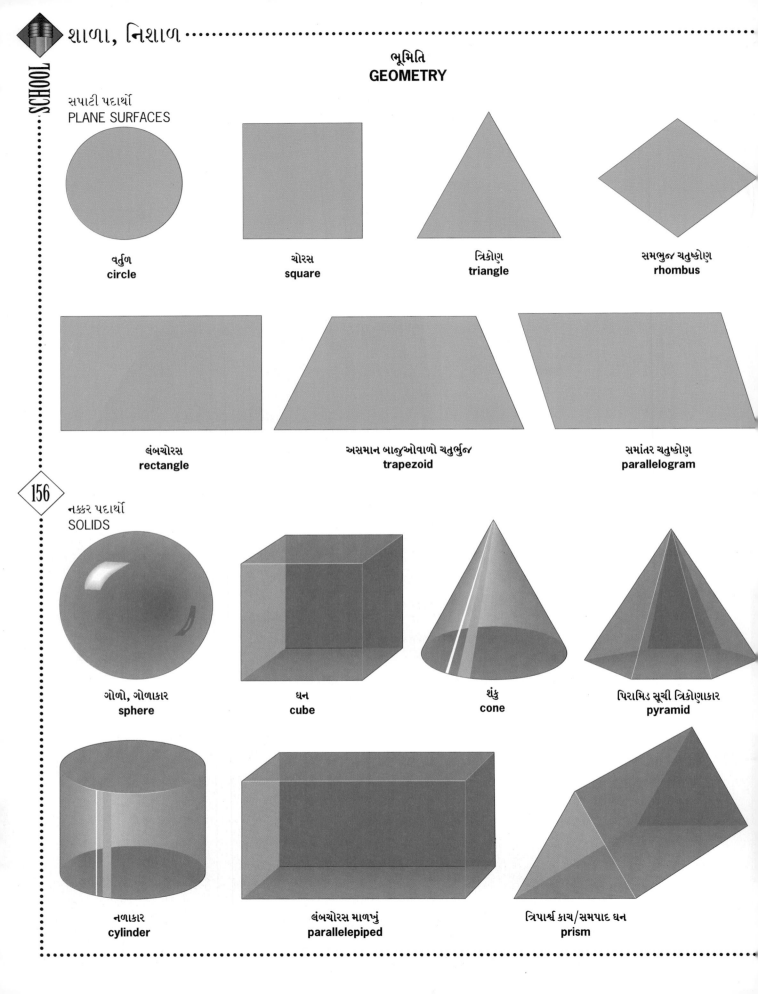

વર્તુળ
circle

ચોરસ
square

ત્રિકોણ
triangle

સમભુજ ચતુષ્કોણ
rhombus

લંબચોરસ
rectangle

અસમાન બાજુઓવાળો ચતુર્ભુજ
trapezoid

સમાંતર ચતુષ્કોણ
parallelogram

156

નક્કર પદાર્થો
SOLIDS

ગોળો, ગોળાકાર
sphere

ધન
cube

શંકુ
cone

પિરામિડ સૂચી ત્રિકોણાકાર
pyramid

નળાકાર
cylinder

લંબચોરસ માળખું
parallelepiped

ત્રિપાર્શ્વ કાચ/સમપાદ ધન
prism

ચિત્રાલેખન
DRAWING

સેકન્ડરી માધ્યમિક રંગો
secondary colors / secondary colours

પ્રાથમિક રંગો
**primary colors /
primary colours**

રંગીન વર્તુળ
COLOR CIRCLE / COLOUR CIRCLE

તૃતીય રંગો/કલર્સ
**tertiary colors /
tertiary colours**

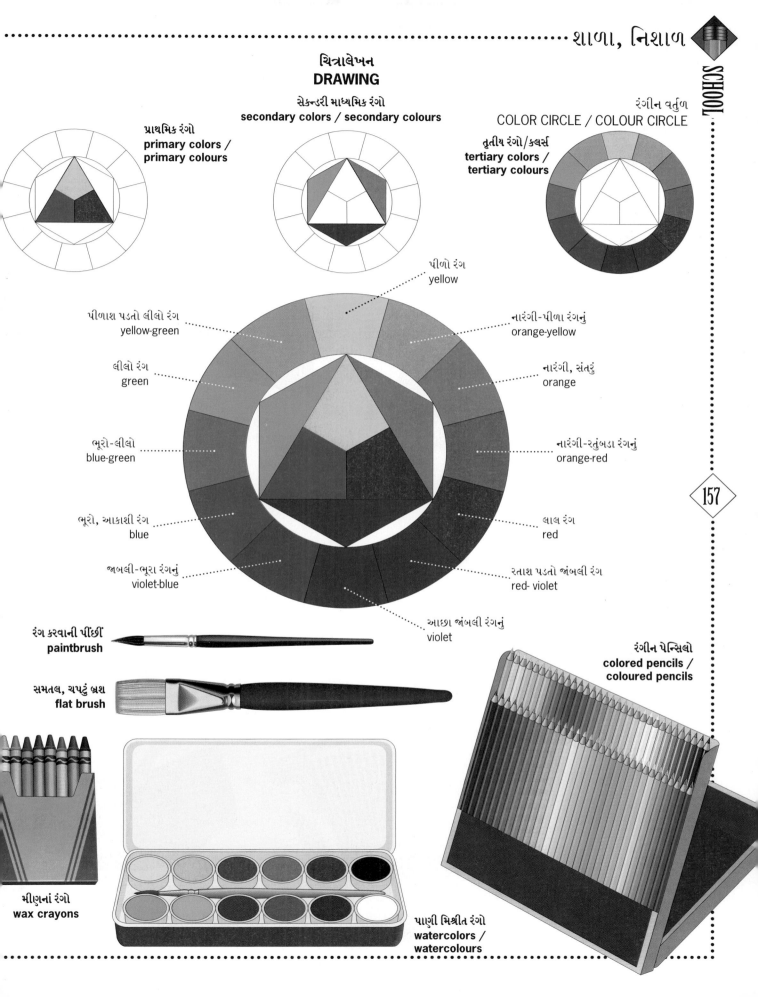

પીળો રંગ
yellow

પીળાશ પડતો લીલો રંગ
yellow-green

નારંગી-પીળા રંગનું
orange-yellow

લીલો રંગ
green

નારંગી, સંતરું
orange

ભૂરો-લીલો
blue-green

નારંગી-રતુંબડા રંગનું
orange-red

ભૂરો, આકાશી રંગ
blue

લાલ રંગ
red

જાબલી-ભૂરા રંગનું
violet-blue

રતાશ પડતો જાંબલી રંગ
red- violet

આછા જાંબલી રંગનું
violet

રંગ કરવાની પીંછી
paintbrush

સમતલ, ચપટું બ્રશ
flat brush

રંગીન પેન્સિલો
**colored pencils /
coloured pencils**

મીણનાં રંગો
wax crayons

પાણી મિશ્રીત રંગો
**watercolors /
watercolours**

સંગીતનાં પરંપરાગત સાધનો
TRADITIONAL MUSICAL INSTRUMENTS

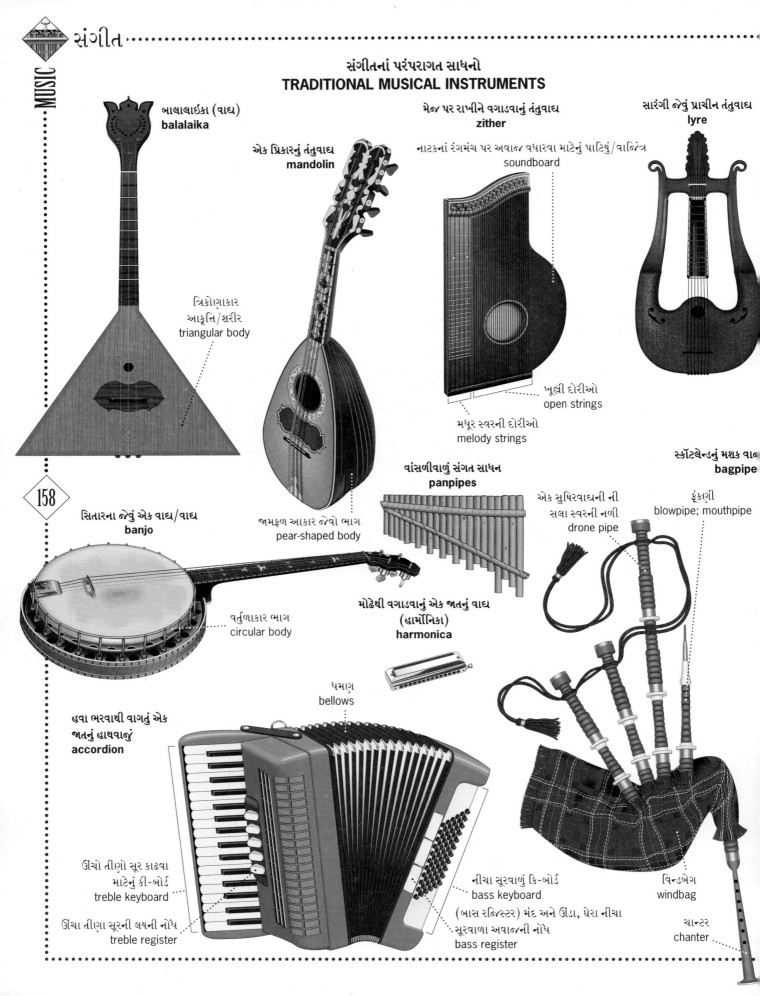

બાલાલાઇકા (વાઘ)
balalaika

એક પ્રિકારનું તંતુવાઘ
mandolin

મેજ પર રાખીને વગાડવાનું તંતુવાઘ
zither

નાટકનાં રંગમંચ પર અવાજ વધારવા માટેનું પાટિયું/વાજિંત્ર
soundboard

સારંગી જેવું પ્રાચીન તંતુવાઘ
lyre

ત્રિકોણાકાર આકૃત્તિ/શરીર
triangular body

ખૂલ્લી દોરીઓ
open strings

મધૂર સ્વરની દોરીઓ
melody strings

વાંસળીવાળું સંગત સાધન
panpipes

સ્કોટલેન્ડનું મશક વાઘ
bagpipe

૧૫૮

સિતારના જેવું એક વાઘ/વાઘ
banjo

જમફળ આકાર જેવો ભાગ
pear-shaped body

એક સુષિરવાઘની ની સલા સ્વરની નળી
drone pipe

ફૂંકણી
blowpipe; mouthpipe

વર્તુળાકાર ભાગ
circular body

મોઢેથી વગાડવાનું એક જાતનું વાઘ (હાર્મોનિકા)
harmonica

હવા ભરવાથી વાગતું એક જાતનું હાથવાજું
accordion

ધમાણ
bellows

ઊંચો તીણો સૂર કાઢવા માટેનું કી-બોર્ડ
treble keyboard

નીચા સૂરવાળું કિ-બોર્ડ
bass keyboard

વિન્ડબેગ
windbag

ઊંચા તીણા સૂરની લયની નોંધ
treble register

(બાસ રજિસ્ટર) મંદ અને ઊંડા, ઘેરા નીચા સૂરવાળા અવાજની નોંધ
bass register

ચાન્ટર
chanter

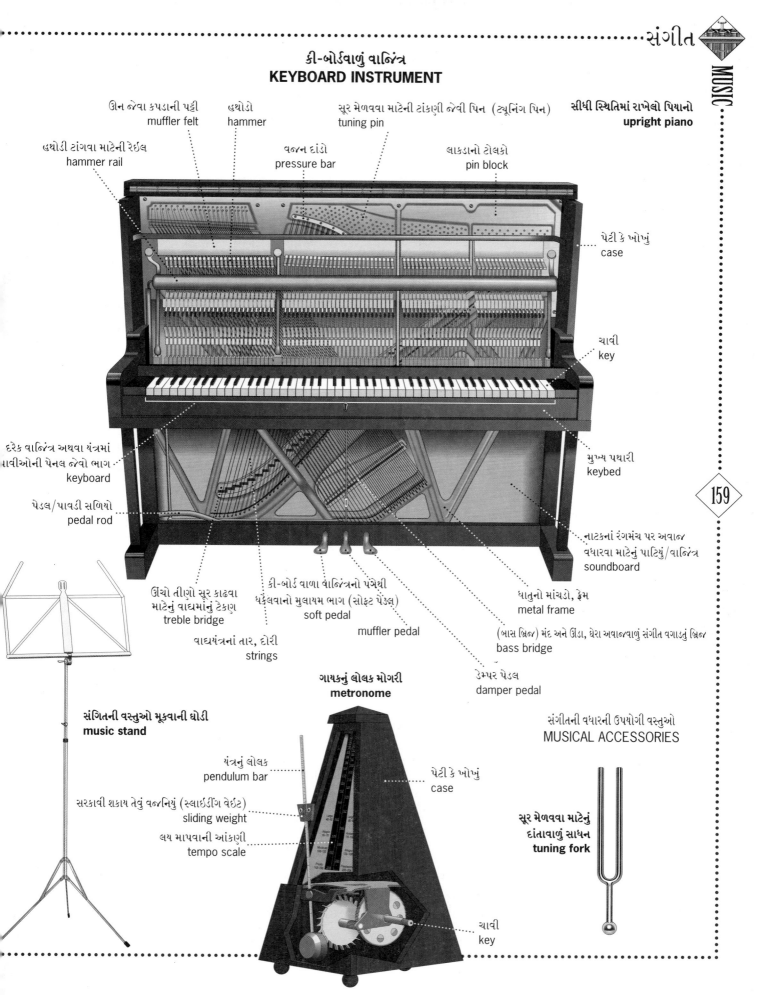

કી-બોર્ડવાળું વાજિંત્ર
KEYBOARD INSTRUMENT

ઊન જેવા કપડાની પટ્ટી
muffler felt

હથોડો
hammer

સૂર મેળવવા માટેની ટાંકણી જેવી પિન (ટ્યૂનિંગ પિન)
tuning pin

સીધી સ્થિતિમાં રાખેલો પિયાનો
upright piano

હથોડી ટાંગવા માટેની રેઇલ
hammer rail

વજન દાંડો
pressure bar

લાકડાનો ટોલકો
pin block

પેટી કે ખોખું
case

ચાવી
key

દરેક વાજિંત્ર અથવા યંત્રમાં ચાવીઓની પેનલ જેવો ભાગ
keyboard

મુખ્ય પથારી
keybed

પેડલ/પાવડી સળિયો
pedal rod

નાટકનાં રંગમંચ પર અવાજ વધારવા માટેનું પાટિયું/વાજિંત્ર
soundboard

ઊંચો તીણો સૂર કાઢવા માટેનું વાઘમાનું ટેકણ
treble bridge

કી-બોર્ડ વાળા વાજિંત્રનો પંગેથી ધકેલવાનો મુલાયમ ભાગ (સોફ્ટ પેડલ)
soft pedal

ધાતુનો માંચડો, ફ્રેમ
metal frame

વાઘયંત્રનાં તાર, દોરી
strings

muffler pedal

(બાસ બ્રિજ) મંદ અને ઊંડા, ઘેરા અવાજવાળું સંગીત વગાડતું બ્રિજ
bass bridge

ડૅમ્પર પેડલ
damper pedal

સંગીતની વસ્તુઓ મૂકવાની ઘોડી
music stand

ગાયકનું લોલક મોગરી
metronome

સંગીતની વધારની ઉપયોગી વસ્તુઓ
MUSICAL ACCESSORIES

યંત્રનું લોલક
pendulum bar

પેટી કે ખોખું
case

સરકાવી શકાય તેવું વજનિયું (સ્લાઇડીંગ વેઇટ)
sliding weight

લય માપવાની આંકણી
tempo scale

સૂર મેળવવા માટેનું દાંતાવાળું સાધન
tuning fork

ચાવી
key

159

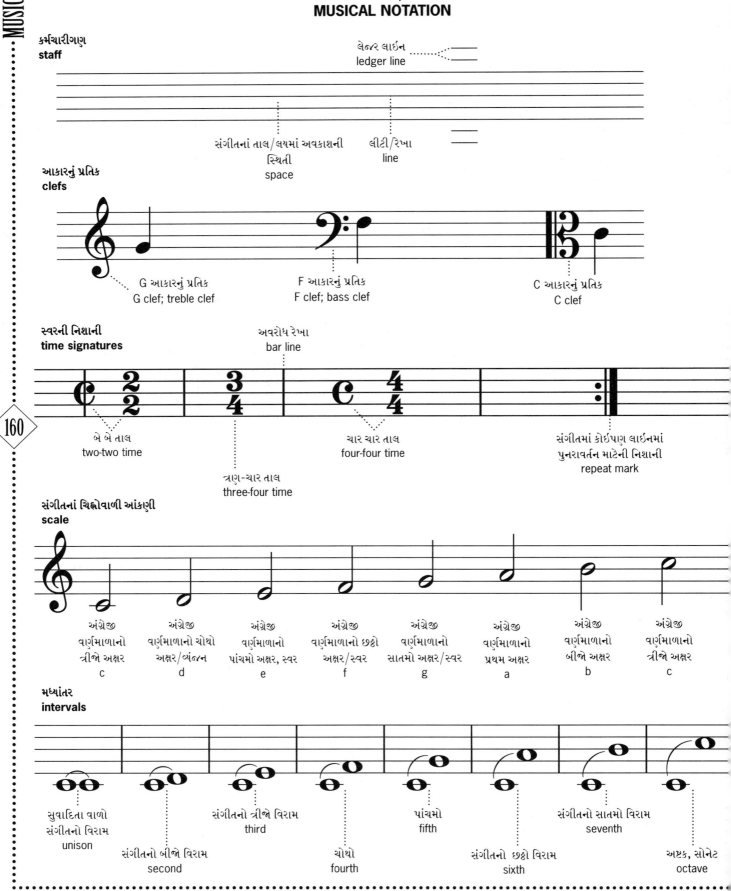

संगीतनां ચિહ્નો/પધ્ધતિ
MUSICAL NOTATION

કર્મચારીગણ
staff

લેજર લાઈન
ledger line

સંગીતનાં તાલ/લયમાં અવકાશની સ્થિતી
space

લીટી/રેખા
line

આકારનું પ્રતિક
clefs

G આકારનું પ્રતિક
G clef; treble clef

F આકારનું પ્રતિક
F clef; bass clef

C આકારનું પ્રતિક
C clef

સ્વરની નિશાની
time signatures

અવરોધ રેખા
bar line

બે બે તાલ
two-two time

ત્રણ-ચાર તાલ
three-four time

ચાર ચાર તાલ
four-four time

સંગીતમાં કોઈપણ લાઈનમાં પુનરાવર્તન માટેની નિશાની
repeat mark

સંગીતનાં ચિહ્નોવાળી આંકણી
scale

અંગ્રેજી વર્ણમાળાનો ત્રીજો અક્ષર
c

અંગ્રેજી વર્ણમાળાનો ચોથો અક્ષર/વ્યંજન
d

અંગ્રેજી વર્ણમાળાનો પાંચમો અક્ષર, સ્વર
e

અંગ્રેજી વર્ણમાળાનો છઠ્ઠો અક્ષર/સ્વર
f

અંગ્રેજી વર્ણમાળાનો સાતમો અક્ષર/સ્વર
g

અંગ્રેજી વર્ણમાળાનો પ્રથમ અક્ષર
a

અંગ્રેજી વર્ણમાળાનો બીજો અક્ષર
b

અંગ્રેજી વર્ણમાળાનો ત્રીજો અક્ષર
c

મધ્યાંતર
intervals

સુવાદિતા વાળો સંગીતનો વિરામ
unison

સંગીતનો બીજો વિરામ
second

સંગીતનો ત્રીજો વિરામ
third

ચોથો
fourth

પાંચમો
fifth

સંગીતનો છઠ્ઠો વિરામ
sixth

સંગીતનો સાતમો વિરામ
seventh

અષ્ટક, સોનેટ
octave

સૂર પ્રતીક
note symbols

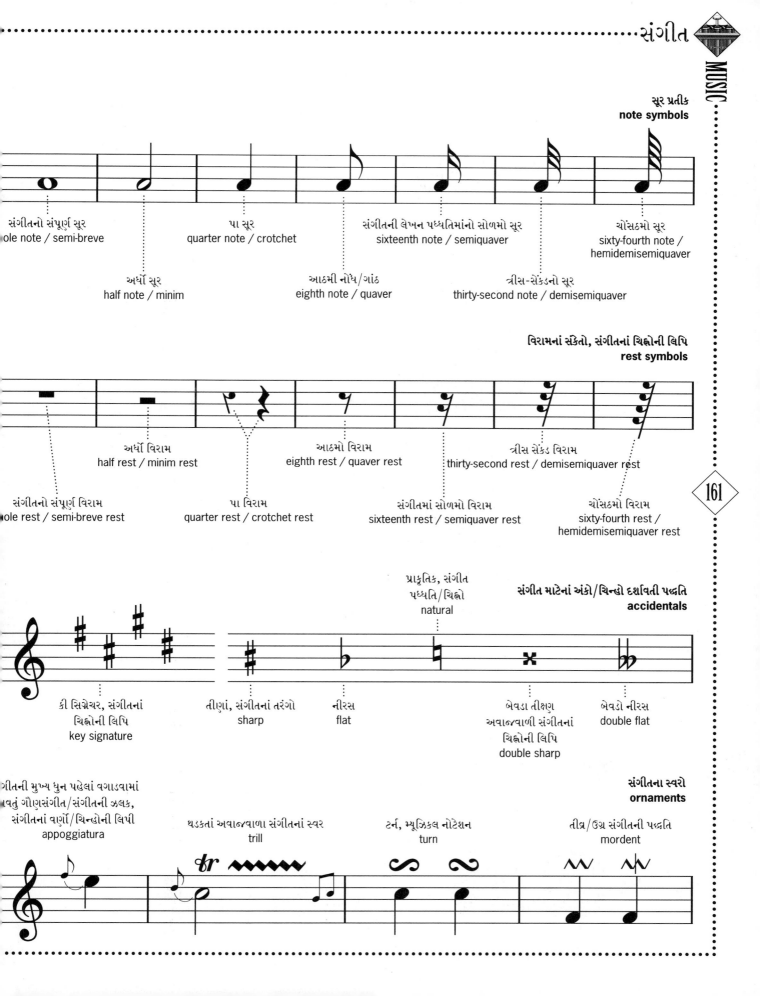

સંગીતનો સંપૂર્ણ સૂર
ole note / semi-breve

અર્ધો સૂર
half note / minim

પા સૂર
quarter note / crotchet

આઠમી નોંધ/ગાંઠ
eighth note / quaver

સંગીતની લેખન પધ્ધતિમાંનો સોળમો સૂર
sixteenth note / semiquaver

ત્રીસ-સેંકડનો સૂર
thirty-second note / demisemiquaver

ચોંસઠમો સૂર
sixty-fourth note /
hemidemisemiquaver

વિરામનાં સંકેતો, સંગીતનાં ચિહ્નોની લિપિ
rest symbols

ole rest / semi-breve rest

અર્ધો વિરામ
half rest / minim rest

પા વિરામ
quarter rest / crotchet rest

આઠમો વિરામ
eighth rest / quaver rest

સંગીતમાં સોળમો વિરામ
sixteenth rest / semiquaver rest

ત્રીસ સેંકડ વિરામ
thirty-second rest / demisemiquaver rest

ચોંસઠમો વિરામ
sixty-fourth rest /
hemidemisemiquaver rest

પ્રાકૃતિક, સંગીત
પધ્ધતિ/ચિહ્નો
natural

સંગીત માટેનાં અંકો/ચિન્હો દર્શવતી પધ્ધતિ
accidentals

કી સિગ્નેચર, સંગીતનાં
ચિહ્નોની લિપિ
key signature

તીણાં, સંગીતનાં તરંગો
sharp

નીરસ
flat

બેવડા તીક્ષણ
અવાજવાળી સંગીતનાં
ચિહ્નોની લિપિ
double sharp

બેવડો નીરસ
double flat

ગીતની મુખ્ય ધુન પહેલાં વગાડવામાં
વતું ગૌણસંગીત/સંગીતની ઝલક,
સંગીતનાં વર્ણો/ચિન્હોની લિપી
appoggiatura

સંગીતના સ્વરો
ornaments

થડકતાં અવાજવાળા સંગીતનાં સ્વર
trill

ટર્ન, મ્યુઝિકલ નોટેશન
turn

તીવ્ર/ઉગ્ર સંગીતની પધ્ધતિ
mordent

161

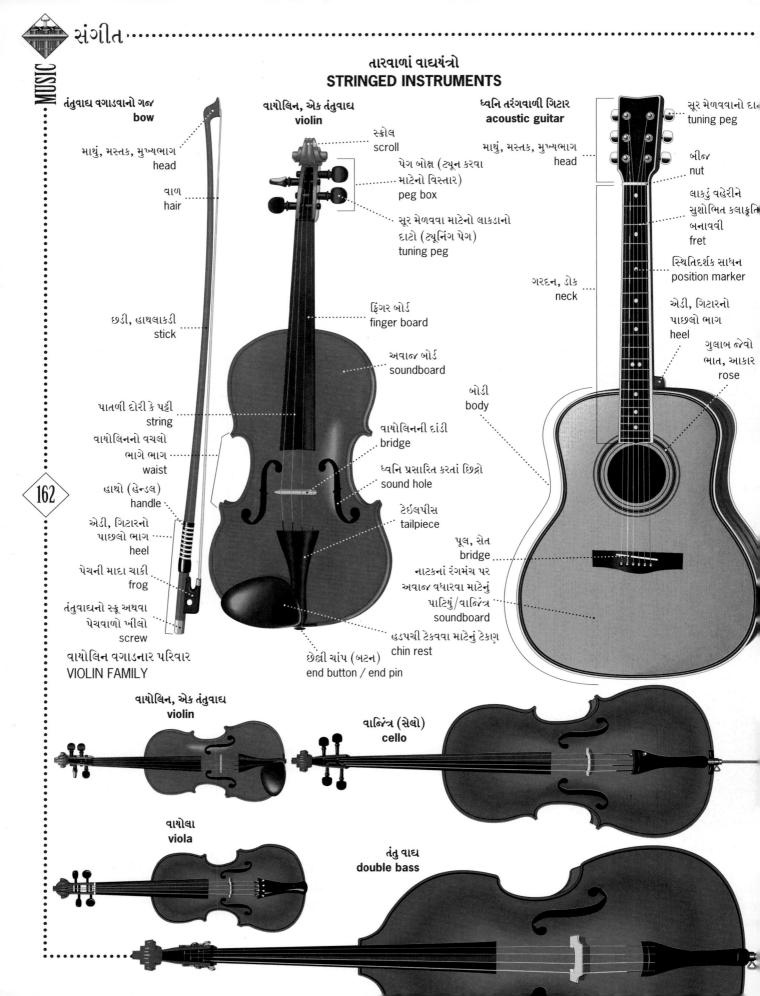

તારવાળાં વાઘયંત્રો
STRINGED INSTRUMENTS

તંતુવાદ વગાડવાનો ગજ
bow

માથું, મસ્તક, મુખ્યભાગ
head

વાળ
hair

છડી, હાથલાકડી
stick

પાતળી દોરી કે પટ્ટી
string

વાયોલિનનો વચલો
ભાગે ભાગ
waist

હાથો (હેન્ડલ)
handle

એડી, ગિટારનો
પાછલો ભાગ
heel

પેચની માદા ચાકી
frog

તંતુવાઘનો સ્ક્રૂ અથવા
પેચવાળો ખીલો
screw

વાયોલિન, એક તંતુવાઘ
violin

સ્ક્રોલ
scroll

પેગ બોક્ષ (ટ્યૂન કરવા
માટેનો વિસ્તાર)
peg box

સૂર મેળવવા માટેનો લાકડાનો
દાટો (ટ્યૂનિંગ પેગ)
tuning peg

ફિંગર બોર્ડ
finger board

અવાજ બોર્ડ
soundboard

વાયોલિનની દાંડી
bridge

ધ્વનિ પ્રસારિત કરતાં છિદ્રો
sound hole

ટેઈલપીસ
tailpiece

પૂલ, સેત
bridge

નાટકનાં રંગમંચ પર
અવાજ વધારવા માટેનું
પાટિયું/વાજિંત્ર
soundboard

હડપચી ટેકવવા માટેનું ટેકણ
chin rest

છેલ્લી ચાંપ (બટન)
end button / end pin

વાયોલિન વગાડનાર પરિવાર
VIOLIN FAMILY

ધ્વનિ તરંગવાળી ગિટાર
acoustic guitar

માથું, મસ્તક, મુખ્યભાગ
head

ગરદન, ડોક
neck

બોડી
body

સૂર મેળવવાનો દા
tuning peg

બીજ
nut

લાકડું વહેરીને
સુશોભિત કલાકૃતિ
બનાવવી
fret

સ્થિતિદર્શક સાધન
position marker

એડી, ગિટારનો
પાછલો ભાગ
heel

ગુલાબ જેવો
ભાત, આકાર
rose

વાયોલિન, એક તંતુવાઘ
violin

વાજિંત્ર (સેલો)
cello

વાયોલા
viola

તંતુ વાઘ
double bass

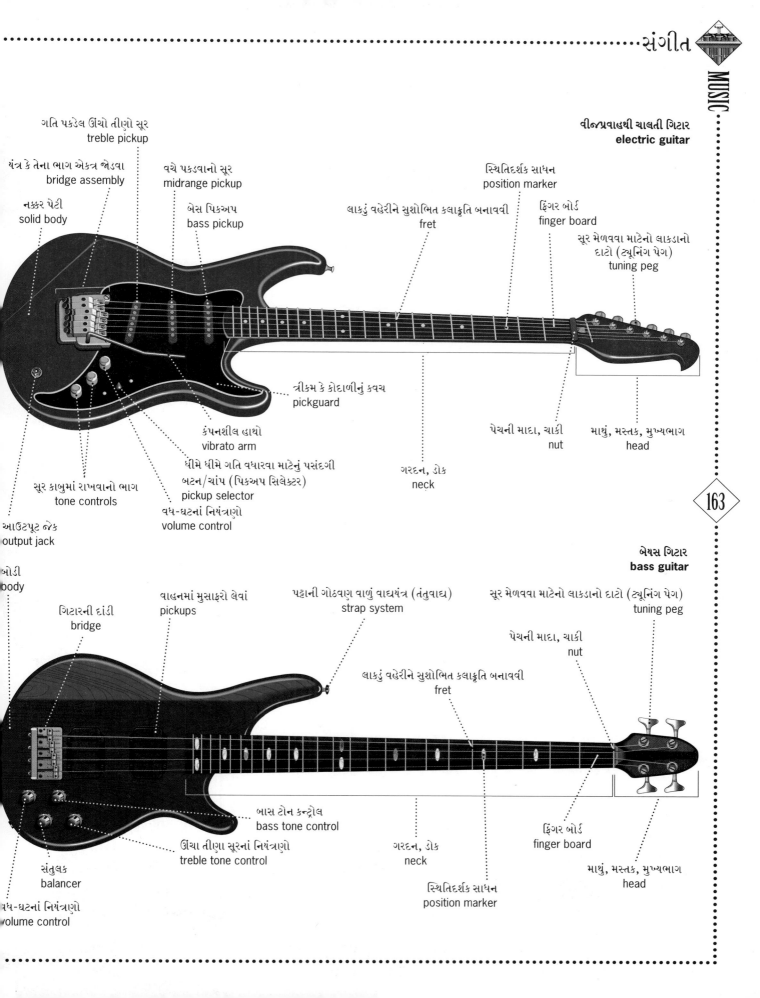

વીજપ્રવાહથી ચાલતી ગિટાર
electric guitar

ગતિ પકડેલ ઊંચો તીણો સૂર
treble pickup

યંત્ર કે તેના ભાગ એકત્ર જોડવા
bridge assembly

નક્કર પેટી
solid body

વચે પકડવાનો સૂર
midrange pickup

બેસ પિકઅપ
bass pickup

સ્થિતિદર્શક સાધન
position marker

લાકડું વહેરીને સુશોભિત કલાકૃતિ બનાવવી
fret

ફિંગર બોર્ડ
finger board

સૂર મેળવવા માટેનો લાકડાનો
દાટો (ટ્યૂનિંગ પેગ)
tuning peg

ત્રીકમ કે કોદાળીનું કવચ
pickguard

કંપનશીલ હાથો
vibrato arm

ધીમે ધીમે ગતિ વધારવા માટેનું પસંદગી
બટન/ચાંપ (પિકઅપ સિલેક્ટર)
pickup selector

વધ-ઘટનાં નિયંત્રણો
volume control

સૂર કાબુમાં રાખવાનો ભાગ
tone controls

આઉટપૂટ જેક
output jack

બોડી
body

પેચની માદા, ચાકી
nut

માથું, મસ્તક, મુખ્યભાગ
head

ગરદન, ડોક
neck

બેયસ ગિટાર
bass guitar

ગિટારની દાંડી
bridge

વાહનમાં મુસાફરો લેવાં
pickups

પક્ષાની ગોઠવણ વાળું વાધયંત્ર (તંતુવાદ્ય)
strap system

સૂર મેળવવા માટેનો લાકડાનો દાટો (ટ્યૂનિંગ પેગ)
tuning peg

પેચની માદા, ચાકી
nut

લાકડું વહેરીને સુશોભિત કલાકૃતિ બનાવવી
fret

બાસ ટોન કન્ટ્રોલ
bass tone control

ઊંચા તીણા સૂરનાં નિયંત્રાણો
treble tone control

સંતુલક
balancer

વધ-ઘટનાં નિયંત્રણો
volume control

ગરદન, ડોક
neck

ફિંગર બોર્ડ
finger board

માથું, મસ્તક, મુખ્યભાગ
head

સ્થિતિદર્શક સાધન
position marker

163

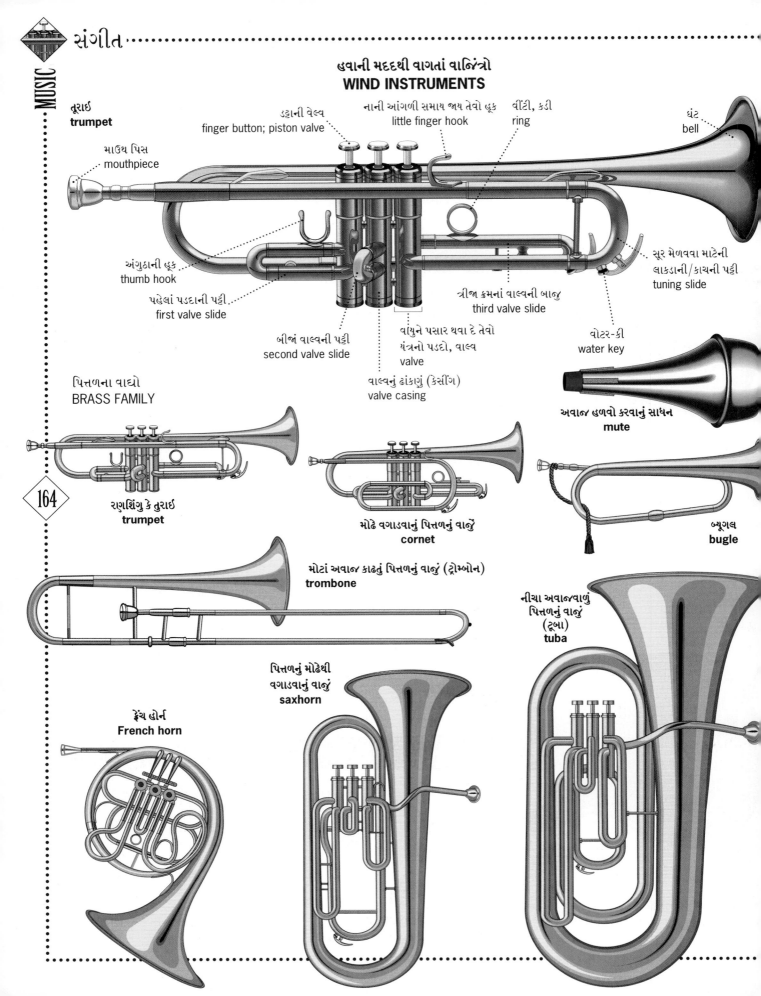

હવાની મદદથી વાગતાં વાજિંત્રો
WIND INSTRUMENTS

તૂરાઈ
trumpet

માઉથ પિસ
mouthpiece

ઉઠ્ઠાની વેલ્વ
finger button; piston valve

નાની આંગળી સમાય જાય તેવો હૂક
little finger hook

વીંટી, કડી
ring

ઘંટ
bell

અંગુઠાની હૂક
thumb hook

પહેલાં પડ્દાની પટ્ટી
first valve slide

બીજાં વાલ્વની પટ્ટી
second valve slide

વાલ્વનું ઢાંકણું (કેસીંગ)
valve casing

વાઘુને પસાર થવા દે તેવો
યંત્રનો પડદો, વાલ્વ
valve

ત્રીજ ક્રમનાં વાલ્વની બાજુ
third valve slide

સૂર મેળવવા માટેની
લાકડાની/કાચની પટ્ટી
tuning slide

વોટર-કી
water key

પિત્તળના વાઘો
BRASS FAMILY

અવાજ હલવો કરવાનું સાધન
mute

રણશિંગુ કે તુરાઈ
trumpet

મોઢે વગાડવાનું પિત્તળનું વાજું
cornet

બ્યૂગલ
bugle

મોટાં અવાજ કાઢતું પિત્તળનું વાજું (ટ્રોમ્બોન)
trombone

નીચા અવાજવાળું
પિત્તળનું વાજું
(ટ્યૂબા)
tuba

પિત્તળનું મોઢેથી
વગાડવાનું વાજું
saxhorn

ફ્રેંચ હોર્ન
French horn

વળાંક, વાકું
crook

ઇજાગ્રસ્ત ભાગને
બાંધવા માટેનો પાટો
ligature

વાંસળી, પાવો
reed

માઉથ પિસ
mouthpiece

વાંસળી, પાવો
REEDS

બેવડી વાંસળી
double reed

સંયુક્ત (એક) વાંસળી
single reed

અષ્ટકની રચના
octave mechanism

ચાવીઓવાળું પિત્તળનું વજું
WOODWIND FAMILY

સેક્સોફોન નામનું ધાતુ અને લાકડાનું વાદ્ય
saxophone

એક જાતની નાની
વાંસળી
piccolo

સેક્સોફોન નામનું ધાતુ અને લાકડાનું વાદ્ય
saxophone

ઘંટ
bell

ઘંટને બાંધવા માટેનો આધાર
bell brace

બોડી
body

165

વાંસળી, બંસી
flute

સંગીત ઉતારનાર રેકર્ડ
recorder

અંગુઠાનું વિરામ
thumb rest

ચાવી
key

વાંસળી જેવું એક વાદ્ય શરણાઇ (ઓબો)
oboe

ક્લેરિનેટ કે તુરાઇ
clarinet

ઇંગ્લીશ શિંગ
English horn / cor anglais

બાસૂન (વાદ્ય)
bassoon

હળવેથી ટપકારવાનાં સંગીતના સાધનો
PERCUSSION INSTRUMENTS

નગારું, પડઘમ
drums

ઝાંઝ કે કાંસીજોડનું એક અંગ
cymbal

ચાલ્સ્ટન સિમ્બાલ તાલ આપવાની ઝાંઝનો એક ભાગ
Charleston cymbal; hi-hat cymbal

ટોમ ટોમ્સ
tom-toms

ઝૂડવાનો, મારવાનો ભાગ
batter head

તારની જાળીવાળું નગારું
snare drum

ત્રણ પાયાવાળી ઘોડી
tripod stand

બાસ ડ્રમ
bass drum

ચીજવસ્તુનો ઘોડો
stand

યંત્ર કે ઓજારનો પગ વડે ધકેલવાનો ભાગ (પેડલ)
pedal

ઊંચા, ઘેરા અવાજવાળું ડ્રમ (નગારું)
tenor drum

લાકડાની નાની હથોડી
mallet

તારવાળી પીંછી (બ્રશ)
wire brush

છડી, હાથલાકડી
sticks

લાકડાની નાની હથોડી
mallets

ત્રિકોણ
triangle

બોંગો (ડ્રમ), એક પ્રકારનું વાજિંત્ર
bongos

પ્રાચીન ઇજિપ્તનું ઘૂઘરા જેવું વાઘ
sistrum

ઘંટડીઓનો સેટ (સમૂહ)
set of bells

બરફ પર સરકતી ગાડીની ઘંટડીઓ
sleigh bells

કરતાલ
castanets

આયલોફોન, કાષ્ઠતરંગ
xylophone

લેટિન અમેરિકન સંગીતમાં દૂધી જેવાં આકારનાં વાઘોની જોડી
maracas

ખંજરી અથવા ડફ નામનું વાજિંત્ર (ટિમ્બોરાઇન)
tambourine

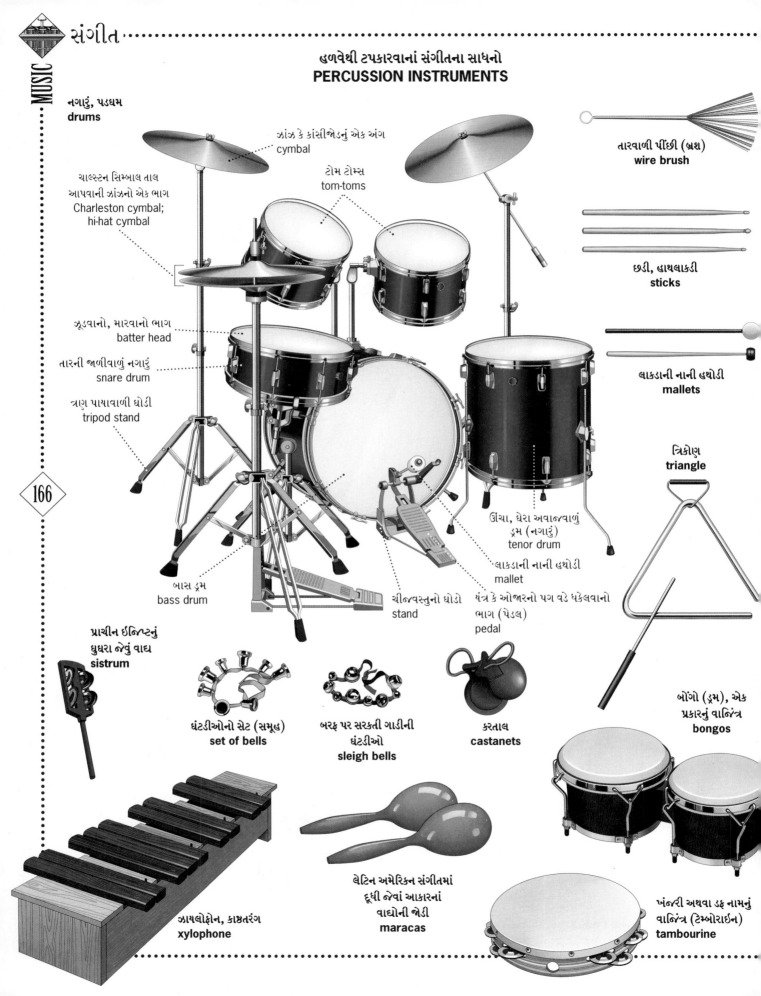

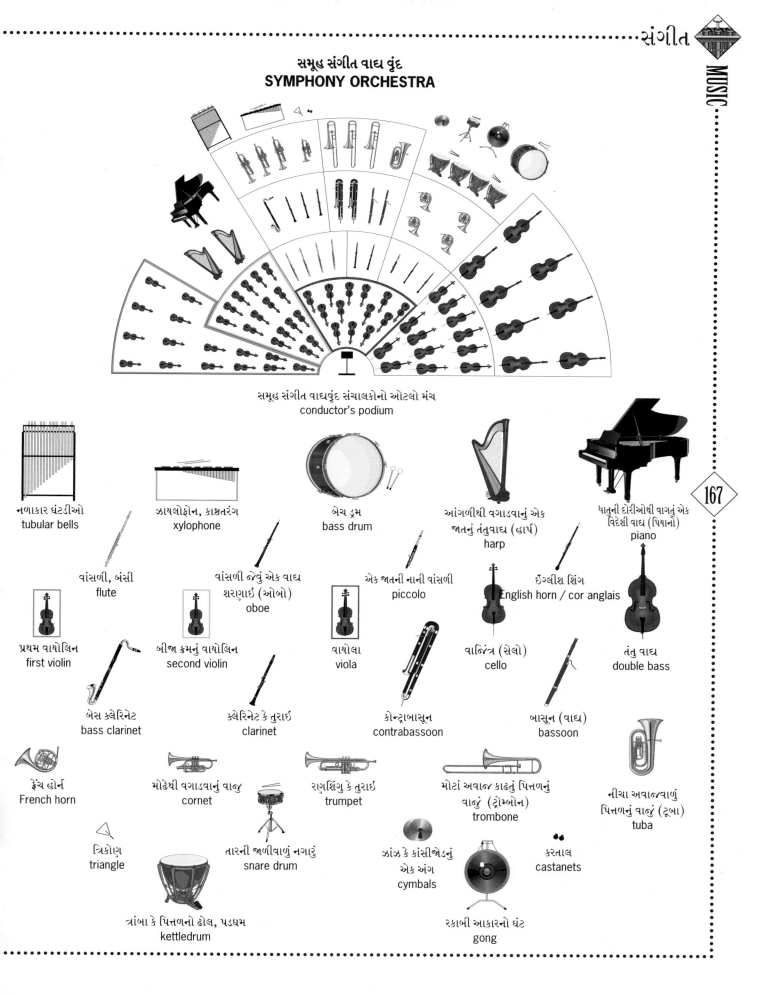

સમૂહ સંગીત વાઘ વૃંદ
SYMPHONY ORCHESTRA

સમૂહ સંગીત વાઘવૃંદ સંચાલકોનો ઓટલો મંચ
conductor's podium

નળાકાર ઘંટડીઓ
tubular bells

ઝાયલોફોન, કાષ્ટરંગ
xylophone

બેચ ડ્રમ
bass drum

આંગળીથી વગાડવાનું એક
જાતનું તંતુવાઘ (હાર્પ)
harp

ધાતુની દોરીઓથી વાગતું એક
વિદેશી વાઘ (પિયાનો)
piano

વાંસળી, બંસી
flute

વાંસળી જેવું એક વાઘ
શરણાઈ (ઓબો)
oboe

એક જાતની નાની વાંસળી
piccolo

ઇંગ્લીશ શિંગ
English horn / cor anglais

પ્રથમ વાયોલિન
first violin

બીજા ક્રમનું વાયોલિન
second violin

વાયોલા
viola

વાજિંત્ર (સેલો)
cello

તંતુ વાઘ
double bass

બેસ ક્લેરિનેટ
bass clarinet

ક્લેરિનેટ કે તુરાઈ
clarinet

કોન્ટ્રાબાસૂન
contrabassoon

બાસૂન (વાઘ)
bassoon

ફ્રેંચ હોર્ન
French horn

મોઢેથી વગાડવાનું વાજુ
cornet

રણશિંગુ કે તુરાઈ
trumpet

મોટાં અવાજ કાઢતું પિત્તળનું
વાજું (ટ્રોમ્બોન)
trombone

નીચા અવાજવાળું
પિત્તળનું વાજું (ટૂબા)
tuba

ત્રિકોણ
triangle

તારની જાળીવાળું નગારું
snare drum

ઝાંઝ કે કાંસીજોડનું
એક અંગ
cymbals

કરતાલ
castanets

ત્રાંબા કે પિત્તળનો ઢોલ, પડઘમ
kettledrum

રકાબી આકારનો ઘંટ
gong

167

ટીમ રમતો

બેસ બોલ
BASEBALL

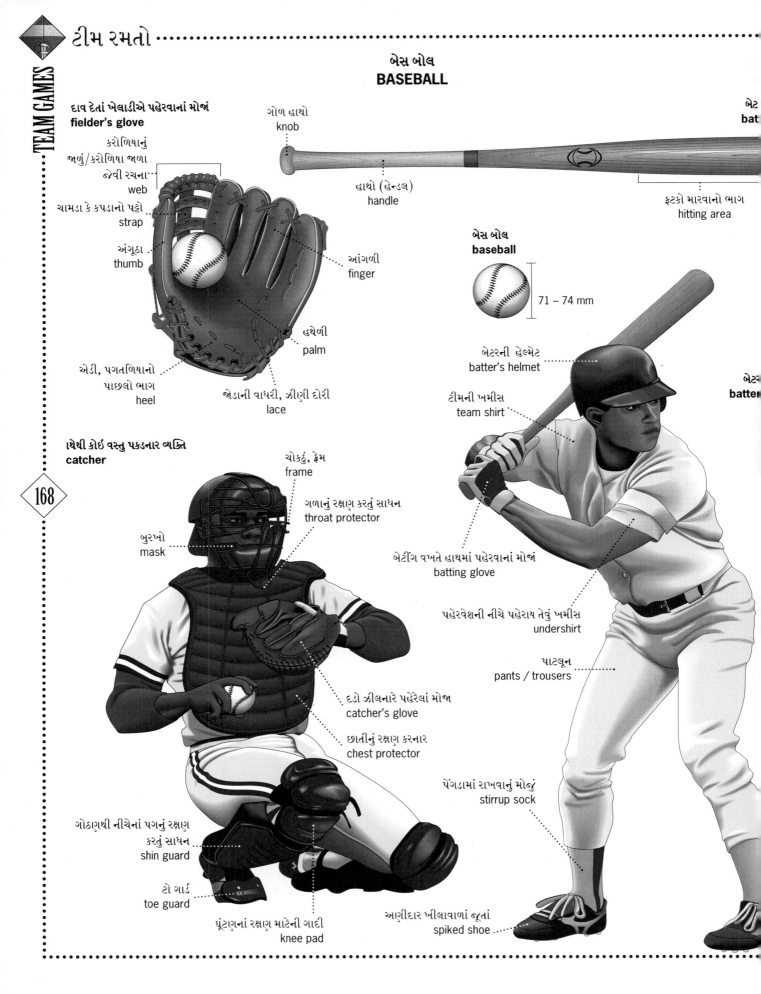

દાવ દેતાં ખેલાડીએ પહેરવાનાં મોજાં
fielder's glove

કરોબિયાનું
જાળું/કરોબિયા જાળા
જેવી રચના
web

ચામડા કે કપડાનો પટ્ટો
strap

અંગૂઠા
thumb

એડી, પગતળિયાનો
પાછલો ભાગ
heel

ગોળ હાથો
knob

હાથો (હેન્ડલ)
handle

આંગળી
finger

હથેળી
palm

જોડાની વાધરી, ઝીણી દોરી
lace

બેટ
bat

ફટકો મારવાનો ભાગ
hitting area

બેસ બોલ
baseball

71 – 74 mm

બેટરની હેલ્મેટ
batter's helmet

ટીમની ખમીસ
team shirt

બેટિંગ વખતે હાથમાં પહેરવાનાં મોજાં
batting glove

પહેરવેશની નીચે પહેરાય તેવું ખમીસ
undershirt

પાટલૂન
pants / trousers

સ્ટિરપ મોજું / પેંગડામાં રાખવાનું મોજું
stirrup sock

બેટ
batter

.થેથી કોઈ વસ્તુ પકડનાર વ્યક્તિ
catcher

ચોકઠું, ફ્રેમ
frame

ગળાનું રક્ષણ કરતું સાધન
throat protector

બુરખો
mask

દડો ઝીલનારે પહેરેલાં મોજ
catcher's glove

છાતીનું રક્ષણ કરનાર
chest protector

ગોઠણથી નીચેનાં પગનું રક્ષણ
કરતું સાધન
shin guard

ટો ગાર્ડ
toe guard

ઘૂંટણનાં રક્ષણ માટેની ગાદી
knee pad

આણીદાર ખીલાવાળાં જૂતાં
spiked shoe

168

બેઝબોલ રમવા માટેનું મેદાન
field

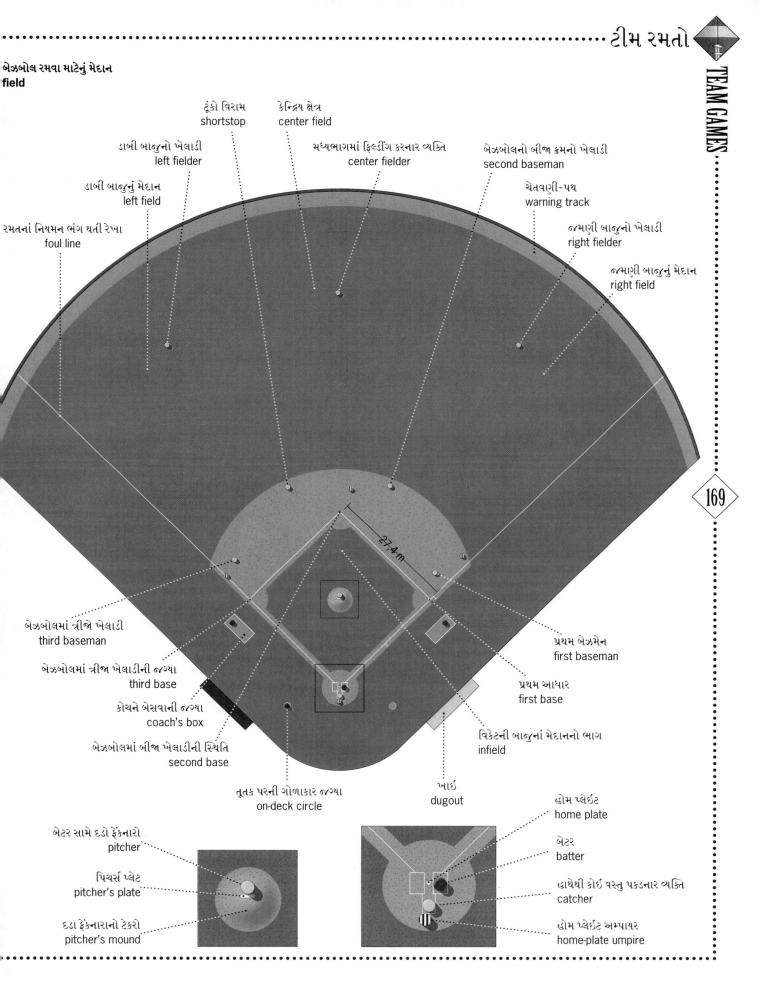

ટૂંકો વિરામ
shortstop

કેન્દ્રિય ક્ષેત્ર
center field

ડાબી બાજુનો ખેલાડી
left fielder

મધ્યભાગમાં ફિલ્ડીંગ કરનાર વ્યક્તિ
center fielder

બેઝબોલનો બીજા ક્રમનો ખેલાડી
second baseman

ડાબી બાજુનું મેદાન
left field

ચેતવણી-પથ
warning track

રમતનાં નિયમન ભંગ થતી રેખા
foul line

જમણી બાજુનો ખેલાડી
right fielder

જમણી બાજુનું મેદાન
right field

27.4 m

બેઝબોલમાં ત્રીજો ખેલાડી
third baseman

પ્રથમ બેઝમેન
first baseman

બેઝબોલમાં ત્રીજા ખેલાડીની જગ્યા
third base

પ્રથમ આધાર
first base

કોચને બેસવાની જગ્યા
coach's box

બેઝબોલમાં બીજા ખેલાડીની સ્થિતિ
second base

વિકેટની બાજુનાં મેદાનનો ભાગ
infield

તૂતક પરની ગોળાકાર જગ્યા
on-deck circle

ખાઈ
dugout

હોમ પ્લેઈટ
home plate

બેટર સામે દડો ફેંકનારો
pitcher

બેટર
batter

પિચર્સ પ્લેટ
pitcher's plate

હાથેથી કોઈ વસ્તુ પકડનાર વ્યક્તિ
catcher

દડા ફેંકનારાનો ટેકરો
pitcher's mound

હોમ પ્લેઈટ અમ્પાયર
home-plate umpire

169

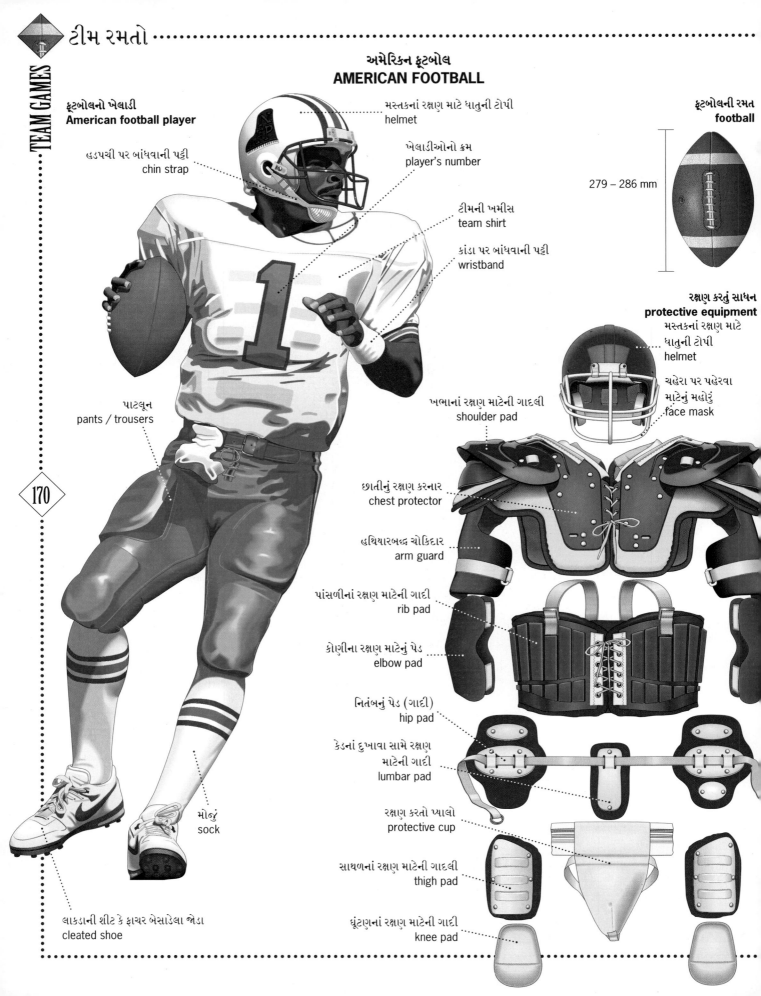

અમેરિકન ફૂટબોલ
AMERICAN FOOTBALL

ફૂટબોલનો ખેલાડી
American football player

મસ્તકનાં રક્ષણ માટે ધાતુની ટોપી
helmet

હડપચી પર બાંધવાની પટ્ટી
chin strap

ખેલાડીઓનો ક્રમ
player's number

ટીમની ખમીસ
team shirt

કાંડા પર બાંધવાની પટ્ટી
wristband

ફૂટબોલની રમત
football

279 – 286 mm

રક્ષણ કરતું સાધન
protective equipment

મસ્તકનાં રક્ષણ માટે ધાતુની ટોપી
helmet

ચહેરા પર પહેરવા માટેનું મહોરું
face mask

ખભાનાં રક્ષણ માટેની ગાદલી
shoulder pad

પાટલૂન
pants / trousers

છાતીનું રક્ષણ કરનાર
chest protector

હથિયારબદ્ધ ચોકિદાર
arm guard

પાંસળીનાં રક્ષણ માટેની ગાદી
rib pad

કોણીના રક્ષણ માટેનું પેડ
elbow pad

નિતંબનું પેડ (ગાદી)
hip pad

કેડનાં દુખાવા સામે રક્ષણ માટેની ગાદી
lumbar pad

મોજું
sock

રક્ષણ કરતો પ્યાલો
protective cup

સાથળનાં રક્ષણ માટેની ગાદલી
thigh pad

લાકડાની શીટ કે ફાયર બેસાડેલા જોડા
cleated shoe

ઘૂંટણનાં રક્ષણ માટેની ગાદી
knee pad

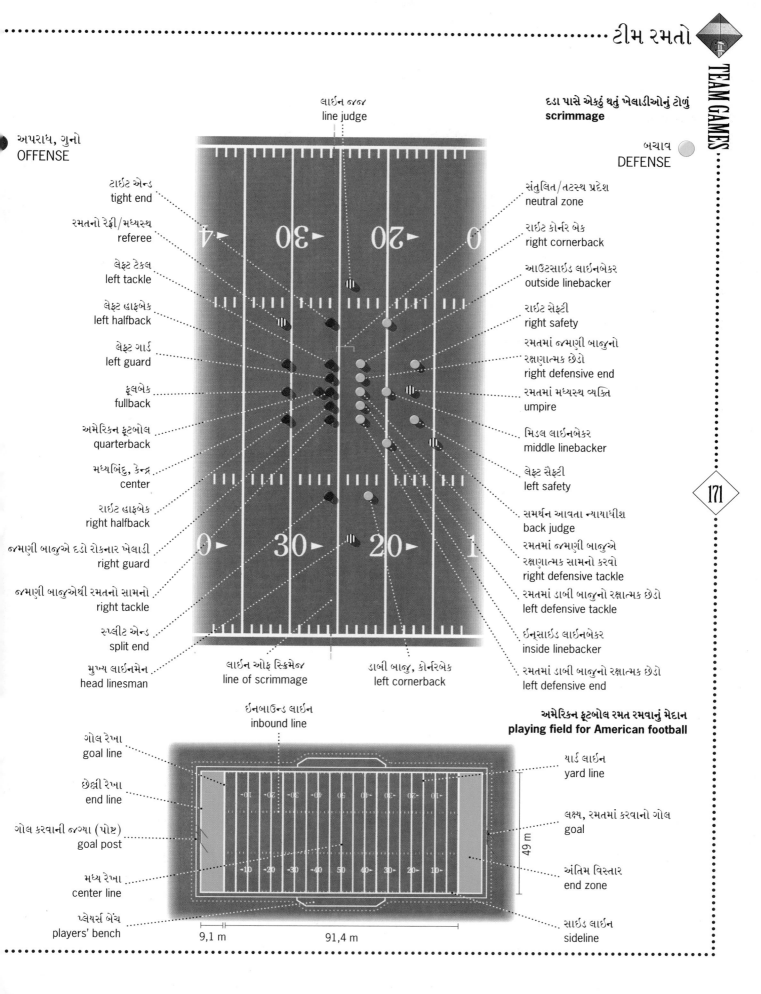

દડા પાસે એકઠું થતું ખેલાડીઓનું ટોળું
scrimmage

બચાવ
DEFENSE

અપરાધ, ગુનો
OFFENSE

લાઈન જજ
line judge

ટાઇટ એન્ડ
tight end

રમતનો રેફ્રી/મધ્યસ્થ
referee

લેફ્ટ ટેકલ
left tackle

લેફ્ટ હાફબેક
left halfback

લેફ્ટ ગાર્ડ
left guard

ફૂલબેક
fullback

અમેરિકન ફૂટબોલ
quarterback

મધ્યબિંદુ, કેન્દ્ર
center

રાઇટ હાફબેક
right halfback

જમણી બાજુએ દડો રોકનાર ખેલાડી
right guard

જમણી બાજુએથી રમતનો સામનો
right tackle

સ્પ્લીટ એન્ડ
split end

મુખ્ય લાઈનમેન
head linesman

સંતુલિત/તટસ્થ પ્રદેશ
neutral zone

રાઇટ કોર્નર બેક
right cornerback

આઉટસાઈડ લાઈનબેકર
outside linebacker

રાઇટ સેફ્ટી
right safety

રમતમાં જમણી બાજુનો
રક્ષણાત્મક છેડો
right defensive end

રમતમાં મધ્યસ્થ વ્યક્તિ
umpire

મિડલ લાઈનબેકર
middle linebacker

લેફ્ટ સૈફ્ટી
left safety

સમર્થન આવતા ન્યાયાધીશ
back judge

રમતમાં જમણી બાજુએ
રક્ષણાત્મક સામનો કરવો
right defensive tackle

રમતમાં ડાબી બાજુનો રક્ષાત્મક છેડો
left defensive tackle

ઇનસાઇડ લાઈનબેકર
inside linebacker

રમતમાં ડાબી બાજુનો રક્ષાત્મક છેડો
left defensive end

લાઈન ઓફ સ્ક્રિમેજ
line of scrimmage

ડાબી બાજુ, કોર્નરબેક
left cornerback

ઈનબાઉન્ડ લાઈન
inbound line

અમેરિકન ફૂટબોલ રમત રમવાનું મેદાન
playing field for American football

ગોલ રેખા
goal line

છેલ્લી રેખા
end line

ગોલ કરવાની જગ્યા (પોષ્ટ)
goal post

મધ્ય રેખા
center line

પ્લેયર્સ બેંચ
players' bench

યાર્ડ લાઈન
yard line

લક્ષ, રમતમાં કરવાનો ગોલ
goal

અંતિમ વિસ્તાર
end zone

સાઈડ લાઈન
sideline

9,1 m   91,4 m

49 m

ફૂટબોલની રમત
SOCCER

ફૂટબોલનો ખેલાડી
soccer player

ફૂટબોલનો દડો
soccer ball

218 mm

ટીમની ખમીસ
team shirt

ચડ્ડીઓ
shorts

ગોઠણથી નીચેનાં પગનું રક્ષણ કરતું સાધન
shin guard

ફૂટબોલ રમતમાં ખેલાડીનાં જૂતાં
soccer shoe / football boot

ઈન્ટરચેઈન્જેબલ સ્ટડ્ઝ
interchangeable studs

રમવાનું મેદાન
playing field

ખૂણાની કમાન
corner arc

રમતનો રેફ્રી/મધ્યસ્થ
referee

લક્ષ્ય, રમતમાં કરવાનો ગોલ
goal

ખૂણામાં રાખવામાં આવેલો ધ્વજ
corner flag

ગોલ કરવાનો વિસ્તાર
goal area

45 – 90 m

રમતનાં ભંગ બદલ દંડ થઈ શકે
તેવો વિસ્તાર
penalty area

પેનલ્ટી એરિયા માર્કિંગ
penalty area marking

પેનલ્ટી સ્પોટ (દંડ સ્વીકારવા
માટેની જગ્યા)
penalty spot

રમતનાં મેદાનમાં જ્યાં બોલ જવાથી
દંડ થઈ શકે તેવું પરિધ/વર્તુળ
penalty arc

90 – 120 m

કેન્દ્રિય ધ્વજ
center flag / centre flag

બહારની બાજુએ જમણી તરફ
outside right

કેન્દ્ર સ્થાન
center spot / centre spot

સેન્ટર ફોરવર્ડ
center forward /
centre forward

અંદરની બાજુએ જમણી તરફ
inside right

રાઈટ હાફ
right half

સ્પર્શ-રેખા (ટચ લાઈન)
touch line

લાઈનમેન
linesman

રાઈટ બેક
right back

ખૂણાની કમાન
corner arc

ડાબીબાજુએ પાછળની તરફ
left back

ગોલરોકનાર ખેલાડી
goalkeeper

કેન્દ્રિય વર્તુળ
center circle / centre circle

મેદાનમાં મધ્ય રેખા
midfield line

અંદરની બાજુએ ડાબી તરફ
inside left

સેન્ટર બેક
center back

બહારની બાજુએ ડાબી તરફ
outside left

લેફ્ટ હાફ
left half

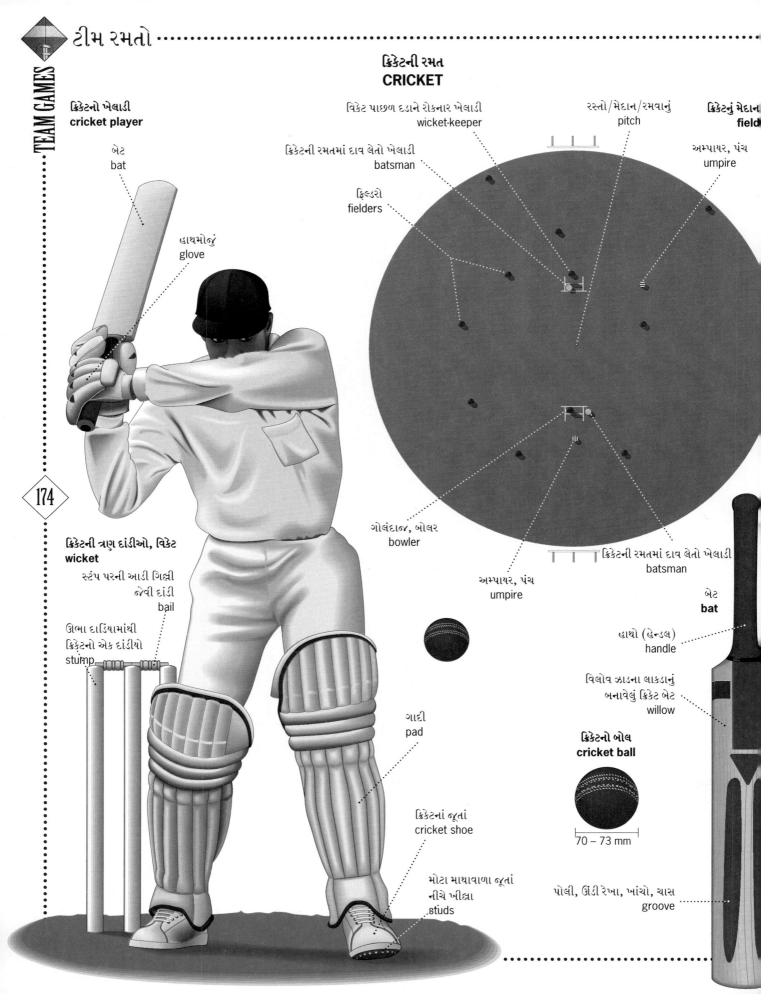

174

ક્રિકેટની રમત
CRICKET

ક્રિકેટનો ખેલાડી
cricket player

બેટ
bat

હાથમોજું
glove

વિકેટ પાછળ દડાને રોકનાર ખેલાડી
wicket-keeper

ક્રિકેટની રમતમાં દાવ લેતો ખેલાડી
batsman

ફિલ્ડરો
fielders

રસ્તો/મેદાન/રમવાનું
pitch

ક્રિકેટનું મેદાન
field

અમ્પાયર, પંચ
umpire

ક્રિકેટની ત્રણ દાંડીઓ, વિકેટ
wicket

સ્ટંપ પરની આડી ગિલ્લી જેવી દાંડી
bail

ઊભા દાંડિયામાંથી ક્રિકેટનો એક દાંડીયો
stump

ગોલંદાજ, બોલર
bowler

અમ્પાયર, પંચ
umpire

ક્રિકેટની રમતમાં દાવ લેતો ખેલાડી
batsman

બેટ
bat

હાથો (હેન્ડલ)
handle

વિલોવ ઝાડના લાકડાનું બનાવેલું ક્રિકેટ બેટ
willow

ગાદી
pad

ક્રિકેટનો બોલ
cricket ball

ક્રિકેટનાં જૂતાં
cricket shoe

70 – 73 mm

મોટા માથાવાળા જૂતાં નીચે ખીલ્લા
studs

પોલી, ઊંડી રેખા, ખાંચો, ચાસ
groove

હોકી રમવાનું મેદાન
FIELD HOCKEY

હોકી, રમતનું મેદાન
playing field

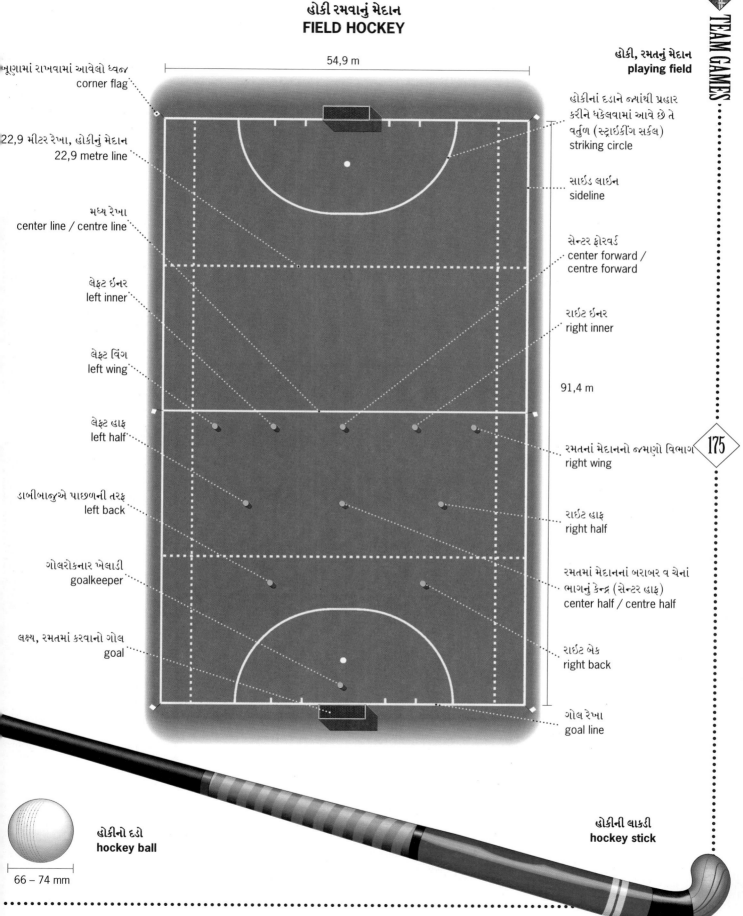

54,9 m

ખૂણામાં રાખવામાં આવેલો ધ્વજ
corner flag

22,9 મીટર રેખા, હોકીનું મેદાન
22,9 metre line

મધ્ય રેખા
center line / centre line

લેફ્ટ ઇનર
left inner

લેફ્ટ વિંગ
left wing

લેફ્ટ હાફ
left half

ડાબીબાજુએ પાછલની તરફ
left back

ગોલરોકનાર ખેલાડી
goalkeeper

લક્ષ્ય, રમતમાં કરવાનો ગોલ
goal

હોકીનાં દડાને જ્યાંથી પ્રહાર કરીને ધકેલવામાં આવે છે તે વર્તુળ (સ્ટ્રાઇકીંગ સર્કલ)
striking circle

સાઇડ લાઇન
sideline

સેન્ટર ફોરવર્ડ
center forward / centre forward

રાઇટ ઇનર
right inner

91,4 m

રમતનાં મેદાનનો જમણો વિભાગ
right wing

રાઇટ હાફ
right half

રમતમાં મેદાનનાં બરાબર વ ચેનાં ભાગનું કેન્દ્ર (સેન્ટર હાફ)
center half / centre half

રાઇટ બેક
right back

ગોલ રેખા
goal line

હોકીનો દડો
hockey ball

66 – 74 mm

હોકીની લાકડી
hockey stick

બરફનાં મેદાનમાં હોકીની રમત
ICE HOCKEY

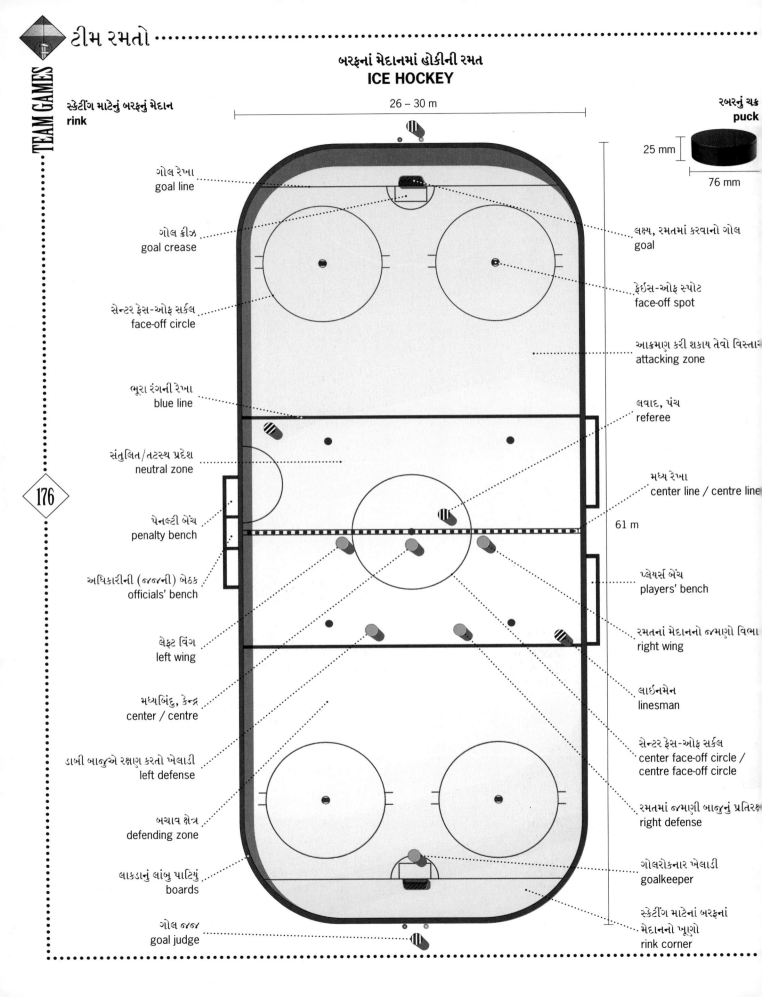

સ્કેટીંગ માટેનું બરફનું મેદાન
rink

26 – 30 m

રબરનું ચક્ર
puck

25 mm

76 mm

ગોલ રેખા
goal line

ગોલ ક્રીઝ
goal crease

સેન્ટર ફેસ-ઓફ સર્કલ
face-off circle

ભૂરા રંગની રેખા
blue line

સંતુલિત/તટસ્થ પ્રદેશ
neutral zone

પેનલ્ટી બેંચ
penalty bench

અધિકારીની (જજની) બેઠક
officials' bench

લેફ્ટ વિંગ
left wing

મધ્યબિંદુ, કેન્દ્ર
center / centre

ડાબી બાજુએ રક્ષણ કરતો ખેલાડી
left defense

બચાવ ક્ષેત્ર
defending zone

લાકડાનું લાંબુ પાટિયું
boards

ગોલ જજ
goal judge

લક્ષ્ય, રમતમાં કરવાનો ગોલ
goal

ફેઈસ-ઓફ સ્પોટ
face-off spot

આક્રમણ કરી શકાય તેવો વિસ્તાર
attacking zone

લવાદ, પંચ
referee

મધ્ય રેખા
center line / centre line

61 m

પ્લેયર્સ બેંચ
players' bench

રમતનાં મેદાનનો જમણો વિભાગ
right wing

લાઈનમેન
linesman

સેન્ટર ફેસ-ઓફ સર્કલ
center face-off circle /
centre face-off circle

રમતમાં જમણી બાજુનું પ્રતિરક્ષણ
right defense

ગોલરોકનાર ખેલાડી
goalkeeper

સ્કેટીંગ માટેના બરફનાં
મેદાનનો ખૂણો
rink corner

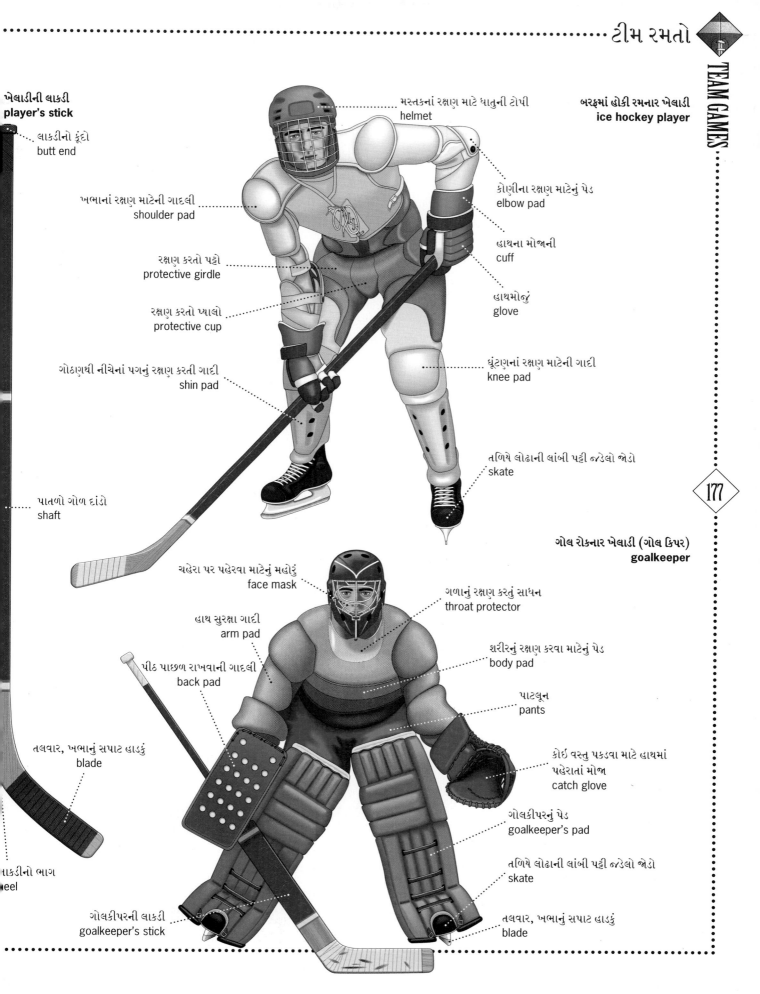

ખેલાડીની લાકડી
player's stick

લાકડીનો કુંદો
butt end

મસ્તકનાં રક્ષણ માટે ધાતુની ટોપી
helmet

બરફમાં હોકી રમનાર ખેલાડી
ice hockey player

કોણીના રક્ષણ માટેનું પેડ
elbow pad

ખભાનાં રક્ષણ માટેની ગાદલી
shoulder pad

રક્ષણ કરતો પટ્ટો
protective girdle

રક્ષણ કરતો પ્યાલો
protective cup

હાથના મોજાની
cuff

હાથમોજું
glove

ગોઠણથી નીચેનાં પગનું રક્ષણ કરતી ગાદી
shin pad

ઘૂંટણનાં રક્ષણ માટેની ગાદી
knee pad

પાતળો ગોળ દાંડો
shaft

તળિયે લોઢાની લાંબી પટ્ટી જડેલો જોડો
skate

ગોલ રોકનાર ખેલાડી (ગોલ કિપર)
goalkeeper

ચહેરા પર પહેરવા માટેનું મહોરું
face mask

ગળાનું રક્ષણ કરતું સાધન
throat protector

હાથ સુરક્ષા ગાદી
arm pad

શરીરનું રક્ષણ કરવા માટેનું પેડ
body pad

પીઠ પાછળ રાખવાની ગાદલી
back pad

પાટલૂન
pants

તલવાર, ખભાનું સપાટ હાડકું
blade

કોઈ વસ્તુ પકડવા માટે હાથમાં
પહેરાતાં મોજા
catch glove

ગોલકીપરનું પેડ
goalkeeper's pad

તળિયે લોઢાની લાંબી પટ્ટી જડેલો જોડો
skate

લાકડીનો ભાગ
eel

ગોલકીપરની લાકડી
goalkeeper's stick

તલવાર, ખભાનું સપાટ હાડકું
blade

બાસ્કેટબોલ, ટોપલા દડાની રમત
BASKETBALL

બાસ્કેટબોલ નામની રમત રમવાનું મેદાન
court

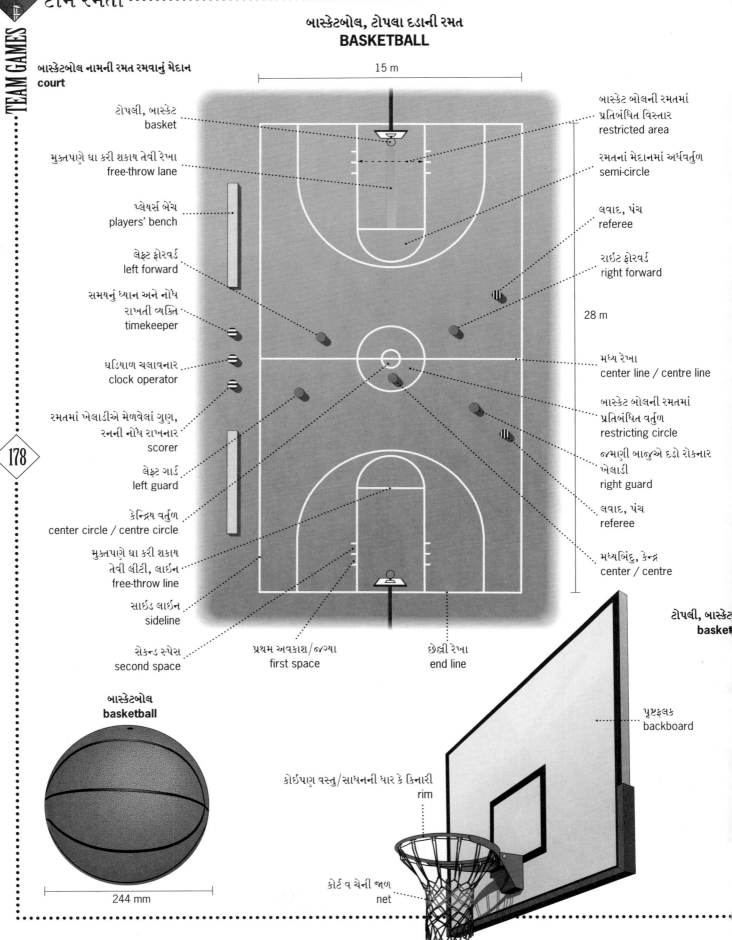

15 m

ટોપલી, બાસ્કેટ
basket

મુક્તપણે ઘા કરી શકાય તેવી રેખા
free-throw lane

પ્લેયર્સ બેંચ
players' bench

લેફ્ટ ફોરવર્ડ
left forward

સમયનું ધ્યાન અને નોંધ
રાખતી વ્યક્તિ
timekeeper

ઘડિયાળ ચલાવનાર
clock operator

રમતમાં ખેલાડીએ મેળવેલાં ગુણ,
રનની નોંધ રાખનાર
scorer

લેફ્ટ ગાર્ડ
left guard

કેન્દ્રિય વર્તુળ
center circle / centre circle

મુક્તપણે ઘા કરી શકાય
તેવી લીટી, લાઈન
free-throw line

સાઈડ લાઈન
sideline

સેકન્ડ સ્પેસ
second space

બાસ્કેટ બોલની રમતમાં
પ્રતિબંધિત વિસ્તાર
restricted area

રમતનાં મેદાનમાં અર્ધવર્તુળ
semi-circle

લવાદ, પંચ
referee

રાઈટ ફોરવર્ડ
right forward

28 m

મધ્ય રેખા
center line / centre line

બાસ્કેટ બોલની રમતમાં
પ્રતિબંધિત વર્તુળ
restricting circle

જમાણી બાજુએ દડો રોકનાર
ખેલાડી
right guard

લવાદ, પંચ
referee

મધ્યબિંદુ, કેન્દ્ર
center / centre

પ્રથમ અવકાશ/જગ્યા
first space

છેલ્લી રેખા
end line

બાસ્કેટબોલ
basketball

244 mm

ટોપલી, બાસ્કેટ
basket

પૃષ્ઠફલક
backboard

કોઈપણ વસ્તુ/સાધનની ધાર કે કિનારી
rim

કોર્ટ વ ચેની જાળ
net

મોટાં દડાં વડે રમાતી રમત, વોલીબોલ
VOLLEYBALL

વોલીબોલ રમવાનું મેદાન
court

9 m

18 m

વોલીબોલની રમતમાં રીટ્રીવર
retriever

ક્લિયર સ્પેસ
clear space

સર્વિસ એરીયા
service area

પાછળનો વિભાગ
back zone

ખેલાડીઓ બાંકડો
players' bench

રમતમાં ખેલાડીએ મેળવેલાં ગુણ, રનની નોંધ રાખનાર
scorer

રમતમાં મધ્યસ્થ વ્યક્તિ
umpire

લેફ્ટ ફોરવર્ડ
left forward

આક્રમણ રેખા
attack line

આક્રમણ વિસ્તાર
attack zone

છેલ્લી રેખા
end line

લાઈનમેન
linesman

સાઈડ લાઈન
sideline

લવાદ, પંચ
referee

કોર્ટ વ ચેની જાળ
net

રાઈટ ફોરવર્ડ
right forward

સેન્ટર ફોરવર્ડ
center forward

ડાબીબાજુએ પાછળની તરફ
left back

સેન્ટર બેક
center back

દડાની સર્વિસ કરતો ખેલાડી (સર્વર)
server

જાળી
net

મોટાં દડાં વડે રમાતી રમત, વોલીબોલ
volleyball

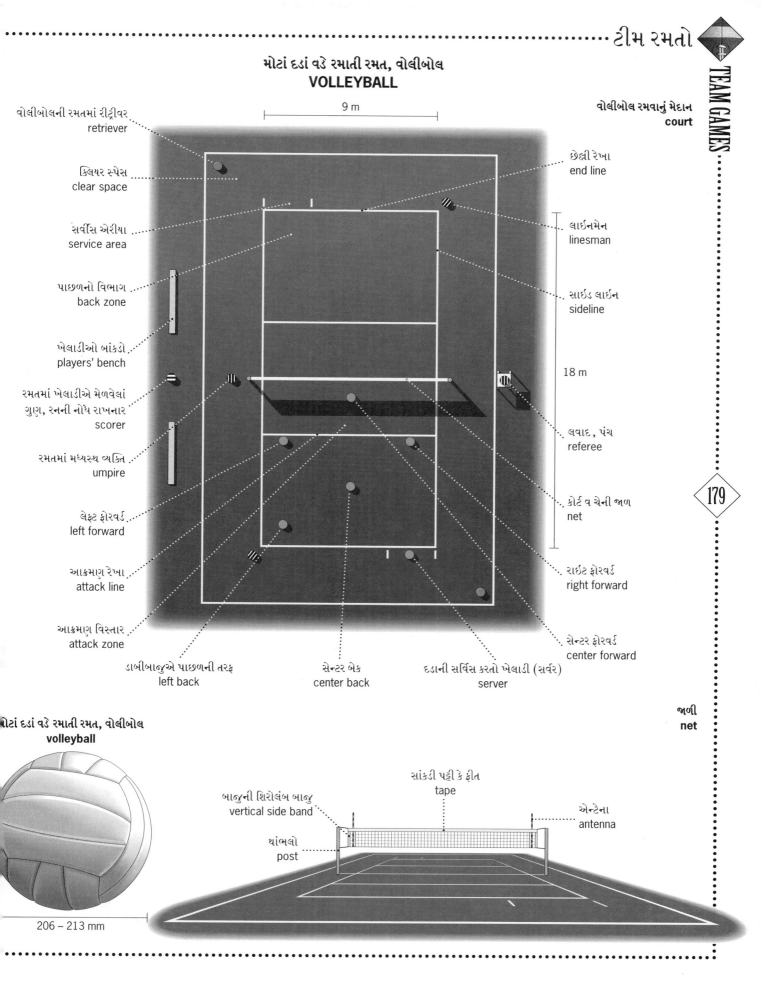

206 – 213 mm

બાજુની શિરોલંબ બાજુ
vertical side band

થાંભલો
post

સાંકડી પટ્ટી કે ફીત
tape

એન્ટેના
antenna

TEAM GAMES

દડા અને જાળીદાર બેટ વડે રમાતી અંગ્રેજી રમત ટેનિસ
TENNIS

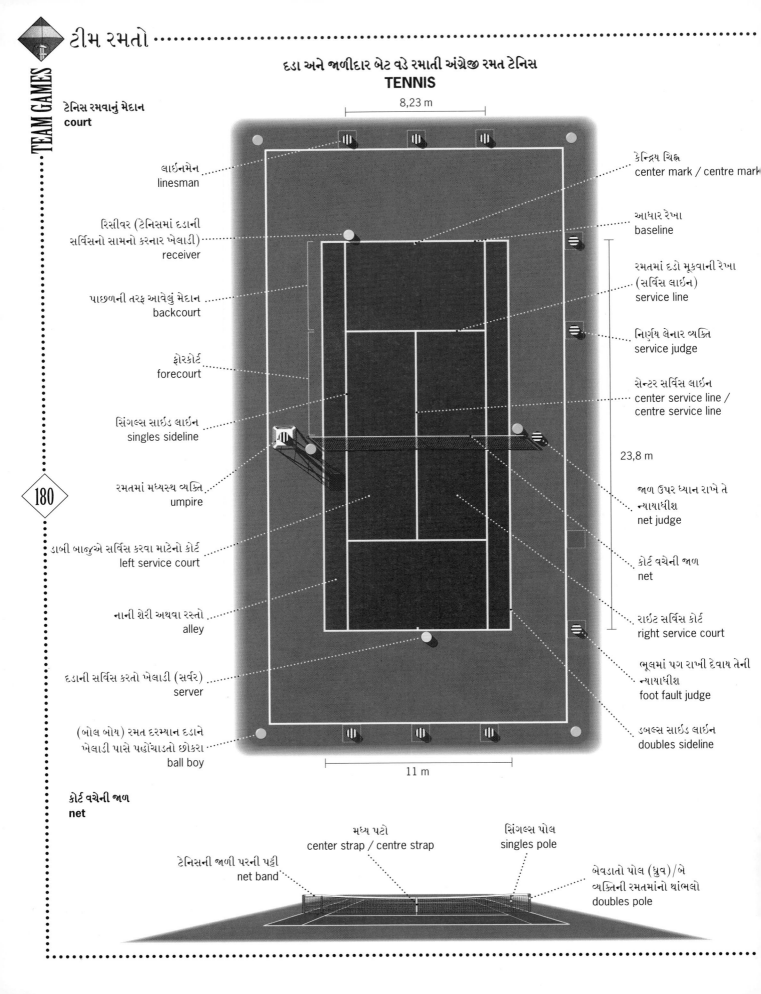

ટેનિસ રમવાનું મેદાન
court

8,23 m

લાઈનમેન
linesman

રિસીવર (ટેનિસમાં દડાની
સર્વિસનો સામનો કરનાર ખેલાડી)
receiver

પાછળની તરફ આવેલું મેદાન
backcourt

ફોરકોર્ટ
forecourt

સિંગલ્સ સાઈડ લાઈન
singles sideline

રમતમાં મધ્યસ્થ વ્યક્તિ
umpire

ડાબી બાજુએ સર્વિસ કરવા માટેનો કોર્ટ
left service court

નાની શેરી અથવા રસ્તો
alley

દડાની સર્વિસ કરતો ખેલાડી (સર્વર)
server

(બોલ બોય) રમત દરમ્યાન દડાને
ખેલાડી પાસે પહોંચાડતો છોકરો
ball boy

કેન્દ્રિય ચિह્ન
center mark / centre mark

આધાર રેખા
baseline

રમતમાં દડો મૂકવાની રેખા
(સર્વિસ લાઈન)
service line

નિર્ણય લેનાર વ્યક્તિ
service judge

સેન્ટર સર્વિસ લાઈન
center service line /
centre service line

23,8 m

જાળ ઉપર ધ્યાન રાખે તે
ન્યાયાધીશ
net judge

કોર્ટ વચ્ચેની જાળ
net

રાઈટ સર્વિસ કોર્ટ
right service court

ભૂલમાં પગ રાખી દેવાય તેની
ન્યાયાધીશ
foot fault judge

ડબલ્સ સાઈડ લાઈન
doubles sideline

11 m

કોર્ટ વચ્ચેની જાળ
net

મધ્ય પટો
center strap / centre strap

સિંગલ્સ પોલ
singles pole

ટેનિસની જાળી પરની પટ્ટી
net band

બેવડાતો પોલ (ધ્રુવ)/બે
વ્યક્તિની રમતમાંનો થાંભલો
doubles pole

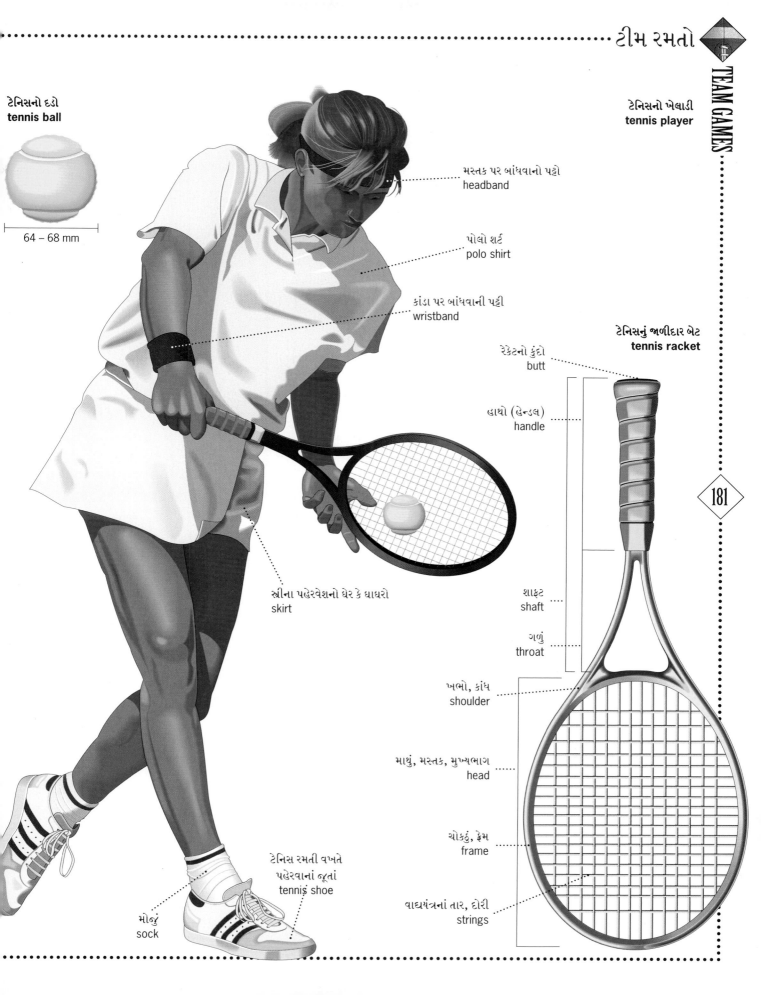

ટેનિસનો દડો
tennis ball

64 – 68 mm

ટેનિસનો ખેલાડી
tennis player

મસ્તક પર બાંધવાનો પટ્ટો
headband

પોલો શર્ટ
polo shirt

કાંડા પર બાંધવાની પટ્ટી
wristband

ટેનિસનું જાળીદાર બેટ
tennis racket

રેકેટનો ફુંદો
butt

હાથો (હેન્ડલ)
handle

શાફ્ટ
shaft

ગળું
throat

ખભો, કાંધ
shoulder

સ્ત્રીના પહેરવેશનો ઘેર કે ઘાઘરો
skirt

માથું, મસ્તક, મુખ્યભાગ
head

ચોકઠું, ફ્રેમ
frame

ટેનિસ રમતી વખતે
પહેરવાનાં જૂતાં
tennis shoe

મોજું
sock

વાઘયંત્રનાં તાર, દોરી
strings

પાણીમાં રમત ગમતો

પાણીમાં તરવું
SWIMMING

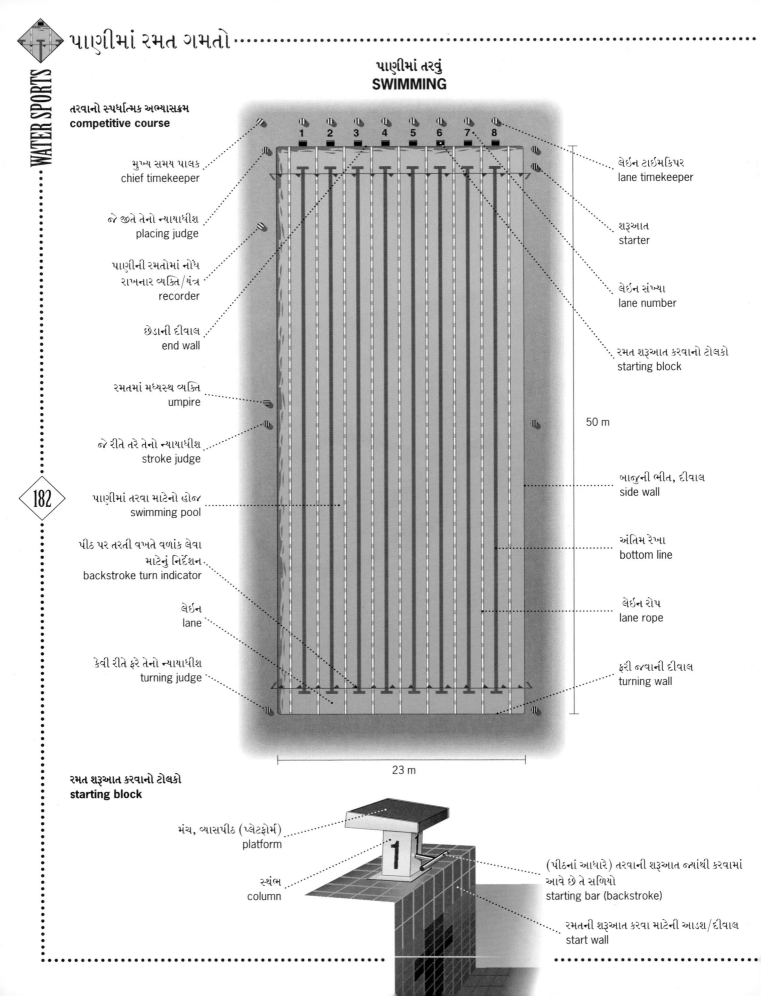

તરવાનો સ્પર્ધાત્મક અભ્યાસક્રમ
competitive course

મુખ્ય સમય પાલક
chief timekeeper

જે જીતે તેનો ન્યાયાધીશ
placing judge

પાણીની રમતોમાં નોંધ
રાખનાર વ્યક્તિ/યંત્ર
recorder

છેડાની દીવાલ
end wall

રમતમાં મધ્યસ્થ વ્યક્તિ
umpire

જે રીતે તરે તેનો ન્યાયાધીશ
stroke judge

પાણીમાં તરવા માટેનો હોજ
swimming pool

પીઠ પર તરતી વખતે વળાંક લેવા
માટેનું નિર્દેશન
backstroke turn indicator

લેઈન
lane

કેવી રીતે ફરે તેનો ન્યાયાધીશ
turning judge

લેઈન ટાઈમકિપર
lane timekeeper

શરૂઆત
starter

લેઈન સંખ્યા
lane number

રમત શરૂઆત કરવાનો ટોલકો
starting block

50 m

બાજુની ભીત, દીવાલ
side wall

અંતિમ રેખા
bottom line

લેઈન રોપ
lane rope

ફરી જવાની દીવાલ
turning wall

23 m

રમત શરૂઆત કરવાનો ટોલકો
starting block

મંચ, વ્યાસપીઠ (પ્લેટફોર્મ)
platform

સ્થંભ
column

(પીઠનાં આધારે) તરવાની શરૂઆત જ્યાંથી કરવામાં
આવે છે તે સળિયો
starting bar (backstroke)

રમતની શરૂઆત કરવા માટેની આડશ/દીવાલ
start wall

182

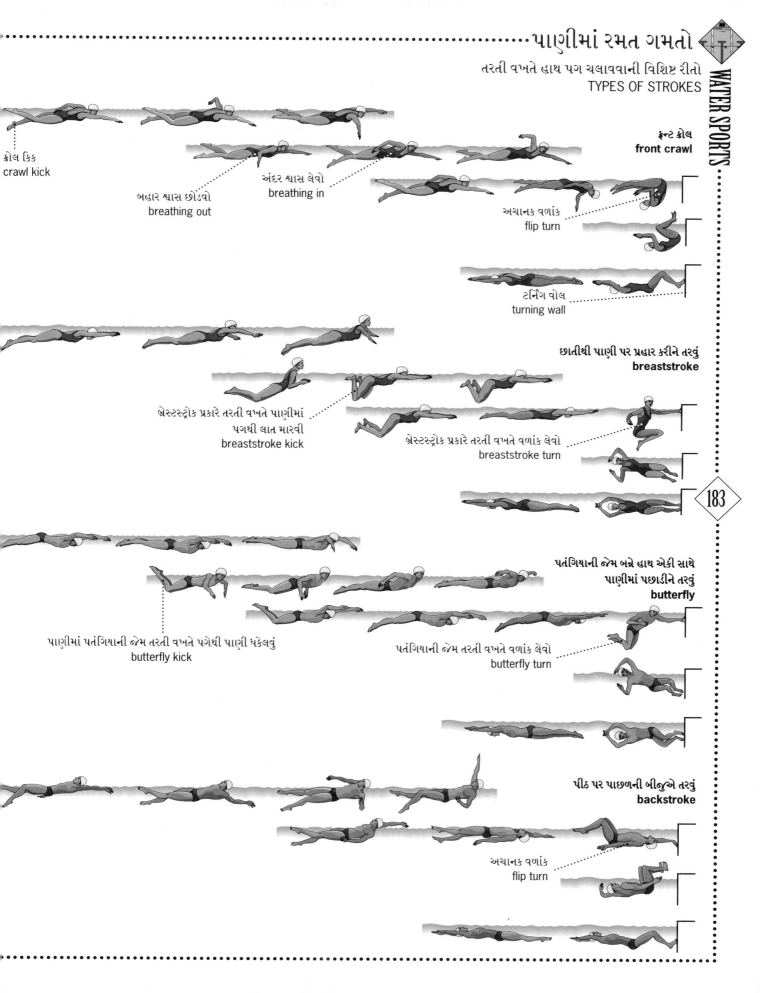

તરતી વખતે હાથ પગ ચલાવવાની વિશિષ્ટ રીતો
TYPES OF STROKES

ફ્રન્ટ ક્રોલ
front crawl

ક્રોલ કિક
crawl kick

બહાર શ્વાસ છોડવો
breathing out

અંદર શ્વાસ લેવો
breathing in

અચાનક વળાંક
flip turn

ટર્નિંગ વોલ
turning wall

છાતીથી પાણી પર પ્રહાર કરીને તરવું
breaststroke

બ્રેસ્ટસ્ટ્રોક પ્રકારે તરતી વખતે પાણીમાં
પગથી લાત મારવી
breaststroke kick

બ્રેસ્ટસ્ટ્રોક પ્રકારે તરતી વખતે વળાંક લેવો
breaststroke turn

183

પતંગિયાની જેમ બન્ને હાથ એકી સાથે
પાણીમાં પછાડીને તરવું
butterfly

પાણીમાં પતંગિયાની જેમ તરતી વખતે પગેથી પાણી ધકેલવું
butterfly kick

પતંગિયાની જેમ તરતી વખતે વળાંક લેવો
butterfly turn

પીઠ પર પાછળની બીજુએ તરવું
backstroke

અચાનક વળાંક
flip turn

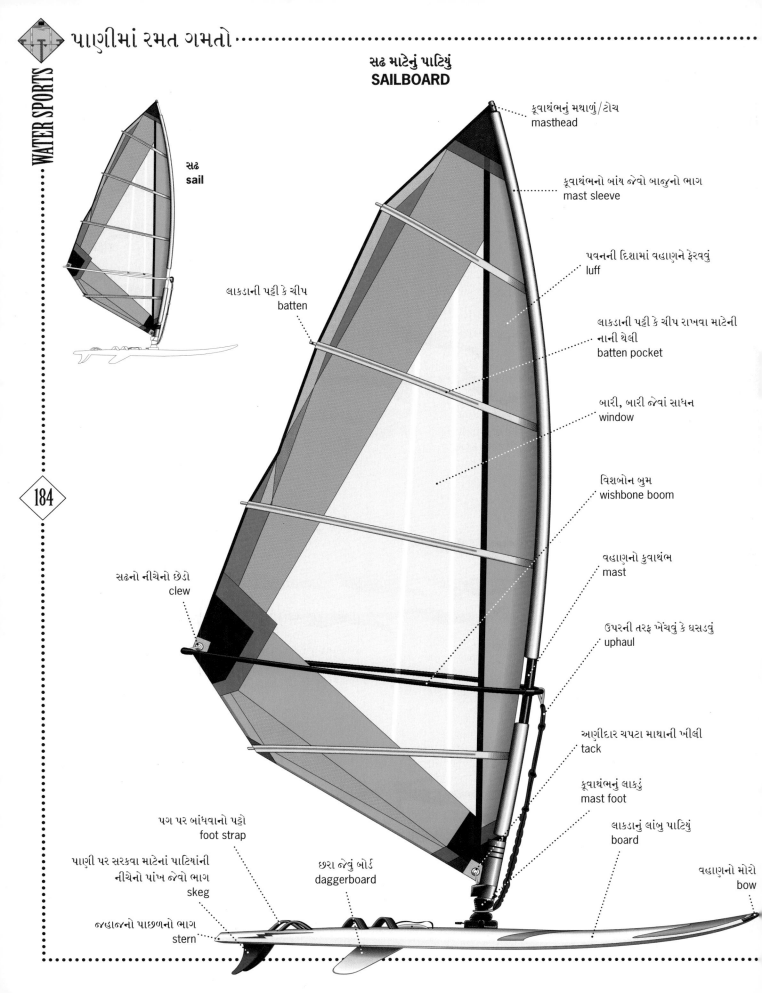

પાણીમાં રમત ગમતો

સઢ માટેનું પાટિયું
SAILBOARD

સઢ
sail

184

કૂવાથંભનું મથાળું/ટોચ
masthead

કૂવાથંભનો બાંય જેવો બાજુનો ભાગ
mast sleeve

પવનની દિશામાં વહાણને ફેરવવું
luff

લાકડાની પટ્ટી કે ચીપ
batten

લાકડાની પટ્ટી કે ચીપ રાખવા માટેની
નાની થેલી
batten pocket

બારી, બારી જેવાં સાધન
window

વિશબોન બુમ
wishbone boom

વહાણનો કૂવાથંભ
mast

ઉપરની તરફ ખેંચવું કે ઘસડવું
uphaul

સઢનો નીચેનો છેડો
clew

અણીદાર ચપટા માથાની ખીલી
tack

કૂવાથંભનું લાકડું
mast foot

પગ પર બાંધવાનો પટ્ટો
foot strap

છરા જેવું બોર્ડ
daggerboard

લાકડાનું લાંબુ પાટિયું
board

વહાણનો મોરો
bow

પાણી પર સરકવા માટેનાં પાટિયાંની
નીચેનો પાંખ જેવો ભાગ
skeg

જહાજનો પાછળનો ભાગ
stern

બરફ પર સરકવાની રમત (સ્કેટીંગ)
SKATING

ઈન લાઈન સ્કેટ
in-line skate

અંદરનો જોડો, બૂટ
inner boot

અપર શેલ
upper shell

સાનુકૂળ બકલ
adjusting buckle

જોડો, બૂટ
boot

ધરી
axle

પૈડું, ચક્ર
wheel

ભારવાહક ગાડી, ટ્રક (ટ્રક)
truck

હિલ સ્ટોપ
heel stop

ઝડપથી સરકવાનું પાટિયું (સ્કેટ)
speed skate

હોકી સ્કેટ
hockey skate

સ્નાયુબંધનું રક્ષણ કરતું સાધન
tendon guard

જોડો
boot

ટો બોક્સ
toe box

આણી, બિંદુ, આંગળી
થી દર્શાવવું
point

બ્લેડ
blade

ફિગર સ્કેટીંગ
figure skate

આંકડો
hook

જીભ
tongue

પાછળનો ભાગ
backstay

છિદ્ર/ગાળ
eyelet

જોડો, બૂટ
boot

ઊભું ટેકાનું
stanchion

જોડાની વાધરી, ઝીણી દોરી
lace

ધાર, છેડો
edge

બ્લેડ
blade

સ્કેટ ગાર્ડ
skate guard

પગનું અથવા પગરખાનું તળિયું
sole

ટો પીક
toe pick

WATER SPORTS

સ્કીની રમત/સરકવું (સ્કીઇંગ)
SKIING

પર્વત પર સરકતી વ્યક્તિ
alpine skier

સ્કીની રમત વખતે પહેરવામાં
આવતી ટોપી (સ્કી હેટ)
ski hat

સ્કીની રમત વખતે પહેરવામાં આવતાં
ચશ્મા (સ્કી ગોગલ્સ)
ski goggles

સ્કીની રમતનો પહેરવેશ (સ્કી સ્યૂટ)
ski suit

સ્કીની રમત વખતે હાથમાં
પહેરવાનાં મોજાં (સ્કી ગ્લવ)
ski glove

કાંડ પર બાંધવાનો કાપડનો પટ્ટો
wrist strap

હાથો (હેન્ડલ)
handle

આણી, આણી જેવા
ભાગ
tip

તળિયું
bottom

શોવેલ
shovel

ટો પીસ
toe piece

જૂતાંની એડી
heel piece

સ્કીની રમતમાં અટકવાની જગ્યા
ski stop

બરફ પર સરકવા માટે લાકડાનું પગરખું (સ્કી બૂટ)
ski boot

જીભ
tongue

ઉપરની પટ્ટી/પટ્ટો
upper strap

બકલ
buckle

સાનુકૂળ કેચ (પકડ)
adjusting catch

નીચલું પડ
lower shell

ઉપલું પડ
upper shell

હિંજ, મિજાગરું
hinge

સ્કીની રમતમાં વપરાતો
લાકડાનો વાંસડો (સ્કી પોલ)
ski pole

ટોપલી, બાસ્કેટ
basket

ધાર, છેડો
edge

પૂંછડી, પૂંછડી જેવો આકાર
tail

પોલી, ઊંડી રેખા, ખાંચો, ચાસ
groove

સ્કી બૂટ
ski boot

લાકડાનાં પગરખાં પહેરીને
બરફ પર સરકવું (સ્કી)
ski

ક્રોસ-કન્ટ્રિ સ્કી
cross-country ski

એડીનાં ટેકા માટેની પ્લેટ
heelplate

આંગળીને બાંધનાર વસ્તુ
toe binding

છેડો
tail

ટો પ્લેટ
toeplate

ચાપડો
clamp

શોવેલ
shovel

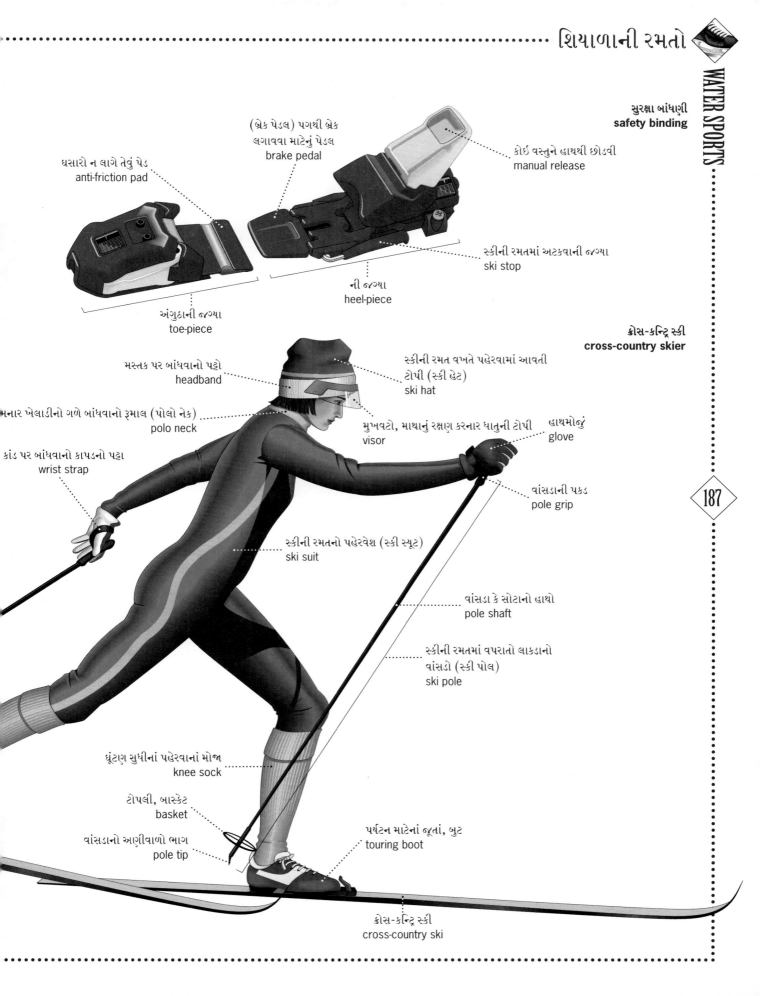

સુરક્ષા બાંધણી
safety binding

(બ્રેક પેડલ) પગથી બ્રેક
લગાવવા માટેનું પેડલ
brake pedal

ઘસારો ન લાગે તેવું પેડ
anti-friction pad

કોઇ વસ્તુને હાથથી છોડવી
manual release

સ્કીની રમતમાં અટકવાની જગ્યા
ski stop

ની જગ્યા
heel-piece

અંગુઠાની જગ્યા
toe-piece

ક્રોસ-કન્ટ્રિ સ્કી
cross-country skier

મસ્તક પર બાંધવાનો પટ્ટો
headband

સ્કીની રમત વખતે પહેરવામાં આવતી
ટોપી (સ્કી હેટ)
ski hat

...નાર ખેલાડીનો ગળે બાંધવાનો રૂમાલ (પોલો નેક)
polo neck

મુખવટો, માથાનું રક્ષણ કરનાર ધાતુની ટોપી
visor

હાથમોજું
glove

કાંડ પર બાંધવાનો કાપડનો પટ્ટા
wrist strap

વાંસડાની પકડ
pole grip

સ્કીની રમતનો પહેરવેશ (સ્કી સ્યૂટ)
ski suit

વાંસડા કે સોટાનો હાથો
pole shaft

સ્કીની રમતમાં વપરાતો લાકડાનો
વાંસડો (સ્કી પોલ)
ski pole

ઘૂંટણ સુધીનાં પહેરવાનાં મોજા
knee sock

ટોપલી, બાસ્કેટ
basket

વાંસડાનો અણીવાળો ભાગ
pole tip

પર્યટન માટેનાં જૂતાં, બુટ
touring boot

ક્રોસ-કન્ટ્રિ સ્કી
cross-country ski

187

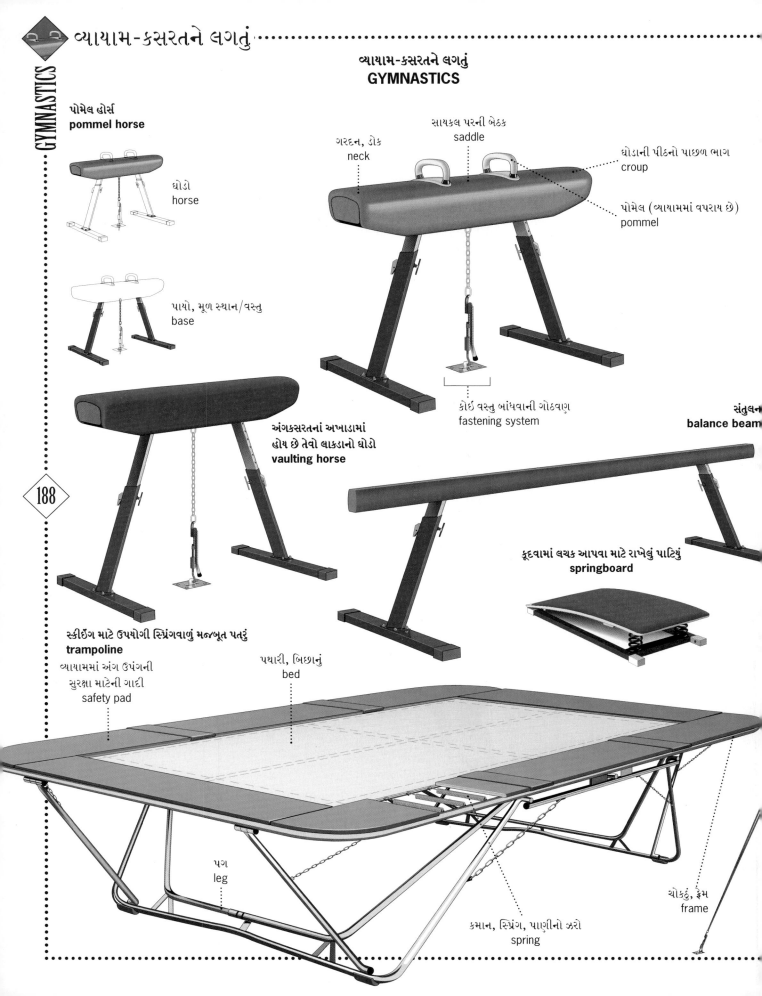

વ્યાયામ-કસરતને લગતું
GYMNASTICS

પોમેલ હોર્સ
pommel horse

ઘોડો
horse

પાયો, મૂળ સ્થાન/વસ્તુ
base

ગરદન, ડોક
neck

સાયકલ પરની બેઠક
saddle

ઘોડાની પીઠનો પાછળ ભાગ
croup

પોમેલ (વ્યાયામમાં વપરાય છે)
pommel

કોઈ વસ્તુ બાંધવાની ગોઠવણ
fastening system

સંતુલન
balance beam

અંગકસરતનાં અખાડામાં
હોય છે તેવો લાકડાનો ઘોડો
vaulting horse

કૂદવામાં લચક આપવા માટે રાખેલું પાટિયું
springboard

સ્કીઈંગ માટે ઉપયોગી સ્પ્રિંગવાળું મજબૂત પતરું
trampoline

વ્યાયામમાં અંગ ઉપંગની
સુરક્ષા માટેની ગાદી
safety pad

પથારી, બિછાનું
bed

પગ
leg

કમાન, સ્પ્રિંગ, પાણીનો ઝરો
spring

ચોકઠું, ફ્રેમ
frame

188

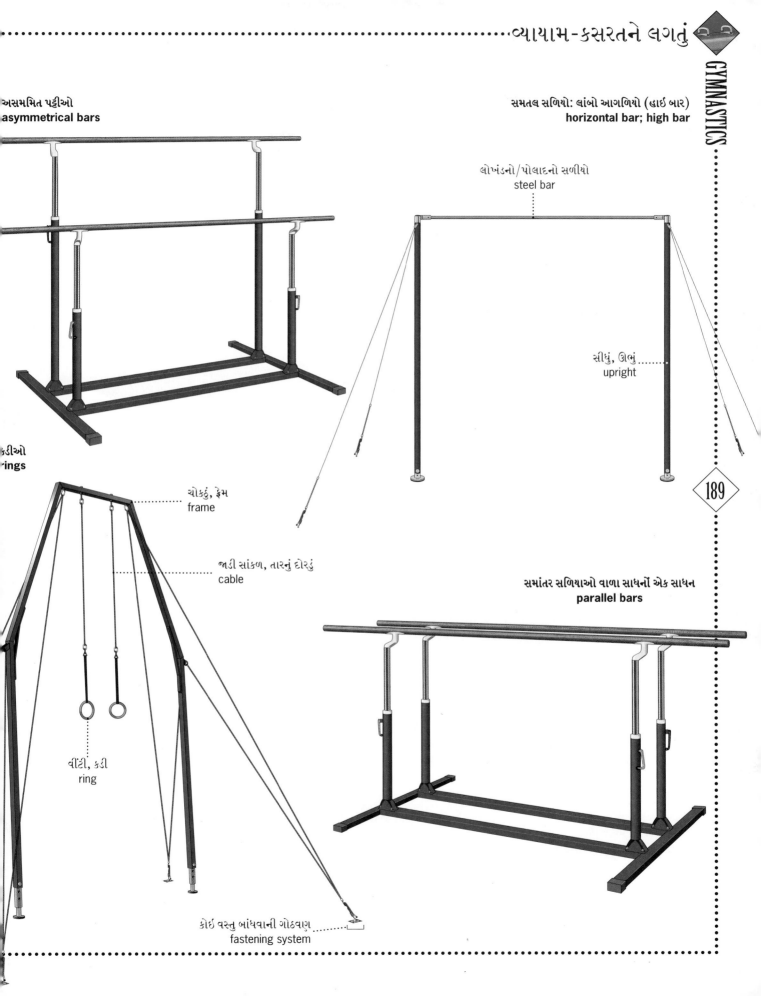

અસમમિત પટ્ટીઓ
asymmetrical bars

સમતલ સળિયો: લાંબો આગળિયો (હાઈ બાર)
horizontal bar; high bar

લોખંડનો/પોલાદનો સળિયો
steel bar

સીધું, ઊભું
upright

કડીઓ
rings

ચોકઠું, ફ્રેમ
frame

જાડી સાંકળ, તારનું દોરડું
cable

વીંટી, કડી
ring

સમાંતર સળિયાઓ વાળા સાધનો એક સાધન
parallel bars

કોઇ વસ્તુ બાંધવાની ગોઠવણ
fastening system

છાવણી, તંબુ રાખીને રહેવું

તંબૂઓ, રાવટીઓ
TENTS

બે વ્યક્તિ સમાઇ શકે તેવો તંબુ
two-person tent

તંબૂના બારણા તરીકે વરસાદથી રક્ષણ મેળવવા માટે વપરાતો કેનવાસનો કટકો (રેઇનફ્લાય)
rainfly / flysheet

બારણું
door

માંડવાની છત (સૂર્યનો તડકો, વરસાદ રોકવા માટેનું છાપરું)
awning

બાંધવા માટેની દોરી
guy line / guy rope

કોઇ વસ્તુ કસીને તંગ કરનાર સાધન (અથવા દોરી)
strainer

ઝિપર, વસ્ત્રનાં છેડા બંધ કરતી દાંતાવાળી રચના
zipper / zip

અંદરની બાજુનો ટેન્ટ/તંબુ
inner tent

આણીવાળી લાકડી
stake / tent pe

તંબૂઓ, રાવટીઓનાં મોટાં પ્રકારો
MAJOR TYPES OF TENTS

ચાર પૈડાવાળી ગાડીમાં બાંધેલો તંબુ
wagon tent

દીવાલ જેટલો ઊંચો તંબુ
wall tent

ગલૂડિયા માટેની રાવટી
pup tent / ridge tent

ધૂમ્મટ જેવો તંબુ
dome tent

આકસ્મિક/તાત્કાલિક ઊભો કરેલો તંબુ
pop-up tent

પરિવાર માટેનો તંબુ
family tent

એક વ્યક્તિ સમાય શકે તેવો તંબુ
one-person tent

સૂવા માટેનાં સાધનો
SLEEPING EQUIPMENT

ખાટલા અને ગાદલા
BEDS AND MATTRESSES

ફોમ પેડ
foam pad

આપોઆપ હવા ભરાઈ જાય તેવું ગાદલું
self-inflating mattress

ઇન્ફ્લેટર
inflator

ઇન્ફ્લેટર – ડિફ્લેટર
inflator-deflator

વાળી શકાય તેવો પલંગ
folding cot / camp bed

થેલા જેવી સૂવા માટેની પથારી
SLEEPING BAGS

સૂવા માટેની નાની પથારી
semi-mummy

સમચોરસ આકારનું
rectangular

હવા ભરેલું ગાદલું, તળાઈ
air mattress / air bed

સૂવા માટેની મોટી પથારી
mummy

છાવણી (તંબુ) માટેનાં સાધનો
CAMPING EQUIPMENT

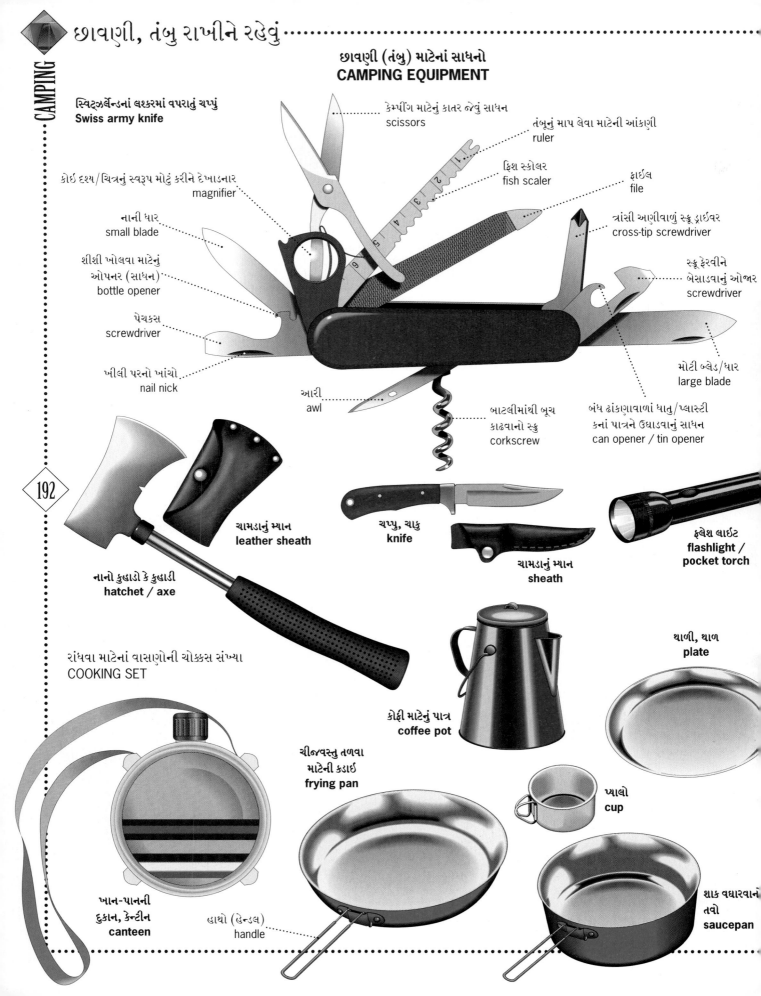

સ્વિટ્ઝર્લેન્ડનાં લશ્કરમાં વપરાતું ચપ્પું
Swiss army knife

કેમ્પીંગ માટેનું કાતર જેવું સાધન
scissors

તંબૂનું માપ લેવા માટેની આંકણી
ruler

ફિશ સ્કેલર
fish scaler

ફાઇલ
file

કોઈ દશ્ય/ચિત્રનું સ્વરૂપ મોટું કરીને દેખાડનાર
magnifier

ત્રાંસી અણીવાળું સ્ક્રૂ ડ્રાઈવર
cross-tip screwdriver

નાની ધાર
small blade

શીશી ખોલવા માટેનું ઓપનર (સાધન)
bottle opener

સ્ક્રૂ ફેરવીને બેસાડવાનું ઓજાર
screwdriver

પેચકસ
screwdriver

ખીલી પરનો ખાંચો
nail nick

મોટી બ્લેડ/ધાર
large blade

આરી
awl

બાટલીમાંથી બૂચ કાઢવાનો સ્ક્રૂ
corkscrew

બંધ ઢાંકણાવાળાં ધાતુ/પ્લાસ્ટી કનાં પાત્રને ઉઘાડવાનું સાધન
can opener / tin opener

192

ચામડાનું મ્યાન
leather sheath

ચપ્પુ, ચાકુ
knife

ચામડાનું મ્યાન
sheath

ફ્લેશ લાઇટ
flashlight / pocket torch

નાનો કુહાડો કે કુહાડી
hatchet / axe

રાંધવા માટેનાં વાસણોની ચોક્કસ સંખ્યા
COOKING SET

થાળી, થાળ
plate

કોફી માટેનું પાત્ર
coffee pot

ચીજવસ્તુ તળવા માટેની કડાઈ
frying pan

પ્યાલો
cup

ખાન-પાનની દુકાન, કેન્ટીન
canteen

હાથો (હેન્ડલ)
handle

શાક વઘારવાનું તવો
saucepan

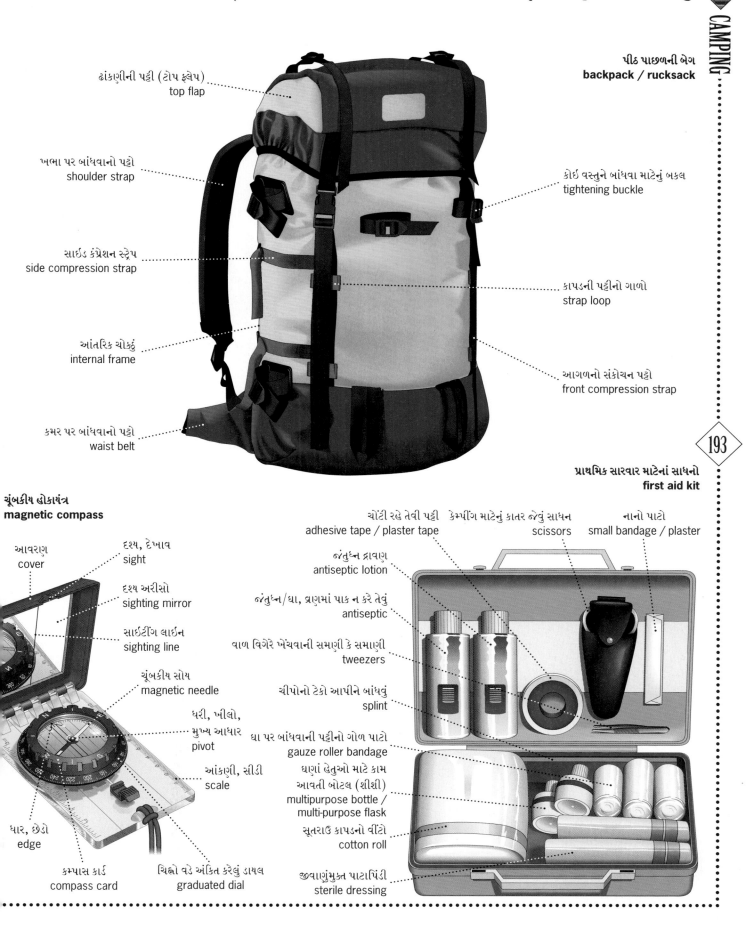

પીઠ પાછળની બેગ
backpack / rucksack

ઢાંકણીની પટ્ટી (ટોપ ફ્લેપ)
top flap

ખભા પર બાંધવાનો પટ્ટો
shoulder strap

સાઇડ કંપ્રેશન સ્ટ્રેપ
side compression strap

આંતરિક ચોકઠું
internal frame

કમર પર બાંધવાનો પટ્ટો
waist belt

કોઈ વસ્તુને બાંધવા માટેનું બકલ
tightening buckle

કાપડની પટ્ટીનો ગાળો
strap loop

આગળનો સંકોચન પટ્ટો
front compression strap

પ્રાથમિક સારવાર માટેનાં સાધનો
first aid kit

ચૂંબકીય હોકાયંત્ર
magnetic compass

આવરણ
cover

દશ્ય, દેખાવ
sight

દશ્ય અરીસો
sighting mirror

સાઇટીંગ લાઇન
sighting line

ચૂંબકીય સોય
magnetic needle

ધરી, ખીલો,
મુખ્ય આધાર
pivot

આંકણી, સીડી
scale

ધાર, છેડો
edge

કમ્પાસ કાર્ડ
compass card

ચિહ્નો વડે અંકિત કરેલું ડાયલ
graduated dial

ચોંટી રહે તેવી પટ્ટી
adhesive tape / plaster tape

જંતુઘ્ન દ્રાવણ
antiseptic lotion

જંતુઘ્ન/ઘા, વ્રણમાં પાક ન કરે તેવું
antiseptic

વાળ વિગેરે ખેંચવાની સમાણી કે સમાણી
tweezers

ચીપોનો ટેકો આપીને બાંધવું
splint

ઘા પર બાંધવાની પટ્ટીનો ગોળ પાટો
gauze roller bandage

ઘણાં હેતુઓ માટે કામ
આવતી બોટલ (શીશી)
multipurpose bottle /
multi-purpose flask

સૂતરાઉ કાપડનો વીંટો
cotton roll

જીવાણુમુક્ત પાટાપિંડી
sterile dressing

કેમ્પીંગ માટેનું કાતર જેવું સાધન
scissors

નાનો પાટો
small bandage / plaster

પત્તાની/ગંજીફાની રમત
CARD GAMES

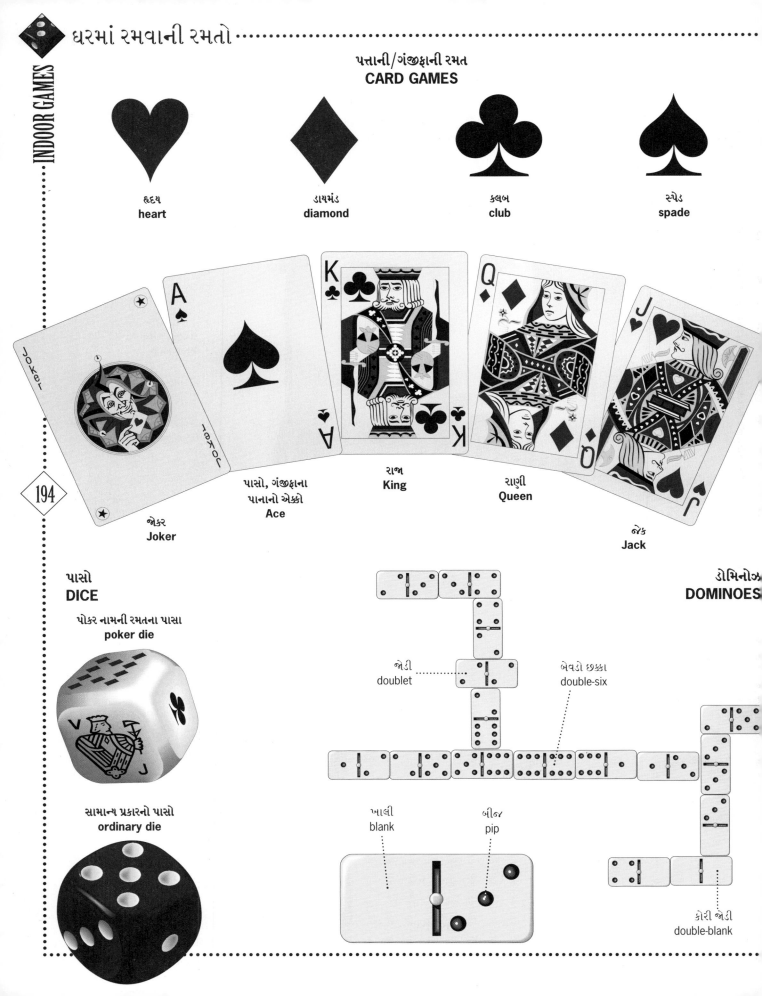

હૃદય
heart

ડાયમંડ
diamond

કલબ
club

સ્પેડ
spade

જોકર
Joker

પાસો, ગંજીફાના
પાનાનો એક્કો
Ace

રાજા
King

રાણી
Queen

જેક
Jack

પાસો
DICE

પોકર નામની રમતના પાસા
poker die

સામાન્ય પ્રકારનો પાસો
ordinary die

ડોમિનોઝ
DOMINOES

જોડી
doublet

બેવડો છક્કા
double-six

ખાલી
blank

બીજ
pip

કોરી જોડી
double-blank

શતરંજની રમત
CHESS

શતરંજ રમવાનું બોર્ડ
chessboard

માણસો, માનવીઓ
MEN

'ચેસ'માં રાણીની બાજુ
Queen's side

રાજાની બાજુ
King's side

કાળો રંગ
Black

શતરંજની રમતમાં
સફેદ ચોરસ ખાના
white square

કાળો ચોરસ
black square

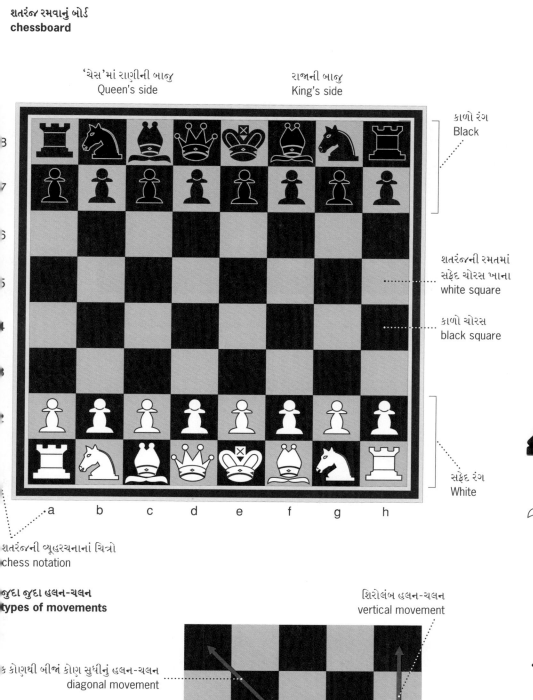

સફેદ રંગ
White

શતરંજની વ્યૂહરચનાનાં ચિત્રો
chess notation

જુદા જુદા હલન-ચલન
types of movements

શિરોલંબ હલન-ચલન
vertical movement

ક કોણથી બીજાં કોણ સુધીનું હલન-ચલન
diagonal movement

ચોરસ હલન-ચલન
square movement

સમતલ હિલચાલ
horizontal movement

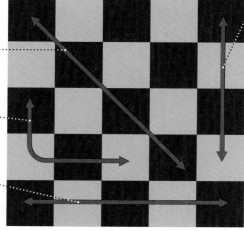

પોન
Pawn

નાઈટ
Knight

બિશપ
Bishop

શતરંજમાં 'કેસેલ'
અથવા હાથીનું મહોરું
Rook

રાણી
Queen

રાજા
King

195

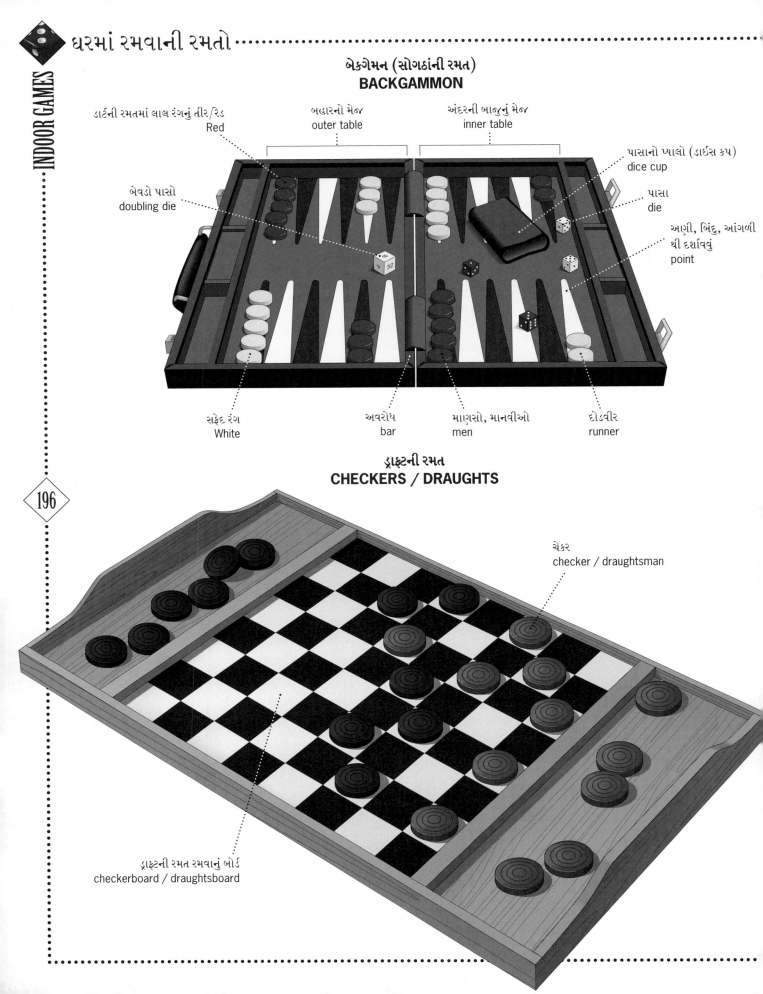

બેકગેમન (સોગઠાંની રમત)
BACKGAMMON

ડાર્ટની રમતમાં લાલ રંગનું તીર/રેડ
Red

બહારનો મેજ
outer table

અંદરની બાજુનું મેજ
inner table

પાસાનો પ્યાલો (ડાઇસ કપ)
dice cup

બેવડો પાસો
doubling die

પાસા
die

આણી, બિંદુ, આંગળી
થી દર્શાવવું
point

સફેદ રંગ
White

અવરોધ
bar

માણસો, માનવીઓ
men

દોડવીર
runner

ડ્રાફ્ટની રમત
CHECKERS / DRAUGHTS

ચેકર
checker / draughtsman

ડ્રાફ્ટની રમત રમવાનું બોર્ડ
checkerboard / draughtsboard

196

વિડિયો દ્વારા મનોરંજનની વ્યવસ્થા
VIDEO ENTERTAINMENT SYSTEM

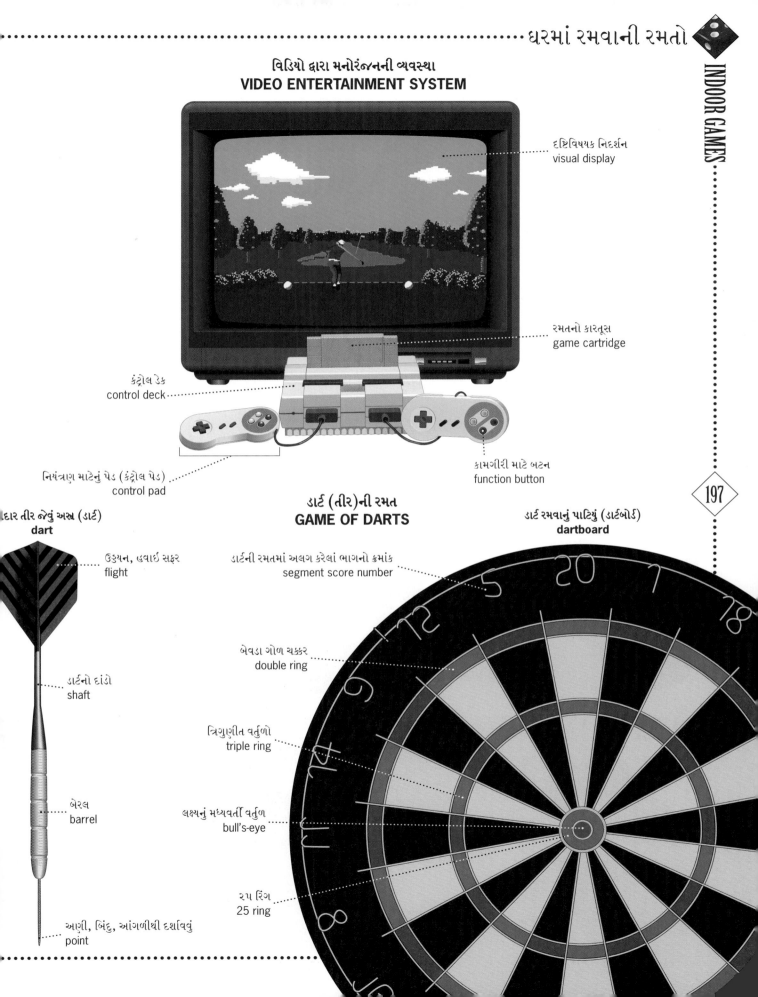

દૃષ્ટિવિષયક નિદર્શન
visual display

રમતનો કારતૂસ
game cartridge

કંટ્રોલ ડેક
control deck

નિયંત્રણ માટેનું પેડ (કંટ્રોલ પેડ)
control pad

કામગીરી માટે બટન
function button

ડાર્ટ (તીર)ની રમત
GAME OF DARTS

દાર તીર જેવું અસ્ત્ર (ડાર્ટ)
dart

ઉડ્ડયન, હવાઈ સફર
flight

ડાર્ટનો દાંડો
shaft

બેરલ
barrel

આણી, બિંદુ, આંગળીથી દર્શાવવું
point

ડાર્ટની રમતમાં અલગ કરેલાં ભાગનો ક્રમાંક
segment score number

બેવડા ગોળ ચક્કર
double ring

ત્રિગુણીત વર્તુળો
triple ring

લક્ષ્યનું મધ્યવર્તી વર્તુળ
bull's-eye

૨૫ રિંગ
25 ring

ડાર્ટ રમવાનું પાટિયું (ડાર્ટબોડ)
dartboard

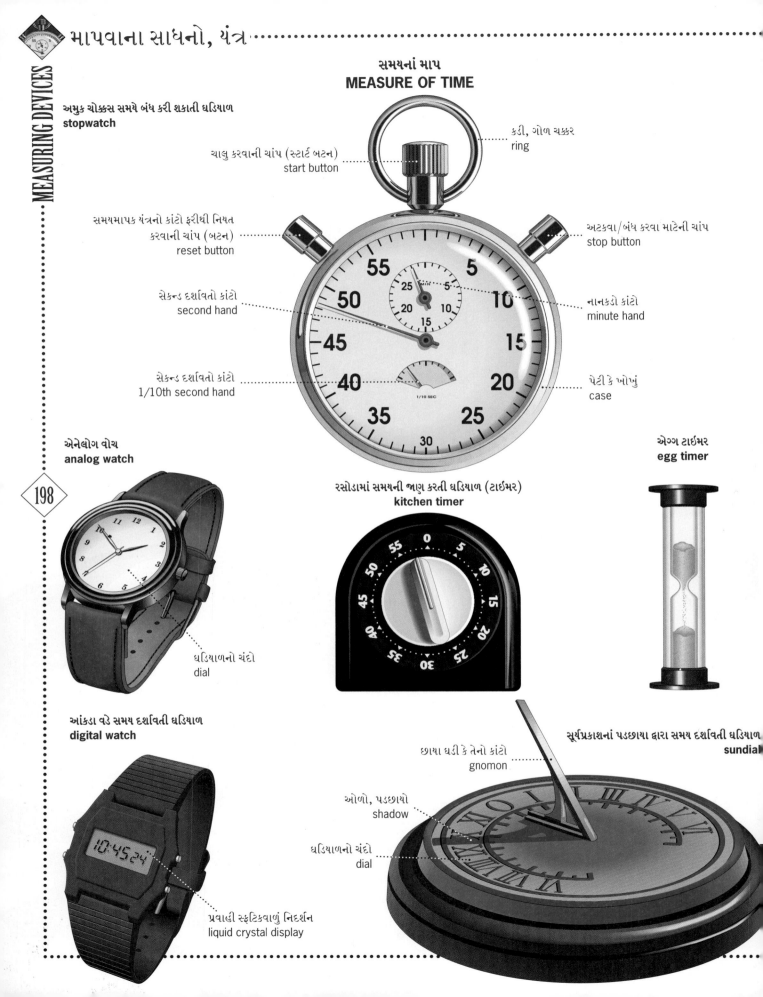

સમયનાં માપ
MEASURE OF TIME

અમુક ચોક્કસ સમયે બંધ કરી શકાતી ઘડિયાળ
stopwatch

ચાલુ કરવાની ચાંપ (સ્ટાર્ટ બટન)
start button

કડી, ગોળ ચક્કર
ring

સમયમાપક યંત્રનો કાંટો ફરીથી નિયત કરવાની ચાંપ (બટન)
reset button

અટકવા/બંધ કરવા માટેની ચાંપ
stop button

સેકન્ડ દર્શાવતો કાંટો
second hand

નાનકડો કાંટો
minute hand

સેકન્ડ દર્શાવતો કાંટો
1/10th second hand

પેટી કે ખોખું
case

1/10 SEC

એનેલોગ વોચ
analog watch

રસોડામાં સમયની જાણ કરતી ઘડિયાળ (ટાઈમર)
kitchen timer

એગ્ગ ટાઈમર
egg timer

ઘડિયાળનો ચંદો
dial

આંકડા વડે સમય દર્શાવતી ઘડિયાળ
digital watch

સૂર્યપ્રકાશનાં પડછાયા દ્વારા સમય દર્શાવતી ઘડિયાળ
sundial

છાયા ઘડી કે તેનો કાંટો
gnomon

ઓળો, પડછાયો
shadow

ઘડિયાળનો ચંદો
dial

પ્રવાહી સ્ફટિકવાળું નિદર્શન
liquid crystal display

198

તાપમાનનું માપ
MEASURE OF TEMPERATURE

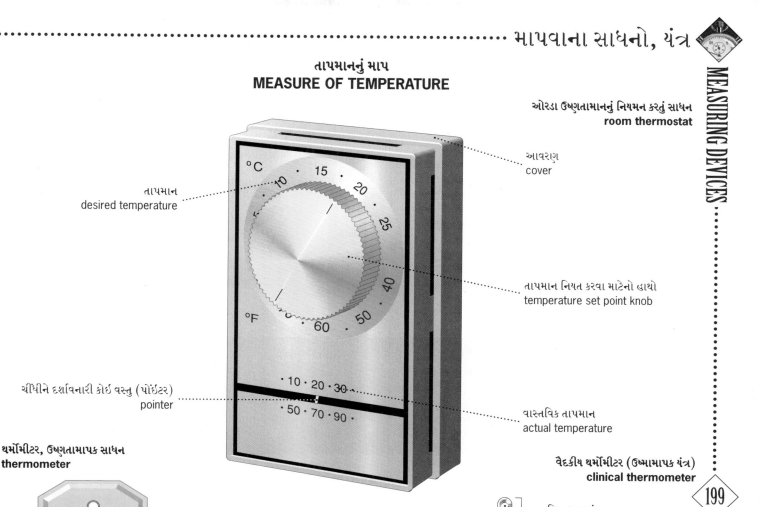

ઓરડા ઉષ્ણતામાનનું નિયમન કરતું સાધન
room thermostat

આવરણ
cover

તાપમાન
desired temperature

તાપમાન નિયત કરવા માટેનો હાથો
temperature set point knob

ચીંધીને દર્શાવનારી કોઇ વસ્તુ (પોઇંટર)
pointer

વાસ્તવિક તાપમાન
actual temperature

199

થર્મોમીટર, ઉષ્ણતામાપક સાધન
thermometer

વેદકીય થર્મોમીટર (ઉષ્ણમાપક યંત્ર)
clinical thermometer

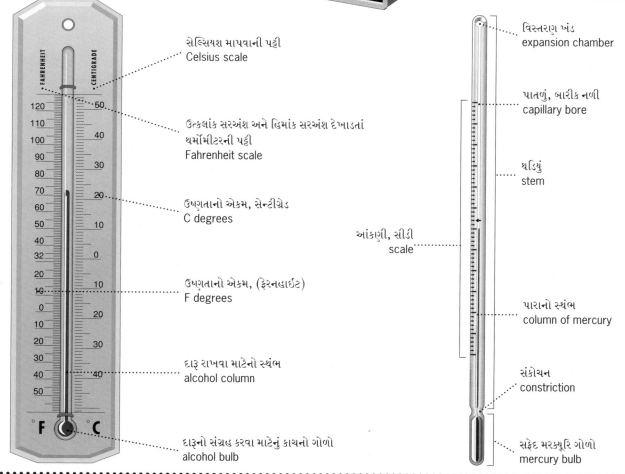

સેલ્સિયશ માપવાની પટ્ટી
Celsius scale

ઉત્કલાંક સરઅંશ અને હિમાંક સરઅંશ દેખાડતાં થર્મોમીટરની પટ્ટી
Fahrenheit scale

ઉષ્ણતાનો એકમ, સેન્ટીગ્રેડ
C degrees

ઉષ્ણતાનો એકમ, (ફેરનહાઇટ)
F degrees

દારુ રાખવા માટેનો સ્થંભ
alcohol column

દારુનો સંચ્રહ કરવા માટેનું કાચનો ગોળો
alcohol bulb

વિસ્તરણ ખંડ
expansion chamber

પાતળું, બારીક નળી
capillary bore

થડિયું
stem

આંકણી, સીડી
scale

પારાનો સ્થંભ
column of mercury

સંકોચન
constriction

સફેદ મરક્યુરિ ગોળો
mercury bulb

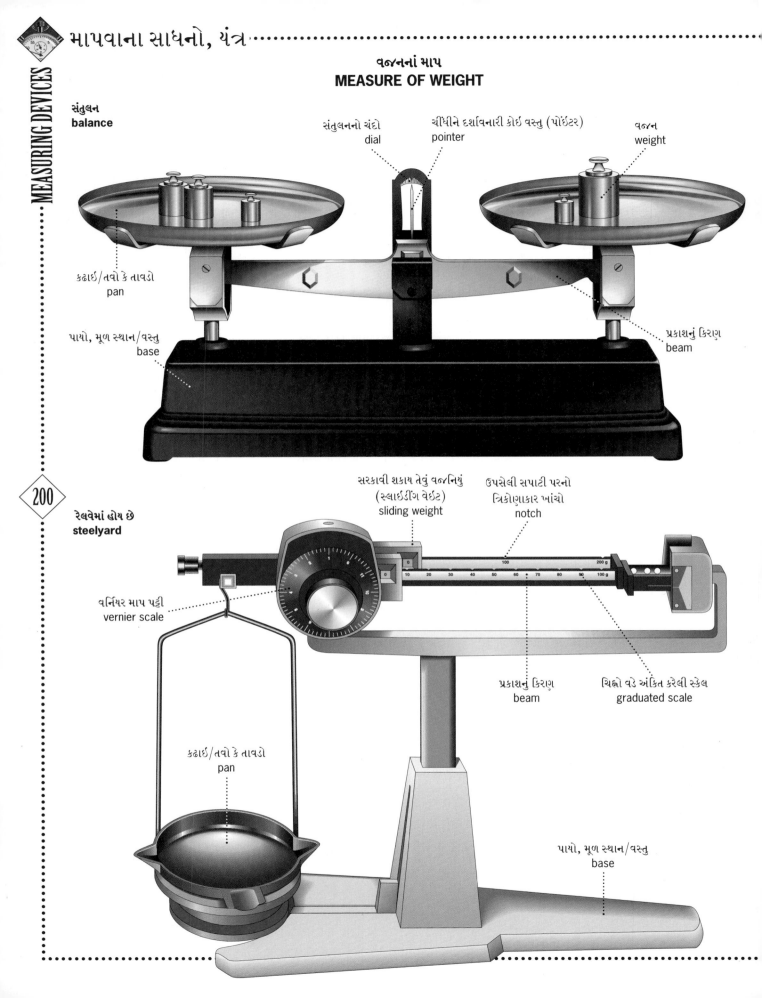

વજનનાં માપ
MEASURE OF WEIGHT

સંતુલન
balance

સંતુલનનો ચંદો
dial

ચીંધીને દર્શાવનારી કોઇ વસ્તુ (પોઇંટર)
pointer

વજન
weight

કઢાઇ/તવો કે તાવડો
pan

પાયો, મૂળ સ્થાન/વસ્તુ
base

પ્રકાશનું કિરણ
beam

રેલવેમાં હોય છે
steelyard

સરકાવી શકાય તેવું વજનિયું
(સ્લાઇડીંગ વેઇટ)
sliding weight

ઉપસેલી સપાટી પરનો
ત્રિકોણાકાર ખાંચો
notch

વર્નિયર માપ પટ્ટી
vernier scale

પ્રકાશનું કિરણ
beam

ચિહ્નો વડે અંકિત કરેલી સ્કેલ
graduated scale

કઢાઇ/તવો કે તાવડો
pan

પાયો, મૂળ સ્થાન/વસ્તુ
base

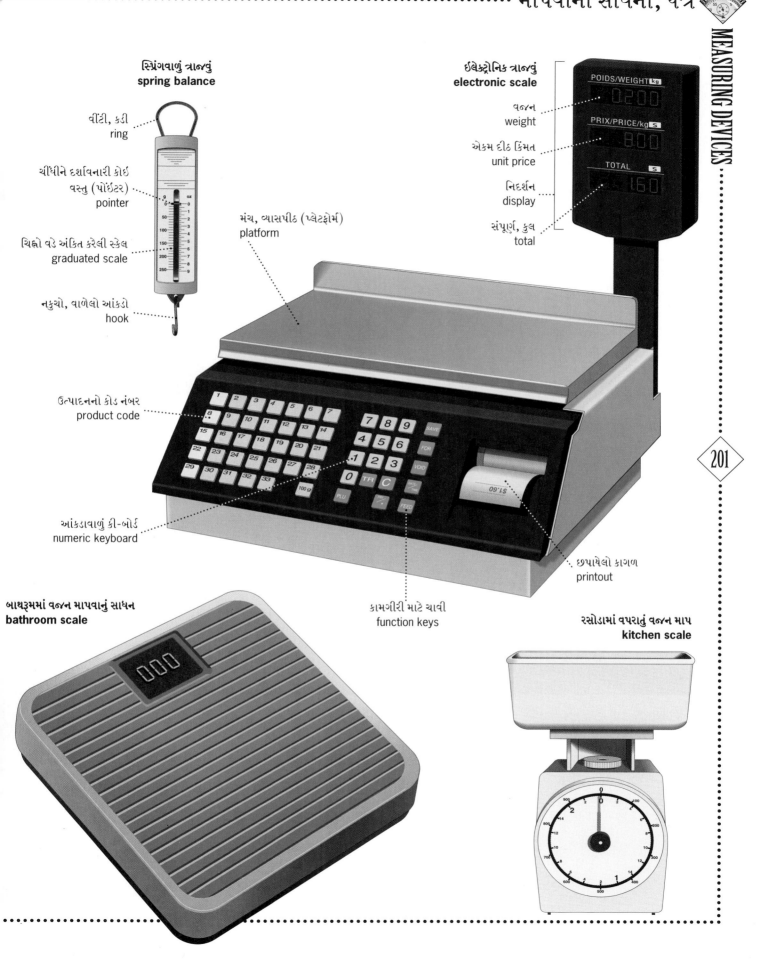

સ્પ્રિંગવાળું ત્રાજવું
spring balance

વીંટી, કડી
ring

ચીંધીને દર્શાવનારી કોઈ
વસ્તુ (પોઇંટર)
pointer

ચિહ્નો વડે અંકિત કરેલી સ્કેલ
graduated scale

નકુચો, વાળેલો આંકડો
hook

ઇલેક્ટ્રૉનિક ત્રાજવું
electronic scale

વજન
weight

એકમ દીઠ કિંમત
unit price

નિદર્શન
display

સંપૂર્ણ, કુલ
total

POIDS/WEIGHT kg

02.00

PRIX/PRICE/kg $

8.00

TOTAL $

1.60

મંચ, વ્યાસપીઠ (પ્લેટફોર્મ)
platform

ઉત્પાદનનો કોડ નંબર
product code

આંકડાવાળું કી-બોર્ડ
numeric keyboard

છપાયેલો કાગળ
printout

કામગીરી માટે ચાવી
function keys

બાથરૂમમાં વજન માપવાનું સાધન
bathroom scale

રસોડામાં વપરાતું વજન માપ
kitchen scale

તેલ, ચીકણું પ્રવાહી
OIL

શોધખોળ કરવું
PROSPECTING

પૃથ્વીની સપાટીની અંદર ખનિજની શોધ કરવી
surface prospecting

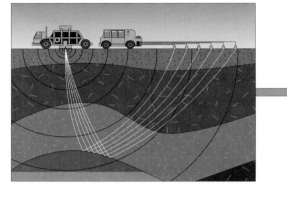

શારકામ કરવું, કાણું પાડવું
DRILLING

શારકામ કરવા માટે શારડી ગોઠવવાની વ્યવસ્થા
drilling rig

જમીન પરનું પરિવહન
GROUND TRANSPORT

પાઇપલાઇન
pipeline

લાંબા દોરડાંથી ખેંચાતું
ટ્રેઇલર/અનુયાન (ટેક ટ્રેઇલર)
tank trailer / road trailer

વિદેશની ધરતી પર ખનીજની ખાણની શોધખોળ કરવી
offshore prospecting / offshore drilling

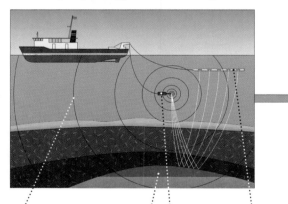

ઉત્પાદન માટેનું પ્લેટફૉર્મ
production platform

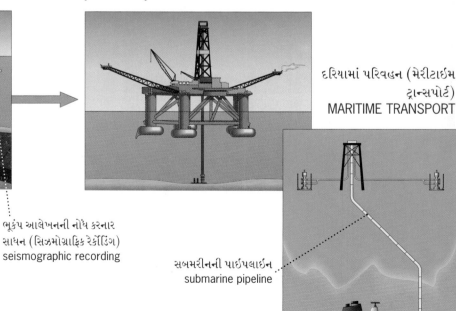

દરિયામાં પરિવહન (મેરીટાઈમ
ટ્રાન્સપોર્ટ)
MARITIME TRANSPORT

જોરદાર આંચકા સાથેનાં તરંગો
(શોક વેઇવ)
shock wave

ભૂકંપ આલેખનની નોંધ કરનાર
સાધન (સિઝ્મોગ્રાફિક રેકૉર્ડિંગ)
seismographic recording

પેટ્રોલિયમ પદાર્થો માટેનાં ભૂગળાનો
ગોળો કે પાશ (પેટ્રોલિયમ ટ્રેપ)
petroleum trap

સ્ફોટક પદાર્થ
blasting charge

સબમરીનની પાઇપલાઇન
submarine pipeline

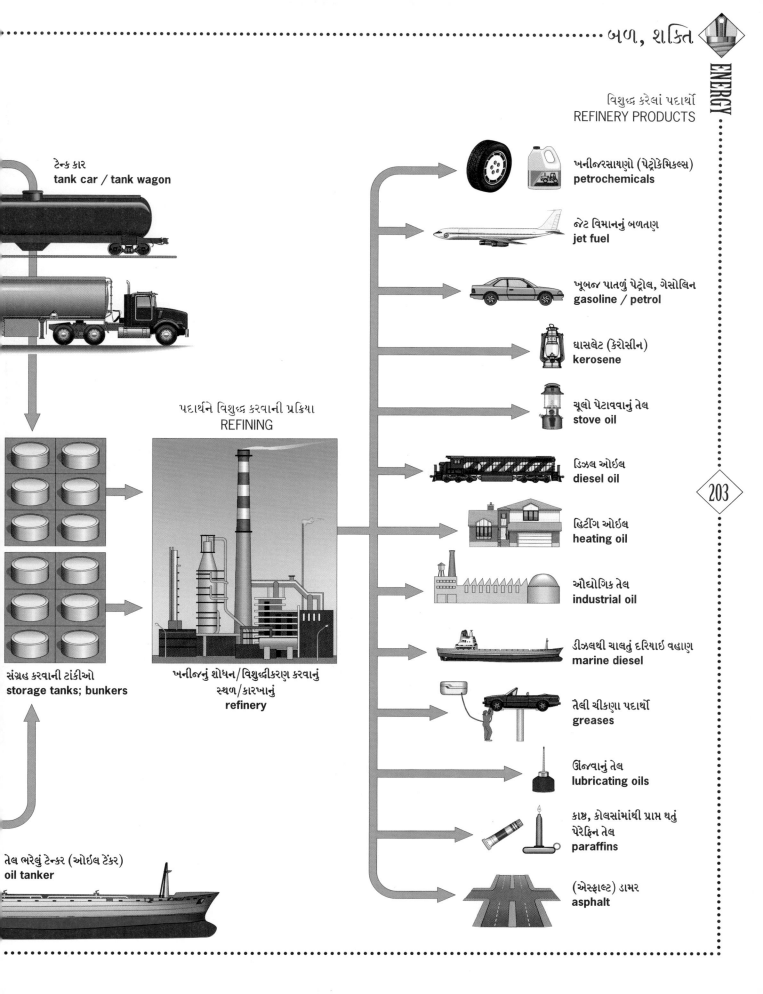

વિશુદ્ધ કરેલાં પદાર્થો
REFINERY PRODUCTS

ટેન્ક કાર
tank car / tank wagon

ખનીજરસાયણો (પેટ્રોકેમિકલ્સ)
petrochemicals

જેટ વિમાનનું બળતણ
jet fuel

ખૂબજ પાતળું પેટ્રોલ, ગેસોલિન
gasoline / petrol

ઘાસલેટ (કેરોસીન)
kerosene

ચૂલો પેટાવવાનું તેલ
stove oil

પદાર્થને વિશુદ્ધ કરવાની પ્રક્રિયા
REFINING

ડિઝલ ઓઇલ
diesel oil

હિટીંગ ઓઇલ
heating oil

ઔદ્યોગિક તેલ
industrial oil

ડીઝલથી ચાલતું દરિયાઇ વહાણ
marine diesel

સંગ્રહ કરવાની ટાંકીઓ
storage tanks; bunkers

ખનીજનું શોધન/વિશુદ્ધીકરણ કરવાનું
સ્થળ/કારખાનું
refinery

તેલી ચીકણા પદાર્થો
greases

ઊંજવાનું તેલ
lubricating oils

કાષ્ઠ, કોલસાંમાંથી પ્રાપ્ત થતું
પેરેફિન તેલ
paraffins

તેલ ભરેલું ટેન્કર (ઓઇલ ટેન્કર)
oil tanker

(એસ્ફાલ્ટ) ડામર
asphalt

જળવિદ્યુત ઊર્જા
HYDROELECTRIC ENERGY

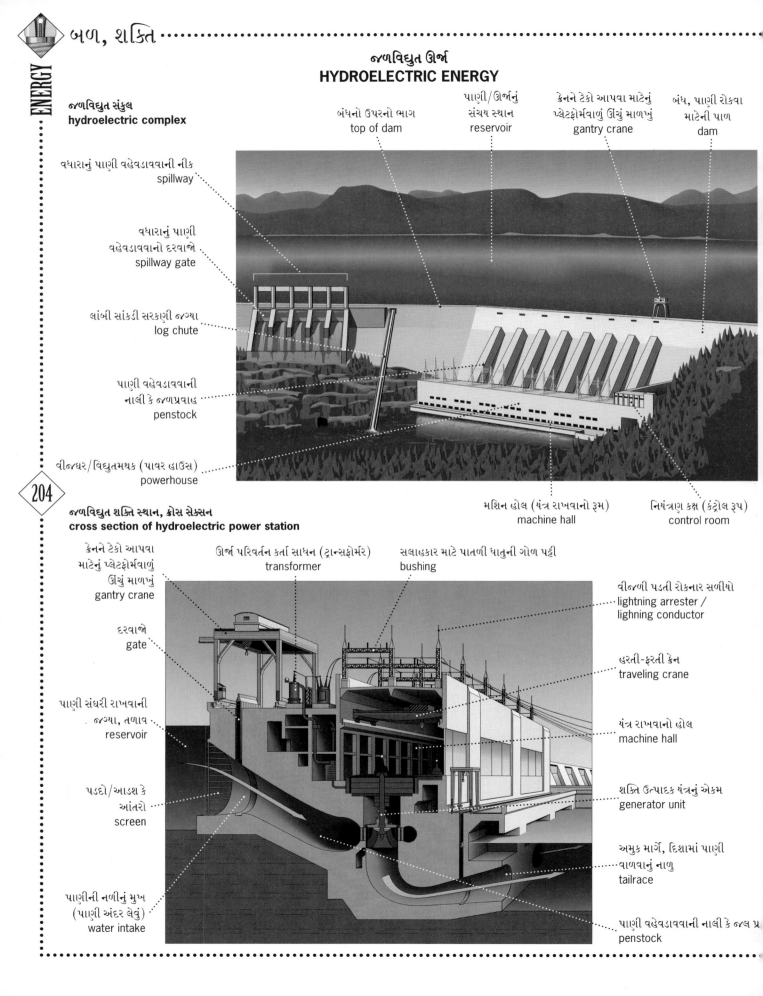

જળવિદ્યુત સંકુલ
hydroelectric complex

બંધનો ઉપરનો ભાગ
top of dam

પાણી/ઊર્જાનું
સંચય સ્થાન
reservoir

ક્રેનને ટેકો આપવા માટેનું
પ્લેટફોર્મવાળું ઊંચું માળખું
gantry crane

બંધ, પાણી રોકવા
માટેની પાળ
dam

વધારાનું પાણી વહેવડાવવાની નીક
spillway

વધારાનું પાણી
વહેવડાવવાનો દરવાજો
spillway gate

લાંબી સાંકડી સરકણી જગ્યા
log chute

પાણી વહેવડાવવાની
નાળી કે જળપ્રવાહ
penstock

વીજઘર/વિદ્યુતમથક (પાવર હાઉસ)
powerhouse

મશિન હોલ (યંત્ર રાખવાનો રૂમ)
machine hall

નિયંત્રણ કક્ષ (કંટ્રોલ રૂપ)
control room

જળવિદ્યુત શક્તિ સ્થાન, ક્રોસ સેક્સન
cross section of hydroelectric power station

ક્રેનને ટેકો આપવા
માટેનું પ્લેટફોર્મવાળું
ઊંચું માળખું
gantry crane

ઊર્જા પરિવર્તન કર્તા સાધન (ટ્રાન્સફોર્મર)
transformer

સલાહકાર માટે પાતળી ધાતુની ગોળ પટ્ટી
bushing

વીજળી પડતી રોકનાર સળીયો
lightning arrester /
lighning conductor

દરવાજો
gate

હરતી-ફરતી ક્રેન
traveling crane

પાણી સંઘરી રાખવાની
જગ્યા, તળાવ
reservoir

યંત્ર રાખવાનો હોલ
machine hall

પડદો/આડશ કે
આંતરો
screen

શક્તિ ઉત્પાદક યંત્રનું એકમ
generator unit

અમુક માર્ગે, દિશામાં પાણી
વાળવાનું નાળુ
tailrace

પાણીની નળીનું મુખ
(પાણી અંદર લેવું)
water intake

પાણી વહેવડાવવાની નાળી કે જળ પ્ર
penstock

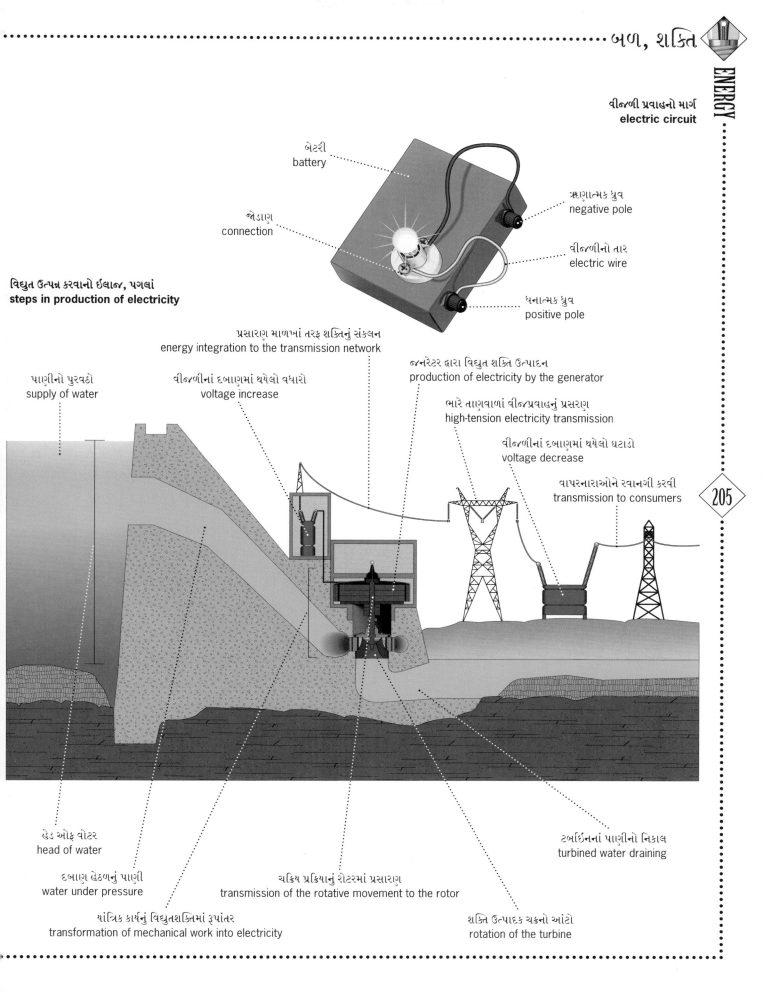

વીજળી પ્રવાહનો માર્ગ
electric circuit

બેટરી
battery

જોડાણ
connection

ઋણાત્મક ધ્રુવ
negative pole

વીજળીનો તાર
electric wire

ધનાત્મક ધ્રુવ
positive pole

વિદ્યુત ઉત્પન્ન કરવાનો ઈલાજ, પગલાં
steps in production of electricity

પ્રસારણ માળખાં તરફ શક્તિનું સંકલન
energy integration to the transmission network

જનરેટર દ્વારા વિદ્યુત શક્તિ ઉત્પાદન
production of electricity by the generator

પાણીનો પુરવઠો
supply of water

વીજળીનાં દબાણમાં થયેલો વધારો
voltage increase

ભારે તાણવાળાં વીજપ્રવાહનું પ્રસારણ
high-tension electricity transmission

વીજળીનાં દબાણમાં થયેલો ઘટાડો
voltage decrease

વાપરનારાઓને રવાનગી કરવી
transmission to consumers

205

હેડ ઓફ વોટર
head of water

દબાણ હેઠળનું પાણી
water under pressure

ચક્રિય પ્રક્રિયાનું રોટરમાં પ્રસારણ
transmission of the rotative movement to the rotor

ટર્બાઈનનાં પાણીનો નિકાલ
turbined water draining

યાંત્રિક કાર્યનું વિદ્યુતશક્તિમાં રૂપાંતર
transformation of mechanical work into electricity

શક્તિ ઉત્પાદક ચક્રનો આંટો
rotation of the turbine

આણ્વિક ઊર્જા
NUCLEAR ENERGY

આણુ શક્તિ મથક
nuclear power station

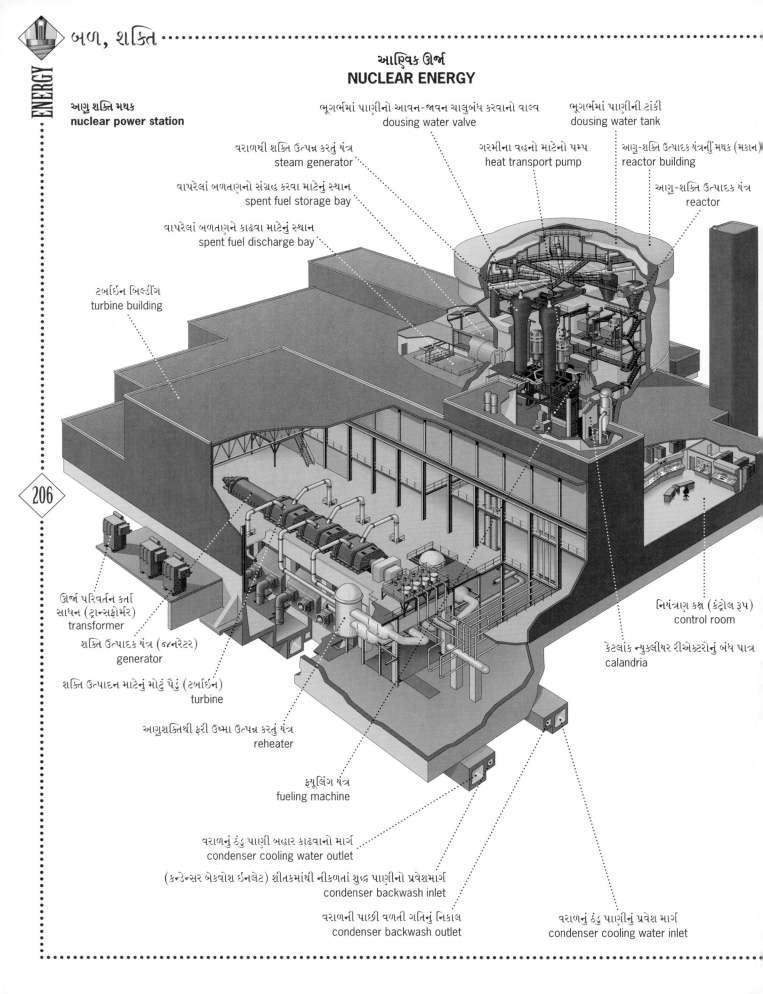

ભૂગર્ભમાં પાણીનો આવન-જવન ચાલુબંધ કરવાનો વાલ્વ
dousing water valve

ભૂગર્ભમાં પાણીની ટાંકી
dousing water tank

વરાળથી શક્તિ ઉત્પન્ન કરતું યંત્ર
steam generator

ગરમીના વહનો માટેનો પમ્પ
heat transport pump

આણુ-શક્તિ ઉત્પાદક યંત્રનું મથક (મકાન)
reactor building

વાપરેલાં બળતણનો સંગ્રહ કરવા માટેનું સ્થાન
spent fuel storage bay

આણુ-શક્તિ ઉત્પાદક યંત્ર
reactor

વાપરેલાં બળતણને કાઢવા માટેનું સ્થાન
spent fuel discharge bay

ટર્બાઇન બિલ્ડીંગ
turbine building

ઊર્જા પરિવર્તન કર્તા
સાધન (ટ્રાન્સફોર્મર)
transformer

શક્તિ ઉત્પાદક યંત્ર (જનરેટર)
generator

શક્તિ ઉત્પાદન માટેનું મોટું પૈડું (ટર્બાઇન)
turbine

આણુશક્તિથી ફરી ઉષ્મા ઉત્પન્ન કરતું યંત્ર
reheater

ફ્યૂલિંગ યંત્ર
fueling machine

વરાળનું ઠંડુ પાણી બહાર કાઢવાનો માર્ગ
condenser cooling water outlet

(કન્ડેન્સર બેકવોશ ઇનલેટ) શીતકમાંથી નીકળતાં શુદ્ધ પાણીનો પ્રવેશમાર્ગ
condenser backwash inlet

વરાળની પાછી વળતી ગતિનું નિકાલ
condenser backwash outlet

નિયંત્રણ કક્ષ (કંટ્રોલ રૂપ)
control room

કેટલાંક ન્યુક્લીયર રીએક્ટરોનું બંધ પાત્ર
calandria

વરાળનું ઠંડુ પાણીનું પ્રવેશ માર્ગ
condenser cooling water inlet

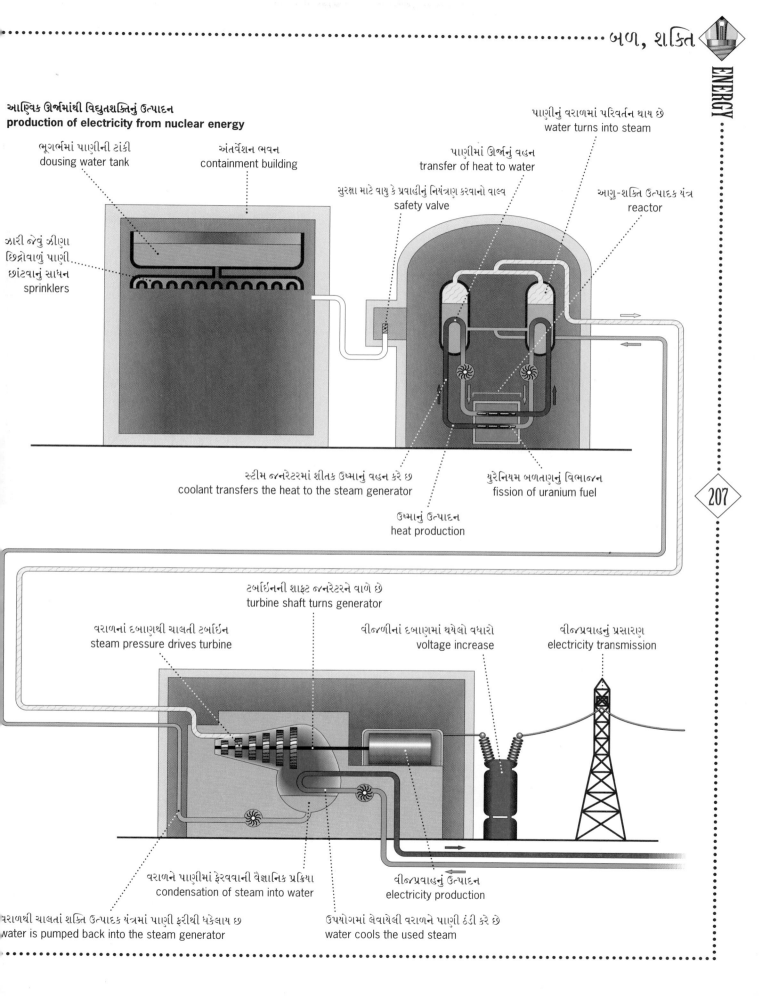

આણ્વિક ઊર્જામાંથી વિદ્યુતશક્તિનું ઉત્પાદન
production of electricity from nuclear energy

ભૂગર્ભમાં પાણીની ટાંકી
dousing water tank

અંતર્વેશન ભવન
containment building

ઝારી જેવું ઝીણા છિદ્રોવાળું પાણી છાંટવાનું સાધન
sprinklers

સુરક્ષા માટે વાયુ કે પ્રવાહીનું નિયંત્રણ કરવાનો વાલ્વ
safety valve

પાણીમાં ઊર્જાનું વહન
transfer of heat to water

પાણીનું વરાળમાં પરિવર્તન થાય છે
water turns into steam

આણુ-શક્તિ ઉત્પાદક યંત્ર
reactor

સ્ટીમ જનરેટરમાં શીતક ઉષ્માનું વહન કરે છ
coolant transfers the heat to the steam generator

યુરેનિયમ બળતાણનું વિભાજન
fission of uranium fuel

ઉષ્માનું ઉત્પાદન
heat production

ટર્બાઈનની શાફ્ટ જનરેટરને વાળે છે
turbine shaft turns generator

વરાળનાં દબાણથી ચાલતી ટર્બાઈન
steam pressure drives turbine

વીજળીનાં દબાણમાં થયેલો વધારો
voltage increase

વીજપ્રવાહનું પ્રસારણ
electricity transmission

વરાળને પાણીમાં ફેરવવાની વૈજ્ઞાનિક પ્રક્રિયા
condensation of steam into water

વરાળથી ચાલતાં શક્તિ ઉત્પાદક યંત્રમાં પાણી ફરીથી ધકેલાય છ
water is pumped back into the steam generator

ઉપયોગમાં લેવાયેલી વરાળને પાણી ઠંડી કરે છે
water cools the used steam

વીજપ્રવાહનું ઉત્પાદન
electricity production

207

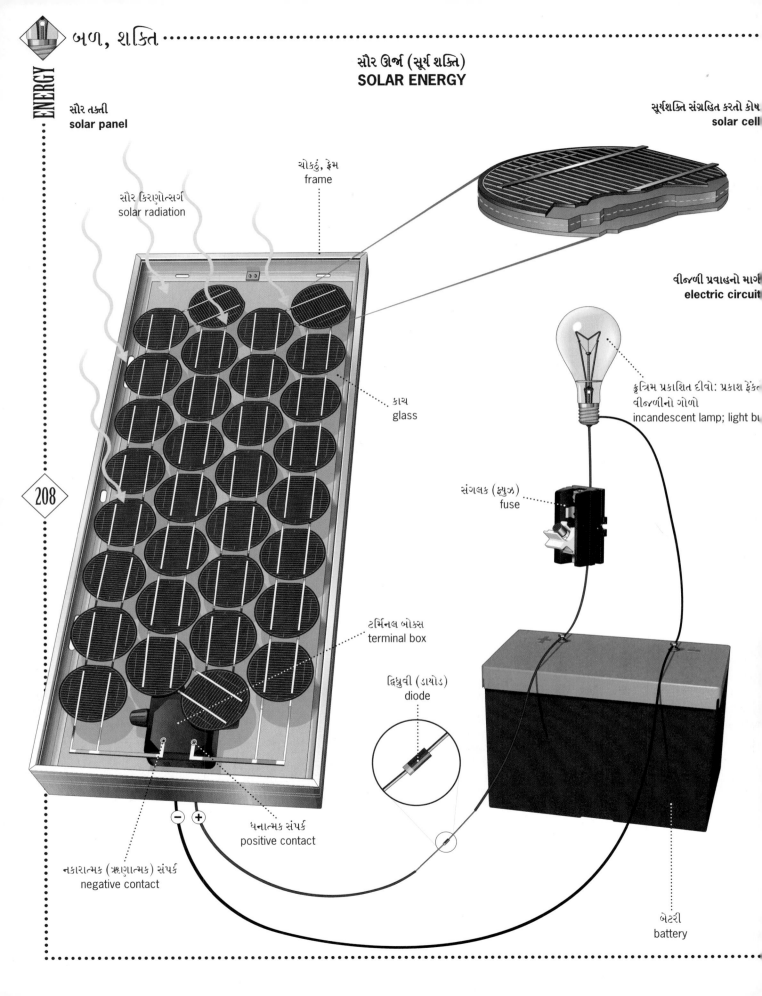

સૌર ઊર્જા (સૂર્ય શક્તિ)
SOLAR ENERGY

સૌર તક્તી
solar panel

સૂર્યશક્તિ સંગ્રહિત કરતો કોષ
solar cell

ચોકઠું, ફ્રેમ
frame

સૌર કિરણોત્સર્ગ
solar radiation

વીજળી પ્રવાહનો માર્ગ
electric circuit

કૃત્રિમ પ્રકાશિત દીવો: પ્રકાશ ફેંકત
વીજળીનો ગોળો
incandescent lamp; light bu

કાચ
glass

સંગલક (ફ્યુઝ)
fuse

ટર્મિનલ બોક્સ
terminal box

દ્વિધ્રુવી (ડાયોડ)
diode

ધનાત્મક સંપર્ક
positive contact

નકારાત્મક (ઋણાત્મક) સંપર્ક
negative contact

બેટરી
battery

પવન દ્વારા ઉત્પન્ન થતી ઊર્જા
WIND ENERGY

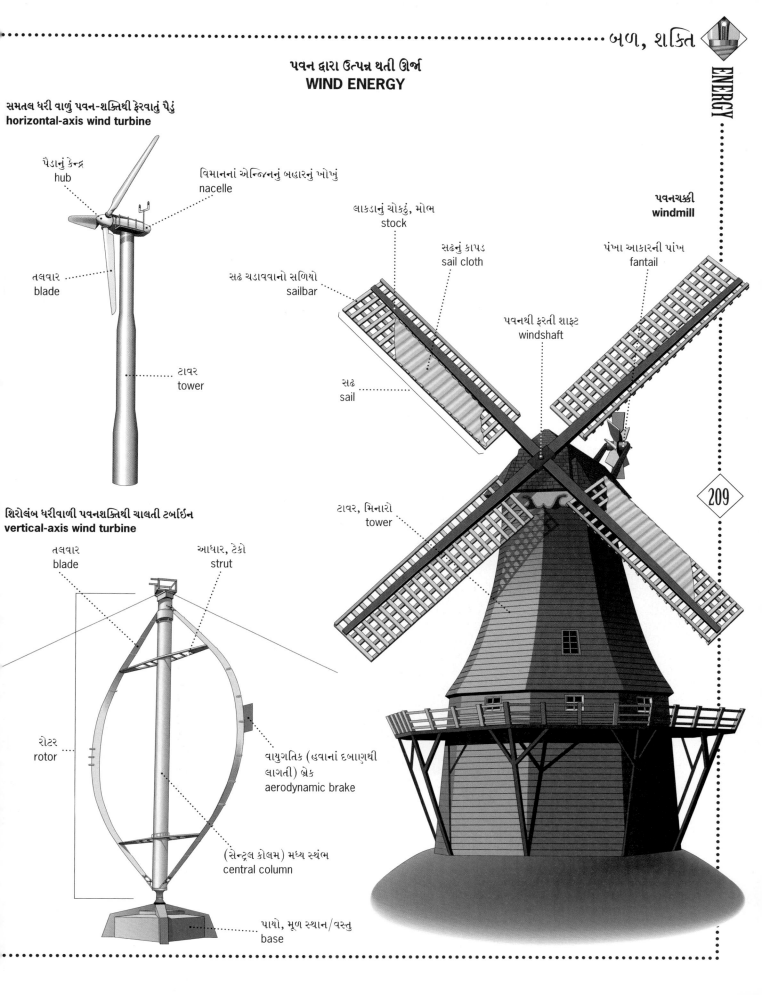

સમતલ ધરી વાળું પવન-શક્તિથી ફેરવાનું પૈડું
horizontal-axis wind turbine

પૈડાનું કેન્દ્ર
hub

વિમાનનાં એન્જિનનું બહારનું ખોખું
nacelle

તલવાર
blade

ટાવર
tower

શિરોલંબ ધરીવાળી પવનશક્તિથી ચાલતી ટર્બાઈન
vertical-axis wind turbine

તલવાર
blade

આધાર, ટેકો
strut

રોટર
rotor

વાયુગતિક (હવાનાં દબાણથી લાગતી) બ્રેક
aerodynamic brake

(સેન્ટ્રલ કોલમ) મધ્ય સ્થંભ
central column

પાયો, મૂળ સ્થાન/વસ્તુ
base

લાકડાનું ચોકઠું, મોભ
stock

સઢનું કાપડ
sail cloth

સઢ ચડાવવાનો સળિયો
sailbar

સઢ
sail

પવનચક્કી
windmill

પંખા આકારની પાંખ
fantail

પવનથી ફરતી શાફ્ટ
windshaft

ટાવર, મિનારો
tower

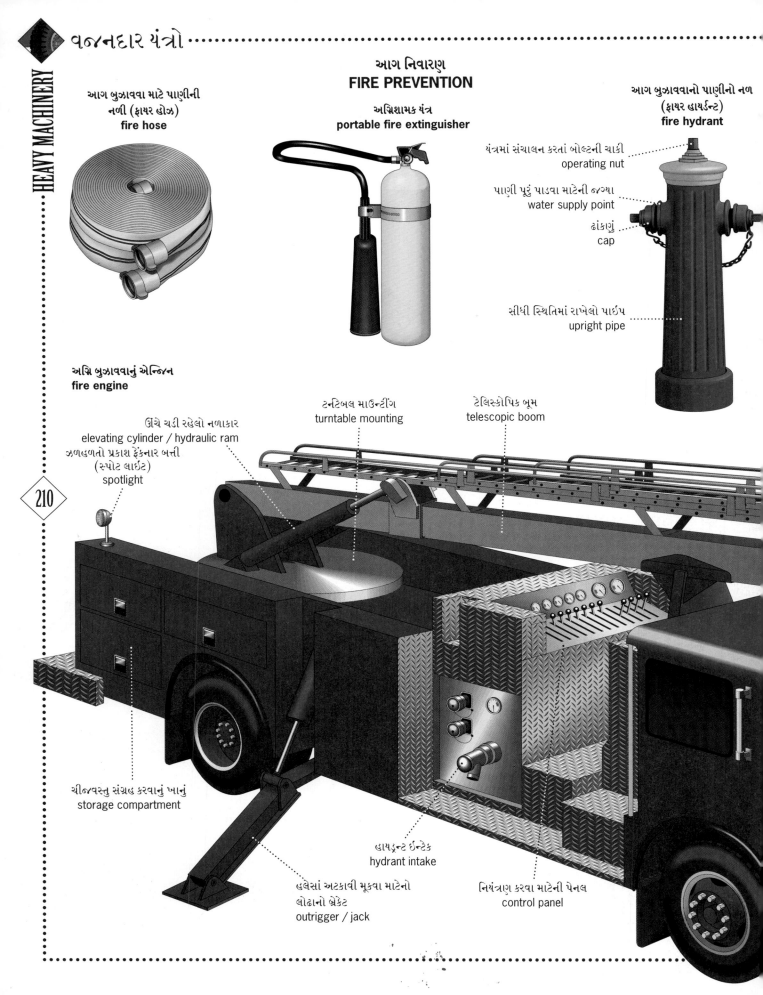

આગ બુઝાવવા માટે પાણીની
નળી (ફાયર હોઝ)
fire hose

આગ નિવારણ
FIRE PREVENTION

અગ્નિશામક યંત્ર
portable fire extinguisher

આગ બુઝાવવાનો પાણીનો નળ
(ફાયર હાયર્ડન્ટ)
fire hydrant

યંત્રમાં સંચાલન કરતાં બોલ્ટની ચાકી
operating nut

પાણી પૂરું પાડવા માટેની જગ્યા
water supply point

ઢાંકણું
cap

સીધી સ્થિતિમાં રાખેલો પાઇપ
upright pipe

અગ્નિ બુઝાવવાનું એન્જિન
fire engine

ઊંચે ચડી રહેલો નળાકાર
elevating cylinder / hydraulic ram
ઝળહળતો પ્રકાશ ફેંકનાર બત્તી
(સ્પોટ લાઇટ)
spotlight

ટર્નટેબલ માઉન્ટીંગ
turntable mounting

ટેલિસ્કોપિક બૂમ
telescopic boom

ચીજવસ્તુ સંગ્રહ કરવાનું ખાનું
storage compartment

હાયડ્રન્ટ ઇન્ટેક
hydrant intake

હલેસાં અટકાવી મૂકવા માટેનો
લોઢાનો બ્રેકેટ
outrigger / jack

નિયંત્રણ કરવા માટેની પેનલ
control panel

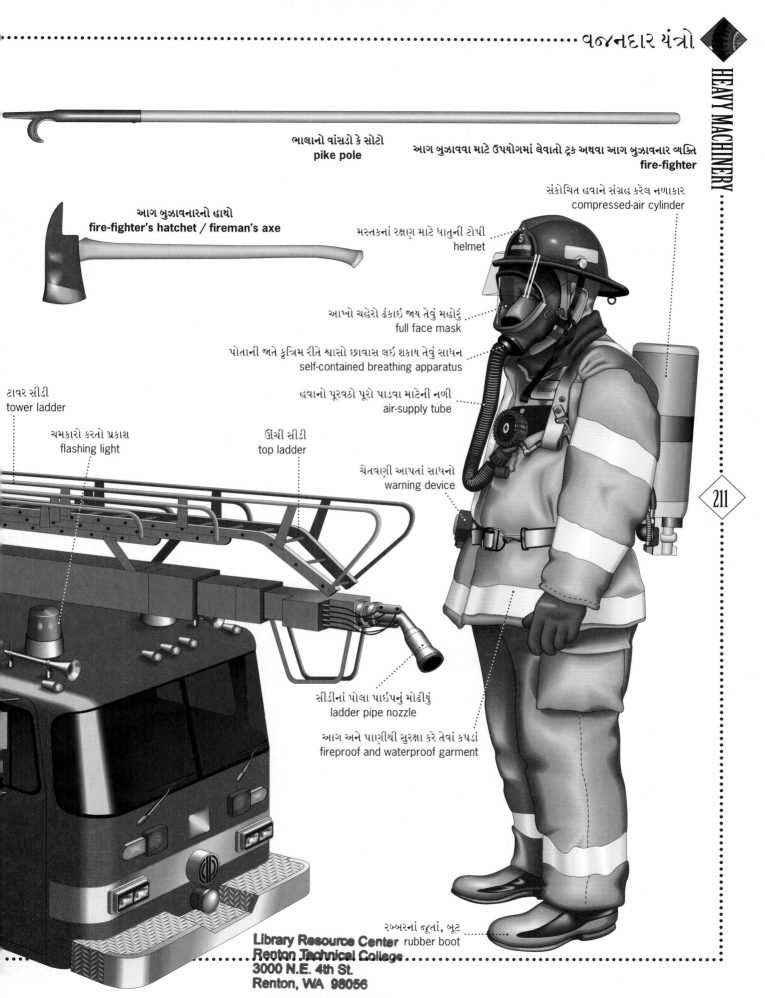

ભાલાનો વાંસડો કે સોટો
pike pole

આગ બુઝાવવા માટે ઉપયોગમાં લેવાતો ટ્રક અથવા આગ બુઝાવનાર વ્યક્તિ
fire-fighter

આગ બુઝાવનારનો હાથો
fire-fighter's hatchet / fireman's axe

સંકોચિત હવાને સંગ્રહ કરેલ નળાકાર
compressed-air cylinder

મસ્તકનાં રક્ષણ માટે ધાતુની ટોપી
helmet

આખો ચહેરો ઢંકાઈ જાય તેવું મહોરું
full face mask

પોતાની જાતે કૃત્રિમ રીતે શ્વાસો છાવાસ લઈ શકાય તેવું સાધન
self-contained breathing apparatus

ટાવર સીડી
tower ladder

ચમકારો કરતો પ્રકાશ
flashing light

ઊંચી સીડી
top ladder

હવાનો પૂરવઠો પૂરો પાડવા માટેની નળી
air-supply tube

ચેતવણી આપતાં સાધનો
warning device

સીડીનાં પોલા પાઇપનું મોઢીયું
ladder pipe nozzle

આગ અને પાણીથી સુરક્ષા કરે તેવાં કપડાં
fireproof and waterproof garment

Library Resource Center
Renton Technical College
3000 N.E. 4th St.
Renton, WA 98056

રબ્બરનાં જૂતાં, બૂટ
rubber boot

ભારે વાહનો
HEAVY VEHICLES

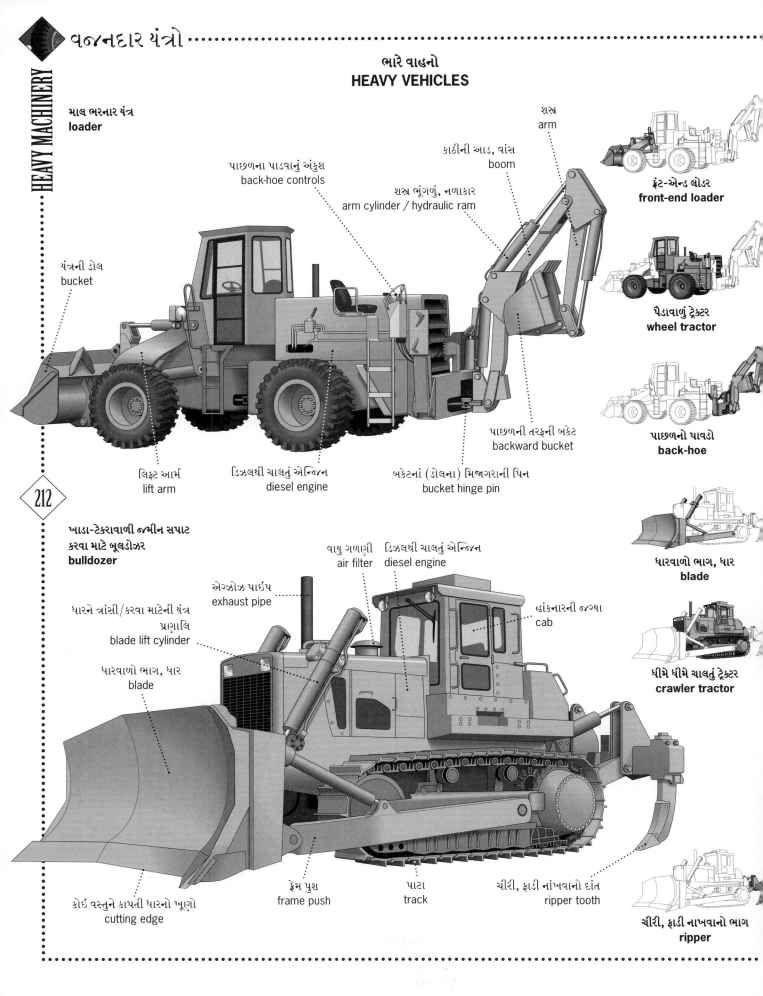

માલ ભરનાર યંત્ર
loader

પાછળના પાડવાનું અંકુશ
back-hoe controls

શસ્ત્ર ભૂંગળું, નળાકાર
arm cylinder / hydraulic ram

શસ્ત્ર
arm

કાઠીની આડ, વાંસ
boom

યંત્રની ડોલ
bucket

લિફ્ટ આર્મ
lift arm

ડિઝલથી ચાલતું એન્જિન
diesel engine

પાછળની તરફની બકેટ
backward bucket

બકેટનાં (ડોલના) મિજાગરાની પિન
bucket hinge pin

ઇંટ-એન્ડ લોડર
front-end loader

પૈડાવાળું ટ્રેક્ટર
wheel tractor

પાછળનો પાવડો
back-hoe

212

ખાડા-ટેકરાવાળી જમીન સપાટ
કરવા માટે બૂલડોઝર
bulldozer

એગ્ઝોઝ પાઇપ
exhaust pipe

વાયુ ગળાણી
air filter

ડિઝલથી ચાલતું એન્જિન
diesel engine

ધારને ત્રાંસી/કરવા માટેની યંત્ર
પ્રણાલિ
blade lift cylinder

હાંકનારની જગ્યા
cab

ધારવાળો ભાગ, ધાર
blade

કોઇ વસ્તુને કાપતી ધારનો ખૂણો
cutting edge

ફ્રેમ પુશ
frame push

પાટા
track

ચીરી, ફાડી નાંખવાનો દાંત
ripper tooth

ધારવાળો ભાગ, ધાર
blade

ધીમે ધીમે ચાલતું ટ્રેક્ટર
crawler tractor

ચીરી, ફાડી નાખવાનો ભાગ
ripper

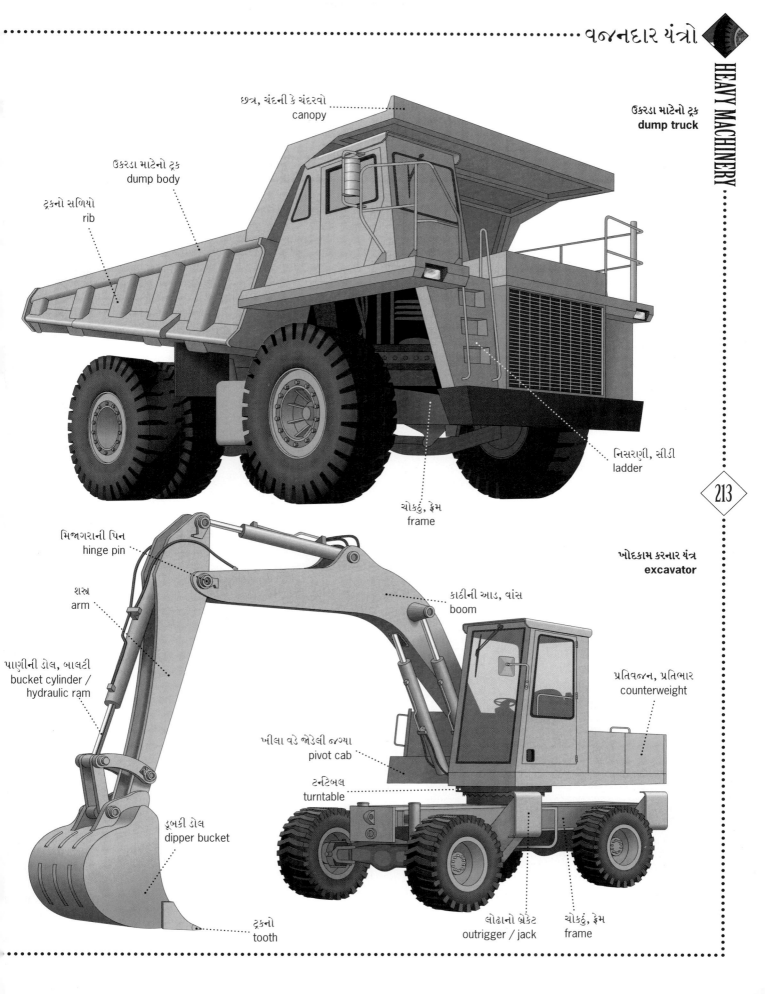

છત્ર, ચંદની કે ચંદરવો
canopy

ઉકરડા માટેનો ટ્રક
dump truck

ઉકરડા માટેનો ટ્રક
dump body

ટ્રકનો સળિયો
rib

નિસરણી, સીડી
ladder

ચોકઠું, ફ્રેમ
frame

213

મિજાગરાની પિન
hinge pin

શસ્ત્ર
arm

ખોદકામ કરનાર યંત્ર
excavator

કાઠીની આડ, વાંસ
boom

પાણીની ડોલ, બાલટી
bucket cylinder /
hydraulic ram

પ્રતિવજન, પ્રતિભાર
counterweight

ખીલા વડે જોડેલી જગ્યા
pivot cab

ટનટેબલ
turntable

ડૂબકી ડોલ
dipper bucket

ટ્રકનો
tooth

લોઢાનો બ્રેકેટ
outrigger / jack

ચોકઠું, ફ્રેમ
frame

ભારે યંત્ર સામગ્રી
HEAVY MACHINERY

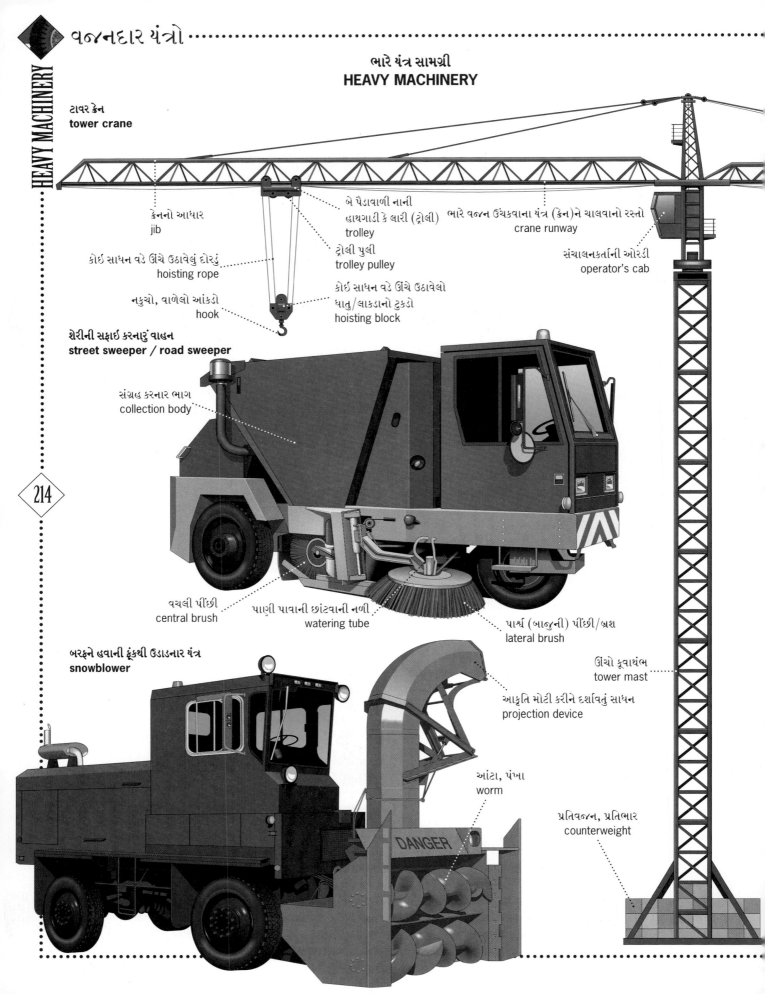

ટાવર ક્રેન
tower crane

ક્રેનનો આધાર
jib

બે પૈડાવાળી નાની હાથગાડી કે લારી (ટ્રોલી)
trolley

ભારે વજન ઉંચકવાના યંત્ર (ક્રેન)ને ચાલવાનો રસ્તો
crane runway

કોઈ સાધન વડે ઊંચે ઉઠાવેલું દોરડું
hoisting rope

ટ્રોલી પુલી
trolley pulley

સંચાલનકર્તાની ઓરડી
operator's cab

નકુચો, વાળેલો આંકડો
hook

કોઈ સાધન વડે ઊંચે ઉઠાવેલો ધાતુ/લાકડાનો ટુકડો
hoisting block

શેરીની સફાઈ કરનારું વાહન
street sweeper / road sweeper

સંગ્રહ કરનાર ભાગ
collection body

વચલી પીંછી
central brush

પાણી પાવાની છાંટવાની નળી
watering tube

પાર્શ્વ (બાજુની) પીંછી/બ્રશ
lateral brush

બરફને હવાની ફૂંકથી ઉડાડનાર યંત્ર
snowblower

ઊંચો ક્વાથંભ
tower mast

આકૃતિ મોટી કરીને દર્શાવતું સાધન
projection device

આંટા, પંખા
worm

પ્રતિવજન, પ્રતિભાર
counterweight

214

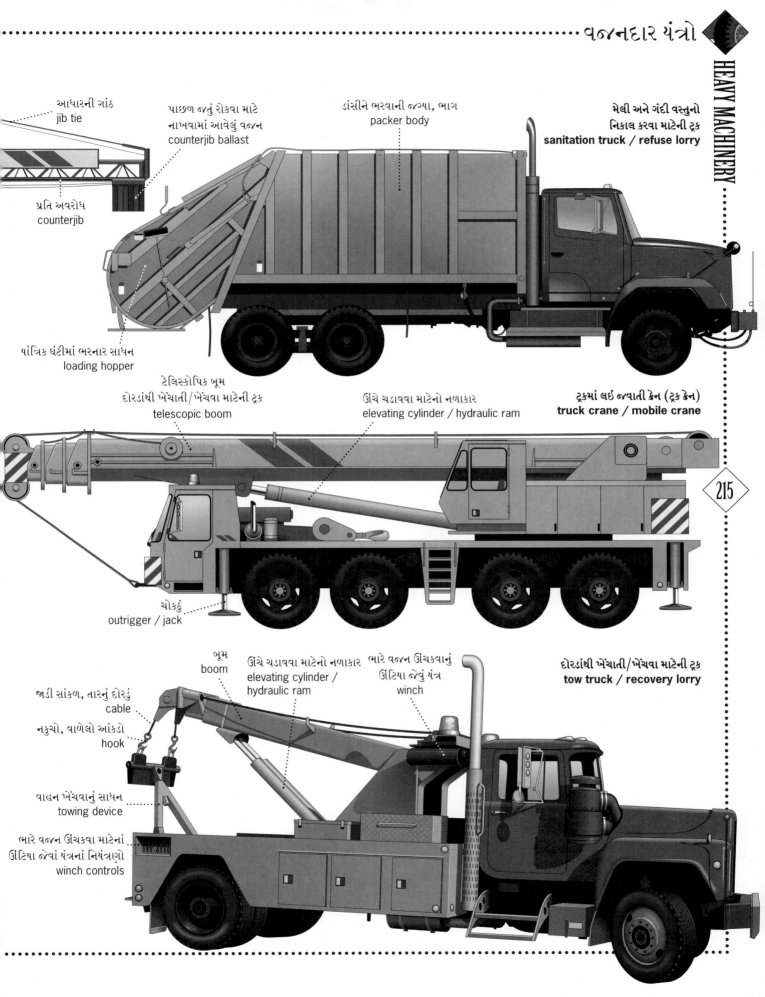

આધારની ગાંઠ
jib tie

પાછળ જતું રોકવા માટે
નાખવામાં આવેલું વજન
counterjib ballast

ડાંસીને ભરવાની જગ્યા, ભાગ
packer body

મેલી અને ગંદી વસ્તુનો
નિકાલ કરવા માટેની ટ્રક
sanitation truck / refuse lorry

પ્રતિ અવરોધ
counterjib

યાંત્રિક ઘંટીમાં ભરનાર સાધન
loading hopper

ટેલિસ્કોપિક બૂમ
દોરડાંથી ખેંચાતી/ખેંચવા માટેની ટ્રક
telescopic boom

ઊંચે ચડાવવા માટેનો નળાકાર
elevating cylinder / hydraulic ram

ટ્રકમાં લઈ જવાતી ક્રેન (ટ્રક ક્રેન)
truck crane / mobile crane

215

ચોકઠું
outrigger / jack

બૂમ
boom

ઊંચે ચડાવવા માટેનો નળાકાર
elevating cylinder /
hydraulic ram

ભારે વજન ઉંચકવાનું
ઊંટિયા જેવું યંત્ર
winch

દોરડાંથી ખેંચાતી/ખેંચવા માટેની ટ્રક
tow truck / recovery lorry

જાડી સાંકળ, તારનું દોરડું
cable

નકુચો, વાળેલો આંકડો
hook

વાહન ખેંચવાનું સાધન
towing device

ભારે વજન ઉંચકવા માટેનાં
ઊંટિયા જેવાં યંત્રનાં નિયંત્રણો
winch controls

સામાન્ય ચિહ્નો
COMMON SYMBOLS

સ્ત્રીઓ માટેનો આરામ-કક્ષ
women's rest room /
women's toilet

માનવીનું આરામગૃહ
men's rest room /
men's toilet

અપંગો માટેની પૈડાવાળી ખુરશી જવા
માટેની સુલભતા (માર્ગ)
wheelchair access

હોસ્પિટલ, ઇસ્પિતાલ
hospital

ટેલિફોન
telephone

ધૂમ્રપાન નહીં કરશો
no smoking

છાવણી (તંબુ)
camping (tent)

છાવણી (તંબુ) નાખવા માટે પ્રતિબંધ છે
camping prohibited

બે રેખાઓનાં છેદનબિંદુ પાસે અટકવું
stop at intersection

સુરક્ષા સંકેતો
SAFETY SYMBOLS

ક્ષય કરનારી વસ્તુ
corrosive

વીજપ્રવાહથી થનારું સંભવિત જોખમ
electrical hazard

વિસ્ફોટક
explosive

જ્વાલાગ્રાહી, ઝટ સળગી ઊઠે તેવું
flammable

ઘનપદાર્થ આરપાર પસાર થઈ શકનારાં અને વિદ્યુત
અસરવાળા અદૃશ્ય કિરણોનું વિસર્જન કરનાર પદાર્થો
radioactive

ઝેરી વસ્તુ/પદાર્થ
poisonous

રક્ષણ
PROTECTION

આંખનું રક્ષણ કરતું સાધન
eye protection

કાનનું રક્ષણ
ear protection

માથાનું રક્ષણ કરતું ઉપકરણ/હેલ્મેટ
head protection

હાથનું રક્ષણ કરતું સાધન
hand protection

પગનું રક્ષણ કરતું સાધન
foot protection

શ્વસન તંત્રની પ્રણાલિનું રક્ષણ કરનાર વ્યવસ
respiratory system protectio

217

The terms in **bold type** correspond to an illustration; those in CAPITALS indicate a title.

INDEX

The terms in **bold type** correspond to an illustration; those in CAPITALS indicate a title.

219

The terms in **bold type** correspond to an illustration; those in CAPITALS indicate a title.

The terms in **bold type** correspond to an illustration; those in CAPITALS indicate a title.

221

The terms in **bold type** correspond to an illustration; those in CAPITALS indicate a title.

222

The terms in **bold type** correspond to an illustration; those in CAPITALS indicate a title.

224

The terms in **bold type** correspond to an illustration; those in CAPITALS indicate a title.

The terms in **bold type** correspond to an illustration; those in CAPITALS indicate a title.

The terms in **bold type** correspond to an illustration; those in CAPITALS indicate a title.

227

The terms in **bold type** correspond to an illustration; those in CAPITALS indicate a title.

The terms in **bold type** correspond to an illustration; those in CAPITALS indicate a title.

229

The terms in **bold type** correspond to an illustration; those in CAPITALS indicate a title.

The terms in **bold type** correspond to an illustration; those in CAPITALS indicate a title.

The terms in **bold type** correspond to an illustration; those in CAPITALS indicate a title.

232

The terms in **bold type** correspond to an illustration; those in CAPITALS indicate a title.

3/05

11525250

$1-

CRAFTS OF MEXICO

LAKE OSWEGO PUBLIC LIBRARY
706 Fourth Street
Lake Oswego, Oregon 97034

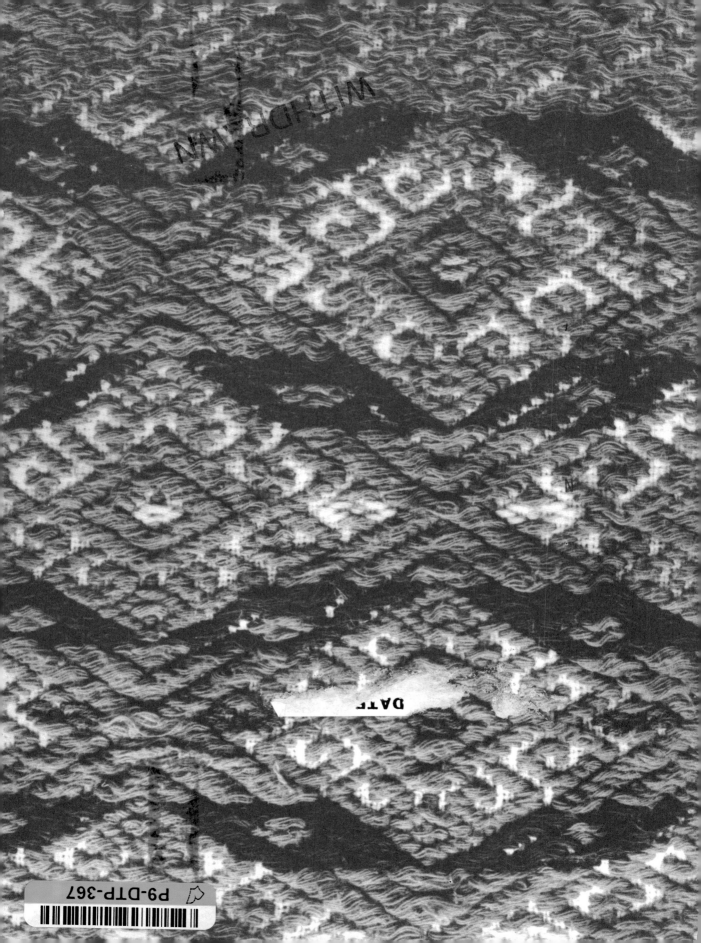

WITHDRAWN

DATE

P9-DTP-367

In remote country areas, however, life continued virtually un- changed and many Indian communities were able to retain their languages and customs intact, producing their own food, satisfying their own needs, and trading locally. Skills such as spinning, weaving, pottery, mask making, and basketry are as important today as they were before the Conquest.

Crafts in Mexico fulfill spiritual as well as practical needs. Through his crafts the artisan, whether mestizo or Indian, expresses his highly personal view of the world, of life, and of death. For the Aztecs and the other nations who once peopled Mexico, life and death were two facets of the same reality, forming an indissoluble whole and playing their part in the cycle of Nature. The dead corn grew up afresh, the sun set only to rise again and out of death came life. The preoccupation with death so frequently displayed by pre-Hispanic sculptors, potters and painters is still a source of inspiration, provok- ing a whole series of grimly humorous pieces and testifying to the continuity that is such a striking and compelling feature of Mexican life and art.

Drawing upon their rich cultural heritage, the craftsmen of Mexico shape the raw materials at their disposal, combining utility with beauty and enriching their own lives, those of their families and of their countrymen.

Inheritors of ancient customs and traditions, the Mexicans express them- selves through colorful celebrations and a rich variety of crafts.

TIJUANA • MEXICALI

SONORA

CIUDAD
JUAREZ

CHIHUAHUA

• CHIHUAHUA

CO

BAJA CALIFORNIA

SINALOA

ZA

DURANGO

DURANGO •

NAYARIT

TEPIC •

GUADALAJA

Tlaquepaqu

JALISCO

Talpa

Pata

COLIMA

MI

Mexico is a land of contrasts. Fertile valleys, tropical jungles, and arid deserts combine with mountain ranges and deep canyons. Mexico is also a land of crafts. Using the materials that nature provides, inhabitants still follow the ancient traditions of their Indian ancestors, shaping pots, weaving cloth, lacquering gourds, or braiding baskets. New methods and materials introduced by the Spanish after the Conquest further enriched the range of handicrafts, and the blending of customs and peoples that followed produced a culture that is wholly Mexican. On the map Mexico resembles a great cornucopia, or horn of plenty, and her wealth of crafts amply bears out this image. Drawing upon their cultural heritage, Mexican craftsmen combine utility with beauty and enrich not only their own lives but those of their countrymen.

● MONTERREY
● Saltillo

SAN LUIS
POTOSÍ

TAMAULIPAS

Santa María
del Río

ANAJUATO

GUANAJUATO

San Miguel

QUERÉTARO

CELAYA   QUERÉTARO   Ixmiquilpan   VERACRUZ
    Tequisquiapan

MORELIA   HIDALGO

ichu   Tzintzuntzan   TLAXCALA   Cuetzalan
apan   Patzcuaro   TOLUCA   MEXICO
    Santa Clara   Metepec   PUEBLA
    del Cobre   MORELOS   Amozoc
CAN   Taxco   CUERNAVACA   Izucar
    Acapetlahuaya   PUEBLA   Ojitlan
    Ameyaltepec   Acatlán   Yalalag
    Olinala
GUERRERO   OAXACA
    Acatlán   Metlatonoc   Teotitlán
                del Valle
ACAPULCO   Xochislahuaca   Coyotepec   Tehuantepec
    Pinotepa de D.L.   OAXACA

MERIDA   YUCATÁN

CAMPECHE   QUINTANA ROO

TABASCO

TUXTLA
GUTIERREZ   ● San Andres
    San Cristobal
    Chiapa
    de Corzo   Amatenango
CHIAPAS   Venustiano
            Carranza

CHAPTER 2
FRUITS OF A GOLDEN AGE

In stunned silence the voyage-weary Spaniards stared at the dazzling sight that lay before their eyes. Spread out across the deck on simple palm mats, glinting and gleaming in the Mexican sunlight, shone a wealth of treasures, gifts from the Emperor Montezuma to the bearded strangers from the sea.

Armbands of gold and silver, pendants, rings, and exquisite necklaces heavy with rubies and emeralds vied in splendor with gem-studded helmets, shimmering breastplates, and rich shields cunningly inlaid with gold or mother of pearl. Two items in particular held the gaze of all present: a solid golden disk, shaped like the sun, "engraved with its rays and its foliage," and another of silver sculptured to represent the moon. Here were marvels indeed and, in the words of the expedition's friar Bartolomé de las Casas, "a present of things so rich and made and worked with such artifice that they seemed a dream and not fashioned by the hands of men."

There were more golden gifts to follow, and the Aztecs recorded with some surprise the reaction of the pale-skinned "gods." "When they were given these presents the Spaniards burst into smiles; their eyes shone with pleasure; they were delighted by them. They picked up the gold and fingered it like monkeys; they seemed to be transported by joy, as if their hearts were illuminated and made new...." Such extreme greed as the strangers exhibited must have been hard for the people of the sun to understand, for in the realm of Anáhuac precious metals were prized less for their value than for their divine attributes, their use being strictly reserved for the priests, warriors, and high-ranking nobles. Gold, "excrement of the gods," was shaped and worked into a dazzling succession of ceremonial objects and offerings, while the iridescent brilliance of silver was intimately bound up with the God of Darkness and of the Night Sky.

Metalsmiths were men of standing and position in Aztec society,

Aztec goldsmiths served the god Xipe Totec, who symbolized spring rain and the renewal of nature. This representation of the golden deity, cast by the "lost wax" method, originally formed the centerpiece of a Mixtec necklace.

Opposite: For hundreds of years, copper has been worked in Santa Clara del Cobre. While one man spins the fiery disk with iron tongs, his companions hammer it out with powerful and rhythmic blows.

justly respected for the delicate precision of their work. Known as Toltecs to show that they were in the direct tradition of the golden age, these extraordinary craftsmen knew how to cast by the "lost wax" method, to weld, inlay or encrust, and to obtain elaborate *répoussé* designs by chiseling metals beaten to paper thinness, all this with a minimum of wood, copper, or stone tools.

Motolinía, a learned and discerning friar, tells us of some of the wonders he saw. "They could cast a bird with a movable tongue, head, and wings, and cast a monkey or other monster with movable head, tongue, feet, and hands, and in the hand put a toy so that it appeared to dance with it; and even more, they cast a piece, one half gold and one half silver, and cast a fish with all its scales, one scale of silver, one of gold. . . ."

Even Cortés was impressed by the beauty and delicacy of such pieces, being moved to write to his king with words of rare praise. "These objects, besides being of great value, are such wondrous novelties and are so unusual that they have no price, nor could anyone believe that a prince in the world today would own something of such quality." Strong sentiments, but in the end it was greed that prevailed. One by one these treasures were melted down and their incomparable workmanship was lost forever.

It was not long before Mexico's new rulers began to exploit the mines, starting with the deposits known to the Indians and going on to discover still richer veins. Vast fortunes were accumulated as New Spain became the most important silver producing country in the world. Skilled craftsmen flocked from the cities of Europe to this golden land where newly acquired affluence found its expression in dazzling secular and religious works of art.

Methods of melting and casting gold are depicted in this ancient Aztec illustration. Metal workers blew through a tube, creating a draft in the charcoal heated furnace.

But what of the Indians, the men whose genius had inspired such wonder and admiration? These native craftsmen were barred by royal decree from working, using, or possessing the precious metals of their country. Not until the seventeenth century could eager Indian apprentices learn the new methods, and they soon rivaled their European masters, entering at last into life on the Street of Silversmiths where the best metal workers were gathered.

As time passed, a succession of Chinese metallurgists was also drawn to New Spain, adding yet another influence to the many, and over the centuries all these different styles have merged and blended to give one that is uniquely Mexican. However, something essentially Indian remains, and the craftsman of today preserves the sense of design characteristic of his pre-Hispanic counterpart.

Gold working is still a noble art in Mexico, and the metalsmiths of Oaxaca City reproduce with exquisite precision the ancient necklaces, pendants, and earrings deposited by their Mixtec forebears in the tombs of Monte Albán. In a more colonial vein are the lovely ornaments of Guanajuato, delicately formed and rich in floral motifs, doves, and turquoise stones. The traditional craft of filigree persists in many regions, local pearls and coral often being added to intricate and lacelike necklaces, bracelets, brooches, and earrings as on the tropical Peninsula of Yucatán.

It is silver, however, that predominates and in the smart city shops fine jewelry inlaid with precious stones and mother of pearl, or elegant coffee pots, trays, and fruit dishes for the home can be seen. Yet nowhere is the workmanship more beautiful than in Taxco, town of the silversmiths, set deep between high mountains in the rugged state of Guerrero.

Well known even before the Conquest for its wealth, Taxco has continued as a major silver producing center. Each year at the Silver Fair the visitor is faced with an array of splendid pieces, many modernistic in style, but others based on classic forms and bearing the plumed serpents and eagles of bygone days. Indeed, metallurgy holds few secrets from these talented craftsmen who hammer and marry metals, emboss and engrave with equal ease, even casting by the lost wax method of executing complicated works of mosaic with turquoise, malachite, mother of pearl, and lapis lazuli. With such skill at their fingertips, the silversmiths of Taxco must surely qualify as the Toltecs of the twentieth century.

In the rural areas of Mexico, far from the cities and the demands of fashion, people follow timeless traditions, preserving their own style of dress and characteristic adornments. The fish is a favorite motif, but nowhere more so than in the lakeside district of Pátzcuaro in southwest Mexico. Famed since early times for the white fish that abound in its waters, the region took on the name of Michoacan, "land of fishes." Tradition still holds strong, for each day the elongated fishing canoes with butterfly-shaped nets can be seen putting out from the villages that surround the lake. Local silversmiths made fish before the Conquest and they make them still, pouring molten metal into molds and finishing off each piece by hand, filing and polishing until the scales gleam. Strung on silver wire with shiny

The goldsmiths of Yucatán specialize in the art of filigree, creating delicate rosaries, earrings, and lacelike necklaces.

With skillful precision, Leonardo Ramos Cobos of Yucatán assembles the golden sections of a filigree flower.

19

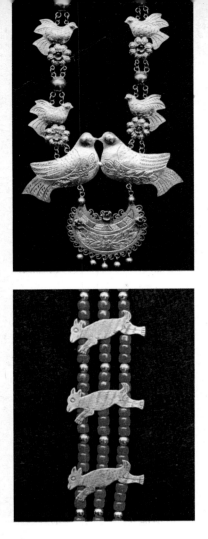

red beads to make necklaces, these cheerful fish are worn by many a local woman on her trips to market. The fish design is popular, too, among the villagers of Tlatlauqui, high in the hills of Puebla. Forged in gold or silver and worn as earrings, the delicate and lifelike fish of the area have a special fascination: they are jointed, just like the classic pieces so admired by Cortés over four hundred years ago.

Tiny suns and moons, of magical significance in earlier days, hang in silver clusters about the necks of the Mazahua women who enter Mexico City daily to sell fruit and nuts of the season. Leaves and flowers are traditional motifs, and in the mountainous state of Oaxaca infinite numbers of animal figures are still worked in silver. Dainty chickens and roosters adorn necklaces or earrings, and the rabbit retains its pre-Hispanic association with the moon whose waxings and wanings were once believed to govern plant life on earth. As for the women in the tiny village of Santa Catarina, they favor a curious motif, an alligator with a fish between its jaws.

With the arrival of the Spanish, a new type of jewelry reached Mexico. Indian women, fascinated by the profusion of gold coins the Conquerors' wives displayed, were quick to copy them. Decked out in a wealth of chokers, necklaces, bracelets, and other ornaments, the colorfully dressed Tehuanas, or women of the Isthmus, are a dazzling and unforgettable sight. Moorish-style earrings, shaped like crescent moons, were adopted with equal enthusiasm and few are the regions today where these pretty decorations are not worn.

No longer allowed to represent their own gods, native peoples were drawn to the medals, rosaries, crosses, and reliquaries that symbolize the Catholic faith. To this day, Yucatán produces fine

Silver is shaped into a variety of motifs. Feathery doves and flowers frequently adorn the necklaces of Mazahua women, and leaping rabbits are combined with red porcelain beads in jewelry from the state of Oaxaca.

A silversmith from Cholula, in the state of Puebla, smooths and perfects mold produced segments before assembling them into earrings.

Ornate crosses such as this one are worn by the women of Yalalag. Cast in silver, they are beaten and embossed by hand.

gold rosaries made from eight-sided hollow beads, and the silver-smiths of Oaxaca City engrave crosses with scenes from the Passion. But perhaps loveliest of all are the compound crosses from the southern Sierra Madre, inspired by those of Salamanca in Spain and introduced into this wild and remote part of Oaxaca by the pioneer friars of the Conquest.

Of cast silver, beaten and embossed by hand, these ornate pieces vary in design from village to village. From the arms and foot of the famous Yalalag crosses hang smaller crosses, replaced elsewhere in the region by crowns, hearts, medals, or Virgins. The silver beads with which the chains are strung combine with red beads of porcelain, colored pompons and animal charms, the more numerous the better. By long tradition mothers present these unique necklaces to their daughters on their wedding day, setting them apart from unmarried companions who may wear only earrings.

Among Indian men jewelry is rarely worn. Abandoning their breastplates, pendants, and armbands, their ancestors watched the new rulers rise to prosperity. With the passing of time huge estates grew up and their owners assumed the wide brimmed hats and richly embroidered clothes, heavy with gold and silver thread and studded with silver buttons, so popular at the time near Salamanca. Known as *charros*, these extravagantly dressed overlords gave rise to an endless series of legends and stories. By the flickering light of an oil lamp, wide-eyed children are still told how the Devil, disguised as a charro, goes riding through the night on a fiery black charger.

Even after Spanish domination had ended in Mexico, the charro remained a national feature symbolizing masculine splendor, and today rich farmers in the north still turn out in full regalia for processions and national festivities. Medieval-style spurs and buckles, exquisitely forged by the smiths of Amozoc in blued steel, and inlaid with engraved silver, complete the costume.

The history of copper in Mexico has been no less far reaching than that of gold and silver, and the Aztecs who prized it greatly were always eager to obtain it, if not by tribute then by trade. Dancers attached strings of melodious bells to their costumes, warriors carried gleaming shields and spears into battle, while the wood carvers and feather workers of Tenochtitlán depended on copper for sharp axes and keen blades. But it was their neighbors, the proud and indomitable Tarascans of Michoacan, who best understood the art of handling copper. Beating it out cold, casting it in molds, or even using the lost wax method, they were able to produce a multitude of bracelets, rings, ornaments, tongs, and other tools that the Spanish admired. They were even more impressed, however, by the rich deposits of the region. Mining started and master coppersmiths arrived from Europe.

The Tarascans found a friend in their Bishop, Vasco de Quiroga. Determined that his protégés should not be exploited, he saw to it that they were taught the new techniques, encouraging them at the same time to continue their traditional skills. In 1553, only a short time after the Conquest, the mountain village of Santa Clara of the Copper was officially recognized and to this day there is hardly a member of the community whose livelihood is not inextricably bound up with this beautiful metal. On a busy day in Santa Clara, the rhythmic sound of hammering echoes through the old and rambling houses that face onto the square, while in the *fraguas*, or working areas at the back, lumps of metal, red hot from the fire, are stretched and beaten on the anvil. As many as nine men participate in the making of large cauldrons, for as one spins the glowing disk with iron tongs, his companions pound it into shape with mighty blows.

The durable pitchers, pans, and tureens of Santa Clara, with their dark gold luster, have always been popular on Mexican farms, and as dusk descends over the fields, tin-lined *cazos*, or cooking pots, simmer on many a kitchen range. But decoration also plays an important role. Gently curving dishes, engraved or embossed with imaginative motifs, elegant candlesticks, and jugs with snakes for handles all testify to the artistry of their creators. Indeed, so smooth and flawless do these pieces appear, it is sometimes hard to remember that they are made by hand.

José Feliz Herrano of Amozoc, in the state of Puebla, devotes his work to the making of spurs, inlaying blued steel with finely engraved silver.

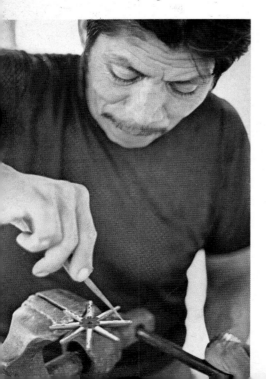

Disks of copper, red hot from the fire, are pounded on the anvil by the smiths of Santa Clara del Cobre. Pieces are then hammered into perfection with deft blows.

Although plentiful in Mexico today, iron and steel were for all practical purposes introduced by the Spanish, even playing a decisive part in the Conquest. Aware that a shortage of these metals could prove fatal, Cortés had the great ships stripped of their fittings, and it was the friendly Indians of Chinantla, famed for their skill with copper, who helped their bearded allies with the casting of weapons. During the long trek across country that followed, a new obstacle arose: the horses needed to be reshod. Silver was found to be both soft and slippery and anguished letters were sent to Spain complaining about the lack of iron. Stores were sufficiently replenished, however, for the would-be conquerors to undertake the building of ships on Lake Texcoco, forging the necessary nails, chains, and anchors for the battle to come. In the end, of course, steel swords triumphed over the obsidian tipped lances of the Aztecs, and heavy iron shackles bound the prisoners of war.

Out of the ruins of Indian townships and temples, imposing cities and cathedrals began to rise, while Spanish galleons plowed back and forth across the seas, bringing much needed iron to Mexico. Local deposits, discovered in due course, were left unmined by order of the Spanish king and prices soared, setting this imported metal on a level with copper or silver. A steady influx of finished articles from

In the peaceful town of San Cristobal de las Casas, local blacksmiths forge iron crosses, decorating them with a mass of symbols. Placed on the roof ridges of houses, they are thought to ward off evil spirits.

In the state of Oaxaca flexible machete blades are decorated with mountainous landscapes and scenes from the bullring. "Horse, machete, and woman, own a good one or own none," reads the motto.

Spain further aggravated the immigrant blacksmiths' lot, causing them to fight fiercely among themselves for a share in the dwindling market. Rivalry was strongest of all on Tacuba Street, where the iron workers of Mexico City were officially situated, and special acts were passed to ensure fair play. Goods could be sold only inside the shops, while to entice a competitor's customer away from him, by word or sign, became a punishable offense.

Yet in spite of the difficulties they encountered, these European metallurgists left fine examples of their work for future generations to admire, and the cities of Puebla, Morelia, Oaxaca, and Guanajuato abound in the lovely wrought iron balconies, gates, grilles, balustrades, and weather vanes so characteristic of colonial architecture. As for the often fanciful ironwork to be found in convents and monasteries, this was generally carried out by Indian craftsmen under the guidance of the friars. Today, iron is forged in many towns, including San Felipe of the Blacksmiths in Michoacan, to produce a variety of garden furniture, door knockers, tools, and ornamental fixtures. Splendid colonial-style lamps, fitted with blown glass of many hues, are a special feature of Mexico City.

In cities and rural areas alike, steel has never ceased to play its vital role and tools of all kinds are manufactured to meet the needs of the community. In the states of Guerrero and Oaxaca, horn handled knives are engraved with lively scenes and well-known mottoes, although similar designs may be achieved with the aid of acid. Amid leafy trees and tall grasses, the tiger hunts the fleeing deer, as underneath we read the words, "The ass wasn't distrustful until he was made so" or still more to the point, "If I say the donkey is striped, it's because I hold his hide in my hand." Each supple and gleaming blade bears its own motto, reminding its owner that "he who keeps company with wolves learns to howl," or that "faces we see, hearts we can never know."

Yet of the many metals worked in Mexico, tin is the most popular.

The seller of miracles is a familiar figure all over Mexico. Once made from silver, but today more often cast in tin alloys, "milagros," or miracles, are offered to saints in churches to serve as expressions of faith and gratitude. The figure of a cow marks its recovery from disease or its fertility in producing young. Arms, legs, ears, or hearts acknowledge that the desired cure has been granted, and a kneeling figure tells the story of a prayer answered.

An experienced craftswoman from Oaxaca City hammers out flexible and gleaming segments of tin on a block. A soldering iron is used to join pieces. Finished creations are left unpainted or further embellished with bright, translucent colors.

Light and flexible, it can be shaped in an infinite number of ways, engraved and embossed, left plain, or painted with bright, translucent colors, and the craftsman is free to follow where his inspiration leads. To enter a tin shop in San Miguel de Allende or Oaxaca City is to enter a wonderland of color and fantasy. Ornamental trees full of birds and fruit, gleaming suns, and elaborately twisted candelabra compete with embossed boxes, mirror frames rich in raised flowers, and eighteen-point lamps that hang from the ceiling like glimmering stars. Minute sailing ships, parrots, angels, and exotic green rocking horses bring to mind a world of enchantment and delight. These ingenious creations seem to express the very spirit of Mexico, a love of beauty combined with great artistry.

MAKING THE CRAFTS OF MEXICO

Throughout this book, you will find "how-to" sections that give instructions for making some of the Mexican crafts you have been reading about. These crafts projects are replicas of authentic Mexican folk crafts and are true to the traditional colors and motifs of the country. The materials and techniques used are as similar as possible to those used by native craftsmen. If materials and tools are difficult to find outside Mexico, we have suggested an easily available substitute. The tools needed to make these crafts projects are likely to be found around the house, or they can be bought inexpensively from craft, art, or hardware stores.

Step by step photographs and detailed diagrams show exactly how to make each craft project. And each how-to section includes a selection of other traditional patterns and motifs so that you can adapt and vary the projects to create ethnic crafts that are both traditional and personal.

Enlarging and reducing designs

Make a drawing or tracing of the original design. Enclose design in a box. Divide the box horizontally and vertically into quarters. Divide the quarters again, and again if necessary, until the whole design is covered with a grid of small squares. Draw another box to the size you want the finished design to be. Divide this into quarters and then into a grid with exactly the same number of squares as in the first box.

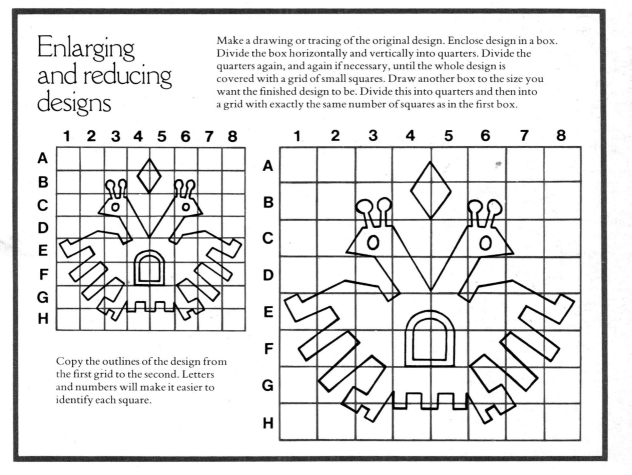

Copy the outlines of the design from the first grid to the second. Letters and numbers will make it easier to identify each square.

TRADITIONAL TINWORK

Among the many metals worked in Mexico, it is tin that is the most popular. Light, flexible, and inexpensive, it can be shaped in an infinity of ways. Whether it is left plain or brightly painted, tin allows the craftsman to follow his inspiration. The soft metal is twisted, punched, cut, and shaped into animals, birds, flower-decked mirrors, embossed boxes, elaborate candelabra, and simple lanterns. Thin aluminum sheet, which can be purchased from metal suppliers and hardware stores, is an easily available substitute for tin. It can be shaped with basic tools—tin snips and improvised punches.

Rainbow-hued butterflies and exotic green elephants are joined by a colorful host of smiling suns, mermaids, stars, parrots, angels, sailing ships, and shimmering fish. Ingeniously shaped and painted with translucent colors, these cut-out tin shapes amuse children and decorate Christmas trees during the festive season.

Punched lantern

Soft candlelight shines through the decorative punched holes in these tin lanterns. They are simple to make from thin aluminum sheet available from metal supply stores. Nails and punches of different sizes are used to create the patterns on sides and roof. Drip hot wax on floor of finished lantern and stand up candle securely.

Materials: 26 gauge (tooling) aluminum, tin can for former, tin snips with curved and straight blades, heavy and light hammers, epoxy glue, nails, countersink, cardboard.

Measure height and circumference of tin can. Make cardboard template (see p. 30) and cut out opening for door. Make roof template. Tape templates to metal, score outline with nail.

Cut out metal shapes with tin snips. Use straight blades for straight lines and rough curves. Use curved blades to make curves neat and for sharp corners.

Tape template to cut-out metal and lightly tap position of all holes through the cardboard. Remove template and punch design in the metal using nails and countersink.

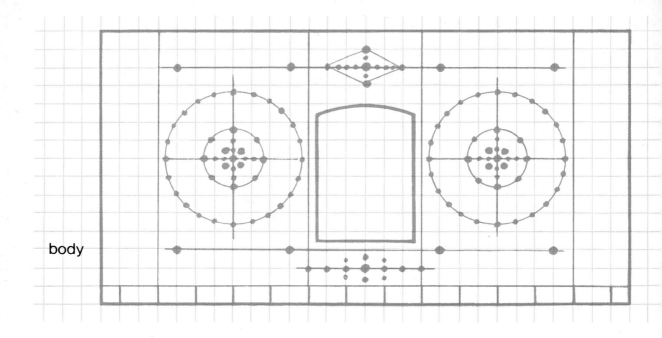

body

Above: Make a template the same height and circumference as the tin can, adding extra at bottom for clipping and turning under and at one end for gluing as shown in the pattern above. Cut out a door in the center and work out a symmetrical punched design, or copy this one.

Right: Use a can opener to start cutting out the door, then use tin snips. Cut the door slightly smaller than final opening. Clip and turn the raw edges to the inside, hammering them flat.

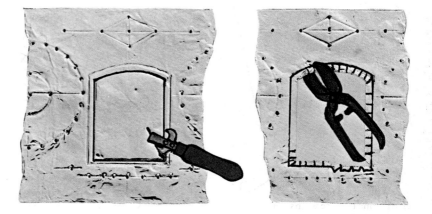

Lightly roughen the surfaces to be glued with sandpaper and roll the punched aluminum around the former, making sure there are no lumps or unevennesss in the metal.

Glue the edges of the metal together and wrap string tightly around it to hold in place. When the glue is set, untie the string and pull out the tin can former.

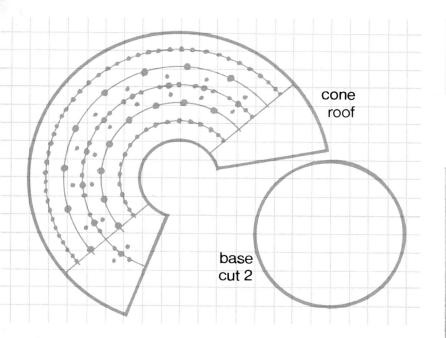

cone
roof

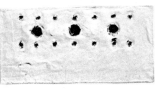

funnel

base
cut 2

4 tabs

handle

Punch a pattern on the cone-shaped roof. Roughen the edges to be glued, apply glue, and fold around. Hold the metal cone in place with strong paper clips while the glue dries.

Cut out and punch a strip for the funnel, fold around your finger, and push into roof. The natural springiness of the metal will keep the funnel in place without any glue.

Cut out base shapes. Clip around base of lantern as shown on template, fold in edges. Glue one base inside lantern and one outside, so folded edges are secured between the two bases.

Glue four tabs inside roof and glue these tabs inside lantern to fix on roof. Cut out handle, glue to lantern as shown. Secure tabs and handle with tape while glue dries.

31

Painted mirror

The scalloped edges of this brightly painted mirror frame are surprisingly simple to cut out with the snips, using a coin as a template. The raised petals are cut out with a hammer and chisel and painted with transparent paints.

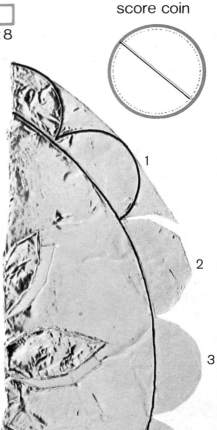

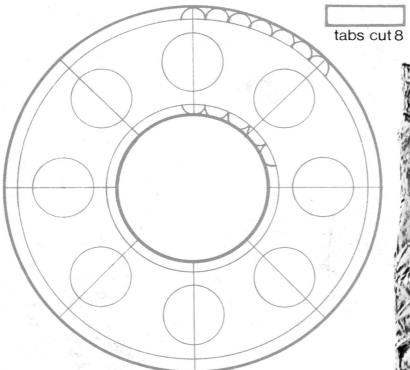

tabs cut 8

score coin

Make a cardboard template (above) for the mirror frame, marking position of flowers and inner circles so scallops can be cut accurately. Score a line across a coin and use this semicircle as template. Cut scallops in three stages, using curved tin snips.

When punching out metal, work on a wooden board. Use straight blade tin snips to cut out a circle roughly, then cut scallops with curved tin snips. Make sure the chisel is kept very sharp so that it punches cleanly through the metal. Remove grease and finger marks with alcohol or vinegar and paint in bright colors.

Cut template of eight-petal flower shape from cardboard.

Materials: 26 gauge (tooling) aluminum, tin snips, $\frac{1}{2}$ in (12 mm) chisel, hammer, cardboard, 1 in (2.5 cm) coin, epoxy glue, transparent paints, paintbrush, round mirror.

Roughly cut out the frame and mark scallops. Cut out flower template; divide back of frame into eight equal sections. Score around flower template in each segment.

Working on the back of the frame, cut out the flower petals. Start at the point and work around each petal as shown, making neat, clean cuts with the hammer and sharp chisel.

For the flower centers, lightly hammer a nail at random on the wrong side of the frame, just enough to texture the metal without piercing it. Practice first on a scrap of metal.

Detail of cut flower shows how three chisel cuts are made on each side of a petal and how flower centers are textured. Detail below shows how to glue tabs around inside of the frame and then fold them over the round mirror to hold it in place.

Cut out scallops and push flower petals through to right side of frame. Paint the scallops, petals, centers, stalks, and leaves as shown in the photograph of the finished frame.

Glue eight tabs on wrong side of frame. Secure with tape while epoxy glue dries. Fold tabs over to secure mirror in frame. To hang frame, punch a hole in the top with a large nail.

CHAPTER 3
FROM THE SPINDLE TO THE LOOM

"She grooms herself and dresses with such care that when she is thoroughly ready she looks like a flower. And to make herself ready she first looks in her glass, bathes, washes, and freshens herself in order to please. She makes up her face with a yellow cream called *axin* which gives her a dazzling complexion; and sometimes, being a loose, lost woman, she puts on rouge. She also has the habit of dyeing her teeth with cochineal and of wearing her hair loose for more beauty. . . . She perfumes herself with an odoriferous censer, and in walking around, she chews *tzictli* making a clacking noise with her teeth like castanets."

These disapproving words, written more than four and a half centuries ago by a Spanish priest Bernardino Sahagún, describe an Aztec lady of easy virtue. Presumably the average Aztec woman took trouble with her appearance, too, and enjoyed her reflection in the polished obsidian or iron pyrites that served as mirrors, without going to the extremes described. Clothes must have held as great a fascination for her as for her female counterparts anywhere – greater perhaps, given that the major part of her time went into the making of them.

The invention of spinning and weaving was attributed to Xochiquetzal, goddess of flowers and patroness of weavers. Many were the beliefs that sprang up linking the weaving process with fertility and with the need for rain. The principal female deities connected with growth and regeneration were depicted with weaving implements. Aztec parents made every effort to ensure that a baby girl would one day be a skilled weaver, presenting her with a miniature spindle or weaving stick and burying her umbilical cord in the house as a symbol that her adult life would be spent at home, creating hard-wearing and beautiful garments for herself or her family, and ceremonial textiles to offer the gods. Such was the respect good

Xochiquetzal, the Aztec goddess of flowers and love, was also the patroness of weavers.

Opposite: The Trique Indian women in the mountainous region of Oaxaca are great weavers, brocading rich and colorful motifs into the fabric of their huipils, which they embellish with a profusion of ribbons.

weaving commanded, that talented slaves were exempted from sacrifice.

Rabbit fur was dyed and spun, feathers were twisted to make colorful yarns or woven into the web of the cloth, and vast quantities of raw cotton were levied in tribute from the peoples who inhabited *tierra caliente*, the hot lands. Finished cloth was eagerly sought after, especially the *centzontilmati* or "cloaks-of-a-thousand-colors" for which the Huastec weavers were famous.

There were many legends about cotton in pre-Conquest Mexico. One tells how at the time of the Creation the Princess Precious Flower gave birth to a child whom she called Well Beloved. To her great grief he died almost at once, but from the ground where he was buried there grew innumerable plants. His fingers became sweet potatoes, his nails maize, and his hair cotton.

People also spoke of a marvelous age, during the reign of Quetzalcoatl, the Plumed Serpent, when pumpkins were as tall as men and cotton grew in brilliant hues. By using a wide range of dyes, women were able to restore some of these mythical colors to the white cotton, while a species of naturally brown cotton, known to this day as *coyuche*, was much admired. The textile section of the great market at Tenochtitlán must have been wonderful to behold with its lengths of cloth woven in all manner of styles, its piles of unspun fiber, and its exotic dyes.

Aztec society was firmly based on a system of hierarchy where every feather in a headdress and every mark painted on the face revealed a man's rank and status. Whole series of adornments, colors, or clothes were restricted to the powerful few, as the following laws indicate:

"Only the King and the Prime Minister Tlacaelel may wear sandals within the palace. No great chieftain may enter the palace shod, under pain of death. The great noblemen are the only ones to

In this scene from domestic life, a young girl learns to weave, watched over by her mother. Over her head the Aztec scribe has drawn two large tortillas, her recommended daily ration.

Colour filmstrip roll 113d. Bodleian Library, Oxford

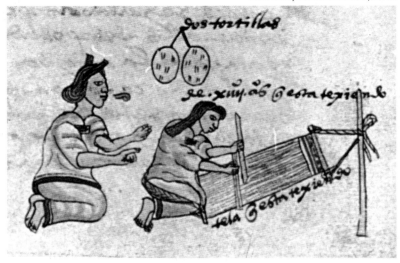

be allowed to wear sandals in the city and no one else, with the exception of men who have performed some great deed in war. But these sandals must be cheap and common; the gilded, painted ones are to be used only by noblemen. The common people will not be allowed to wear cotton clothing under pain of death, but only garments of *maguey* fiber." This fiber, known as *ixtle*, is obtained from the spiky leaves of the maguey cactus. Spun and woven it gives a cloth with an open, netlike appearance and Aztec women liked to decorate it with embroidery, using needles of copper or bone and even the thorns of the maguey itself.

In ancient Mexico costume differences not only set the rich or privileged apart from the poor, they also testified to the wearer's tribe and place of origin, enabling soldiers on the battlefield to tell friends from foes.

Centuries have rolled by, but Indian communities still adhere to a particular style of dress, while within such communities each village may have its own variations. Now, as in the past, mothers teach their daughters to spin and dye, weave, and embroider, ensuring that these traditions will not be lost. Ixtle is still used, particularly among the Otomi Indians who embroider it with animal or flower designs in the style of their ancestors. But it is cotton that is the most common fabric, for the restrictions of the ancient Aztec code were canceled out by the Conquest.

Ixtle, or maguey fiber, is still much used in Mexico. Portions of the fresh plant are pulled between two sticks so that the pulp is scraped away, leaving tough white fibers that can then be dyed. Strands are wound onto a frame in a figure eight, prior to weaving.

Dexterously twirling her spindle in a half gourd, Yolanda Pérez Vasquez from the Oaxaca region spins her freshly carded yarn to make smooth and even thread.

When the cotton pods are ripe and ready for gathering, the fibers are carefully removed from the husk and all impurities or short, useless strands discarded. Then follows the beating, once thought of as a way of punishing the goddess Xochiquetzal, forcing her to aid the weaver with her work. A palm mat is placed under the newly cleaned cotton, which becomes soft and pliable under the blows.

The spinning process is no less laborious. The spindle, a smooth round stick with a whorl of wood, clay, or bone, is twirled in a half gourd or pottery dish. Many women remember their first lessons as small girls and the scoldings they received. "If you can't learn with your head, I'll punish your hands," irate mothers exclaim, bringing down the spindle on their daughters' knuckles. "One day you'll marry and know what it is to be beaten by a mother-in-law because you can't make even thread." And yet to see an Indian woman, spinning as she sits in her doorway nursing a child or talking with a neighbor, one would think it an effortless task.

Now the cotton is ready for coloring and in remote areas techniques have persisted unchanged for hundreds of years, while each community has its own special secrets and traditions. Roots, wood, bark, and berries provide good vegetable dyes, creating a wealth of different shades. Blue is obtained by combining the leaves of the acacia with black clay, or more commonly with the help of the indigo plant. The longer the yarn is left to soak, the deeper the tone. The yellow of the country dahlia or the mustard tinge of the *mora*

In remote regions, natural dyes are still used. The indigo plant is popular, and here a weaver from the Chiapas Highlands spreads out her newly dyed yarn in the sun to dry.

Roots, bark, berries, and leaves are used by the weavers of Magdalenas, in the state of Chiapas, to produce a subtle range of colors.

tree are popular, and the *peña* root with its range of ochers can always be recognized by the permanent but not unpleasant odor that remains in the cloth. When red is desired, logwood or the berries of the *capullín* tree are used. Natural brown cotton is still cultivated in several regions, though a similar effect is achieved by impregnating white cotton with the juice of the *huixtololo* root. Additional colors are created through successive immersions: yellow followed by blue produces green; violet is the result of blue followed by red.

Chief among the animal dyes is cochineal, exported in vast quantities to Europe by the Spanish during their rule. This tiny parasite is to be found on the prickly pear cactus and when crushed yields a brilliant shade of crimson. To make a pound of coloring matter, about 70,000 insects are required. Another animal dye comes from the sea snail, which lives along the coastline of Oaxaca and periodically causes the Chontal Indians to leave their villages and journey to the shores of the Pacific. For a month at a stretch whole families camp out on the beach, engaged in the dyeing of their raw cotton. As each successive tide withdraws, men, women, and children search the rocks for the snails, blowing on their shells, and dipping the yarn into their colorless secretion. It doesn't remain colorless for long, however. Contact with air turns the cotton first green and then a marvelous lilac. Cloth dyed in this way never loses the tang of the sea.

Minerals and earth dyes are numerous, often producing interesting variations when added to other natural colors. Mordants, too, play a vital role. Saltpeter, alum, lemon juice, and urine all serve to fix the different tones into the yarn.

The method of dyeing known as *ikat* is still practiced in the northern town of Santa Mariá del Rió. Stiffening the warp threads with corn dough, weavers separate certain sections, tying them tightly for protection. Submersion in the dye follows. When the yarn has dried out thoroughly, new sections are bound and the process continues as the desired colors are absorbed in successive stages. The dyed cotton is then measured out as needed, and the warp threads are wound onto a frame. Certain weavers, in addition to their calculations, symbolically "feed" the yarn with beans or maize to ensure that it will not run out.

The waist strap loom, used extensively in Mexico even today, is traditionally known as the *telar de otate*, or loom of bamboo rods, for when dismantled it is little more than a bundle of sticks, varying in length, size, and thickness. The weaver sits either on a low stool or on the ground, kneeling only when her work requires unusual strength. The width of the cloth produced is determined by the weaver's arm span. One end of the loom is attached to a tree or a post, while the other fits around the waist.

Mothers often accompany daughters who are learning to weave on pilgrimages to the local church, lighting candles for the Virgin and showing Her samples of the young girls' handiwork. "I did as my mother told me," one woman recalls. "I asked the Virgin to put the art of weaving into my hands and my heart, and She must have heard me for it wasn't long before I made my first shawl. When my child is older I shall take her in the same way."

Techniques can be very complicated and delicate, for the design is actually brocaded into the fabric in combinations of color, while additional weft threads are frequently included to form exquisite

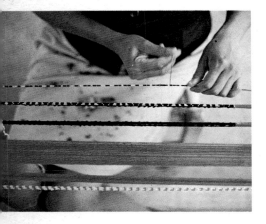

The rebozo weavers of Santa María del Río practice the ikat method of dyeing. Tightly binding the silk thread in sections before immersing it in dye, they produce a dappled effect.

Ikat dyed thread was used to weave this belt from Toliman, in Querétaro.

Before this woman from Pinotepa de Don Luis, in Oaxaca, can begin weaving an enredo, she must measure out her thread onto a winding frame. Cotton, blue-black from the indigo plant and lilac from the sea snail, is combined with cochineal-dyed silk.

raised motifs. The weaver needs no diagram or model, working as she does from memory alone. In some parts of Mexico figured gauze is achieved in brilliant white and the beauty of the patterning can only be fully appreciated by holding the cloth up to the light.

By twisting the warp with the fingers and crossing the odd threads with the even, a lacelike effect is obtained, popular among the women of Cuetzalan in the mountains of Puebla. The decorative possibilities of weaving on a waist strap loom are many: when thicker weft threads are incorporated into the fabric, ribbed bands are produced. If a puckered appearance is desired, then the warp should be pulled tight, for when the garment is washed, the cotton will shrink and crinkle.

An ancient skill retained by the Otomis and Totonacs of Puebla is that of weaving in a curve. By using the warp threads as weft, they are able to give the cloth a rounded edge. The Otomis who inhabit the states of Hidalgo and Mexico are no less gifted, for they specialize in weaving double. Two series of threads, in contrasting colors, are used to provide superimposed layers that remain partially separate, joining only when the colors are interchanged. Animal motifs are often featured, and if a horse shows up white on one side, it will be black on the other.

Other looms are also to be found, the rigid heddle type being favored in certain villages for the making of belts, while both the

The waist strap loom is widely used in Mexico and weavers make their own clothes and those of their families. Working without diagrams or models, they often brocade complex designs into the fabric in striking colors.

41

The pre-Columbian art of working feathers into the cloth has not been altogether lost. It survives to this day in the village of Zinacantan, set deep in the heart of the Chiapas Highlands. This wedding huipil is interwoven with fluffy white down.

Mayos of Sonora and the Tarahumaras of Chihuahua are adept at ring weaving. Producing their cloth on a circular framework, they release it by cutting, leaving luxuriant fringes at each end.

Although in some communities men occasionally operate these different looms, taking over what is traditionally the women's role, treadle weaving is an essentially male occupation. Introduced after the Conquest, the European loom with its spools, pulleys, and shuttles soon became an integral part of the textile industry that sprang up in cities and towns. Indian women are often only too glad to buy strips of cloth wider than those they can make themselves on a waist strap loom.

Wool proved another welcome importation, giving rise to the *sarape*. During the Colonial period the towns of Saltillo and San Miguel de Allende achieved great fame as sarape production centers. There rich overlords set up special workshops on their land, employing talented craftsmen to provide them with these much valued blankets, which they draped over their horses to go riding. So colorful did these weavings appear, that they reminded the Indians of rainbows. Gradually, however, the sarape was adopted by the ordinary man who uses it still, covering himself with it at night or wearing it like a mantle in cold weather.

Woolen garments were soon adopted in cold and mountainous regions where they are woven on the waist strap loom in the usual manner. The women of San Juan Chamula, in Chiapas, treat their wool in a special way, beating it to give it a feltlike texture. Great pains are taken not to remove the natural oils during the cleaning stage, with the result that their thick, warm clothing is virtually rainproof.

In areas where methods and techniques have changed so little, it is hardly surprising to find that many of the styles of dress worn before the Conquest are still in use. Simple to make, these garments are

Weaving on a treadle loom is an essentially male skill. Beautiful woolen sarapes or blankets are made and used in most parts of Mexico.

assembled from squares or rectangles straight from the loom, and cutting is avoided wherever possible.

Today, as in pre-Hispanic times, the Indian woman favors the *enredo*, which is basically a skirt without a waistband. Although single, treadle loomed lengths are becoming increasingly popular, the usual procedure is to stitch two or three panels made on a waist strap loom together, wrapping the resulting strip of cloth around the waist, sarong-style. The lengths can also be sewn up at the edges to make a tubular skirt. Adjusting it in the style of her village, the wearer doubles the cloth over upon itself to make deep folds. The skirts of Michoacan, woven in black or red wool, are a striking variation, often weighing six pounds or more. The heavy pleating at the back is obtained by dampening the fabric and leaving it for several days under a *metate*, or grinding stone.

The waist sashes that hold these enredos in place are an indispensable and often highly decorative feature of female dress, while a *soyate*, or belt of woven palm, is sometimes used underneath for extra strength. Fitting comfortably inside the enredo, or left to hang loose over it, is the *huipil*. This tuniclike garment, made from one, two or, more commonly, three lengths of cloth, is both elegant and practical, allowing great freedom of movement. The *quechquemitl*, today worn over a blouse, was associated in the distant past with goddesses and women of high rank. There is in addition a rounded type of quechquemitl produced by the Otomis and Totonacs of Puebla who specialize in the curved method of weaving. With her magnificently brocaded huipil or her delicately patterned quechquemitl, the Indian woman is wearing what her ancestors would have considered aristocratic dress.

Spanish influence, however, has been responsible for certain changes. Before the Conquest, country women often went bare breasted – as they still do, very occasionally, in certain remote villages

Ceremonial dress is worn at this meeting of village dignitaries in San Juan Chamula, in Chiapas.

Belts woven in Santo Tomás Jalieza are worn throughout Oaxaca.

43

of Oaxaca – and the friars were quick to condemn this custom. The use of the quechquemitl on its own was thought to be no less immodest and Indian women were strongly encouraged to adopt the blouse. This they did, adapting it to suit their tastes by adding a wealth of tucks and embroidery.

The *rebozo*, or shawl, has come to form such an integral part of female costume that it is sometimes hard to remember it was only introduced during the Colonial period. With the spread of Christianity, Indian women were taught to cover their heads for mass, and a length of cloth from the loom proved an ideal solution. The rebozo has since acquired many additional uses, securing the newly born baby to its mother's back or serving as a carrying cloth when heavy goods are transported to and from market. The rebozo industry flourished under Spanish rule, and the town of Santa Mariá del Rió grew famous for its silken ikat dyed creations, which were often so finely made that they could pass through a ring. The multicolored shawls woven on a waist strap loom by the men of the village of Mitla, in Oaxaca, are particularly warm and attractive, but every community has its own special style and there are few markets where rebozos are not on display.

Male clothing has become far more European in style than that of women, perhaps because men so frequently have to leave their villages, trading or working in centers where Indian dress is a curiosity.

The pre-Hispanic articles of clothing included the long and decorative loincloth with its fringes or tassels, and the *tilmati*, or rectangular cloak. Lavishly embellished with woven motifs, embroidery, and shells, it was worn knotted over the chest or the right shoulder. Wall paintings and sculptured figures both testify to the

The pre-Hispanic huipil has been retained by many communities, although in Jalapa de Diaz, in Oaxaca, trimmings are added to form sleeves.

Villagers from Zinacantan, in Chiapas, often come down from the hills to trade in the market at San Cristobal de las Casas. This man has adopted European pants but he still favors a palm hat streaming with ribbons and a jorongo, or tunic. His wife wears a cape embellished with tassels.

richness of the costumes in use among the nobility and to the feathers and other adornments that were popular. When the Spanish settled, establishing large towns and cities, they issued a law forbidding the Indian to enter built-up areas without pants. One reads how enterprising tradesmen would position themselves on the highroads leading into the towns and renting pants to the Indians as they came down from the hills.

In the mountainous states of Oaxaca and Chiapas, however, it is possible even today to find remote communities where a traditional style of dress is favored. Until fairly recently, the Mayos and the Tarahumaras of the North, still wore the loincloth, wrapping blankets around themselves in the manner of the Navahos.

In the dense and virgin forests of Chiapas, which border Guatemala, live the Lacandon Indians, last survivors of the pure Mayan race, and here the male covers himself with a huipil of unbleached cotton. In the same state, the Zinacantecos and the Chamulas use a garment not unlike shorts, retaining the pre-Hispanic sandals with a leather strip that rises from the heel up the leg. In nearby Huistán, loose pants are formed from uncut, handloomed lengths of cloth and worn looped up in front over a waist sash. Many neighboring communities have conserved equally picturesque costumes, often characterized by elegant palm hats, streaming with ribbons and pompons and inspired perhaps by the elaborate headdresses of old.

Belts are an important and beautiful feature everywhere, ranging from narrow woolen bands to wide ceremonial sashes knotted at the front in the style of the ancient loincloth. Woven squares, folded about the hips in a triangular fashion, are still worn over pants in a few communities. As for the rectangular cloak of maguey fiber, it serves in many areas as a carrying cloth. The *morral*, or shoulder bag, came into being as pre-Columbian dress had no pockets. Woven today from cotton, wool, or numerous vegetable fibers, it has lost none of its popularity.

Until this century pants were still produced on the waist strap loom, but now the tendency is to buy them ready-made. Shirts are generally more decorative, often being hand-woven and ornamented with brocaded motifs or embroidery. The sarape, of course, contributed greatly to male dress, providing a welcome series of variations. A blanket with a head opening becomes a *jorongo* and, when sleeves are added, a *cotón*.

Elegant yet functional, the clothing of Indian men and women is ideally suited not only to their way of life but also to the geographical and climatic conditions of their country. Many are the hours of hard work that go into the making of just one garment. Great is the skill and knowledge involved. But where quality and beauty are desired, chemical dyes, commercial thread, and machine weaving have a hard job competing. Costume in Mexico continues, as it always has done, to link the individual with his people and to play a social and even magical role.

Waist sashes are an essential feature of male and female attire. On the left is a woman's belt from Cuetzalan, in Puebla, adorned with woolen tufts, lace, and sequins. The Tarahumara man's belt on the right is distinguished by long braided fringes at each end.

In the village of Huistán, in Chiapas, traditional dress is still worn.

HUIPILS AND QUECHQUEMITLS

These elegant pre-Hispanic garments are still widely worn in Mexico and dimensions vary from region to region. A huipil either tucks into a skirt or hangs loose in graceful folds, sometimes almost to the ground. The lengths of cloth are joined with satin stitch or other decorative stitching and motifs are either woven into the cloth or embroidered on after the garment is sewn together. Ribbons may be attached to the neckline and left to flow in colorful cascades. The V-shaped quechquemitl is worn over a blouse with the points lying from side to side or more often facing front and back. To make a huipil or quechquemitl, decide on the style and length and adapt the pattern to the size of the wearer and the desired fit.

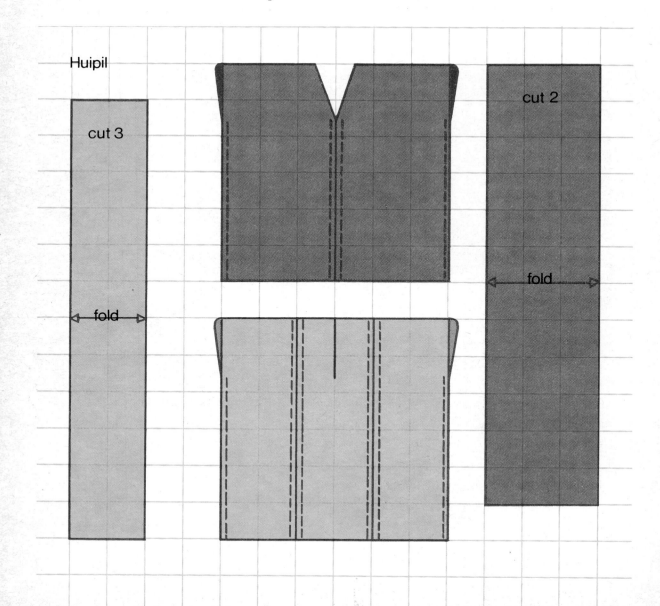

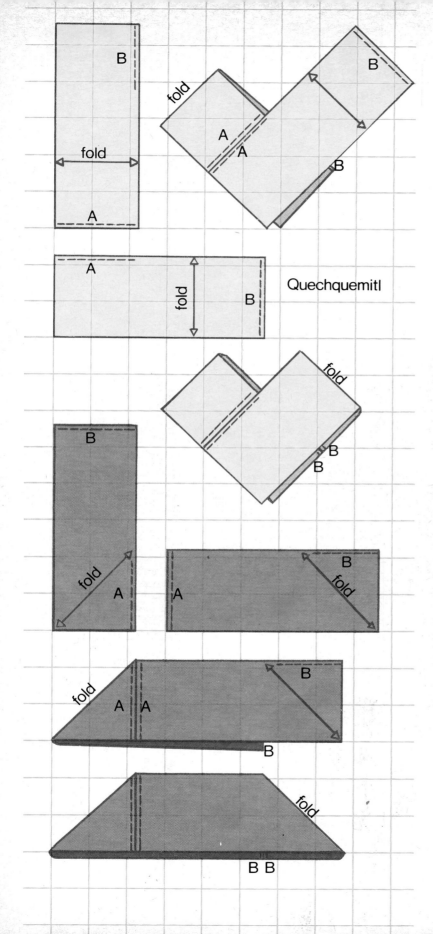

Quechquemitl

In Cuetzalan, white and gauzy quechquemitls are worn over charmingly embroidered blouses. On festive occasions the pre-Hispanic *rodete* or woolen turban is used and frequently topped with a second quechquemitl.

CHAPTER 4
FANTASY IN THREAD

Once upon a time, long long ago, the mother of the sun and the moon was weaving to clothe the creatures of the earth, the air, and the water. She clothed the birds, the insects, the fish, and the beasts of the forest. But while she was working on the armadillo her thread ran out, and to this day the armadillo has remained rough and unfinished.

This legend tells of the creation of the world and of the part that weaving played. Today's Indian woman is no less creative than this mother goddess of ancient Mexican mythology, for she, too, conjures up a world – a magical and colorful world where birds, snakes, and curious animals abound, and where exotic flowers are captured in full bloom. No two designs can ever be the same, even if conceived by the same imagination and shaped by the same hands. Every village has its own traditions it is true, but within that tradition each woman is free to follow her inspiration.

Decorated textiles fall into two categories. Either the decorative motifs, with their subtleties of shade and texture, are worked into the fabric while it is still on the loom, or they are applied afterward. The range of woven designs in Mexico remains amazingly rich and varied. There is, however, one important limitation: only straight lines can be executed on a loom, although fine and skillful weaving may, of course, suggest curved ones. Since the turn of this century, brocaded patterning has been getting steadily more colorful and elaborate. Readily available commercial wools and embroidery threads are responsible for this trend and women are often happy to combine them with home produced, hand spun cotton.

The use of embroidery is also on the increase for much the same reason, and brilliant store bought yarns may be re-spun where delicate work is involved. Each community has its own special motifs, and embroidery enables women to put their mark on cloth

In the Chiapas Highlands, social position is often expressed through dress. This wife of a village dignitary in Tenejapa wears a magnificently brocaded huipil during a fiesta.

Opposite: This little girl from Chiapa de Corzo, in Chiapas, wears her colorful and richly embroidered costume at fiesta time.

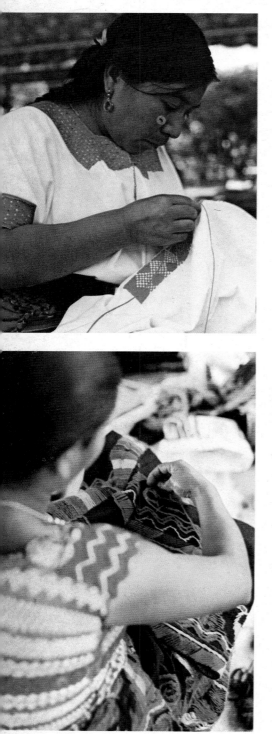

Embroidery has a long history in Mexico and communities adhere to their own special motifs and stitches. Here, two women from Chiapas are busy sewing.

that has been treadle loomed in the local town, or woven on a waist strap loom in a neighboring village.

Popular in pre-Conquest times, embroidery received new impetus under Spanish rule when additional methods and styles were introduced. The cross stitch and the running stitch are both widely practiced, as is the satin stitch. High in the Sierra of Puebla the weavers of Cuetzalan like to adorn the corners of their white and lacelike quechquemitls with feather stitching, knotting the loose threads into tiny tassels. As for the Nahuas of San José Miahuatlán, they buy their cloth ready-made, saving their energy for the deep and heavy bands of embroidery with which they embellish their huipils. Reversible satin stitch, cross stitch, and a particularly complicated type of looped pile stitch are just a few of the techniques favored by these talented needlewomen, and it is not unusual for these horizontal bands to be transferred from a worn-out garment to a new one.

Embroidery can also be functional. Blanket and buttonhole stitching serve to strengthen necklines or arm openings, and the satin stitch is ideal for joining lengths of cloth together, providing an added decoration.

Before the arrival of the Spanish, elaborate designs were as freely painted onto textiles as they were onto pottery. There was also a cloth printing system involving rollers and stamps of clay. Nothing remains of this today, although the women of Ixtayutla, in Oaxaca, use their fingers and thumbs to smear their brocaded capes with the juice of the cactus fruit or with *fuchina*, a purple aniline dye. In the not so distant past when Lacandon Indians still wore huipils of beaten tree bark, they favored a similar style of decoration, celebrating certain feast days by streaking each others' robes with the red juice of berries.

There are a few instances of dyeing taking place after weaving, and tie-dyeing, called *plangi*, is not unknown among the Otomis of Querétaro State. In Oaxaca, the Chinantec women of San Felipe Usila traditionally place their colorful and richly patterned huipils on a frame, staining the central panel with fuchina to obtain a whole set of new and subtle tones. Another complex procedure is current among the Tepehua weavers of Huehuetla in the state of Hidalgo. Not content with their predominantly white quechquemitls, worked with flowers and bands of purple, they achieve additional patterning in the following way. First they wet the garment, impregnating it with soap and folding it with care so that the plain sections press against the design. Then they bind it tightly with leaves and place it near the heat of the fire. When the garment is unwrapped, the color will have imprinted itself on the rest of the cloth.

The Spanish love of trimmings and ornamentation was no greater than that of the Indians, who were quick to adopt novel styles of decoration while retaining their own. Tassels are an eye-catching feature. Cascades of red wool brighten up the dark huipils of the

The skilled embroiderers of Acatlán, in Guerrero, cover their woven enredos with a host of lions, eagles, and lambs all worked in artificial silk.

This detail shows how the Tepehua women of Huehuetla, in Hidalgo, succeed in imprinting the colors of central motifs over the rest of their white quechquemitls.

Chamula women, and in Yalalag long, brilliant strands of artificial silken thread enhance the huipils of white cotton. Fringes are even more popular and warp threads are often left loose to allow for knotting and tying. Many a fine rebozo or sarape is finished off in this way. Warp threads on waist sashes are frequently braided most skillfully, as among the Tarahumara Indians whose fringes seem to flow like water. On market day in Cuetzalan men's belts are sometimes sold unadorned and awaiting final knotting.

Ribbon proved a welcome and colorful importation, silk giving way to rayon in this century. Inserted at the seams to disguise joins or stitched in star-shaped layers around the neckline, ribbon plays a useful and decorative role, demanding far less effort than embroidery. Lace, once hand made but usually store bought today, is often com-

The warp threads of rebozos are often left loose to allow for knotting and tying. Here a highly skilled crafts-woman from Santa María del Río interweaves the silk strands with her fingers, creating delicate and varied patterns.

The Chinantec women of San Lucas Ojitlan embroider their huipils with feathery birds. Such is the angularity of the stitching, that these ancient designs give the appearance of having been woven.

bined with ribbon to form little sleeves, giving a blouse-like appearance to many huipils. Much used by the women of Huautla de Jimenez, these two synthetic materials are gradually taking over from weaving and embroidery, covering ever larger areas of the huipil.

In spite of European influences, however, many ancient motifs, both woven and embroidered, have survived the passage of time. Geometric design has always been important, and the step and fret patterning, triangles, rhomboids, and chevrons that were such a feature of pre-Conquest architecture and painted pottery continue to appear regularly on sashes, shoulder bags, sarapes, and huipils. Vertical or horizontal stripes are a favorite form of decoration, while a rectangle or square, worked halfway down the front and back panels of a huipil, is in the purest pre-Hispanic tradition. As for the serpentine lines that often embellish woven textiles, these suggest snakes, lightning, and rain.

Stylized plant designs are popular among the Amusgo weavers of Xochislahuaca who specialize in eight-petaled flowers and vine or fernlike patterns, brocading them into the fabric of their long huipils. Animal, bird, and insect motifs persist in many places, but the totemic significance they once possessed has been largely forgotten. The double headed bird is not based, as visitors to Mexico often imagine, on the Hapsburg eagle. Its frequent appearance on the seals, spindle whorls, and pottery of bygone days affirms that it was as widely used then as it is now. Cut off from the outside world by steep and rugged mountains, the Chinantec women of San Lucas Ojitlan wear one of the most colorful and striking costumes of Oaxaca, embroidering their huipils with sinuous snakes, strange creatures, and feathery double headed birds with outstretched wings.

Indian dress may be decorative but it is often magical as well and nowhere is this more true than in the highlands of Chiapas. The peoples who inhabit this remote and hilly region have retained the customs of their Mayan ancestors to a remarkable extent, believing as they do in a cubic world that rests eternally on the shoulders of four gods. When one grows tired, he shifts the weight to the other shoulder, causing tremors and earthquakes. Each day Father Sun goes around the world, marking out anew the four cardinal points that dominate religious thinking and textile design alike. Complex geometric formations combine with key colors to convey a cosmic

Until recently, marvellous effects were achieved by sewing beads onto blouses, patterning them with shimmering birds, flowers, and animals. Made in Puebla, this blouse is a magnificent example.

Costume often has a magical significance in the Chiapas Highlands. In these weavings from Tenejapa, Bochil, and San Andres Larrainzar, complex geometric patterning combines with vivid colors.

vision. Red predominates, symbolizing the east. White is associated with the north, yellow with the south, and black with the west. As for green, its use suggests regeneration upon earth and fertility. Among the frets and diamonds, it is possible to discern plant motifs, while the densely woven Magdalenas huipil bears mysterious animal figures. One person might see frogs and bees, and another spiders and bats. Yet both would be right, for it is this very ambiguity that characterizes pre-Hispanic design.

So it is that in Mexico, descendants of ancient civilizations continue to favor the old symbols, looking on them as a means of spiritual protection. Sometimes, of course, a woman may not be aware of the precise reason why she weaves a particular pattern. If asked, she might well reply, "I do it because it's the custom."

On the other hand, many of the motifs that are popular today have clearly been inspired by European models and adapted to suit Mexican taste. Large and colorful flowers are a feature of the *Chiapaneca* costume worn by the mestizo girls of Chiapa de Corzo at fiesta time. By contrast, the satin stitched floral decorations that adorn the velvet skirts and huipils of the Tehuana women are Oriental in style, and were suggested by the highly ornate Manila shawls that the Spanish imported during their rule.

In country districts near Mexico City, dancers at fiesta time traditionally adopt the charro image, appearing in magnificent costumes worth thousands of pesos each and richly embroidered in gold and silver thread with scorpions, fighting cocks, roses, eagles, and leaping horses. While celebrations last, these villagers can enjoy impersonating the foreign grandees who once dominated Mexico, indulging at the same time in a degree of caricature, for the wax masks that are worn, with their colorful beards and moustaches of braided horsehair, lend a decidedly comic touch.

Using natural and undyed wool, the sarape weavers of San Francisco Xonacatlán create with their treadle looms veritable landscapes on which dogs, horses, deer, birds, and flowers abound. Teotitlán del Valle is no less famous as a sarape producing center. In the blankets of this region, a large red rose with rounded petals

During the week, women from Acatlán, in Guerrero, often wear their embroidered enredos wrong side out to save wear and tear, reversing them on Sundays or for festive occasions.

Eagles, fighting cocks, bulls, and toreadors embroidered in gold and silver thread adorn the costumes worn at fiesta time by dancers in country districts outside Mexico City.

A rainbow profusion of fairy-tale creatures and plants, inspired as much by fantasy as by observation of nature, covers this embroidered cloth from Tenango de Doria, in Hidalgo.

is often woven with a black background. Blouses are invariably made from industrial cotton cloth and embellished with frills, tucks, and embroidered designs. The women of Cuetzalan specialize in bird, animal, and flower motifs all done in running stitch. In the neighboring village of Huauchinango, the embroidery often spreads down the bodice of the blouse. Sometimes lettering is added to spell out the wearer's name or even a much-publicized trademark.

There are other types of decorations, however, and these appear to spring quite simply from observation of nature. A profusion of birds, worked in shellfish-dyed thread, are brocaded into the cloth by the Huaves on the coast of Oaxaca, while the huipils of Metla-tonoc feature a splendid parade of plume-tailed horses and other creatures. Birds, animals, and rows of human figures holding hands appear on the gauzy napkins and huipils woven in Venustiano Carranza in Chiapas.

Birds are joined by crabs, cats, scorpions, spiders, and rabbits on the man's costume of Santa Maria Zacatepec in Oaxaca. These minuscule creatures are massed around the neck in numerous rows and embroidered with multicolored thread. The wedding huipil from Pinotepa Nacional on the coast is also beautifully decorated. The neck is trimmed with a band of wild silk, bought at a distant fair on the third Friday of Lent and adorned with a multitude of tiny animals, insects, fish, and flowers, worked in chain stitch.

In the rugged and infertile state of Hidalgo, magnificent napkins and tablecloths are embroidered, suggesting a world apart where curious birds, their shimmering wings outstretched, soar and dive. Huge butterflies alight on flowery boughs, and fairy-tale beings, half man, half plant, hang suspended in mid-air. In these unique land-scapes nature and the imagination merge to give some of the most fantastic and colorful designs in the vast field of Mexican textiles.

A bird on a flowery bough forms part of a landscape depicted on a woolen sarape from Santa Ana del Valle, in Oaxaca. Only vegetable dyes have been used.

EMBROIDERY MOTIFS

Red and green are popular colors with the women of Cuetzalan who adorn the neckline and sleeves of their blouses with bird, animal, and flower motifs worked in running stitch.

Opposite: On market day the women of Cuetzalan display blouses of industrial cotton cloth embroidered with traditional motifs and further embellished with a profusion of tucks.

Embroidery has a long history in Mexico. Popular in pre-Hispanic times, it received new impetus under Spanish rule when additional methods and styles were introduced. Today, flowers, leaves, birds, animals, stars, and geometric designs are worked in a wide variety of stitches. Most communities have their own traditional motifs and favor certain combinations of color. Weavers frequently double as skillful needlewomen, embellishing their home-loomed huipils, quechquemitls, skirt lengths, rebozos, and napkins with a wealth of embroidery motifs. Displayed overleaf are some of the imaginative designs that decorate the splendid huipils worn by the women of Metlatonoc, in Guerrero. Invariably made from industrial cotton cloth, blouses offer great scope to the embroiderer and are imaginatively adorned with a mass of decorative patterning. This is typical in the village of Cuetzalan.

All the motifs shown here are made by darning the embroidery thread over and under varying numbers of threads on the background fabric. The stitch used throughout is a simple running stitch. Each vertical and horizontal line on the graph paper represents one woven thread of the background fabric.

To embroider the motifs, choose a fabric with a regular, even weave. The size of the finished motifs will vary according to the coarseness of the fabric. For example, a motif worked on heavy linen will be larger than one worked on an embroidery fabric with a much finer weave. Use a blunt-ended tapestry needle that will go between the woven threads of the fabric without splitting them. Four strands of cotton embroidery floss are suitable for finely woven fabrics; thicker thread or tapestry wool are ideal for coarser woven cloth.

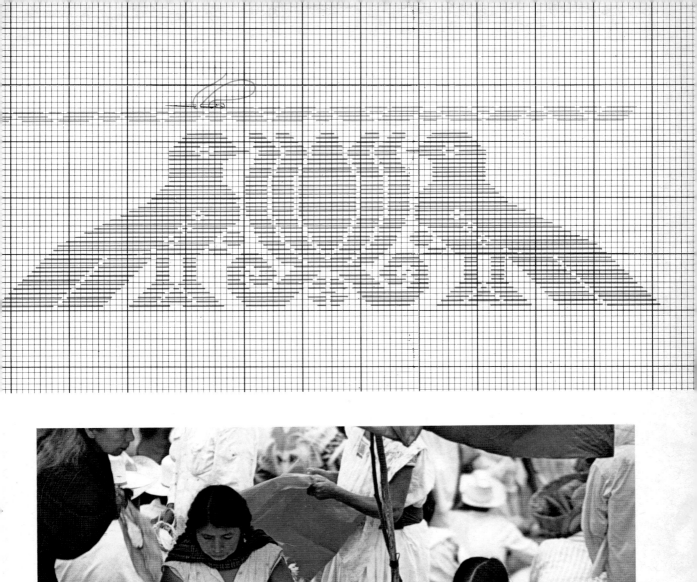

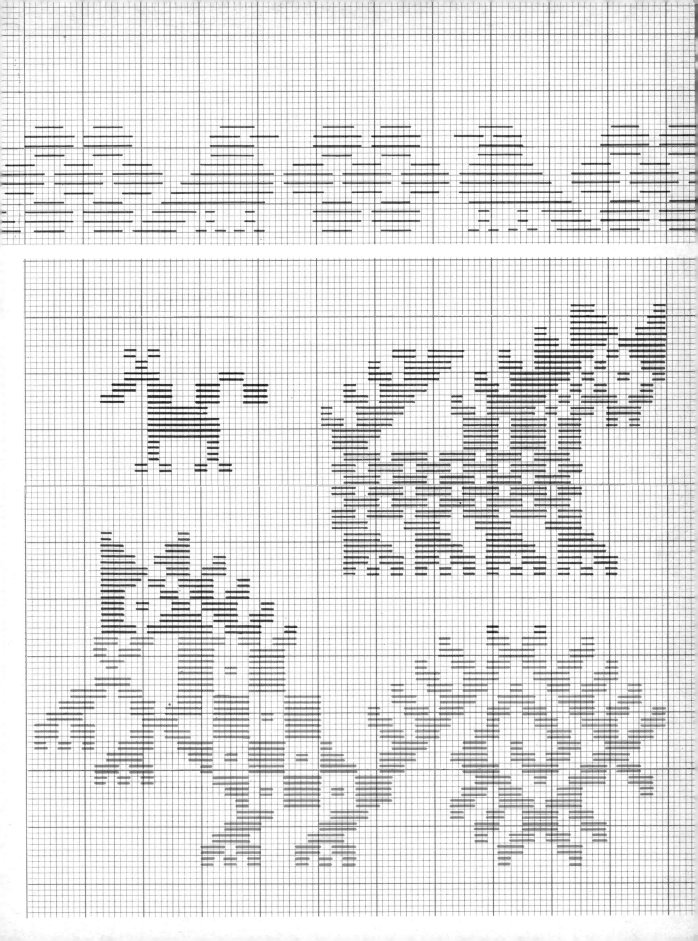

CHAPTER 5
LACQUERS OF THE RAINBOW

In the ancient town of Chiapa de Corzo, lacquered gourds are embellished with garlands of flowers.

Opposite: In rural areas, gourds still serve as natural drinking vessels and water containers. Harvested gourds are left to dry in the sun and then placed in water until the insides rot and the gourd shell can be scraped clean.

Thousands of years before the rise of the great Mexican civilizations, nomadic hunters roamed across the vast and fertile central plateau in pursuit of game, equipped with only the most rudimentary tools, and gathering wild plants or fruit. The simple gourd provided them with vessels for eating and drinking. Cut in half and worn upon the head, the round gourd offered protection against the sun's rays, while the bottle-shaped gourd served as a natural water container. As villages grew and developed into towns and ceremonial centers, myths circulated; in the forests of the South, the Mayas thought of the sky as a great and luminous gourd of blue which hung suspended above the earth.

It is not known when the Indians first began to use lacquer, but in ancient tombs gourds have been found with traces of color still visible. By the early sixteenth century, lacquer was a flourishing art and the Spanish chroniclers described the gleaming array of highly varnished gourd bowls and dippers they saw on sale in the great Aztec market, commenting particularly on the fine colors and elaborate patterning.

Today lacquer working is still practiced in a few regions. Implements, techniques, and even basic ingredients have changed little in hundreds of years, and the gourd continues to play a vital role.

Tradition holds firm in the small and picturesque village of Acapetlahuaya, set deep in a valley and surrounded on all sides by the rolling hills of Guerrero. Here, the lacquered gourd is a part of daily life, preferred to all other drinking vessels and closely associated with *atole*, the hot and delicious gruel made, as in pre-Hispanic times, from the toasted seeds of a local shrub.

Efrain Martínez Zuloaga comes from a long line of lacquer workers or, as he likes to refer to them, "painters," the word lacquer being unknown in the area, and he explains the methods involved.

Lacquered gourds from Acapetla-huaya, gleaming with a final coat of chia oil, are laid out to dry in the hot Mexican sun.

First, the gourd must be cleaned and prepared for use. This is a long and laborious procedure. Harvested in October or November, the fruit is left to dry out completely, then cut down the middle and placed in water until the insides rot. The seeds are planted and the gourd itself is scraped until only the hard rind remains. A second period of drying follows, for even the smallest degree of moisture will affect the lacquer. A great deal of care and patience are required. Stones and graters remove all roughness and the gourd is now smooth and ready for the next stage.

Don Efrain begins by toasting and pounding the tiny *chia* seeds, even squeezing them in his powerful hand. Eventually adding a few drops of water to this oily substance, he stores it away in a glass jar

Don Efrain reduces a local mineral to a fine powder. Combining it with a red pigment and water, he will coat the waiting gourds, which have already received a base coat of chia oil and brown earth.

until it is needed. A brown earth, found on the outskirts of the village, is ground on a great flat slab of stone. So, too, is a white mineral. Reducing it to a fine powder, he mixes it with water and obtains a paste to which he adds a brilliant red pigment. Made commercially today, this powder would once have been derived from another type of local earth or mineral, but the secret has long since been lost.

Lacquering is a protracted process and takes place largely during the dry months when the sun can be depended on to shine daily. Seated outdoors on a low stool with his clean and polished gourds beside him on the ground, Don Efrain begins the initial treatment, lining each one with sun-warmed chia oil before applying the finely ground brown earth. Taking a porous stone, he rubs it over the newly anointed surface, leaving it smooth and even. Three days pass, during which time this base coat is allowed to dry. He then goes on to the next stage. Using a deer's tail he smears the gourd with the newly mixed red paste. When the first layer becomes hard, a second is applied.

Market women in the state of Oaxaca serve frothy chocolate in red lacquered gourds from Olinala.

The lacquered gourd is now ready for painting. Don Efrain gets out his homemade brushes and prepares the new colors, adding the store bought pigments to the white paste as before. Floral and animal motifs are popular, and with deft movements he adorns each gourd with a leaping rabbit, a bouquet, a bird, or perhaps a squirrel eating a nut. While he works he talks of ancient times and of the Aztecs who used to demand vast quantities of lacquered gourds as tribute from the people of Acapetlahuaya. When the paint is completely dry, Don Efrain gives the gourd a final coating of chia oil. This seals the lacquer, making it both heat-resistant and waterproof, thereby setting it apart from all others produced in Mexico today making it sought after throughout the country.

I ask if his sons have learned the art, but he shakes his head. "No, no. . . . The work is far too hard and demanding. Cleaning out the gourds is the worst part. Why, sometimes my hands are rubbed raw. What modern man would want to do such a job?" And yet, in spite of his words, he is a proud man for he is conscious of being a fine craftsman and one of the last in his village. When dusk comes, Don Efrain will sit down with his family and they will drink hot atole from the beautifully laquered gourds, just as they have always done.

Lacquer has a long history, too, in the ancient town of Chiapa de Corzo, and during the time of the Viceroys elegant chests, lecterns, frames, and crosses were made here, examples of which are on display in the local museum. Today, however, with the exception of a few wooden boxes and crosses, lacquer work is confined almost exclusively to the gourd.

Methods differ a little from those of Acapetlahuaya, instead of chia oil the fat of the *aje* is used. These tiny parasites, which live on trees and suck their sap, are cultivated by the Indians of Venustiano Carranza many miles away. During the dry season their eggs are kept in gourds or cornhusks where the larvae form cocoons. When the rains begin, these are placed on a host tree and left to hatch. The minuscule insects are harvested, washed, and boiled. The fat that is strained off and left to stand is subsequently cooked and strained yet again to give a yellow and rancid-smelling wax. Wrapped in cornhusks this is then sold to the lacquer workers of Chiapa de Corzo.

Used by the Aztecs themselves, this much prized ingredient is rubbed well into the gourd and followed by two coats of a finely ground earth called *tizate*, which is found in the nearby riverside caves. Once smoothness has been achieved, aje is applied again, serving as a fixative for the dry, colored powder. Red earth is still used occasionally, and until not so long ago earth or charcoal produced black. Layer alternates with layer until, after much polishing, a glossy and protective sheen is achieved.

In this town the men cut and clean the gourds, leaving everything else to their womenfolk. To visit the home of Doña Luvia Macías

The craftswomen of Chiapa de Corzo use the fat of the aje insect to fix numerous layers of colored powder, achieving a smooth and brilliant finish. Doña Luvia paints lacquered gourds and boxes with traditional floral motifs using cats' hair brushes and the tips of her fingers.

Encrusted lacquers are a feature of Uruapan. When the lacquer has hardened, designs are incised with sharp instruments and sections are hollowed out. The fat of the aje insect, kept inside a cornhusk, is applied and alternated with layers of brightly colored powder.

Ferns and flowers are popular motifs and finished pieces resemble gleaming mosaics.

de Blanco is to find innumerable lacquered gourds drying in her garden, while she herself sits quietly painting in the shade. Floral garlands are the traditional design, but none are more delicately executed or more colorful than those of this skillful and talented craftswoman.

Commercial pigments have replaced the earths and plant dyes of the past. Doña Luvia uses mineral powders from Mexico City, which she combines with linseed oil. Painting directly onto the lacquered surface of a gourd, she frequently puts down her brush of cats' hair and blends the colors together with the tips of her fingers. Red meets white, lending a realistic pink glow to the petals of a rose. "Usually," she confesses, "I don't have a clear idea how a piece will turn out. I just begin and go on from there." Laying aside the half-painted gourd to dry, she takes up a wooden box, gleaming with fresh lacquer. Unhesitatingly she shapes the first flowers. "My mother painted lacquer and I used to watch her, hour after hour. Then when I was twelve, out of curiosity, I began to paint too."

In Pátzcuaro, in Michoacan, lacquered surfaces are elaborately painted with oil colors and gold leaf. Rodolfo Rodriguez adheres to special methods. Using a mordant, he paints on ornate designs, pressing down sheets of gold leaf that become part of the pattern.

Sold during the festival of Corpus Christi in neighboring Tuxtla Gutiérrez, the capital of Chiapas, the lacquered gourds of Chiapa de Corzo often travel long distances. They are particularly sought after by the Tehuana women of the Isthmus who carry them on their heads, piled high with candies, toys, and mangoes that they distribute among the crowd at the time of the annual fruit throwing ceremony.

The elaborate and difficult technique of incrustation is carried out exclusively by the skilled craftsmen of Uruapan in the state of Michoacan. Gourds, or in many cases large wooden trays of resinless wood, are coated with size, a mixture of aje and linseed oil, and then dusted with pigment. As always, local earths play an important part, being added to the size and also to the colors themselves, brightening them up considerably.

When the various layers have hardened and the polishing rag has brought a brilliance to the even surface, the design is incised with a sharp instrument. If blue lacquer is to be applied, all the sections that require this color are hollowed out. Gradually a mosaic forms, the lighter shades being inlaid last. Crescent moons, birds, animals, or human figures predominate, accompanied always by a profusion of flowers. An experienced craftsman can even reproduce the veins on a leaf or the feathers of a crest.

Early on in their rule the Spanish began to import Oriental lacquer work into Mexico, and this explains the markedly Chinese influence that prevails in the lakeside town of Pátzcuaro. Here, both gourds and trays carry charming, fairy-tale scenes painted with gold leaf and specially imported oil colors. Across these smoothly lacquered surfaces fly elegant birds, while timid rabbits play among luxuriant grasses and butterflies sip nectar from exotic flowers. At the tip of the paintbrush lies a world of enchantment.

Rodolfo Rodriguez is one of the few artisans who still adheres to the old secrets and traditions of working with gold leaf, and these are passed down from father to son. First, a mixture must be made that will serve to fix the gold. This mordant, which contains finely ground copper oxide, pine tree resin, garlic, and the oils from both chia and aje, is blended with yellow ocher and silver white paint before being left to settle by the light of the moon for three months. The wood of the arbutus tree is boiled to rid it of all resin and lacquered in the usual way with a mixture of aje and linseed oil. With a pencil, the artisan lightly outlines his design, painting it over afterward with the top part of the fixative and discarding the rest. Twenty-four hours later, the gold leaf may be applied, but only after the lacquered surface has been wiped over with magnesium carbonate to remove all grease. Then, cutting the 24-carat gold sheet to a manageable size on a piece of suede with a razor blade, Don Rodolfo deftly presses it down onto the design using a wad of cotton. The gold adheres to the fixative and becomes delicate traceries and curling fronds while the residuum disintegrates and is lost in the air. Should the gold leaf ever become chipped, however, or peel away, the fixative beneath with its silvery yellow tones will serve to conceal the accident.

The lacquer workers of Olinala, in Guerrero, travel long distances, selling colorful trunks, gourds, and boxes at far-off fairs and markets.

In the village of Olinala, which can be reached during the rainy season almost exclusively by minuscule passenger planes, the greatest variety of lacquer work is to be found. Cut off from the outside world by dense forests and the high Sierra Madre del Sur mountains, this thriving and artistic community devotes itself to an enduring craft. Families work together, children help their parents from an early age, learning their skills, and each object passes through many hands before its completion.

During the Colonial period, lacquered trunks were much in demand and they are still an important feature. From the tropical zone of Guerrero comes a fine and sweet-smelling wood called *linaloé*, and linen stored in these chests retains a lingering perfume.

Decorative trays and plates, small boxes, ingenious toys, animal figures, and colorful clusters of ornamental fruits are also produced here. As for the ever useful gourd, it is halved or skillfully cut to form a container with a star-shaped lid.

No less than five local earths, all of them known by their old Aztec names, are used in the lacquering process. As in Acapetlahuaya, chia oil serves as fixative and industrially produced, vivid pigments are re-ground for greater fineness. Layer by layer, a resistant coat of lacquer is built up, left to harden, and polished with a soft cloth or wad of cotton. Designs that feature a profusion of flowers, foliage and birds are applied with homemade brushes of cats' hair, and paints are obtained by mixing the commercial pigments with linseed oil. Francisco Colonel favors chia oil, however, rightly believing that the brilliance it lends far outweighs the added expense. This extraordinary painter, winner of countless competitions, specializes

Grooved lacquers are a feature of Olinala. A second layer is applied on top of the first, then partially scraped away. The raised motifs that remain depict a multitude of birds, fish, animals, and flowers.

In high relief against the black background on this grooved lacquer tray, green parrots stretch their feathery wings amid a profusion of fronds and veined leaves.

Wrapped in cornhusks and secured with grasses, these lacquered gourds from Olinala arrive without a scratch at the yearly market at Tepalcingo, in Morelos.

in elegant flower motifs, downy white doves, tigers with curly tails, and delicately fronded ferns. He also enjoys working with gold leaf, obtaining dazzling and magical results. A quiet man, Don Francisco paints from early morning until sunset, always striving after a perfection his many admirers feel he has already achieved.

Another method that has brought fame to Olinala is the grooving technique. When one layer of lacquer has been applied and left to dry, a second follows in a different color. The design is drawn with a thorn onto the unpolished surface and a feather is used to dust away the loose powder. The bottom coat is then exposed by scraping away the top one. Leaping deer, fish, cavorting rabbits, butterflies, doves, and long-legged cranes are just a few of the delightful creatures that swarm across gourds and boxes in eye-catching combinations of color.

The inhabitants of Olinala are devout Catholics and have made their church one of the most beautiful in all Mexico. Walls and altar are paneled with a mass of gleaming lacquer, and the old lampshades have been replaced by richly decorated gourds that hang suspended from the ceiling.

At markets and fiestas up and down the country, the craftsmen of Olinala sell their unique and brilliant wares. The yearly spring fair at Tepalcingo in the state of Morelos is a great occasion lasting almost a week, and lacquer is a particular feature. Carefully packed in straw and cornhusks, gourds, boxes, and even huge trunks arrive without a scratch, fresh and bright after the long bus journey. Once bought, these lovely pieces will be taken by their owners to other villages, or even to Mexico City.

No less keen on traveling are the lacquer workers of Temalacatzingo and with greater reason, for although their village lies relatively near to Olinala, it can be reached only by mule or on foot. These imaginative craftsmen are anxious to find a market for their goods and to make a name for their village, feeling that the fame of Olinala will otherwise overshadow them entirely. The rivalry that they feel exists has been wonderfully productive, driving these resolute craftsmen to think up ever more ingenious ways of expressing themselves through their art. The visitor to Tepalcingo is greeted by a gay and fantastic profusion of lacquered animals carved out of wood, mother hens and their brood pieced together from gourds, airplanes, masks, and gourd handbags charmingly painted with owls and flowers.

Fashions may come and tastes may change, but lacquer working with its long tradition remains one of the most vital and imaginative crafts in Mexico.

From Temalacatzingo come lacquered toys and gleaming gourd handbags, imaginatively painted with flowers and birds.

LACQUER
OF OLINALA

A profusion of birds and flowers embellish the smoothly lacquered surface of this gourd, which features a petal–shaped lid.

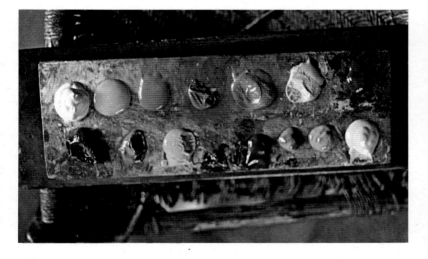

Deep in the heart of the mountains of Guerrero lies the picturesque village of Olinala, famous throughout Mexico for the splendor of its lacquers. Layers of finely ground local earth and colored powder are alternated with chia oil to produce a lacquered finish. Linseed oil is added to commercial pigments and birds, animals, leaves, ferns, and flowers are painted onto the smooth and even surfaces. Families work together to decorate a gleaming succession of trunks, boxes, gourds, trays, dishes, rattles, and other toys, which are sold at distant markets and fairs.

Center: The delicate brush strokes of the work of Francisco Colonel conjures up colorful and enchanted landscapes.

Above: From the richly decorated church of Olinala comes this lacquered and brightly painted wall plaque.

On the left, a Mexican gourd lacquered with colored earths and other local materials; on the right, our wooden box lacquered by the same process, but using materials easily available in art shops. Oil paints are used for the bird and flower design on top of the box.

Materials: Powder paint, artists' gesso, fast drying linseed oil, wooden box or cigar box, old saucepan, cotton rags, oil paints, paintbrushes, mortar and pestle.

Warm the oil in the saucepan. With a wadded rag, rub oil into the wood. Keep the oil warm while working. Let the oil sink into the wood so that only a thin coat remains on the surface.

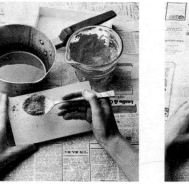

Grind two parts gesso to one part powder paint as fine as talcum powder. Sprinkle the oiled surface of the wood evenly and generously and then tap off the excess powder.

Rub pigment into the oiled wood, building up a smooth, shiny coat. Smooth the surface with your fingers or a rag. Alternating oil and pigment, build up at least six thin coats of each.

Lacquering is a very messy process, so cover the working surface with newspaper. Prepare the box by removing any hinges, fastenings, or labels. Scrub and sand it if necessary to make the surface smooth. Lacquer only one surface of the box at a time. You will need at least two sessions to complete the box, so that the sides lacquered in one session have time to dry out before being handled during the next session. Build up the coats of lacquer, making each one as thin and smooth as possible. Lightly oil the wood first, generously sprinkle on the pigment, then tap off the excess before rubbing it in. Rub the pigment into the oil with your fingers or with clean soft cotton rags, which should be changed frequently.

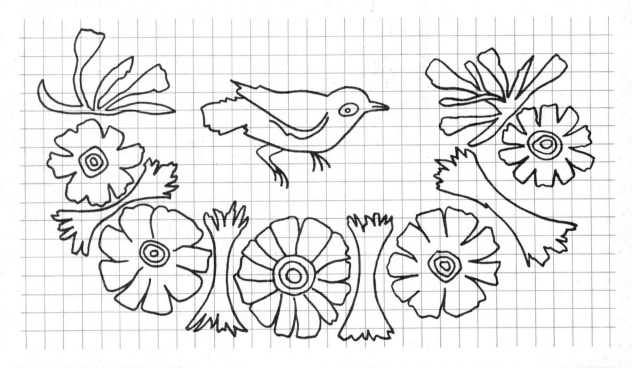

Keep each coat as smooth as possible. Lumps will build up, especially on the edges. Smooth them off right away. The surface should remain smooth, not sticky or gritty.

Allow the lacquer to dry for two days before decorating the box. Transfer design by lightly incising the soft lacquer with a sharp pencil through tracing paper.

Decorate box with oil paints. Allow finished box to dry for at least a week before use, so that the paste of gesso and oil can dry thoroughly and harden into a tough lacquer.

Grooved lacquer work

In Olinala surfaces are coated with earth and chia oil, left to dry, and polished with a stone. Oil and a mixture of earth and pigment are then applied.

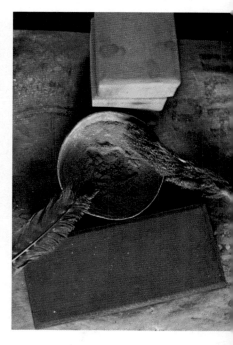

When the first layer of lacquer has set hard, artisans proceed to build up a second in a different color. Coats of powder, applied with the hand or with deer tails, are alternated with oil.

Five local earths, known by their old Aztec names, are used in the lacquering process. Colored powders are industrially produced and re-ground for greater fineness.

Using a thorn or a needle embedded in a quill, artisans skillfully scratch their designs onto the lacquered surface, starting with a geometric border.

Gradually the pattern reveals itself more clearly. During the scraping, loosened powder is brushed away with the tip of the feather.

Red rabbits and long legged dogs bound across the lid of this box, in relief against the blue background. Friction with wads of cotton will leave surfaces gleaming.

When an artisan has finished scratching on his design, he begins to partially scrape away the top layer of lacquer with a quill, revealing the contrasting color that lies beneath.

CHAPTER 6
THE MAGIC WORLD OF THE HUICHOLS

Deep in the heart of the wild and mountainous Sierra Madre of the West live the Huichol Indians who are, without doubt, the purest indigenous group in all Mexico.

Now, as in the past, the Huichols tend to live in isolated family groupings but each community, no matter how small, builds a house for its deities, traveling long distances at fiesta time to reach the nearest ceremonial center and filling the temple with offerings. In addition to these man-made shrines there are sacred caves where the gods reside. Pilgrims bring them flowers, feathers, and gifts, requesting special favors, bathing in the holy water, and often taking some away in special vessels. Outside, the rugged landscape is dotted with other natural shrines, for the "ancient people" frequently dwell in rocks, stones, or springs, and they too demand their share of offerings.

During the rainy season, this inhospitable terrain, with its deep canyons and abrupt slopes, becomes virtually impassable, while at other times of the year a plane ride or a journey on foot or horseback lasting several days must be undertaken to reach the most peripheral of the Indian settlements. Surroundings like these provide excellent protection, and the Huichol people remained unconquered by the Spanish until well into the eighteenth century. Even then victory was in name only, for the Huichols have systematically rejected any attempt to change either their beliefs or their traditions. Divided into five autonomous communities, each with its own civil and religious authorities, they follow a pattern of life that has remained unchanged for centuries, cultivating the barren land, hunting, and serving their gods.

Related to the Aztecs, the Huichols came long ago from the North, but they have their own mythological view of history, and on ceremonial occasions the shamans, or spiritual leaders, sing of the

The god's eye, or tsikuri, allows the supplicant to communicate with his deities. Strands of yarn are stretched onto bamboo crosses to form lozenge shapes through which the gods may view their followers, keeping them in health and life.

Opposite: The maraakame, or shaman, acts as mediator between the Huichols and their gods, interpreting their divine will and singing their legends.

past and of the first times when gods, animals, and men were one. They tell of the deluge that devastated the earth and of the Huichol who escaped in a boat with his dog. The dog turned into a woman who bore him many children and re-peopled the world. And inevitably they tell of the short lasting but marvelous period when the ancestors of their race enjoyed the favors of the corn maiden.

Once upon a time, so the legend goes, the Huichols had no corn. Then one day a boy called Ucá heard that there were men living on the other side of the mountains who had corn in plenty. Tired of the hunger that reigned in his house, Ucá set out to cross the mountains. On his way he met a group of men who offered to accompany him, and they all went on together. Night fell, and sleep overcame the boy. Awakening alone beneath a tree, he found that the men, who were really ants, had eaten his clothes, his hair, and even his eyelashes. A white dove above him in the tree came to his aid, telling him that she was the mother of corn and inviting him to go home with her. Regaining her human form, she invited him inside, fed him, and introduced him to her five daughters, each one of whom represented a different type of corn. "You may choose one to be your

The Huichols seek to win the favor of their deities with splendid festivals and ceremonies. During the Fiesta of the Ripe Fruits, participants thank the gods for the new crop. Here the shaman bestows his blessing upon the sacred offerings.

bride," she told him. Passing over the yellow, the red, the white and the mottled, Ucá chose the blue corn because she was the most beautiful. "Never make her work," the mother told him, "but cherish and protect her always."

When Ucá arrived home with his new bride, his own mother was angry, scolding him for bringing her an extra mouth to feed. "Do not be afraid," said the corn maiden. "From now on there will always be enough to eat." And there was. Their bowls overflowed with corn, and Ucá built his wife an altar to sit upon. Then one day when he was out, his mother, unable to conceal her jealousy any longer, ordered her daughter-in-law to grind the corn. "I'm tired of your idleness," she said. "Today you shall work." Weeping, the corn maiden climbed down from her altar and began to grind, but blood flowed from her tender hands and she left the house, never to return. From that day, the Huichols have had to tend their fields, raising their corn by the sweat of their brows.

An agricultural people, the Huichols continue to depend on corn, along with beans and squash, for their livelihood, seeking to enlist the aid of their gods with splendid festivals and ceremonies. There

During Holy Week wooden masks are worn by dancers who play the part of "neighbors" or non-Indians.

Food, drink, flowers and a multitude of gifts are offered to the gods during the Fiesta of the Ripe Fruits. Altars are adorned with fluffy, white wads of cotton to symbolize the rain clouds that bring life and health to the community.

79

The Fiesta of the Ripe Fruits celebrates fertility and children play an important part. Their heads are adorned with feathers and god's eyes, and faces are painted with rain and peyote symbols. Here a little girl shakes her gourd rattles while the shaman's assistant beats the ceremonial drum.

are fiestas for the Rain, for the Purification of the Crops, for the Ripe Fruits, for the Toasted Corn, for the Goddess of Fertility, for the Sun, and for Peyote, the hallucinatory cactus that inspires the Huichol throughout his life, enabling him to communicate directly with his deities.

The peyote fields lie far outside Huichol territory and once a year groups of chosen men leave their homes and families to go on the long pilgrimage to Wirikuta, "hunting down" the cactus with bows and arrows. According to Huichol mythology, the god Peyote first appeared on earth as a giant deer, causing small plants to spring up wherever he trod. Corn, an incarnation of both peyote and the deer, completes this sacred trinity upon which all religious belief centers.

The *maraakame*, or shaman, is both healer and prophet, interpreting the will of the gods and averting their wrath. Birds' feathers, attached to a stick, are important symbols of his office. Birds are attributed with magic powers: it is thought that they can hear and see everything that passes on earth. Their wing and tail feathers are eagerly sought, for it is believed they confer wisdom. With their help the shaman can cure the sick, ward off evil, guide the soul of the departed on the long journey that awaits it, and converse with the gods.

The fiestas, pilgrimages, and other collective expressions of faith that take place under the guidance of the shaman are only one aspect of religious life. In addition, the gods expect selfless service from the individual, demanding a whole series of private ceremonies and gifts in return for their favor and protection. The nature of these offerings is clearly laid down in the following myth.

In the long distant past when the god Nariwame was still a small child, he wept without ceasing and would not be consoled. At length his mother, tired of his tears, sent him out into the world. Nariwame began to walk, taking the path that led toward Wirikuta where the peyote grows. His brother, the Wind, went in pursuit of him, anxious to know what had caused his grief, and Nariwame confessed that he yearned for many things. Questioned further by his brother, Nariwame listed his requirements, which included a shrine, a prayer bowl, a god's eye, a *nierika*, and an arrow, promising faithfully to return home within five days if these things were granted him. When the Wind told the other gods of Nariwame's requests, they agreed that henceforth he should have all the things he asked for.

The arrow, for which Nariwame wept, serves to convey the prayers of the individual to the gods. Shaped like a bird with outstretched neck, it possesses all the magic powers attributed to the bird. The gods, too, have their arrows, but these take the form of rattlesnakes, scorpions, and meteors. "We make ceremonial arrows in order to gain life," a Huichol once told the Norwegian anthropologist Carl Lumholz. Fathers make arrows for newly born children, hoping to win health and divine protection for them. No project is ever contemplated without the preparation of an arrow, and special requests are symbolized by miniature objects tied to the shaft. When an arrow is sticking upright in the ground it is considered "sacrificed," and the supplicant knows that his prayer has been heard.

The god's eye, or *tsikuri*, offers the Huichol another way of communicating with his deities. Tightly stretched onto a bamboo cross, strands of colored wool are made to form a rhomboid or lozenge shape through which the gods may view their followers, keeping them in health and protecting them from harm. Gods' eyes have a special association with children, and fathers dedicate them to deities on behalf of small sons and daughters, each rhomboid signifying a year. Two eyes count as two years, and five eyes as five years. After this age, however, the child must discharge his own religious obligations and make his own tsikuri. As with the arrows, colors are important, serving as prayers in themselves and representing gods or holy places.

Among the ceremonial arrows and gods' eyes that abound in caves and beside natural shrines, there are always large numbers of votive bowls. Lined with beeswax, these half gourds display strange shapes and symbolic pictures formed with seeds, corn grains, minute pebbles, shells from the seashore, feathers, and fluffy white wads of cotton. The depiction of a deer by a hunter signifies a prayer for fortune in the chase. Decoration with seeds and grain shows that the supplicant desires a good harvest that will banish hunger, while the representation of a sick person is a petition for divine intervention for a speedy recovery. It is believed that when the gods finally come

God's eyes have a special association with children, and fathers dedicate them to the deities on behalf of sons and daughters. Each rhombus signifies a year in the child's life.

to use these bowls they will drink in the prayers of the people.

Glass beads, introduced into Mexico by the Spanish, greatly affected the art of votive bowl making and today, many bowls are elaborately embellished with beads. The tiny, translucent beads are picked up, one by one, on the point of a needle or maguey thorn, and dexterously pressed down into the soft beeswax lining. Gourds display magical and colorful landscapes, featuring suns, birds, animals, butterflies, and flowers. Gods are depicted and myths or ceremonies are evoked in the patterns.

The enormous skill and creativity of the Huichols, devoted always to a religious end, find yet another outlet in the nierika, or "countenance." Fashioned from stone, from reeds interwoven with thread, or from small wooden boards covered with beeswax and yarn, these round or square offerings depict the "face" of the wind, of the deer, King of the Beasts and Elder Brother of the Huichols, of the Sun Father, of the regenerative and life giving rain, of peyote, of the ripe corn, and of the other forces and beings that surround mankind. Representations of serpents, waves, and water gourds express a wish for rain and it is believed that the gods, when presented with such picturesque and tangible prayers, will be obliged to take heed and

Yarn paintings are built up in sections like a mosaic. Artists outline their designs, pressing strands of yarn onto beeswax covered boards, then filling in spaces.

Belts, bags, armlets, and necklaces of netted beadwork display colorful and symbolic motifs that protect the wearer from harm.

grant what is asked. The last few decades have seen the emergence of the yarn painting based upon the nierika. Wooden boards are smoothly coated with beeswax, and designs are scratched on with a sharp instrument. The artist then lays down the outlines with strands of yarn, pressing them down firmly into the wax and methodically filling in all the spaces. Built up like a mosaic, the finished pictures show the magic world that is the inheritance of the Huichol race, depicting legends in dazzling combinations of color and re-creating visions seen during peyote rituals.

Religious belief is also expressed through dress, and in the whole of Mexico there is no other group where the men deck themselves out as elaborately or as splendidly. "A fine Huichol man in costume is what first enabled the sun father to rise in the sky and shine," a shaman once told a visiting anthropologist.

Today, the Huichol man wears wide pants, a long open-sided shirt and a square shoulder cape, folded corner to corner. Made from industrial cotton and profusely embroidered, these articles of dress are accompanied by one or more woven waist sashes of wool, below which hangs a row of flat, embroidered bags on a belt. Numerous embroidered or woven shoulder bags are also worn. Wide brimmed, low crowned palm hats are adorned with small crosses formed from short strips of red flannel, woolen pompons, and clusters of feathers, while tassels, seed pods, or bead droplets dangle from the rim, according to the whim of the wearer. Colorful necklaces, pendants, armlets, and belts of netted beadwork, skillfully worked with symbolic motifs, complete the costume.

Women favor simplicity, dressing in skirts, blouses, and quechquemitls, and devoting their energy to embroidering and weaving for their sons and husbands. Before embarking on a piece of handiwork, Huichol women invariably seek the support of the gods by embroidering a small figure on a fragment of cloth and attaching it to a ceremonial arrow or god's eye. Another magical ritual was described by Carl Lumholz in his book *Unknown Mexico*: "When a Huichol woman wants to weave or embroider anything, her husband catches a large serpent, the neck of which he places in the split of a stick, and the reptile is thus held up while the woman strokes it with one hand down the entire length of its back; then she passes the same hand over her forehead and eyes, that she may gain the ability to do beautiful work."

Reptilian markings are, in fact, deliberately reproduced during the weaving of sashes. These narrow bands, easily identifiable with snakes, are in themselves a prayer for rain. Zig-zag lines that suggest lightning and water bottle gourds are also associated with rain, while the white *totó* flower that grows during the wet, corn producing season is both a petition for and a symbol of corn. Another popular motif is the royal eagle. Guardian of the corn, the young female eagle is thought by many to hold the world in her talons, and representations seek to enlist her goodwill while at the same time expressing adoration of Grandfather Fire to whom she belongs. Delicately worked in cross stitch with industrially produced thread that has been re-spun, these and many other designs protect the wearer against harm and evil spirits.

For the Huichols, religion and art are inextricably bound together. Inheritors of a magic world, they joyfully put their exceptional skill and boundless creativity at the service of their gods, secure in the knowledge that in return they will receive food, health, and life itself.

Dress serves as an expression of faith. The garments are profusely embroidered in cross stitch with the two-headed Royal Eagle as a popular motif, although it is not considered perfect unless both sides of the head are shown.

YARN PAINTING

The creativity and skill of the Huichols find their expression in yarn painting, which has emerged over the last few decades, inspired by the traditional nierika, which means countenance, or face. Beeswax, softened by the sun's heat, is spread evenly over a wooden board. Using a sharp instrument, the artist scratches on the design and lays down the outlines with brightly colored strands of wool. Spaces are filled in and the yarn is pressed firmly down into the wax. In the above example, Father Sun smiles benignly, suspended above the house of the gods. On the left, the shaman sits on his ceremonial chair, wielding his sacred plumes, a candle, and a deer's tail, while at his feet incense burns. Behind him stands his wife. From her candle emanate a prayer arrow and a rod carved in the likeness of a deer. In her bag are five ceremonial tortillas. From the rocks above her head grow candles, sacred plumes, and a lightning arrow. To the right sits the shaman's assistant, holding a god's eye, an arrow, and a nierika. Behind him his wife supports a candle, and her bag also contains five tortillas. Above her the Kieri plant rises from a heap of rocks combining its magic powers with those of the sacred plumes, the arrow, and the god's eye to bring into being a person.

Built up like a mosaic, this fine yarn painting depicts a Huichol ceremony.

Overleaf: Inspired by the visions that the gods send during peyote rituals and ceremonies, artists express themselves with complex symbols and brilliant colors depicting the myths and legends of their people.

85

Enlarge the sun motif to required size following instructions on page 27.

Spread a warm mixture of 1 lb (½kg) beeswax melted with a 4oz (113 gms) jar of petroleum jelly onto required size piece of plywood. Prick design outlines in wax through paper with tailors' wheel or pin.

Press yarn into warm wax with a fingernail. Keep wax warm, ideally by working in sunshine, or shine a strong light bulb over wax to keep it malleable. Begin work on central motif.

Place the strands as close together as possible. Twist the end of the yarn to begin or end a length. Spiral the yarn tightly round and round when finishing off an area of color.

HUICHOL BEADED BOWLS

Seeking to win the favor of their gods, the Huichol Indians make elaborate votive bowls by coating the inside of dried half gourds with beeswax and forming symbolic pictures with seeds, kernels of corn, minute pebbles, shells, fluffy feathers and white wads of cotton. Glass beads, introduced into Mexico by the Spanish, greatly affected the art of bowl decorating, and today many gourds are entirely lined with them. Picking up the tiny beads one by one on the point of a maguey thorn or needle, and pressing them deftly down into the soft wax, Huichol men and women create magical landscapes full of animals, birds, flowers, and suns in dazzling combinations of color, evoking myths, depicting their gods, and giving a graphic form to their desires. Votive bowls are placed in temples or beside springs, natural rock formations, and in secret caves. It is hoped that when the deities come to use these bowls they will drink in the prayers of supplicants and grant what is asked.

A close-up of a Huichol bowl shows how the beads are placed tightly together, in even rows with holes all facing upward. To fill awkward spaces, beads can be placed sideways.

Materials: Dried gourd or bowl made of wood, glass, china, or plastic. Tiny seed beads, approximately 1oz (28g) of each color, plastic clay, tracing paper, fine needle.

Place a flat ball of plastic clay in the bowl and smooth it up the sides and over the rim, making an even coating about ⅛in (3mm) deep. Be sure to smooth out any air bubbles.

Mark the quadrants in the bowl with the needle to help in positioning the motifs. Make tracing of major motifs, prick outlines in clay, or draw free-hand with point of needle.

Position first bead in center of bowl. Pick up each bead on the needle, stick needle in position, and slide bead down into place. Work central motif first, then motifs around sides.

Bottle-shaped beaded gourds, color-fully embellished with traditional designs, are among the many cere-monial offerings to be dedicated to the gods.

Left: A multitude of eagles, scorpions, suns, and flowers adorn these votive bowls, while one shows the sacred path followed each year by the peyote gatherers on their way to Wirikuta.

Deftly this Huichol woman adorns the rim of a votive bowl, adding the last few beads one by one on the point of a needle. Around her neck hang colorful ropes of threaded beads.

CHAPTER 7
A LAND OF POTTERS

Inspired by the squash, this delicately fluted pot of polished redware, which rests on three bird-shaped legs, was modeled in the small state of Colima before the thirteenth century.

Opposite: In villages where water still has to be carried from a well or nearby river, clay pots play a vital role.

He who animates the clay
with penetrating eye amasses
and shapes it.
The good potter
puts effort into things,
teaches the clay to lie,
converses with his very heart,
breathes life into objects, creates,
knowing everything as if he were a Toltec,
he makes his hands dextrous.
The bad potter
dull-witted, clumsy in his art,
seems dead in life.

This Aztec poem clearly reveals the esteem felt for the art of ceramics, an art that goes back many thousands of years to the time when corn was first domesticated. In the hands of the early inhabitants of Mexico, clay was transformed into water storage jars inspired originally by the squash and the bottle gourd, pots of varying shapes and sizes, dishes, incense burners, and ritual vessels for the temple, idols and figurines depicting animals, birds, and human beings often engaged in everyday activities.

Long before the Aztec era ceramics had acquired the status of a great art, and although farming communities in rural areas habitually produced pottery for their own use, in the towns and important centers professional potters underwent a lengthy training to learn the skills and secrets involved. Pieces were hand modeled, although molds were used with great ingenuity, and methods of decoration were imaginative and varied. A smooth, shiny appearance was achieved by burnishing or polishing pottery with a stone or lump of

A humming bird perches on the rim of this ancient, exquisitely painted bowl modeled by a Mixtec potter.

metal, while the background color of a piece could be changed by dipping it in a wash made from strongly colored earth mixed with water. Incising with shells or sharp instruments, roller stamping, and textile impression with woven net or cloth were all popular ways of embellishing pottery before firing. High-relief decoration was another important skill, and pots and vessels were frequently adorned with elegant birds, flowers, leaves, animals, or representations of gods' heads. Alternatively, the entire pot might be modeled in the shape of a fish or a dog.

Painted designs ranged from geometric patterning and naturalistic or symbolic depictions of animals, human beings, and plants to pictographic motifs or scenes derived from history or religion. Some of the decorative techniques practiced by these dedicated pre-Hispanic potters were elaborate in the extreme, as when the clay was incised after firing and the design hollowed out. The spaces were filled in with different colors and the effect achieved was a veritable mosaic.

Glazing was unknown with the exception of a type of pottery known as Plumbate, which gleamed with a rainbow-hued sheen rich in lead residues. This process, which was popular for a short time only, involved a special method of firing. Otherwise firing was a haphazard affair. Families baked small pieces in the ashes on their hearths, and large-scale firings were effected either on the surface of the ground, bonfire-style, or else in pits dug deep into the ground. Placed at the bottom, the hard, sun-dried pots would then be alternated with layers of broken pottery. The wood, piled on top of this carefully arranged stack, was then ignited. By such means as these, consistent temperatures could not be obtained, yet the passage of time has proved the durability of these clay objects, many of which are still being excavated thousands of years after their creation.

Today Mexico is still a land of potters: the skill and aptitude displayed by those ancient craftsmen has never been lost. Every day before dawn, all over the country, potters set out with their wares for market. Protected by deep cane baskets or swathed in corn husks and dry grasses, these fragile pieces are transported long distances by mule or, more frequently, on the back of the man or woman who is making the journey.

In remote areas, where the pattern of life has changed little, pottery continues to play its vital role in the domain of cooking, eating, and storage and traditional forms persist. Every home has its water jars, its pots for cooking beans and stews, its *comal*, or flat round griddle for heating tortillas, and its *molcajete*, or crisscross bottomed bowl, specially roughened for grating chilli peppers and the other ingredients needed to make spicy sauces. Jugs and gently rounded mugs for gruel and the liquor *pulque* hang from nails driven into the wall. Occasionally, the branches of a nearby bush or the arms of a cactus serve as a natural support for pitchers, bowls, and cooking pots.

Not only have many of the ancient forms remained unchanged, but numerous techniques have proved equally enduring. In the purest Indian tradition are the various types of pottery that are hand modeled and fired under primitive conditions. In the forests of Chiapas, the Lacandon Indians fashion the local clay, wetting it and kneading it until it is pliable. The women shape cooking pots, and are joined by their menfolk and children in the making of toys. Tigers, armadillos, human figures, and birds are baked hard in the ashes of the open fire. The Lacandons in the Lacanjá area still serve the old Mayan gods and every man is his own priest, building a house for his deities and fashioning a series of pots, each one featuring the head of the god to whom it is dedicated. Once fired, these pots are whitewashed and streaked with red and black earth dyes. During religious ceremonies they are used for burning incense, and as the smoke rises up toward the sky the white garbed Lacandon, his long black hair flowing free, sings for his gods.

Also in the state of Chiapas is the picturesque village of Amatenango del Valle, which provides the entire region with water storage jars, pots, dishes, and toys. The clay is dug up locally and brought to the village by the menfolk. After that they return to their labor in the fields, and pottery making is left entirely to the female members of the family.

While women devote themselves principally to the making of pots, building them up in various stages, their daughters learn to

In many communities potters grind local earths and minerals, mixing them with water to make paints and washes.

Fragile pottery pieces are carefully transported over long distances to be sold at markets and fairs.

95

In Amatenango, pots are built up over several days in various stages. Water and sifted sand are added to finely ground clay and the mixture is kneaded until it is pliable. Fashioned into long tubes, the clay is coiled around and pressed down with the fingers.

Recently modeled pots, complete with flaring lip and handles, wait in the shade protected by a cotton cloth.

The surfaces of the pot are polished with a stone from the riverbed, which the potter wets continually in a dish of water at her side. Left to harden, the pot is polished again with a stone, this time without water.

Dry pots are carefully scraped with a sharp blade for greater smoothness. The scrapings are not disregarded; they will be used in the making of another pot, once mixed with water.

Colors for painting are made by dissolving locally found earths with water in the hollow of a stone. Natural clay has an ivory tone when fired, but some potters like to give their pieces a coat of orange.

A twig, a feather, a homemade brush, or a finger serve to paint on the snakelike lines, flowers, and leaf motifs that adorn the pots. During firing, yellow will turn to red and red will darken to brown.

Before being fired, pieces are set out in the sunshine to warm up; otherwise they would crack in the heat of the flames.

Pieces are piled up on the patio or out on the public highway, covered with a mound of wood, cow dung, and corn-husks and fired for up to 30 minutes. These pots and toys are sold locally and in the market at San Cristobal.

In Amatenango, small girls learn to handle clay by modeling and painting toy animals. A broken leg or horn is cheerfully glued on with a touch of saliva.

In the shady interior of her home in Atzacoaloya, this potter walks around her pot, adding finishing touches to the base.

handle clay by fashioning cows, bulls, birds, piggy banks, and antlered deer. Shade and coolness are necessary if the clay is to remain moist, and the colorfully dressed women and girls of Amatenango seat themselves in the patio under the overhanging eves of their grass roofs, often suspending a blanket for extra protection. Finished pieces are scraped with a sharp blade, polished with a stone, and painted with natural earth colors. Firing takes place in the patio or out on the public highway and on a busy day smoke rises up on all sides from the many bonfires that burn throughout the village.

Most of the women of Amatenango use what is known as the "Zapotec wheel" to help them with their pot making. This pre-Hispanic device entails the placing of the pot on a board or pottery tray, which rests in turn on a stone or upturned bowl. The potter is, therefore, able to remain seated and to rotate her pot as she fashions the walls. In the village of Atzacoaloya in the state of Guerrero, however, women still walk around the pot, which sits on a table, coiling it as they go. Whereas in most places potters start with the bottom and finish with the neck, in Atzacoaloya it is customary to leave the base until last. Resting on a flat temporary bottom, the walls are built up stage by stage. Then when the top is reached and completed, the pot is turned upside down and the base is remade. Working in the dark and cool interior of her home, the potter dexterously coils her clay into a gentle dome, moving inward. Gradually the hole grows smaller until the last knob of clay causes it to disappear altogether, and the smooth surface gives not a clue as to the order of its making.

Another very ancient method of firing is that favored in the small potting village of San Bartolo Coyotepec, just a few miles from Oaxaca City. Water jars of all sizes, globular containers for the agave liquor called *mezcal, pichanchas*, or perforated pots for the washing and straining of maize, toy whistles in the shape of mermaids, fish, birds, and deer, bells with a metallic tone and flutes are all characterized by their wonderful black and brilliant sheen.

Left to dry out, the local clay is trampled underfoot until it is ground to a fine powder, then soaked in water overnight, making it ready for use. Pots are lump formed. The potter pushes her hand into a ball of clay that is supported by her other hand. Twisting her fist with great strength she succeeds in hollowing out the clay. Then she proceeds to build up the walls from the inside, adding more clay and wetting her hands. A piece of broken pottery is used for smoothing surfaces. Balancing her pot on a saucer, which rests on a second upturned saucer, she is able to spin it, fashioning the top part with coils of clay and making the lip flare with the help of a piece of wet leather. The pot is then set aside to dry for several days before being scraped with a strip of tin.

After another drying period, the pot is polished with a lump of quartz or even with a hardened reed. If the potter wishes to give her

piece a particular decoration she can polish it in sections. Alternatively, she can scratch on a motif, add high relief figures such as birds, or perforate the clay wall with tiny lozenges and stars. Toys and figurines are hand modeled with great skill and imagination or else produced in molds and perfected afterward. The minutest piece then receives its polishing.

The kiln, circular in form, lies in a pit with its opening at ground level, while a second pit, dug alongside, allows the potter to descend and feed the furnace below. With great ingenuity the sun warmed pieces are accommodated on the platform, and the heat from the wood fire begins to rise. The kiln is then covered with pottery shards. Often lit just before dusk, the fire is left to burn gently for a couple of hours. Then more wood is added to increase the temperature and the kiln is entirely sealed off with mud. All through the night the pieces bake. The fire, choked by lack of oxygen, emits clouds of smoke and soot that impregnate and color the clay. When the mud and shards are removed the next morning, the pieces are stained black and friction with a rag soon removes the grime, revealing the metallic brilliance beneath. This phenomenon, due both to the presence of lead oxide in the clay and to the method of firing, is further helped by the polishing already given to the pieces. Unpolished pottery would emerge not black but gunmetal gray. On the other hand, should the temperature rise too high during firing, the pieces would lose their newly acquired blackness. Firing in San Bartolo Coyotepec might seem a risky business but these experienced potters seem to have a sixth sense.

The European kiln, introduced by the Spanish, provided the Mexican potter with a more reliable method of firing his pieces and was soon in common use. Cylindrical, open topped, and with the fire grate below, the majority of kilns are built of adobe and stand out in the potter's yard. Resinless woods are favored for burning, but where trees are scarce, kerosine is an acceptable substitute.

In San Bartolo Coyotepec, kilns are circular and built underground. When pieces have been accommodated and the fire beneath lit, the opening to the kiln is sealed off with broken shards and mud. During the firing, pottery absorbs the soot and smoke and emerges deep black.

A potter from San Bartolo Coyotepec sells her gleaming wares.

99

In the state of Puebla, however, the potters of Acatlán traditionally use the cactus plants that grow in profusion throughout the surrounding countryside. Rich in resin, they burn well and Herón Martínez admits to using ten different varieties. This master potter, who began his career making pots and water jars in the style of his village, has since dedicated himself to the creation of fantastic and beautiful sculptures. Hand modeled, polished, and adorned with red and brown earth markings, his pieces attest to his extraordinary skill and imagination. Pyramids of animals and elaborate candelabra incorporating deer, foliage, birds, mermaids, and moons leave his kiln to reappear in shops and exhibitions up and down the country.

The candelabrum was a Spanish importation and over the years that followed the Conquest other pottery forms were added to the Indian range. Tea sets and dinner services imposed themselves on a domestic level, pre-Hispanic idols were supplanted by angels and saints and by depictions of the Virgin and the Devil, while soldiers, men on horseback, dogs, and cows replaced the figurines of old, offering new inspiration to potters.

Over the centuries, European influence has led the men, women, and children of Metepec, in the state of Mexico, to evolve their own unique style. Adding the dried flowers of rushes to the local clay, these ingenious craftsmen produce winged horses, flower bedecked oxen under the yoke, nativity scenes, guitar playing mermaids, and smiling suns. But it is the tree of life that has most strongly prompted their creative instincts. These ornate candle-bearing sculptures, which range from tiny to gigantic, are fired in vast ovens, given a white base coat and painted with vivid colors.

Although the potters of Metepec model the basic structure with their hands, they depend on molds for the production of smaller figures, dusting the clay with the ashes of burnt cow dung to prevent

European-style kilns are used today by most potters and wood remains the staple fuel.

The women potters of Aguasuelos, in Veracruz, provide surrounding villages with hand-coiled pots and bowls decorated with raised or incised motifs and painted with natural earth colors.

With delicate brush strokes, Alfonso Castillo Horta of Izucar de Matamoros, in Puebla, adorns a whitewashed candlestick with floral motifs.

it from sticking. A popular device in pre-Hispanic times, the clay mold is still used extensively in many parts of Mexico. Mushroom-shaped molds are ideal for fashioning deep plates, bowls, or mug bottoms. Pots are often made in concave molds and joined vertically; alternatively, the base may be mold formed and the upper part coiled by hand. Some potting villages favor combinations, using one mold for the bottom and another for the top section, while others use the same one twice. As for figurines and toys, these are nearly always made in molds.

In the state of Jalisco, the potters of Tlaquepaque specialize in producing miniatures. Musicians, wedding parties, men and women on their way to market, and even pottery vendors are captured in the midst of their activities. Some even bring the past to life, for many of the molds that are used to form bodies and heads date back to the Colonial era. Arms and legs are hand modeled, however, often on tiny wires. Oil paints have replaced water colors, but otherwise tradition holds firm in this aptly named village, for Tlaquepaque means "makers of pottery."

New pottery forms and the enclosed kiln were far from being Spain's only contributions in the field of ceramics, however, and today variations of the European-style wheel are found in a few centers, worked exclusively by men and constructed at home from spare automobile parts or operated by kicking a wooden wheel on the ground. Glazing proved an even more important innovation and its introduction was greatly welcomed. Silica, sand, and lead oxide are the chief ingredients for most Mexican glazes. Boiled together they turn into a liquid glass, which is then poured over the clay. Fired once, glazed and fired again, pottery becomes water retentive and stronger. In every market piles of low-priced dishes, mugs, and cooking pots are displayed, gleaming in the sunlight.

Mottoes are a feature of the tankard sized pulque mugs that are made in Tecomatepec in the state of Mexico. "Women are devils

When pottery molds are used, clay is dusted to prevent it from sticking.

The potters of Izucar de Matamoros specialize in making ornate and colorful candlesticks for festive occasions and for the Day of the Dead.

LAKE OSWEGO PUBLIC LIBRARY
706 Fourth Street
Lake Oswego, Oregon 97034

Made from *barro de olor*, or aromatic clay, the beautifully painted jugs and drinking vessels from Tonalá, in Jalisco, are much valued for the special flavor they impart to the water.

The famous glazed *petatillo* ware of Tonalá is distinguished by a network of fine crisscrossing lines and by a profusion of animals, birds, ferns, and flowers.

when they wish to wed," warns one with wry humor. Spirited scenes often adorn these much sought after mugs, and tigers hunt down deer or fight among themselves, well protected by a coat of transparent glaze.

Highly practical, glazing can also be a decoration in itself. Potters from the Barrio de la Luz, translatable as the "District of Light," in the city of Puebla, glaze their heavy cooking vessels, pitchers, and platters to a golden brown, then drip glaze them with black, achieving an attractive streaky effect. Drip glazing is also popular in the city of Oaxaca, where molten blue, green, and yellow oxides are poured over the wheel-thrown, white-coated kitchenware, giving it a careless and cheerful rainbow appearance. The evenly glazed pottery produced in Santa Fé de la Laguna in Michoacan seems sober by contrast. Elaborate candelabra, embellished with high-relief flowers and leaves, and punch bowls hung with tiny cups are enriched with a silvery black sheen.

Green glazes are favored in many pottery villages. Traditional methods are time consuming and entail the burning of copper wire with lemon and salt. Particles are finely ground and mixed with lead oxide at the time of glazing. Today most potters confess to buying their copper oxide ready prepared, thereby saving themselves con-

siderable labor. Green glazing has long been popular in the village of Patamban in Michoacan. Tableware, punch bowls, and wonderful pineapple-shaped water containers, their surfaces covered with spines, are given a white coating, fired for eight hours, glazed a brilliant green, and fired for another three and a half hours.

Tin glazing is essential to the art of Majolica, introduced by the Spanish soon after the Conquest. The recently founded city of Puebla, with its rich deposits of both clay and silica, proved an ideal location and factories soon sprang up, providing the new inhabitants with high quality tableware. Methods of production have remained unchanged. Now, as then, two types of clay are blended together. Beaten, trampled underfoot, washed, and kneaded, the mixture is carefully stored and left to ripen before being shaped on the wheel. After the first firing, the pottery is submerged in an opaque liquid glaze. The sun-dried pieces are then decorated with mineral colors, often ground in the factory. Designs are traditional and represent a combination of Islamic, Spanish, Chinese, and Mexican styles. Flower and bird motifs or rural scenes depicting people and animals are charmingly painted in delicate shades of green, blue, yellow, black, and rust. Equally popular are the undulating leaf patterns in cobalt blue on a white background. Once dry, the pieces are fired for up to thirty-six hours. Gleaming with their enamel-like glazes, vases, dishes, and lidded jars adorn the homes of Puebla, while churches, houses, and fountains are resplendent with facades of tiles.

The range of Mexican pottery is vast indeed, deriving as it does from ancient Indian traditions and further enriched by Spanish importations. But all pieces, whether functional, ceremonial, or purely decorative, have one thing in common: all are made from clay, modeled and worked with loving care, and it is their very fragility that lends them such charm and fascination.

Green glazing is popular with the potters of Patamban, in Michoacan. Pineapple-shaped water containers are fired, glazed, and fired again.

During the Colonial period, the art of Majolica blossomed in the city of Puebla and buildings were adorned with splendid tiled facades.

METEPEC TREE OF LIFE

Colorful and ornate, the trees of life from Metepec are famous throughout Mexico. The theme, which originated in the Middle East, was brought by the Moors to Spain where it took on a Christian significance. Introduced into Mexico after the Conquest, the tree of life became popular with the potters of Metepec in the state of Mexico. From their dexterous hands come elaborate candle-bearing sculptures, ranging in size from tiny to gigantic, which commemorate the divine Creation and conjure up the era before the Fall when Adam and Eve knew perfect happiness in the Garden of Eden. Sometimes not life, but death, is depicted in these colorful trees, and grinning skeletons cavort among the green and leafy boughs. Seascapes are a variation on the tree of life.

Doves and brilliant flowers surround the central figures of Adam and Eve, while the cunning serpent winds itself sinuously around the apple-laden branches of our tree of life.

Below: Tracing pattern for cardboard tree shapes. See page 27 for instructions on how to enlarge. Keep clay damp while working. Between sessions, or if clay starts to dry out, cover it with a damp cloth and plastic bag. Mold and smooth clay around the cardboard branches of the tree of life with wet fingers.

Materials: 7lb (3kg) self-hardening clay, three pieces heavy cardboard, low wide tin can, craft knife, glue, garden cane, florists' wire, round-nose pliers, wire cutters, poster paints, fine and medium paintbrushes, epoxy glue, clear varnish.

Cut out three cardboard tree shapes, glue together and secure in can with clay. Strengthen trunk with canes stuck in can at front and back. Cover tree with clay from base upward.

Work up center trunk then down each side. Roll strips of clay for candle holders and mold clay into place. Cover frame generously with clay, rounding and smoothing branches.

Make leaves from ball of clay pressed into shape between finger and thumb. Scratch veins on leaves, push wire into leaves and fruit, let clay dry, and paint.

Mold birds in the stages shown from a small fat roll of clay. Shape wings like leaves and smooth onto body. Push U-shaped piece of wire into body, allow to dry, paint.

Attach birds, leaves, and fruit while covering tree skeleton. Hold in place and with pliers, twist wire around to back of branch. Cover wires with clay to secure.

Allow tree to dry and paint it. Make flower petals from flattened balls of clay, mold petals and centers together. Flowers will be glued to tree, so flatten the backs. When dry, paint flowers.

The snake's curves must fit in with Adam and Eve during final assembly, so trace the snake, lay roll of clay on tracing, and form into curves using the tracing as a guide. Paint snake.

Opposite: The potters of Izucar de Matamoros, in Puebla, also specialize in trees of life. Basing their designs on cacti, they adorn pieces with birds, animals, fruits, and exotic flowers.

Adam and Eve: Form trunks from wedge-shaped pieces of clay, attach limbs as shown. For hair, make "wigs" of clay and smooth on. Flatten backs of figures so that they can be glued on.

To attach snake, figures, and flowers, lay tree flat on crumpled newspaper. Attach pieces with epoxy glue. Allow glue to dry. Touch up paint, add gold highlights, and varnish.

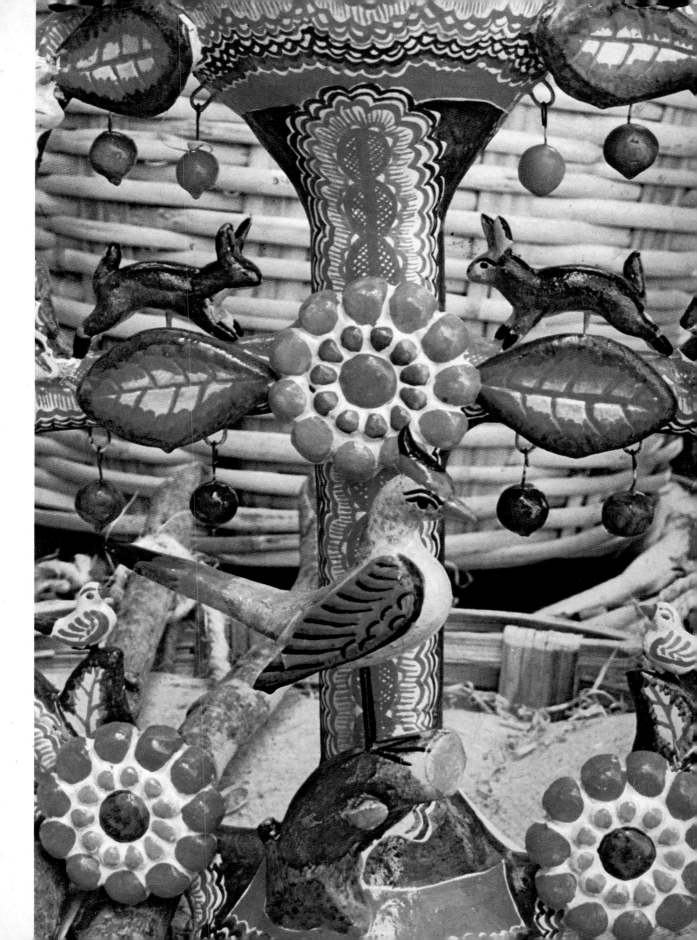

CHAPTER 8
MINIATURES AND MATRACAS

Mexican people never outgrow their delight in the colorful and the fantastic. Perhaps that is why toy makers bring such love and enthusiasm to their work, giving a free rein to their imagination and conjuring up a world of dreams and magic.

For the baby, enveloped in the folds of its mother's shawl, there are brightly lacquered gourds from Olinala, painted with swans and flowers, or braided palm leaf rattles, bedecked with brilliant feathers and shaped to suggest exotic birds.

Like their counterparts anywhere, little girls love dolls, many of which tempt passersby at fairs and markets up and down the country. From the town of Celaya in Guanajuato State comes a dazzling succession of papier-mâché figures with articulated limbs and bright blue eyes. These unlikely beauties, reminiscent of Hollywood chorus girls from the twenties, proudly bear their names in glitter across their chests. Rag dolls present a softer image as they smile winningly from the depths of wicker baskets. In more remote areas, children often make their own dolls, and the Indian girls of the Chiapas Highlands like to model figures of clay, decking them out in miniature huipils and wrap-around skirts, or to fashion dolls from cornhusks, giving them long corn silk braids entwined with strands of brightly colored yarn.

Animals also play their part. Bushy tailed pottery squirrels, speckled wooden birds, paper anteaters, and palm leaf lizards, together with a variety of creatures not to be found in any zoo, are cared for and played with by their youthful owners. Many clay animals have additional attributes. A glistening black fish with legs may turn out to be a useful money box, while a green and yellow striped tortoise doubles as a whistle.

Musical toys are a special feature. Whistles come in every imaginable guise, emitting notes that range from a high-pitched squeak to a

As the wheels turn, his brightly painted toy airplane delights this small Mexican boy.

Opposite: From the pottery village of Ocumichu, in Michoacan, comes a host of imaginative money boxes and whistles.

Dolls are popular throughout Mexico and rags, braided palm, clay, and corn-husks are just some of the materials used to make them.

Children help their parents from an early age. This boy potter from Ocumichu knows that painting clay toys can be as much fun as playing with them.

low and resonant boom. Leather covered drums, shiny wooden violins, and gaily painted guitars combine, though not always melodiously, with clay trumpets and flutes to complete the orchestra.

It is an intriguing fact that although the Indians of ancient Mexico discovered the wheel, they applied it only to children's toys and offerings, never realizing its greater potential. Today this fascination with movement can be seen in any market. Tiny, jointed wooden snakes, their red, forked tongues protruding, wriggle realistically. Delicately formed feathered birds wage battle, vibrating on slender wires like fighting cocks. Bizarre boxing matches take place between Death and the Devil at the touch of a button, while colorful wooden chickens peck from acorn-cap dishes. As for the skilled artisans of Tzintzuntzan, they can create an entire fun fair, using only wheat straws to produce carousels with prancing horses, swings, and the big wheel itself.

From an early age children are expected to help their parents. Daughters are taught how to pat tortillas into shape, to spin, and to carry water from the well in small clay pots. Sons help in the fields and learn their fathers' craft. But before the full weight of adult responsibility descends, children enjoy a whole range of imitative games, playing at being grown-up. Little girls carry their dolls on their backs, feeding them tamales of leaves and mud gruel. Little boys build houses and temples, filling them with clay families and saints, and enacting splendid fiestas and rituals. Diminutive baskets, hammers, and tools of all kinds, brooms, copper cauldrons, wooden shelves stacked with minuscule pottery plates, tables, chairs, grinding stones, and spoons, all exact replicas of day-to-day objects, are patiently fashioned by local craftsmen to supply the needs of this make-believe world.

The minature is a Mexican speciality and the glass centers of Mexico City and Guadalajara often resemble Noah's Arks. A caval-

Children in a party mood amuse themselves with a wheat straw carousel from Tzintzuntzan and jointed paper dolls from Celaya. A musical accompaniment is provided by a gaily painted guitar.

cade of tiny translucent creatures covers shelves and counter. Green mother alligators nurse their little ones, and antlered deer keep company with fluffy poodles; nor are human figures absent from the scene. Mariachis in wide brimmed hats and charros on horseback mingle with heavily laden women on their way to market amid a forest of trees, while in the background a stately galleon sails out to sea.

Castles with turrets and rugged mansions set deep into the mountainside are deftly carved from the wood of the *pochote* tree by the villagers of Tepoztlán in Morelos, but it is among the inhabitants of Puebla State that the miniature has found most favor. Minute purple pigs with curly tails, patchwork lizards, and lop-eared rabbits are just a few of the endearing and imaginative animals to be created from strips of dyed palm by the artisans of Santa Mariá Chicmecatitlán. Enticing little dishes piled high with rainbow fruits and tempting chicken dinners garnished with rich brown sauce and sesame seeds turn the shop windows of Puebla City into delectable restaurants. Even more skillfully contrived, however, are the tiny Puebla kitchens, complete with old-style ranges. The walls are hung from floor to ceiling with cooking pots, while in the foreground plump and smiling cooks of painted clay chop food on wooden tabletops. Some of these charming domestic tableaux are set into glass-fronted wooden boxes but others, smaller still, fit snugly inside a walnut shell.

Seasonal festivities, of which there are many, play a large part in the life of the Mexican child. Easter is an exciting time, and the paper workers of Celaya and Mexico City are kept busy fashioning red-

The brightly lacquered gourd rattles from Olinala travel long distances. Here, a Trique Indian mother in Oaxaca watches her small son at play.

111

Craftsmen supply the Mexican child with a profusion of miniatures, exact replicas of day-to-day objects.

Salvador Sevilla, who lives in Mexico City, shapes glass into tiny figurines. With the heat of the blow torch, sticks of glass are transformed into translucent animals, fish, balloon sellers, and fairy-tale galleons.

painted devils and grotesque cardboard dolls called Judases. Smaller figures are shaped directly onto a mold, but larger ones are assembled limb by limb.

The workshop of Ignacio López Barrera and his wife Loreto Luna in Celaya is a strange and surrealistic place to visit. Arms, legs, heads, and bodies, painted and unpainted, lie around in mounds waiting to be brought to life. Sold in markets and outside churches up and down the country, these colorful creations are kept by their new owners until Easter Saturday, known as the Saturday of Glory. As night falls, the Judases, gaily decked out with fireworks, are brought out into village and city squares. When the paper fuse is lit these ill-fated figures disintegrate in a shower of stars and golden rain accompanied by the whirring noise of the *matraca*, or Easter rattle. Made from wood or tin and brightly painted, these noisy toys are an indispensible feature of all such celebrations.

In June comes the feast of Corpus Christi. During the Colonial period, the inhabitants of Mexico were required to pay their dues to the Church on this day, tethering their mules outside the building. It became customary, as a result, for children to receive tiny mules made of palm, straw, rushes, or cornhusks, bearing panniers packed with fruit and candies. Mestizo parents also take great delight in dressing up their small sons and daughters Indian-style. In the courtyards of churches and cathedrals little girls gather, wearing colorful shawls and embroidered blouses, accompanied by boys with sarapes, sandals, and painted moustaches. Completing the costume is the *huacal*, or bamboo frame that is worn on the back and hung with a multitude of tiny pots, gourds, baskets, and other typically Indian objects.

A mood of jollity reigns as photographers entice the children to enter specially constructed scenarios like miniature film sets. For the girl there is a kitchen tableau with its grinding stone and pile of fresh tortillas, while for the boy-charro a donkey awaits bedecked with flowers.

The Totonac children of Veracruz enjoy an unusual and fragrant series of playthings at this time of the year. In honor of Xanat, the Vanilla Goddess, a ten day festival is held, and during this period the fresh and sweet-smelling pods are cunningly shaped into flowers, fishes, scorpions, and lizards or braided to make hearts, lovers' knots, and tiny baskets.

An infinite variety of toys and candies are made everywhere for the Day of the Dead in November. In the cities, as the day approaches, bakers announce their festive breads and buns by covering their windowpanes with slogans and drawings of cavorting skeletons. The markets fill up with an amazing selection of playthings inspired by the theme of Death. There are clay skulls with movable lower jaws and cardboard skeletons that dance at the pull of a string. From Guanajuato come coffin bearing priests on a moving belt; with the

As Easter time draws near, the paper workers of Celaya and Mexico City fashion grotesque figures called Judases, which are sold in markets and outside churches.

During the feast of Corpus Christi, mestizo children are decked out Indian-style by their parents.

113

turning of a handle the funeral procession glides swiftly into the gaping jaws of Hell.

In the city of Oaxaca small painted theaters of wood are constructed and peopled with rakish cotton haired skeletons. Again, the turning of a handle at the side lends life to the proceedings. As one grinning skeleton rises up in his coffin, a companion jerkily raises a glass to his bony jaws. The miniaturists of Puebla are skilled in the making of exquisite altars for the dead. Every detail is perfect, right down to the wax candles, the dishes of clay fruits, and the lace frill on the altar cloth. But strangest and most fantastic of all are the tiny clay skeletons portrayed in the midst of everyday activities. These grimly humorous figures include wedding couples, policemen

These two boys are making traditional vegetable fiber mules for Corpus Christi. These mules, with their panniers filled with fruit and candy, are often bedecked with flowers for this holiday.

Colorfully dressed for Corpus Christi, this little girl displays her *huacal* hung with a multitude of miniatures and typically Indian objects.

running, women making tortillas, or selling chickens and vegetables in the market place. There are even skeletons praying on their knees at the graveside of a dead relative!

But no less imaginative than the toys are the candies that are specially made for the Day of the Dead. From Guanajuato, Puebla, and Toluca come lions, lambs, deer, doves, angels, baskets of flowers, crosses, souls in purgatory, tiny pairs of sandals, and decorative name-bearing skulls made from sugar or marzipan. These colorful and tasty creations are offered up to dead children and enjoyed by the living.

As Christmas draws near, the markets of Mexico City take on the appearance of miniature forests as excited children play hide-and-seek among the freshly cut green firs. More traditional than the Christmas tree, however, is the nativity scene that takes pride of place in every home, and each year new pottery figures are acquired and added to the existing collections. Although Jesus in His manger is always represented, He is often overshadowed by an unlikely succession of elephants, writhing snakes, devils, and maguey plants.

Children look forward particularly to a series of parties known as *posadas*, which take place on the nine successive nights leading up to Christmas. The object is to re-enact the journey that Joseph and Mary made from Nazareth to Bethlehem, and in each house where the posada takes place a procession is held. Led by Joseph and Mary, the pilgrims make their way through the house chanting a litany and pausing eventually in front of a door to beg for posada, or lodging:

"In heaven's name,
I beg for shelter.
My wife tonight
Can go no further,"

sings Joseph, only to be greeted by the following reply from the other side of the door:

"No inn is this,
Begone from hence;
Ye may be thieves,
I trust ye not."

A dialogue ensues until at length the inmates open their door and grant hospitality to the pilgrims. The ninth night of the posadas falls on Christmas Eve and is celebrated with especial pomp and joy to commemorate the birth of the Savior.

Christmas day passes in a whirl. There are visits to church, festive meals, and reunions with family and friends. But when Mexican children go to sleep on Christmas night they are not regretting that the fun is over. Instead their minds are already racing ahead to the Feast of the Three Kings on the sixth of January, for it is then that they will receive their presents. Manuel longs for a wooden horse, José for a spinning top, while Maria is already fast asleep, dreaming of a doll.

The balloon seller is a familiar figure in the cities and towns of Mexico. Secured by a network of strings, the multihued globes fill the sky with color.

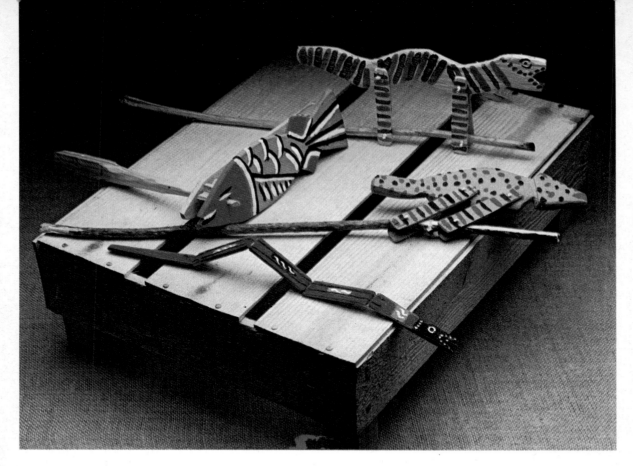

WOODEN FOLK TOYS

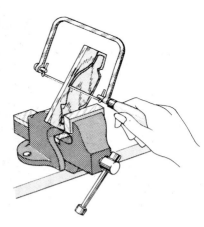

After drawing the outline of each shape onto the wood, hold wood firmly in a clamp or vise and cut out the shape with a coping saw, cutting just outside the penciled outline.

Ingenious yet simple to make, Mexican toys create a world of color and enchantment. Brightly painted animals leap backward and forward on sticks. Jointed wooden snakes wriggle realistically, and the whirring noise of fish- or bird-shaped matracas accompanies Easter celebrations.

These simple wooden toys are made from pieces of fruit crates, which can be picked up free in markets. To make the four toys shown, you will need at least two crates to allow for split and imperfect pieces of wood. Pull the crates apart with a hammer and pliers. Throw away split wood and nails or staples.

For the animal bodies, choose strong, thick boards from the sides of the crate. Glue two together to make the bodies for the sea snake and the hyena. Clamp the pieces and let the glue dry. When the shapes have been cut out with the saw, round the edges with a sharp craft knife and then smooth with sandpaper. You will need a hand drill with at least three different bits – small for the string-jointed snake, medium for the sea snake and hyena on sticks, and medium and large for the fish matraca.

The sea snake and hyena are mounted on long sticks, or pieces of dowel or bamboo, and held together with knotted string. Drill the holes as indicated on the patterns. Make sure all the legs of the toys are the same length so that they will balance on their sticks. Sand pieces smooth before assembling and paint the toys with bright poster paints or enamels.

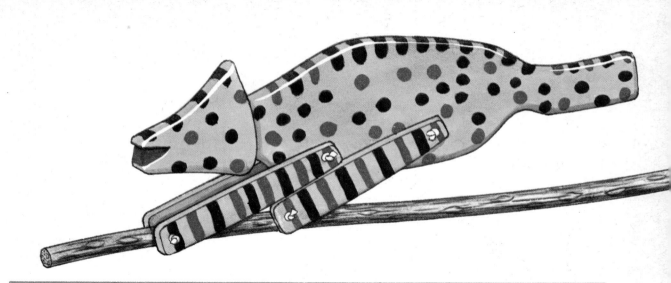

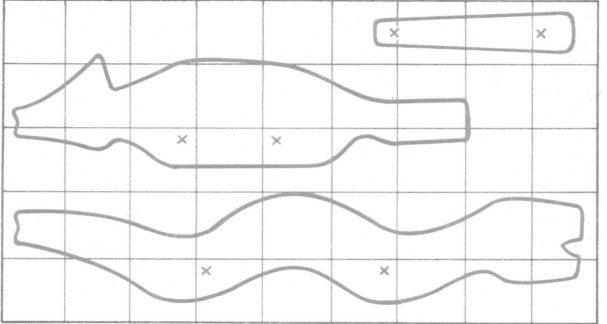

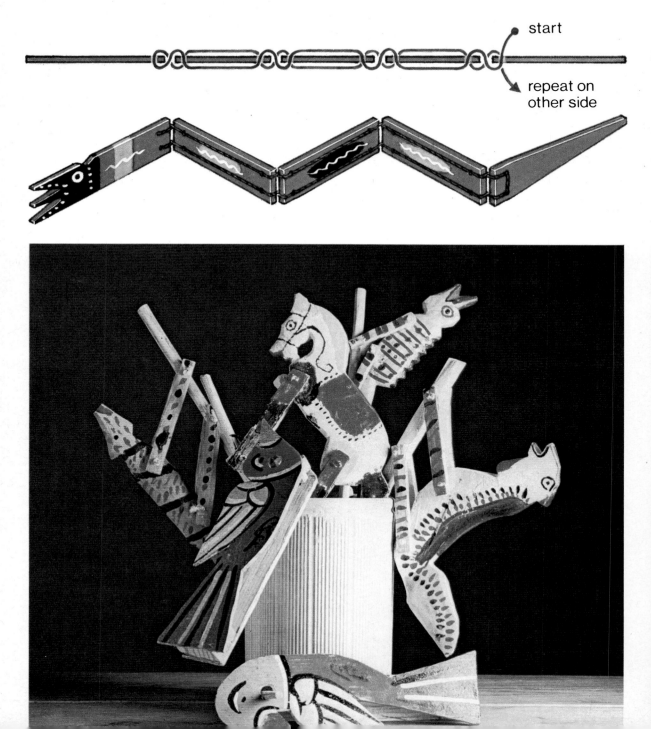

cut 3

start

repeat on
other side

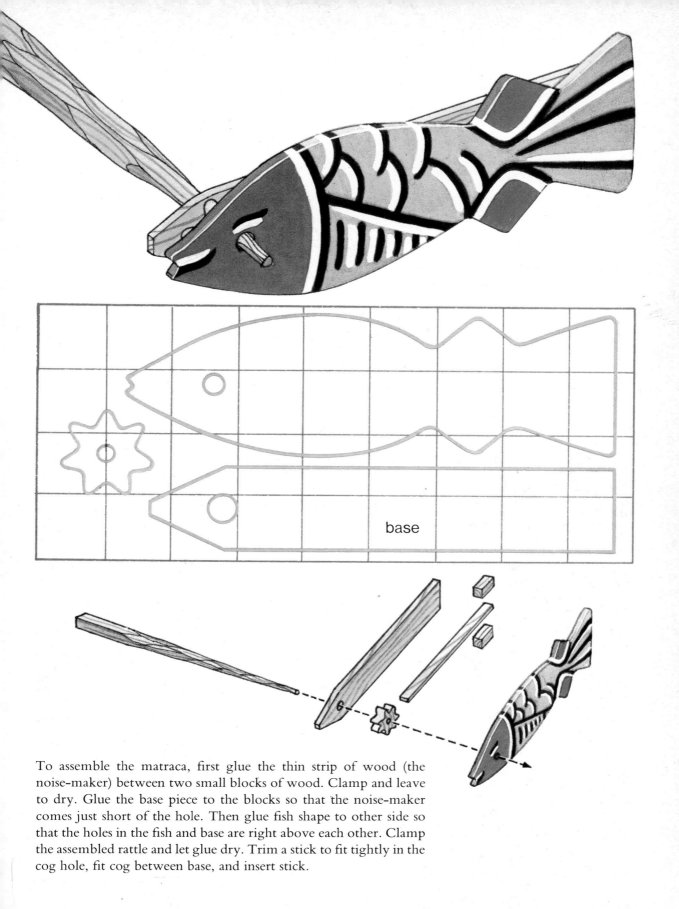

To assemble the matraca, first glue the thin strip of wood (the noise-maker) between two small blocks of wood. Clamp and leave to dry. Glue the base piece to the blocks so that the noise-maker comes just short of the hole. Then glue fish shape to other side so that the holes in the fish and base are right above each other. Clamp the assembled rattle and let glue dry. Trim a stick to fit tightly in the cog hole, fit cog between base, and insert stick.

base

CHAPTER 9
AN ABUNDANCE OF FOLK CRAFTS

On sale at markets and fairs up and down the country, hats are an indispensible feature of male attire. Here, miniatures are displayed beside adult-sized hats.

Opposite: With speed and dexterity, a skilled craftswoman from Toluca interweaves brilliantly colored strips of palm, creating rainbow hats and baskets.

We have seen how the Mexican weaves, makes pots, forges his metals, lacquers his gourds, and amuses his children. But these are only some of the ways in which he satisfies his urge to create, and there seems to be hardly a substance that is not made to serve a useful, ceremonial, or decorative purpose.

Plant fibers and other vegetable products have long been a part of life, and every community knows how best to use its natural resources. Wheat and rice straw, reeds, bamboo, flexible twigs and branches, maguey fiber, and strong grasses are all important materials, and to visit a palm growing area is to see men, women, and children braiding palm leaves. Even as they walk or sit talking in the shade, their fingers move ceaselessly, producing one smoothly braided palm strip after another. If a stranger were to ask the distance to the next village he might well be told that it lay "half a hat" or even "a whole hat" away, according to the amount of work that could be accomplished on the way.

Hats are, of course, an essential feature of Mexican male attire, and they come in a wide range of shapes and styles. The cream-colored strips are sewn together, often at special semi-industrialized centers that rely on the local people to provide them with great coils of hand-braided palm. The finest hats are made in the southern states of Yucatán and Campeche where the palm is worked in caves because the cool, damp atmosphere lends greater flexibility.

According to archaeological findings, both in Mexico and throughout the rest of the world, basketry anticipated pottery and textile weaving by several thousand years. This is logical as all nomadic peoples wish to carry their possessions with them. Baskets have remained a major necessity and each region favors different methods and materials. Willow baskets demand a lot of preparation, for the brown skin that covers the supple twigs of the young tree

An Indian from San Andres Larrainzar, in the highlands of Chiapas, twists vegetable fiber on his knee to make the twine needed for the netlike shoulder bags used throughout this region.

must be peeled away. Some craftsmen prefer to loosen the skin first by soaking the twigs in hot water, but this shortcut brings a brownish tinge to what would otherwise be an ivory whiteness.

Palm is often used in basketwork. On the coast of Oaxaca the women specialize in interweaving dark and light strands to form beautifully patterned round containers called *tompeates*, while in the village of Juchitan on the Isthmus, the palm is dyed brilliant shades, braided, and stitched to make rainbow-colored baskets and bags. No less eye-catching are those of Santa Ana Tepaltitlán, sold on market day in neighboring Toluca only a few miles from Mexico City. Multihued palm strips are wrapped around coarse grasses and these long tubes are tied securely together. Color is matched with color to form the cats, deer, eagles, and human figures that decorate the thick walls of these durable baskets.

The nomadic Seri Indians of the Sonora coast depend upon the *torote* tree when weaving their ingenious water-retaining baskets. Stained various shades of brown with natural plant dyes, the fiber is worked with awls of deer bone to give a handsome geometric design. Known as *coritas*, these baskets are not unlike those of the Pimas or the Apaches.

Hard-wearing netlike bags that expand the more they have to carry are popular among the Indians of Chiapas, and in the state of Guerrero shoulder bags are woven from local fiber and painted with motifs and humorous scenes. "My love is work," proclaims one, its lettering intertwined with brilliant flowers, while another shows a pink and green striped donkey with a yellow head smelling a rose.

The materials that are used so dexterously in making bags and baskets also serve, as they have always done, to satisfy the needs of the Indian home. Interiors are simple, often consisting of one room only, the light entering through the doorway. The floor is of earth and furnishings are few. Suspended from the ceiling, a hanging

On market day in the town of Chilapa, in Guerrero, the seller of grass brooms takes up his position in the main street.

basket holds possessions and protects food from ants and other scavengers. In the Southeast, fine hammocks are woven from cotton and sisal, but almost every region has at least one *petate* producing center.

These palm or rush mats are an integral part of life, each member of the family having his own, which is spread out at night and kept rolled up during the day. Under Aztec rule, subjugated peoples brought their tribute to Tenochtitlán in petates or *petatls*, and today they are still used to wrap presents, even serving on occasion as a shroud. In the village of Tuxpan in Jalisco, a bridal party traditionally carries a new petate to the church to symbolize the union, and inhabitants of Mochitlan in Guerrero, celebrate the feast of Santa Ana by parading a long and flower bedecked petate through the streets, eventually dedicating it to the saints.

Not far from Mexico City, the craftsmen of Lerma specialize in working with rushes, making not only petates but also round stools and comfortable armchairs of ancient design. On Sundays, motorists entering the capital by certain roads are likely to see impromptu furniture stores set up along the grass verge.

Markets remain the normal outlet for most wares, however, and the visitor is faced with a tantalizing display of tortilla baskets, individual place mats, bunches of twigs for scouring plates, sandals of maguey fiber, lengths of rope and twine, brooms, ingenious toys, and colorful fans for the fire. A profusion of wicker cradles, lampshades, and decorative sewing baskets with a chicken or an owl for a lid are produced in the village of Tequisquiapan in Querétaro and sold in the picturesque market of San Juan del Rió. Still more imaginative are the ornamental cane birdcages contrived in the arid and mountainous state of Hidalgo. Topped with splendid turrets and domes, these magical creations often stand more than two feet high.

Tzintzuntzan, once the capital of the Tarascan Empire, is as

From the state of Oaxaca come gaily colored hammocks of maguey fiber. Strands of fiber are attached to two horizontal bars, enabling this experienced craftswoman to interlace them in elaborate patterns.

Wheat straw is transformed into angels, airplanes, stars, and sailing ships in the hands of Gudelia Cuanas Camacho of Tzintzuntzan, in Michoacan.

famous today for its basketry as for its pottery. Wheat straw, known locally as *panicua*, is used in the making of delicate and charming angels, figures of the Virgin, nativity scenes, and diminutive landscapes complete with houses and trees. No less adept at working with rushes, these skillful craftsmen often fashion life-size figures of charros, mariachis, and women on their way to market.

Flowers and even vegetables become highly decorative materials in the hands of the Mexicans. Ornate and ephemeral archways of fresh flowers and leaves are erected over church doorways at fiesta time, and the inhabitants of San Antonino in the state of Oaxaca are adept at threading tiny everlasting flowers of yellow and white on wires to make doves, angels, lyres, stars, and garlands for the adornment of their altars. For the Fiesta of the Radishes, which falls on the twenty-third of December, the men and women of Oaxaca carve fantastic figures and humorous toys, using the elongated radishes that grow locally. As for the many varieties of berries and seeds found everywhere, these are ingeniously incorporated into colorful and decorative necklaces.

One of the strangest and most unlikely vegetable substances to be worked in Mexico must surely be the gum or *chilte*, which is extracted during the winter months from the tall and corpulent trees that grow in the forests of Jalisco. Aniline dyes are added on the spot before the milky liquid solidifies. The collector then carries the hardened gum to the nearest stream where he beats it with a wooden hammer and washes away any excess color. In nearby Talpa de Allende, women carvers reduce the solid blocks of chilte to paper-thin layers, rolling them out with the aid of heavy glass bottles filled with hot water. These layers are separated into strands and modeled with infinite patience and dexterity. During the annual fair in honor of Our Lady of the Rosary, the women of Talpa present Her with their fragile and beautiful offerings, which include minute gardens, fountains, figures of the Virgin, and lacelike baskets of fruit or flowers, all made from chilte.

Although the art of working chilte probably developed fairly recently, the tradition of paper making dates back to Aztec times and earlier. The inner bark of certain trees was soaked in water. Then the fibers were separated from the pulp and beaten. Resin or gum served as an ideal binding material and gradually the fibers emerged as a rough sheet. When dry, this paper, called *amatl* or today *amate*, was coated with a chalky varnish that whitened it, leaving it smooth and ready to receive the symbolic picture writing of the scribes.

The Otomi Indians of San Pablito in Puebla, have always made paper, boiling the tree bark with water and lime in great copper cauldrons and pounding out the softened strands on flat wooden boards. Amate paper serves as a magic ingredient in many pagan rituals and ceremonies that the Catholic missionaries never succeeded in banishing.

Earth, Air, Fire, Water, Sun, and Seeds are all protective gods whose favor must be sought and won. There are, in addition, malevolent forces that have to be placated. They include the Devil, Bad Currents of Air, which bring sickness and disease, the Moon, whose eclipses threaten women, and the Rainbow, killer of expectant mothers.

Dark bark is a power for evil, and light for good. The Otomis depend upon male sorcerers to effect cures, which they initiate by offering white papers to the gods. Some even claim to be able to bring the spirit of a dead person back to earth by means of paper cuts and candles. Evil sorcerers are much feared for they practice witchcraft, sticking pins into effigies of dark paper and casting spells. In their anxiety to ward off black magic and harmful spirits, householders often pin white paper figures depicting the sacred Bird of the Mountain over their doorways.

Life in San Pablito is highlighted by many communal ceremonies, but perhaps the most important is the Baptism of the Seeds. In spring, when the crops are planted, villagers prepare complicated figures, using commercially manufactured papers as well as amate. These they cut into a variety of shapes, investing them with a haunting and primitive beauty. Some figures represent corn, coffee, or sugarcane, and others chickens, cattle, honeybees, and men. Carrying these offerings, the Otomis make their way to a sacred cave that lies over the border in the state of Hidalgo. Entering the

Vendors of sturdy baskets and fine palm mats watch passersby at the yearly fair of Tepalcingo, in Morelos.

In the village of San Pablito, in Puebla, paper is still made from tree bark. Boiled with water and lime, the softened strands are methodically spread out on a flat wooden board and pounded into a smooth sheet.

This colorful detail from a painting on bark by Francisco Garcia, of the state of Guerrero, features an artist at work surrounded by a profusion of people, animals, and plants.

cave alone, the chief sorcerer addresses the gods, enlisting their aid and protection for the seeds as represented by the paper cuts. During the return journey, the pilgrims treat the paper cuts with great veneration. On the following day they are symbolically fed with gruel and taken to a distant lake to be baptized. The village officials are then entrusted with the paper cuts for safe keeping.

The Otomis, ever careful not to offend their gods, make payment for everything they require. The mountains receive ceremonial tribute in return for trees, which are needed for house building and, when the crops ripen, the earth is repaid with offerings and paper cuts.

In the state of Guerrero, villages such as Ameyaltepec, Xalitla, and Tolimán have taken to buying up bark paper in large quantities, and men and women who once dedicated themselves only to pottery now paint colorful landscapes full of animals, birds, and flowers. Combining fantasy with realism, they conjure up vivid and delightful scenes. As a wedding procession wends its way toward the church, watched over by a smiling sun, harvesters gather luscious fruits in golden fields, a farmer chases his runaway donkey, and bright macaws are dwarfed by giant butterflies.

The painstaking art of *popote* is still practiced in Mexico City by a few dedicated craftsmen. Fine straws are placed in boiling water and stained with aniline dyes, before being left to dry. The artist then coats a sheet of paper with beeswax and applies the colored straws, mosaic fashion, one by one. Among the few remaining popote workers, Arturo Hernandez must surely count as one of the best. With patience and imagination he builds up charming landscapes and highly decorative skulls bedecked with fronds and flowers.

Gratitude often drives the many devout Catholics of Mexico to present their saints with paintings on sheets of tin, wood, paper, and even copper. These votive offerings, or *retablos*, acknowledge in pictorial form a cure or blessing conferred, and may be specially commissioned from the village *retablero*, or painted by the giver himself. Miraculous escapes from illness, accidents, fires, falls, and drownings are depicted with a dedicated regard for detail.

Paper has inspired many skills, and the houses of the paper flower makers of Guadalajara and Mexico City resemble tropical bowers pulsating with exoticism and color. The capital is also the home of the talented Linares family. In addition to fashioning the grotesque Judas figures that amuse children every Easter, Pedro Linares and his sons delight in modeling strange and wonderful creatures called *alebrijes*, using cardboard and heavy brown paper. Molds are never used and each piece is unique. Imaginatively painted dragons with forked tongues and curling tails, two headed monsters with gaping jaws, and winged fish on legs are just some of the fairy-tale creations to leave their untidy workshop.

Among the ancient peoples of Mexico, feathers were highly

A flower-bedecked skull is depicted with a mosaic of tiny straws.

Bark cut outs from San Pablito symbolize coffee, bananas, beans, and pineapples, good spirits like the Little Monkey Bird, and the evil spirit Lord of the Land.

Fairy-tale creatures are modeled from cardboard and paper by the Linares family who live in Mexico City.

Creations are whitewashed before being painted with a rainbow profusion of markings. Here Miguel Linares gives a coat of color to a two-headed dragon.

prized, even venerated, and the feather workers of the Aztec capital comprised one of the most important guilds, sharing with the gold- and silversmiths the honorary title of Toltecs. These respected and privileged craftsmen lived in a self-contained community near the temple, serving their patron god Coyotlinaual, or He-who-is-disguised-as-a-wolf.

Women dyed and sorted out the feathers while the men were engaged in shaping fans, tassels, and armbands, or in knotting and sewing long plumes to form banners, cloaks, and glorious head-dresses. The art of feather mosaics required great skill and ingenuity. Carefully following his design, the craftsman glued an initial layer of medium-sized feathers onto a base of cotton cloth, topping it with a second made up of smaller ones. This was the technique employed in the creation of the exquisite ceremonial shield that Montezuma presented to Cortés on his arrival in the city.

After the Conquest, the art lingered on in the shape of religious images and ornamental pictures. Today it is possible to find exotic feathered birds gracing calendars and greeting cards, while the plumed dancers who participate in *Los Concheros*, or the Shell Dance, remind spectators of vanished splendor.

Among the Aztecs, precious stones were more highly valued than silver or gold, and lapidaries were also known as Toltecs. With infinite patience they cut through jade, onyx, rock crystal, malachite, and serpentine, using implements of copper or rawhide string and depending on moistened sand to create friction. Carving was achieved with the aid of obsidian, stone, or jade chisels. Drills of bone, horn, wood, or copper served to bore holes where necessary, and by chipping away at the stone between the holes the craftsmen were able to hollow out elegant bowls and vases, smoothing and polishing them with sand and cane.

Jade bore the name *chalchihuitl*, which meant precious, and was set high above all other stones, but amethysts, carnelians, opals, topazes, and turquoise were much admired. Indeed, the art of mosaic work centered upon the turquoise, and small fragments were combined to cover masks, breastplates, shields, wooden and pottery vessels, knives, helmets, and scepters, held in place by a cementlike mixture or by wax.

Healing powers were attributed to certain stones. The blood stone was believed to stop bleeding through the nose. Finely ground obsidian was placed on wounds. As for jade, it was regarded as the symbol of life itself, and when an Aztec died, relatives placed a piece of jade in the mouth of the corpse to serve as a heart, enabling the

In this ancient picture, an Aztec artisan glues feathers onto cotton cloth.

For the Dance of the Conquest, performers dress up as Aztecs and Spaniards, re-enacting the battles of old. This dancer from Guadalajara, with his magnificently plumed head-dress, portrays a fearless Aztec warrior.

129

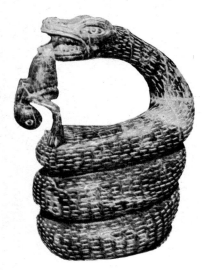

Exquisitely carved by a craftsman in Guerrero, this stone snake was inspired by pre-Hispanic examples.

Grinding stones and mortars are used all over Mexico for pounding chilli peppers and other ingredients to make hot and spicy sauces. From Comonfort, in the state of Guanajuato, come these stone mortars hewn in the shape of animals.

soul to pacify the fearsome beasts of the Seventh Hell during the long journey to Mictlan, the eternal resting place.

Today, semiprecious stones are cut and polished in Querétaro and San Juan del Rió, while the skilled craftsmen of Taxco delight in the delicate arts of stone setting and mosaic work. Serpentine, jadeite, and rock crystal carvings are a feature of Iguala in Guerrero. Here ornamental animals and snakes, heavy necklaces, and imaginative rings depicting cats, birds, and wolves are fashioned in pre-Hispanic style. As for onyx, it is worked with ingenuity by the inhabitants of Tecali and Tescala in the state of Puebla, where it is converted into handsome vases, boxes, goblets, animal figures, chess sets, and ornamental bowls of colored fruits.

Few examples of pre-Conquest wood carving have survived. Under Spanish rule, furniture achieved great elegance and splendor, and today colonial-style pieces are still produced in many centers including Mexico City and Cuernavaca, the flowery capital of Morelos. In the small town of Cuanajo in Michoacan, lovely dressers, tables, chairs, and chests are hewn from the soft white wood of the pine tree and beautifully hand carved with flowers, birds, angels, and decorative friezes. One piece of furniture that has survived without change since ancient times is the *equipal*. This comfortable armchair, made from strips of natural wood and featuring a seat of furry hide, was once reserved for Aztec dignitaries.

Up and down the country, in large cities and tiny hamlets, wood is worked in an infinity of ways, and no market is complete without its piles of spoons and chocolate beaters. Using the wood of the quince tree, the craftsmen of Tlaxcala make sturdy walking sticks, painting them brilliant colors, while the town of Paracho in Michoacan has won fame for its resonant guitars. Charming orangewood combs are sold in the city of Oaxaca, and from Santa Mariá del Rió come inlaid boxes designed to contain fine silk rebozos. Realistic doves, lizards, deer, and birds of prey are carved in Iguala from hard and attractively grained tropical woods, and in the state of Mexico, duck and swan–shaped salt shakers are hollowed out.

The woodworkers of Oaxaca delight in the creation of cavorting skeletons and strikingly humorous scenes from the Dance of Death. In a different vein are the endearingly naïve tigers, flaxen-haired mermaids, speckled owls, and grinning orange and yellow lions, which are carved and painted with great imagination in Arrasola and San Martín Tilcajete, not far from Monte Albán, the great Zapotec burial site. Different yet again are the highly stylized and polished figures of *palo de fierro*, literally ironwood, produced in recent years by the Seri Indians of the Sonora Coast. Drawing their inspiration from their surroundings, they carve out powerful dolphins, turtles, sinuous snakes, and deadly stingrays.

Since prehistory, man has shaped numerous tools from bone, and the many knives, necklaces, and spatulas, often engraved, that have been excavated suggest that this was a much used material among later Mexican civilizations. Today in Teocaltiche in Jalisco, bone is carved as finely as ivory to make exquisite chess sets and paper cutters, while Roberto Ruiz Pérez from Mexico City specializes in miniatures. The horns of deer and other animals were also used in early times, and the introduction by the Spanish of cattle prompted the craftsmen of San Antonio la Isla in the state of Mexico to dedicate themselves to working with cow horn, soaking, heating, and flattening it before cutting it into charming combs and hair ornaments featuring fishes, prancing horses, parrots, and bushy tailed squirrels. In the state of Guerrero, horns are sometimes engraved with pictures or geometric designs and serve as containers for *mezcal*, the fiery liquor derived from the agave plant.

Coastal peoples traded with shells before the arrival of the Spanish, often using them as money. In the Aztec capital, the low and vibrant tone of the conch summoned citizens to ceremonies and battles. Shells continue to provide material for necklaces and other adornments, while mother of pearl is much sought after. In the rugged state of Hidalgo, the Otomis of Ixmiquilpan produce delicate brooches, mirror frames, and miniature mandolines, guitars, and violins, inlaying the wood of the walnut tree with mother of pearl and building up intricate and minute pictures of doves and flowers. In and around Taxco, craftsmen apply mother of pearl to metal, making not only jewelry but also articulated fish with scales that shimmer and glisten realistically, and jaws that serve to open bottles.

And so the Mexican continues to give free rein to the creative impulse that drives him. Using whatever materials are at hand, no matter how unlikely they may seem, he makes objects that are both useful and beautiful.

Wood is worked all over Mexico in a multitude of ways. This craftsman from Ixtapan de la Sal, in the state of Mexico, carves a tiny salt shaker with a fearsome scythe of steel.

Duck- and swan-shaped vessels, spoons, and dishes from Ixtapan de la Sal are on sale in the markets of Mexico City.

CHAPTER 10
FIESTA!

Fidel Navarra of Acapetlahuaya serves neighboring communities as well as his own by carving saints and masks.

Opposite: At fiesta time, colorful paper cuts adorn the entry to the magnificently tiled church of San Francisco Acatepec in the state of Puebla.

In the rural areas of Mexico life can be hard. Caught up in the eternal cycle of planting and harvesting, men spend their days in the fields, leaving their womenfolk at home grinding corn, fetching water from the well, spinning, weaving, or washing clothes in a nearby river. And then, suddenly, it is fiesta time! Day-to-day occupations are forgotten as the whole community throws itself into a whirl of preparation. For the fiesta marks the high point of village life, just as it did in ancient times.

The eighteen month solar year of the Aztecs was made up of a complex series of different festivals dedicated to the gods of the earth, water, fire, sun, and maize. No sooner had one festivity ended than the black-robed priests began to anticipate the next, believing that only in this way could the People of the Sun hope to secure the goodwill of their deities.

Spanish chroniclers described in vivid terms the festivities they witnessed in the great Aztec capital. On the day of the fiesta an endless stream of men, women, and children would file past the pyramids, their arms full of flowers, feathers, or baskets of food. The idols, lavishly dressed and bedecked with jewels, were brought forth from the temples and held up for all to see and admire. In the main square there was dancing and music, while on all sides thick columns of incense rose up toward the sky, filling the air with a heavy sweetness. Human sacrifice, the inevitable climax of such festivities, is happily a feature of the past, but the Indian continues to express his religious belief through the fiesta.

As the fiesta time approaches, the mask maker in the village is kept increasingly busy. Neighbors file in and out of his house, bringing him old masks to repair, ordering new ones, or discussing terms for renting a mask. Mask makers, who double as *santeros*, or saint carvers, are adept at working with local woods, shaping and

Masks are indispensable to most fiestas and local woods are skillfully carved and painted. In the state of Morelos, performers in the dance of *Los Chinelos* wear masks of wire mesh with pointed beards of horsehair. Horsehair is also used to adorn the fine wax masks that are worn outside Mexico City with wide brimmed hats and richly embroidered costumes.

This dancer from the state of Guerrero plays the part of the tiger in the ancient agricultural dance of *Los Tlacololeros* and his mask is made of leather.

painting them as tradition demands and often incorporating real teeth and hair. Leather, paper, wax, and even wire mesh take the place of wood in some villages and are no less ingeniously fashioned.

The making of wax masks is complicated, and craftsmen guard their secrets jealously. A strip of cotton gauze is spread over a mold of stone and dampened with starch. When it dries and hardens, the mask maker paints in the pink flesh tones, the red of the lips, and the eyes, complete with lashes. Then, seated in the heat of the sun, he coats the painted cloth with thin layers of wax. Using a hot needle, he pricks fine holes, delicately inserting strands of horsehair. When a dancer wishes to wear his mask he will first let the sun soften it: it will then take on the contours of his face.

In pre-Hispanic times, masks acted as a bridge between the natural world and that of the spirits, and ritual personification was thought to endow a dancer with special powers. Animals, birds, and reptiles were believed to possess secret knowledge and masks were shaped in their likeness. Bat, tiger, rabbit, and deer masks have remained a feature of many dances and are connected with ancient agricultural, hunting, and fertility ceremonies. The Spanish introduced Christian themes into Mexico, and inspired a new series of masks with fair skins, beards, and blue eyes. The dancers take their roles seriously, aware that they are performing a religious duty on behalf of the community. Costumes have to be repaired or fresh ones improvised, and if there is a spoken text, rehearsals will be initiated under the guidance of a village elder or schoolteacher.

The house of the firework maker is an exciting place to visit during this time of preparation. Helped by his family, he is sure to be hard at work, stuffing bamboo tubes with gunpowder and producing various rockets and pinwheels. Friends and excited children drop in to watch the proceedings and to admire the great *castillo*, or castle, which waits in the patio, surrounded by *toritos*, or little bulls. These elaborate bamboo structures will not be brought out until the fiesta begins.

If the village goes in for potting, special candlesticks and incense burners will be lovingly modeled and baked. If not, these important items, bought at some distant fair or market, will have been preserved with care. Cloths for wrapping tortillas are woven or embroidered, and trips are made into the nearest town to buy ribbons, candles, and other necessary articles.

Fluttering gently in the breeze, colorful paper cuts adorn the entry to the church, while inside a profusion of flowers greets the eye. In the Chiapas Highlands, the saints are decked out with mirrors and hand-woven textiles. The greatest honor a weaver can receive is to be allowed to present the Virgin with Her new ceremonial huipil. Food also plays an essential part, and the women are kept busy grinding corn for tortillas and tamales, pounding chillies and plucking chickens. Whatever may be lacking at other times of the year abounds in these days of celebration.

The day comes at last, and soon after dawn the Virgin and the Patron Saint of the village receive their first visitors who bring them gifts of flowers and incense. Before long the church is ablaze with candles, while outside in the porch the musicians and dancers begin to assemble. Suddenly the sound of a rocket pierces the silence. Fiesta has begun!

All at once, as if by magic, the square is full of people and a mood of infectious gaiety takes over. The dancers, a mass of color, begin to

A young craftsman in Michoacan shapes ornate wax candles.

Luis Vivanco of Puebla hammers sharp blades through layers of colored paper to make lacy decorations.

135

A path of flower petals, sawdust, and sand leads to this church in the state of Puebla.

A ceremonial procession wends its way through the village of Ocumichu, in Michoacan, stopping at houses where the saints are lodged.

sway in time to the music that echoes through the church. Next comes the procession. Dancers and musicians lead the way, followed by swarms of eager children as through the winding streets they go, taking in the whole village. Families gather at every corner to watch the fun and some dancers make sallies among the crowd, provoking screams of laughter from younger onlookers. Every few seconds a new rocket blasts off, leaving a thin white trail of smoke in the cloudless sky.

Despite its jollity, the procession is devoutly religious, and participants keep to a carefully mapped-out route, pausing before certain houses to pay their respects to the saint who is lodged there. Each year, different families are honored by being given the sacred task of sheltering and serving the saints, and at fiesta time duties are many. A shrine, bedecked with candles, flowers and paper cuts, must be erected for the saint who is in their keeping, and the celebrants are received with food and drink. They in return bring gifts for the householder and offerings for the saint. Eventually the procession returns to the main square, coming to a halt outside the church. The sun is high and it is time to eat.

In the house of the *mayordomo*, or headman, all is bustle and preparation. In the patio the women of the family are hard at work, stirring rich-smelling stews and sweet gruels in great cauldrons, and shaping golden tortillas. Traditionally the mayordomo opens his doors to the entire village during these days of fiesta, and everyone is welcome to eat and drink their fill. The musicians strike up, liquor flows like water, and mounds of tortillas disappear as fast as they are made.

As the shadows begin to lengthen, the villagers assemble once again outside the church, the women bearing dishes of food and

baskets heaped high with fruit, bread, and candies. Held high by willing hands, the Virgin and the saints are brought out into the square and ceremonially paraded in all their finery, before being returned once again to their niches.

With the darkness comes the firework display. Stepping forward, the firework maker lights the fuse at the bottom of the towering castle, and the crowd watches with mounting excitement as the fuse burns slowly upward from storey to storey, setting off the rockets and pinwheels that burst like myriad flowers and stars, filling the sky with cascades of light and color. No sooner has the flame reached the topmost turret, expiring in a gentle glow, than the first of the toritos rushes forward. Rearing and diving like the bull he represents, the boy carrying the bamboo framework of the torito runs among the spectators. Fireworks fly and the horns send out showers of golden rain. He is followed by a second and a third. Sometimes as many as twenty or thirty ''bulls'' loose themselves on the crowd which scatters, laughing and screaming, into the night. Inside the church a few candles still burn, going out one by one. Tomorrow, fresh flowers will arrive and the whole pattern will begin again.

Time has wrought many changes. Among town or city dwellers the handwoven huipil is replaced by a nylon dress and the clay pot by one of aluminum or plastic, but the fiesta lives on. Once a year in the town of Huejotzingo in Puebla, inhabitants give themselves over to *carnaval*, re-enacting from start to finish the resounding defeat that the French troops suffered at the hands of the Mexican people when they attempted to stage a conquest during the nineteenth century. Magnificently arrayed in colorful costumes, ornate headdresses, and leather masks, participants play their roles, some

The ancient *Quetzal* dance is still performed in the highlands of Puebla. Flaring out from a conical cap, is a framework of reeds interlaced with multicolored strips of paper or ribbons and tipped with feathers.

During this day of fiesta, this woman and her husband have welcomed friends and relatives to their house, feeding them and seeing to their wants. Now, as dusk descends, she brings especially baked breads bedecked with fruit to the Virgin and the saints in the church of Ocumichu.

impersonating arrogant French officers and others warlike Mexican soldiers, and as the battle rages, culminating at last in the town center, the square resounds with musket fire. A dramatic sub-plot is provided by the capture and death of a fierce bandit. Followed by his men, he rides into the square and abducts the daughter of a rich landowner, carrying her off to a nearby hut of branches. No sooner has a mock wedding been performed than troops attack the hideout, burning it to the ground and killing the bandit.

By tradition, the second of November belongs to the Dead. Indians and mestizos alike believe that on this day the deceased are granted celestial permission to visit friends and relatives on earth. It is imperative that the dead should be welcomed with ceremony and respect, for they have achieved the status of intermediaries who may intercede for the living with the saints.

Absent relatives frequently travel long distances to be with their families, for this is a time of reunion of the living with the living, and more important still, of the living with the dead. All over Mexico tombs are made tidy and adorned with wreaths of marigolds, candles, and other offerings, which include cigarettes, tequila, fruits, candies, and specially baked breads, often patterned with white sugar to simulate bones.

Tired dancers in Mochitlan, in the state of Guerrero, rest during a procession.

With the darkness comes the firework display. A fuse burns its way up the giant bamboo castle, setting off fireworks that fill the sky with light and color. When the castle has burned, boys carrying bamboo frameworks shaped like bulls, will shower the crowd with gold and silver rain.

In the home, an altar is erected, featuring a mass of flowers, paper cuts, elaborately fashioned candlesticks, and incense burners. When night falls, the family presents its invisible guests with hot food served in the best clay dishes. Great care is taken to ensure that the aroma is strong, for it is the aroma or essence that the dead extract. Later, these offerings are consumed in a more material way by the living, and the children, after a decent interval of time, will greedily devour the sugar skulls and marzipan doves.

In certain regions the Night of the Dead is spent in the graveyard itself. As dark descends, the whole family makes its way to the cemetery, bearing gifts and flowers. The tomb is decorated and the candles are lit. Sometimes altars of fragile and transient beauty, made from sticks of sugarcane and hung with marigolds and candies, are brought from home in honor of the dead, but even the poorest of graves is sanctified. Petals are sprinkled on the bare earth and a solitary candle is left burning. While small children sleep rolled up in blankets, the adults keep vigil, lighting fires to keep out the cold and to heat tortillas. The graveyard becomes a magical place on this night with flowers and candles everywhere.

In Michoacan, the dead are presented with beautiful altars of sugarcane hung with flowers, candy, and fruit.

To an outsider such celebrations might seem surprising but in Mexico death is seen to be a part of life, just as it was in pre-Hispanic times. The dead are never forgotten because once a year they return to earth to take their place beside the living, to enjoy the fruits and flowers of the earth, and to drink tequila.

Christmas is a time of great rejoicing and in many villages *pastorelas* are held. These are religious plays introduced by the Spanish friars soon after the Conquest to commemorate the birth of Christ. Casts are large and include a host of gaily dressed shepherds and shepherdesses, devils, angels, kings, and deadly sins. Watched by friends, neighbors, and visitors from local villages, the participants recite lines that are centuries old.

A favorite feature of the Christmas season is the colorful piñata, enjoyed by children in cities and villages alike. Ships, stars, fish, and animals are just some of the fanciful shapes that are modeled out of paper and cardboard to hold clay pots, packed to the brim with candies, fruit of all kinds, and exciting small toys. One by one the children are blindfolded. Stick in hand they lash out at the piñata as it swings dizzily from the branch of a tree, high above their heads. The excitement builds up until a sudden crash is heard. The pot, broken at last, pours out its contents while the contestants, screaming and laughing, dive forward in pursuit of treasures.

Ever present throughout the year, the Mexican concern with beauty becomes supreme at fiesta time. Creations may be intended to last a short while only, perhaps no more than a day or a night, yet the Mexican craftsman puts all his skill and imagination into the making of these ephemeral works of popular art, aware that by serving his religion he is serving his community and enriching the ceremonial life of his people.

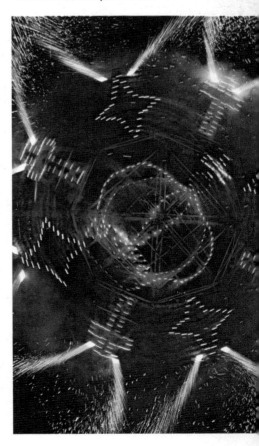

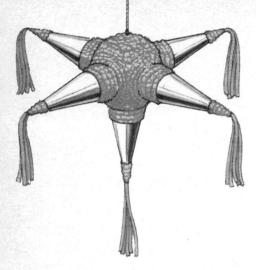

TOYS MADE TO BE BROKEN

Suspended high above the fruit and vegetables in one of the covered markets of Mexico City hangs a host of colorful piñatas. Horses and giant ducklings vie for attention with grinning clowns and stars.

A favorite feature of the Christmas season is the colorful piñata, enjoyed by Mexican children in cities and villages alike. Made to be broken, these exotic creations are nevertheless fashioned with enormous care. Ships, stars, flowers, fish, birds, and animals are just some of the fanciful shapes that are modeled out of paper and cardboard to hold clay pots packed to the brim with candies, fruit, nuts, and small toys. One by one the children are blindfolded. Stick in hand, they lash out at the piñata as it swings dizzily from the branches of a tree, high above their heads. Often a parent joins in the fun, pulling the rope to raise and lower the piñata. The excitement builds up until a sudden crash is heard. The pot, broken at last, pours out its tempting contents while the contestants, screaming and laughing, dive forward in pursuit of treasures.

Materials: Wallpaper paste, news-paper, beach ball, petroleum jelly, five sheets each thin cardboard and silver paper, 15 sheets tissue paper, scissors, adhesive tape, glue with brush, spoon.

Grease ball with petroleum jelly and cover with pieces of newspaper dipped in paste. Cover ball with about 10 layers of this papier-mâché, leaving a gap so that the mouthpiece is exposed.

When the mâché is dry and hard, deflate the ball and pull it through the hole in the paper shell. Thread a loop of string through holes pierced on each side of the opening.

Cut out five cardboard triangles and roll each into a cone shape, securing the edges with tape. Make even cuts around the base of each cone and fold the flaps out.

Cut out five curved rectangles of silver paper and roll each one around the middle of a cone. Secure the silver paper with tape stuck over the join in the cardboard.

Lay the 15 sheets of tissue paper on top of each other and cut them into 2in (5cm) wide strips. Set aside five bunches of strips for tassels. Cut deep fringes in remaining strips.

Taking one strip at a time, curl the tissue paper fringes by pulling each one individually over the back of a spoon. With practice you will soon be able to work speedily along each strip.

Brush glue over cardboard and, starting at base of cone, stick on paper curls. Attach one row at a time, tear off extra tissue paper on each strip and start a new row right above it.

Cut a bunch of 15 tissue paper strips in half, making 30 long thin strips. Tape them together at one end. Cut the tip off each cone and insert tassels, attaching with tape.

141

Other shapes can be made by adapting the papier-mâché and cardboard method used for the star piñata. Use the basic ball shape for bird and animal bodies and flower centers.

Left: Pattern shape for cardboard and silver paper. See page 27 for instructions on how to enlarge to the required size.

Opposite: Children all over the world will find a piñata as exciting as do the children of Mexico.

When all five cones have been decorated with fringes and tassels, fill the papier-mâché shell with a selection of lightweight toys, candies, and small party favors.

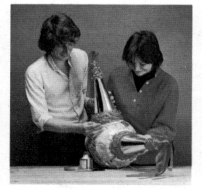

Spread the flaps at the base of each cone with glue, and stick the cones onto the body, securing with tape if necessary. Get a friend to hold the piñata body steady for you.

Balance the piñata on two chair backs and cover the body with tissue paper curls. Glue the curls first around the base of each cone and then over the rest of the body in neat rows.